"We've always wanted something to trust and believe in, and in the modern world that has been 'the brand'. Ridley Scott was one of the first to see it when he painted the dystopian future of Blade Runner *with rain-soaked neon images of brands like Atari. This was way before the days of Apple and Google, and proved to be truly prophetic in terms of how we have raised the logo and what it represents to almost religious levels.*

A great logo resonates with its audience and provides an easy identifier in the contemporary visual world of social media and marketing. Call it luck or serendipity, but something brought Rian and I together to create one of the most iconic logos in dance music. I've seen it tattooed on various body parts, made into wall art, discussed in design magazines and sold on millions of CDs. It featured heavily in our club decor; many of the production pieces we used were stolen and then turned up for vast sums on eBay.

Rian's work nailed what Hed Kandi was about in its earliest and most successful period. It's a truly memorable piece of art, and I can't imagine starting that label without it."
– Mark Doyle, Hed Kandi

"A fervent typographic expressionist."
– Steven Heller

"Try a death tango in the upper atmosphere with smoky Cyrillic logos wrapped around your fuselage and raw Letraset moiré crackling in the rear-view and then maybe you'll earn my respect the way Rian Hughes earned my respect ages ago."
– Grant Morrison

"Rian Hughes is Brit-Pop for typography at its best."
– signalgrau.com

"Rian is typographical Jedi. Inspired and inspiring, he understands the mercurial magic that fuels the mind-twisting propaganda machines that drive our cultures."
– Frazer Irving

"Rian's typefaces are unique because he is unique – a type designer that can actually draw."
– Jonathan Barnbrook

"Rian is the rare visualist whose sharp, eye-pleasing design playfully evokes the past while boldly defining the future."
– Jim Lee

"It's next to impossible for me to do any more than gush over the startling brilliance that is Rian Hughes' work. To put it bluntly, if the comics for which he provided logos and cover concepts were actually worthy of his skills and attention, this would be the true golden age of comics."
– Howard Chaykin

"I was a big Rian Hughes fan before I ever worked with him. His skills helped pull comics kicking and screaming into the 21st century. The depth and breadth of the work found here is truly staggering."
– Joe Casey

"Your book simply isn't dressed unless it's wearing Hughes!"
– Duncan Fegredo

"Rian's fresh and witty design combines with his deep and knowledgeable love of pop culture."
– Dave Gibbons

"Rian Hughes, the man who's done more for comic book design than anybody else, ever."
– talkaboutcomics.com

"Rian Hughes' dashing, dapper design work enhances every project he's involved with. He's the designer's designer with impeccable taste, charm and good hair!"
– Sean Phillips

"I was simply struck by his talent: whatever he touches turns out to be funny, cool and amazingly functional. More is better. Keep it coming."
– Erik Spiekermann

"I want to give a massive round of applause to the cover and logo designer of the [James Bond] *series, Rian Hughes. The simple, striking cover and elegant logo that stands apart from the film series or any of the iterations of the novels is stunning. I can't praise Hughes enough."*
– Geek Syndicate

"The James Bond logo is sleek and stylish and we're thrilled with it."
– Ian Fleming Publications

"Simply put, [Avengers: Endless Wartime] *this is the best-looking Marvel book I've seen in a long time. From the trade dress to the spine to the front and back covers to the spiralling design elements and infinite loop of Avengers logos on the endpapers, it all reflects* [the book's theme]*, the never-ending, self-sustaining cycle of warfare."*
– Comic Book Resources

"Chances are you've seen his work somewhere if you're at all plugged into pop culture . . . rife with style and energy."
– YPP.com

"Rian Hughes is one groovy bastard. Fact."
– www.venusberg.org

"The influential designer."
– The Guardian

"Striking . . . stylish . . ."
– New York Times

"Bravissimo designer inglese . . ."
– www.yo-yoll.net

"To say that Rian Hughes can design logos in his sleep is not an overstatement. He once sent me a logo that he'd designed in a dream and worked up on awakening. It was good, but maaaan, was it weird!"
– Steve Cook

"You expect me to go into a meeting and show them this shit?"
– Unnamed art director at unnamed British high-street retailer

RIAN HUGHES LOGO-A-GOGO
KORERO

Thank you

In no particular order, huge thanks are due to the publishers, artists, musicians, DJs, art directors and writers with whom I have collaborated. They have listened to my outré ideas, given me enough rope, helped steer projects through to completion, indulged my obsession with typographic detail and consistency, listened to my gripes, pushed me further than I would have gone otherwise, and without them none of this would have been possible: Yahya El-Droubie at Korero; Curtis King, Mark Chiarello, Richard Bruning, Shelly Bond, Karen Berger, Julie Rottenberg, Bob Wayne, Maria Cabardo, Amie Brockway, Robbin Brosterman, Tom Peyer, Kenny Lopez, Georg Brewer, Mike Marts, Scott Nybakken and Janice Walker at DC Comics; Steve Cook at 2000AD/DC Comics; Scott Dunbier, John Nee and Jim Lee at Wildstorm/DC Comics; Dinesh Shamdasani, Josh Johns, Hunter Gorinson, Alejandro Arbona, Robert Meyers, Lauren Litzhusen, Warren Simons, Jody LeHeup and Kyle Andrukiewicz at Valiant Entertainment; Ivan Brandon; Geri Halliwell; Yvonne Neumann; Josh Palmano at Gosh!; Rachel Vale; Jamie Hewlett; Allan Amato; Tony Fletcher; Professor Elemental; Colin Smith; Mark Irwin at Insight Comics; Frazer Irving; Sean Phillips; Frank Quitely; Kelly Sue DeConnick, Valentine De Landro, Lauren Sankovitch and Kit Cox at Milkfed Criminal Masterminds; Todd Klein, letterer supreme and historian of logos; Dean Motter; Keith WTS Morris at Chapterhouse; Mark Millar; Mark "Haven Stables" Doyle; Duncan Fegredo; Dave Gibbons; Eric Stephenson at Image; Bill Wallsgrove; Erik Spiekermann, Petra Weitz and Joan Spiekermann at FontShop; Midge Ure; Joe Casey; Sean Mackiewicz at Skybound; Jeremy Pearce, John Warwicker and Graham Tunna at A+M; Tony Bennett and Carol Bennett at Knockabout; Nick Landau, Leigh Baulch, Chris Teather, Jo Boylett, Laura Price, Andrew James, Steve White and Mark Cox at Titan; Jon Harrison at Forbidden Planet; Alan McKenzie, Steve MacManus Richard Burton (ex-Thargs), John Tomlinson, Audrey Wong, Igor Goldkind and Michael Bennent at 2000AD and Crisis; Peter Hogan at Revolver; Matt Smith at Rebellion; Bill Prady at The Big Bang Theory; Amy Sterling Casil; Geoff West at the Book Palace and Illustrators Magazine; Bryce Carlson and Mel Caylo at Boom!; Frank Wynne and Tom Astor at Deadline; Matt Haley; Ross Furlong at Furlong PR and Blogstar; Howard Chaykin; Nathan Fairbairn; Grant Morrison for the foreword and long-time collaboration; Mike McKone; Warren Ellis; Rick Remender; Charlotte and Peter Fiell; Amadeus Mozart at Music Factory; Joe Illidge at Lion Forge Comics; Richard Silberman, Paul Budgen and Kate Sadler at Remedy; Mike Ford and John Barber at IDW; Joseph Rybrandt and Jason Ullmeyer at Dynamite; Didier Pasamonik; Peter Milligan; Dave Johnson; Jeremy Banx; John McCrea; Chris Kerr; Billy Hawswell and Alan Parks at London Records; Alison Padley at Scholastic; Alex Buono at Third Person; Rob Levin, Paul Morrisey and Stephen Christy III at Archaia; Russell Coultart and Lawrence Cooke at Transient Records; Rob O'Connor at Stylorouge; Patrick Craig at Tensai for legacy file format conversion; Chris Groll, Andrew Faw, Isabel Garcia and Stavit Young at Nickelodeon; Gustav Temple at The Chap; Axel Alonso, Alejandro Arbona, David Bogart, Mark Paniccia, Tom Brevoort, Jennifer Grunwald, Ellie Pyle, Lauren Sankovitch, Nick Lowe, Jeanine Schaefer Wilson Moss, David Bogart, Jennifer Grünwald, Emily Shaw, Lauren Sankovitch (now at Milkfed Criminal Masterminds), Daniel Ketcham, Stephen Wacker and John Barber at Marvel; Dick Hansom and Cefn Ridout at Acme; David Price for scans; Jaime Hernandez; Chris Foss; Darwyn Cooke; Cameron Stewart; Dave Johnson; Mark Millar; Hunt Emerson; Gilbert Sheldon; Serge Clerc; John Freeman; Dave Gibbons; Ra Kahn; Steven Lo Presti and Pablo Gargano at Eve.

Copyright

Colophon

Published by Korero Press Ltd
www.koreropress.com
First published in 2017

A CIP catalogue record of this book is available from The British Library.

ISBN-13: 9780993337420
10 9 8 7 6 5 4 3 2 1
Printed in China

Set in Korolev, a Device font
Book design by Rian Hughes at Device
Science Service approved

www.devicefonts.co.uk
www.rianhughes.com
Contact: info@rianhughes.com
Twitter: Rianhughes
Instagram: @RianHughes

Foreword

You can't judge a book by its cover, 'they' tell us, but this book proves conclusively that you can judge a book by its logo, when that logo is the work of Rian Hughes.

Designer, artist, culture commentator and author, Rian is a 21st-century Renaissance Man whose participation in a project is a guarantee of its excellence. Rian's graphic illustration work has been so prolific, generous and widespread and his distinctive style has been sampled and copied so repetitively it's become as ubiquitously recognizable as a James Brown riff.

Even if you don't know Rian Hughes, you know Rian Hughes.

In what amounts to his spare time, our square-jawed hero of the future has realized some of the most memorable comic book mastheads of the last 30 years, collected here as demonstrative proof of his taste, his panoramic range of influences, and his ability to deliver genius every time.

From the Serge Clerc-inflected days of *Escape* to the 21st-century dazzle of his mind-evaporating Alt.end-history hyper-modernist novel *XX*, Rian has never failed to excel or to express our momentary times in type.

For three decades, Rian has been my go-to creative mind when it comes to realizing the graphics of my comic book stories. This collection shows why his work has always appealed to my sensibilities.

From the rugged dissonance of the **Nameless** logo, which draws its bleak inspiration from the black-and-white pulp horror magazines of the 1970s, to his iconic **The Invisibles**, with its *Invaders*-esque callback to 1960s spy-fi TV shows. From **Batman Incorporated**'s tasteful, corporate business card approach, to the exuberant, cartoon-show, colour-blocking simplicity of **Batman and Robin**. From the bubblepop, seapunk style of **Seaguy** to the shredded punkzine graphics of **Doom Patrol**, and the school-encyclopedia-style of **The Multiversity** design with its offshoots – the neo-1930s-pulp of **Society of Super-Heroes**, trash mag aesthetic of **The Just** – Rian's incredible, clever logo designs never fail to complement, distil and express the content, the characters, and the stories of the books he graces.

Some of the designs on display here, like his logos for **Spider-man** or **The Spirit**, seem to encapsulate the entire scope and tone of a feature, and even suggest possibilities for new, unwritten, undrawn adventures.

As this book demonstrates, each of these is the product of a massive applied intelligence, each finished product selected from dozens of brilliant alternatives which he meticulously conceives and provides. Lesser artists would struggle to create the masterpieces Rian discards in his search for the perfect expression of a book's heart and soul.

Grant Morrison
Argyll, Scotland

Rian Hughes on the *Stubnitz*
Photo by Allan Amato
2013

Introduction

Countdown #22
Polystyle Publications
Weekly British comic
Cover art by John M. Burns
1971

Countdown
Cover art by Rian Hughes
c1971

Throughout, items shown in **medium** are featured elsewhere in this book

Long before I'd heard the term 'graphic design', long before I grappled with gainful employment, lettering had me in its thrall.

I was a font-spotter. I was copying the type I saw in my weekly issues of *Countdown* – 'The Space-Age Comic!' I could recognise almost every typeface in my rebound Letraset catalogue from a short word or two on a paperback book cover or a record sleeve.

The logos I remember were not from the corporate world, they were part of popular culture: the decals on Matchbox cars, skateboard brands, bubble gum cards and stickers, Gerry Anderson's Supermarionation title sequences. They fizzed with wild colours and outré type styles. The logos for the banks, estate agents and supermarkets on the high street seemed oppressively utilitarian by comparison; they reminded me of the covers of dull, old-fashioned school textbooks, and promised nothing but stifling conformity. Not so the logos that had caught my imagination – Commander Ed Straker from the SF show *U.F.O.* had a stylish S.H.A.D.O. logo over the breast of his Nehru-collared beige jumpsuit, and those free badges that came in packs of Sugar Puffs had the nifty *Star Trek* insignia on. Or the mastheads of Alan Class' range of cheap black and white comic reprints, in which I discovered Steve Ditko and Jack Kirby monster/mystery tales that were already ten to twenty years old. Then there were band logos, which we copied in the margins of school exercise books, and Bond's iconic 007 gun emblem. They promised adventure, they spoke of tomorrow, they were the gang colours for the coolest gang in town.

The mark, the symbol, the icon. It has always had a seductive power. Like some kind of magical sigil, the logo serves as a visual shorthand – it encapsulates, it stands in for. Communicating simply and powerfully, it is the comic character reduced to an icon, the company marque, the badge worn on the school blazer lapel as a signifier of tribal affiliation. It's why our prehistoric ancestors tattooed themselves with a bespoke skin. It's why we rally behind a flag.

How does this magical power work? Part of the secret is familiarity, what we have learned by association. When designing a logo, there is often a legacy to consider, previous iterations that have earned a valuable resonance with the audience. There are many logos that would not fare well today in a marketing focus group, yet are known and loved and should not be changed. Others may just need refining, bringing to the surface the essence which has become buried under an encrustation of stylistic quirks.

More often there is no precedent to consider. Something new needs to be created from fresh cloth that fits snugly, that looks right. If it's a comic masthead, the logo has to express the essential character of the star(s) of the book. A publisher's identity might be more of an umbrella under which disparate characters or products can coexist, so should be more universal. The word I often use to describe a logo that seems right is 'inarguable'. It should look like there's nothing you could add or take away that would improve it.

Is there a formula for this? Yes and no. Yes, I think there are some general rules that seem to work. No, they are not applicable in all cases, and simply applying them indiscriminately is not going to lead to original results.

In this book, I'll try and explain this process on a case-by-case basis. I'll show some of the ideas that were rejected, sometimes by me (in which case the client didn't get to see them), sometimes by the client; I'll discuss how others took the design in a new direction, and explain how the final version was arrived at.

Just like comics, another of my favourite artforms, logos often combine type and image. Of course a logo may be purely typographic, purely pictorial, or a combination of the two, but even in cases where it solely consists of type it can still be considered a 'word picture': the type is not neutral, even when it's attempting to be neutral. Unaccompanied by imagery, it still has a visual appearance, a *style*, the part of the type that communicates non-verbally – the *look* of the thing, and what that look *means*.

What does the style of the letters say? This can be a matter of historical precedence, of referencing recognised tropes to leverage a certain effect: a classical serif, a moderne geometric sans, a Gothic blackletter. All have a given set of connotations that can be pressed into use, or twisted in some new and unusual way. Other forms have no such cultural baggage and come as they are.

Even so, every font choice must mean something. Every line must serve a purpose, and you must be able to articulate that purpose – to explain to the non-designer why it's there. Logo design is one of the purest and simplest forms of communication, and you need just the right amount of stuff on the page to say what you need to say (or avoid saying something else) and no more. If you can't justify it, take it out.

Does this mean there's no room for ornament? Of course not. But decoration for decoration's sake is not meaningful decoration. If you need to apply a density of detail to suggest a certain craft, evoke a certain period or communicate a concept, this is meaningful decoration. I sometimes see logos that I've designed given the Photoshop filter treatment post-delivery; brushed chrome is a particular favourite, one that even I've indulged in on occasion. But a logo should first and foremost work 'bare', like a good tune without the orchestral backing. You can't polish a turd, though some visually tone-deaf clients do love an aqua effect and a drop shadow.

Appropriate design emerges from an understanding of the conceptual underpinning of the project itself. Ask if it should be elegant, or brutal, or rational, or chaotic. Perhaps it should be bold and shouty, or aristocratically refined? Perhaps it presses into use abstract shapes taken from a character's costume or profile, or colours from Neapolitan ice-cream or military camouflage. Will you need both a

Star Trek Captain
Badge
Free gift with Sugar Smacks cereal
c1969

Century 21 Productions logo
Badge
c1974

S.H.A.D.O logo
Bubble gum card
'Supreme Headquarters Alien Defence Organisation' insignia from the TV show U.F.O.
1970

Apollo 7 mission patch
Cut from back of a cereal packet
c1972

portrait version for the business card and a landscape version for the shopfront? Is size important? That logo might need to be used at ten point on a book spine. Or on the wing of a plane. Can it do both?

Punchy bold capitals, or a retiring fineline serif? An urgent italic? Are curves essentially feminine and angles masculine? Many of these connotations are just conventions lifted from our shared culture, the memetic stew in which we all marinate. Others arise by reference to the human experience – blood is red, grass is green, the sky is blue. If we were Vulcan (and we wore a nifty *Star Trek* badge), our blood would be green, and if we were Martians, the sky would be pink – and thus what these colours signified would also be different.

However, underlying all these manipulations of our orthographic back catalogue, there are the universal harmonic relationships of shape and colour that form the bedrock of aesthetics. Unfashionable though the idea may be, this is what we sense when we say something is *beautiful*. Here, we're into the abstract elemental realm charted by the likes of Wassily Kandinsky, Piet Mondrian and Kazimir Malevich, from which new symbols and visual languages whose final meaning has yet to be codified are formed.

My guess is that, like a pure note in isolation, no colour or shape is essentially more beautiful or ugly than any other; they achieve this only in *combination*. Beauty is a *relationship* – a harmonious chord on a piano, perhaps, in which the sound waves that move our eardrums come in mathematically related ratios. A beautiful arrangement of shapes and colours might obey some similar but less well defined mathematical logic, one we don't have to understand in order to recognise.

Though many artists might disagree, strip away the memetics and it all comes down to mathematics. If a cat walks across a piano, the result will be disharmonious, and design is no different – within the small confines of a simple logo, every element must relate to every other element. It is a careful balance of form on which the higher-order semiotic message is then carried.

Much of this sleight-of-hand is best left to do its work invisibly, under the hood. If you've been commissioned to design a logo for a new flavour of potato crisp, talk of universal Platonic colour relationships will only get you weird looks in a meeting.

Sometimes innovation is entirely surplus to requirements; you develop a sixth sense for such cases. "We like this font", for example, is not an idea. This is working from the outside in, not the inside out – if the concept is sound, the font choice will naturally follow. "We are an anarcho-cyber Belgian folk quintet who dress in skin-tight leopardskin", on the other hand, is positively replete with ideas.

Even while studiously trying to avoid trends, young bands or similar clients whose knowledge of design stretches as far back as last week can catch you out; try and steer them away from a 'flavour of the month' solution. That this may be entirely appropriate for their 'flavour of the month' music is not lost on me – but I'd hope they'd at least like to *think* their album will hold up years from now, and so should their logo. Though a superficial solution may fly, it's always more rewarding to delve a little deeper. The result will undoubtedly be more original.

As has been said elsewhere, the solution is in the problem. If a solution isn't apparent, often it's because the problem hasn't been stated clearly enough.

En route to that final logo, a designer will explore interesting dead ends, produce beautifully executed options that are completely inappropriate for the job in hand, deal with inarticulate clients who you have to coax and cajole, and negotiate briefs that shift dramatically like a lurching dreadnought beneath you.

Sometimes, for reasons that remain opaque, the client chooses the logo you threw into the mix at the eleventh hour to make up the numbers. There is a lesson to be learned here: don't submit anything you'd not want used.

Other times there is but one perfect solution, and so you only deliver that one option. This can be a risky all-or-nothing strategy, but I find that if I've produced more than a dozen or so concepts it may be because I've not defined the criteria the logo needs to fulfil clearly enough, and so I'm not quite sure if I've answered the question – or perhaps the question was not clearly articulated in the first place. In these cases, it's helpful to have a more detailed discussion – what does it need to *say?* Who *is* this character? Where will it appear? Who does it need to speak to?

Sometimes the client may be able to answer these questions; other times you may need to use MI5 interrogation techniques to help them firm up the project in their own mind. This is just as much a part of the design process as what happens in front of a computer screen.

Some clients are not that articulate: "My music speaks for me!" Yes, maybe it does, but I'd still like to hear what it means directly from you. What are you trying to say? Who are your influences? How would you like to be perceived? Bands, comic book artists and writers usually love to tell you about what they do. Have this conversation before you start designing. Logos can often be visualised completely in the mind's eye during this process, leaving only the execution.

When presenting alternatives, beware that the client might not always make what you think is a reasoned choice. However, they may be seeing something in the design that you're not, or conversely may be aware that your design is not saying something they need it to say. The exploratory designs are the basis for a back-and-forth conversation that the designer and client must both willingly and enthusiastically engage with.

Sometimes, three or four rounds of concepts in, you can sense you're no closer to a resolution. The client has told you what they're about; you've done a little research, and come up with a few solutions that you feel say what they need to say. Only what they need to say is not what they originally told you they needed to say. It's now something a little different . . . and you can end up chasing a mirage. I have been sent a dozen logo examples to illustrate what a client is after, the only common denominator being that they were all for hugely successful companies, each completely different, each one only suited to the company in question.

There have been times when, out of sheer desperation, I've thrown anything I can think of, however clichéd, at the wall to see what will stick. This is not the best way to produce good work. If you're just shuffling shapes or idly browsing through the font menu for inspiration, step away from the keyboard and do some thinking.

Arriving at an appropriate solution also requires that the chain of command is short; ideally, you'll be dealing with the decision-maker directly. Pleasing one layer of a bureaucracy with whom you've had all the relevant conversations only to find that someone higher up has your design dropped on their desk for a simple yes or no without any insight into the thinking behind it can be disastrous. If feedback is along the lines of "the person upstairs likes this colour/shape/font, and I'm afraid it's up to us to make it work" and there can be no further discussion, the design process can be undermined entirely.

Experience has taught me that clear communication is vital. It helps hone your own thinking, forces you to step up to the mark and justify every choice you have made – and you *should* have a solid reason for every choice you make.

Matchbox Collector's Catalogue
1973

Alfa Carabo toy car packaging
c1974

Kinky Dan/Crazy Zoo
Stickers and wrapper
c1974

The best logos are the ones where the client has pushed me further than I would have gone otherwise. Sometimes, with a new client, there can be a bit of muscular back-and-forth in which we check each other out. They may test you; somewhere between being an autocrat and a pushover is a sweet spot that works best for both parties, and out of which the most original and striking work will come.

Lest this seem overly critical, there is another scenario: I've misunderstood the brief entirely. Learn to pay attention. For **Manifest Destiny**, for example, the script I was sent to read still had the working title, *Lewis and Clark,* as did my first round of designs. Cue bemused client. Entirely my own fault – it was clearly called **Manifest Destiny** in the brief. Start again, do not pass Go, do not bill extra.

For a logo that will accompany other visual material – a comic book logo, for example – there are some practical concerns I've learned through trial and error. Too much pictorial imagery in such a design can clash with the art, and as the designer might have a limited influence on what that art will look like from issue to issue on an ongoing title, stripping out anything that may be problematic will make it more versatile and thus ease the job of the in-house designer, who you'd prefer not to be cursing you every month. Some of my favourite **Batman** logos shown in this book, especially those which incorporate a cape and cowl, did not work so well in situ.

To that end, I'll always place comic or magazine logos in a representative layout. This is the only way you can reliably see what works and what doesn't. The same is true of the colours you may use – in the hands of a sensitive designer, these can change to key to the art each issue. While corporate logos have a preset colour palette, one that can't be altered, many comic logos have to be more versatile.

In addition to the logo, I'll often produce master 'trade dress' templates in Indesign or Illustrator. These have to be robust enough to accommodate fluctuating word counts, changing credits and different styles of art. They include all the necessary page furniture: the barcode position, the price, the company logo, the web address, etc., preferably in a minimum number of fonts and point sizes.

A good example of this holistic approach in action is the **Valiant** comic book line. Consistent design can really build a company's brand recognition, helping to cross-promote their titles and give them a strong shelf presence.

Once a template is set, good artists will very quickly get a handle on how much space needs to be left up the top (or, less often, up the side or along the bottom), and they will often playfully run elements over the logo or otherwise customise it in interesting ways. This is to be encouraged.

The design of the covers on ongoing titles often falls to the in-house designers, who make it all work month in and month out. They choose sympathetic colours for the logo, for the most part adhere to the templates I've provided, and hopefully don't gripe too much when it turns out I've forgotten some essential bit of cover copy that needs to be added at the last moment – or we suddenly have an anthology title that needs to accommodate credits for ten people, all with double-barrelled surnames. You make it all happen.

The less said about the occasions where you add a starburst or a corner flash or a big #1 in a random free font the better. If I find you've imported my Illustrator vector files into Photoshop because that's the only program you're familiar with, and stretched ten-point type to fit a measure while giving it an outline and drop shadow, I may need to have a few words. Maybe I should collate the emails in which I've had to explain the very basics of grid-based, conceptually consistent design into a book for beginners.

While my involvement often ends with delivery of the logo or trade dress, other times I'm art directing and conceptualizing a project in its entirety. The most cohesive and successful designs in this book have come about in such cases, where it's possible to exert that extra authorial control. Being that I'm also an illustrator myself, one who has been poorly served by designers on occasion, where possible I'll try and involve the artist in the process from the outset, especially if I intend to manipulate their work in any way. I'll show them what I intend to do and ask for their feedback. I'm often surprised at how receptive they can be, and how they can run with the idea and turn it into so much more than I anticipated.

The **Iron Man** covers by Salvador Larroca for **Marvel** or the **Challengers of the Unknown** covers with Howard Chaykin for **DC Comics** are cases in point. I discuss these in more depth on the relevant pages.

For **Bitch Planet**, Kelly Sue DeConnick's women-in-space-prison series from Image, I run cover artist Valentine De Landro's art through the wringer, adding textured ink effects and misregistration to mimic the printing of vintage exploitation movie posters. Val deserves an award for generously allowing me to do all this in the service of the Big Concept.

The **James Bond** series was an interesting case study. The art for several of the first issue's variant covers had been commissioned before the Fleming estate had approved my logo and layout, and had to be adjusted to fit within the squarer format I'd created. Once the artists had seen the first issues in print, they worked within (and creatively pushed the boundaries of) the chosen design, but for that first tranche of covers I did have to make a few tight crops and art extensions in order to weave a symphony out of what could have been inelegant compromise. Apologetic emails had to be sent to artists, who I thank for their understanding.

Sometimes a project may involve a half-dozen illustrators, and still need to come across with a single voice, cohere as a single project with a consistent design aesthetic. The **Tangent Comics** series was just such a case. I mocked up several covers to illustrate the design approach I had in mind, and very graciously, under the capable aegis of art director Curtis King, the artists all produced a set of covers that held together seamlessly.

One reason this project worked is that within the constraints of the concept the artists still had enough leeway to flex their creative muscles. It's a team effort, and as long as one person isn't trying to dominate the proceedings with the visual equivalent of an inessential drum solo, the result is more than the sum of its parts.

Many other logos are used primarily in isolation: on a letterhead, on a T-shirt, in a corporation's lobby. Here it makes more sense to use specific colours, and not to change them for each application. A simple 'bible' may be in order, in which the Pantone or cyan, magenta, yellow and black values are specified, and details such as the minimum amount of empty space around the logo are set out. The logo itself need not compete with a complex background, as it often does on a comic or book cover, where sometimes a strong outline or panel is needed to lift it out so it reads clearly.

I studied Graphic Design at The London College of Printing (now The London College of Communication). The college has been refurbished in the last ten years, but back then it was a dusty brutalist tower block on a large traffic interchange in Elephant and Castle, just off the Old Kent Road, the cheapest property on the London version of the Monopoly board. During the final year we were set a brief to design a logo and single bag for **DIY Records**, a new label to be run by Chrysalis. Peter Saville,

something of a design hero of mine through his work for Factory and **Ultravox**, my favourite band at the time, was one of the judges. My design was chosen, along with one by fellow Double Crown Club member Ian Chilvers. Peter handed me a scrap of paper with his address and phone number on (I rather expected an immaculately set business card) and invited me to his studio.

Peter is not known for his timekeeping, and it was three visits before I actually got to show him my work; in the meantime, Brett Wickens took Polaroids so I didn't feel my trip was completely wasted. The proof for New Order's *Power, Corruption and Lies* lay on a desk in an otherwise sparsely furnished 1930s industrial unit in Ladbroke Grove. A couple of other designers whose names I didn't pick up on sat at drawing tables by the windows doing, I assumed, the actual hands-on work. I leafed through my portfolio, and he made wise and erudite comments on the state of Radio 4, rock journalism (a bizarre article on his Factory Records work had just appeared in the style press) and my use of Gill Sans. Though he was complimentary about my work a job offer was not forthcoming, and shy and gauche as I was, I thought it inappropriate to ask.

We got to talking about French illustrator Serge Clerc, whose work was then appearing in the *New Musical Express,* a copy of which Peter had to hand. Serge's marriage of *ligne claire* cartooning and off-centre compositions that featured large blocks of black set against angular trapezoids of Letratone was then a big influence on my own work. His was illustration that was *almost graphic design,* that interesting area between disciplines I have continued to explore. Peter suggested I visit the company directly below – **Knockabout Comics**, the UK publishers of the **Fabulous Furry Freak Brothers** – so on my way out I dropped in unannounced on Tony and Carol Bennett.

In complete contrast, their space was overcrowded, stacked high with underground comics, posters, books and hippie paraphernalia on Dexion shelving. I showed them my work, was presented with a fine selection of Sheldon and Crumb comics, and a working relationship began that continues to this day. In 2007, they published **Yesterday's Tomorrows**, a hardback collection of my early comic strip collaborations with Grant Morrison, Raymond Chandler and others from *2000AD,* **Revolver** and elsewhere.

Knockabout later moved to Acklam Road, Notting Hill, in a studio complex under the Westway that also housed a club we frequented called Subterrania. Design company Town and Country Planning were neighbours, and I would meet them again when they merged with Stylorouge, with whom I would share studio space several years later in nearby Salem Road.

For **Knockabout** I designed Robert Crumb and Gilbert Sheldon collections in-house, and at lunchtime I'd rummage along Portobello Road Market for books, comics, furniture and Homemaker crockery for my new flat. One day I found a box of 1950s and 1960s American 'Artype' sheets, a product that predates rub-down lettering like Letraset. Artype is printed on a thin self-adhesive sheet from which the letters are cut and assembled, and I began to use them extensively on **Knockabout**'s books.

All the while I was taking on more illustration work. Some months before graduation I was freelancing at *Smash Hits,* designing abstract patterns to be dropped behind song lyrics and spreads for bands like the Belle Stars and Jimmy the Hoover. Editor David 'Scoffer' Bostock would send my page layouts off to be duplicated by a union-approved designer who would stamp them on the reverse with his special Union Stamp, which he guarded like the One Ring. Without it, the printers would refuse to print the magazine. The (much resisted) introduction of the Mac into their closed shop eventually made this sort of protection racket untenable.

I was offered illustration work at *Just Seventeen* because it was launched by the same publisher as *Smash Hits* and they needed some imagery for the dummy issue. They were both based in Emap's Carnaby Street office, above shops selling bongs and Union Jack Doc Martens to tourists, back when Emap consisted of just two magazines and could fit into one office.

My illustration and comic strip work make the occasional appearance in the present volume, but fall outside its logo design remit. Interested readers are pointed towards the collections *Art, Commercial,* **Soho Dives, Soho Divas**, **Yesterday's Tomorrows** and **Tales from Beyond Science**.

During these early days I also began to design book jackets and album sleeves for smaller labels, beginning with the **Manowar** album *Sign of the Hammer* for 10 Records. The art director had spotted my work at my degree show, and asked me to come in and present my portfolio. I was completely green when it came to the process of art directing a sleeve and preparing the artwork, so he suggested that another designer they were working with step in to help me out. I needed PMT (photo-mechanical transfer) prints, typesetting and scanning – none of which I'd had any experience with. He organised all these for me; a few days later I realised I needed the logo resized, so I turned up at his place of work to get a new print done. What I didn't realise was that he'd been helping me out on the side and I'd just inadvertently alerted his employers, who were not happy. I remember calling him to apologise, and getting short shrift in return. I laboured on with the artwork, not really knowing what I was doing. After I delivered it, 10 Records had to bring my work up to a professional, printer-friendly standard. They didn't use me again, although the sleeve turned out nicely, and is included here. I think it won an in-house award, but I wasn't around to get a pat on the back.

In 1988 I collaborated with Dave Gibbons on Madness' album *The Madness.* I had been a fan since *One Step Beyond,* and the band themselves were keen comics readers, *2000AD* being a particular favourite. Their label, **Zarjazz**, is named in imitation of *2000AD* editor Tharg's alien Betelgeusian slang.

My first full-time job after graduation was at a small design agency in Angel, Islington, North London. I got lost on the way to the interview, it was raining heavily, and I finally arrived forty-five minutes late, soaking wet. Thinking it couldn't get much worse, I was ushered up to the boardroom where I lifted my portfolio off the wheeled contraption I used to carry it around. That's when I noticed there was something brown on my white shirtsleeve – something smelly.

In the rain I'd inadvertently run the wheels through some soggy dogshit, which had splattered up all over the portfolio and had now been transferred to my sleeve and the immaculately polished boardroom table. The directors had to open the windows to let the stench out. Despite this, they offered me the job.

There were three directors, two of whom weren't on speaking terms. One of them, as a prank, had called the other's garage, claiming that his scooter needed to be recalled because the brakes were faulty. This went all the way up to Vespa's HQ in Italy, where they stopped the production line. When they discovered it was all a practical 'joke', they threatened to sue for lost production.

Health was no concern. In the design department, we had an unfolded cardboard box taped to the wall in lieu of a spray booth. Sheets of layout paper would be pressed against the stalactites of glue that had built up, and spray mount would be liberally waved around. In the hermetically sealed room, after a dozen

Letraset catalogue
c1971

Countdown
Sheet of Letraset rub-down transfer lettering (missing the letters that I used on schoolbooks, toys, comics, Matchbox cars, etc.)
Designed by Colin Brignall, 1965
c1975

The Race into Space
Brooke Bond Tea picture cards
and album
1971

Galactic Defence League
Membership card for schoolboy
SF club, produced with Letraset
and a photocopier
c1977

Uncanny Tales #131
Alan Class
c1976

Secrets of the Unknown #157
Alan Class
c1976

Tracker Trucks
Sticker
Skateboard truck brand
c1977

or so sheets had been mounted for a big presentation we were high as kites. My lungs are probably still lined with the stuff. The artwork department, housed in a separate building across Camden Passage, spent their free time with the PMT camera collaging the director's heads onto hardcore Swedish pornography.

I quit three months in, after the same director tore up my mock-up for a wetsuit company brochure in a meeting because "his four-year-old daughter could do better". In a pique of adolescent unprofessionalism, I told him to fuck off in front of all present and left the room. He later sent one of the other directors up to the studio to apologise (he, of course, couldn't do this himself) and the company even offered me a sizeable raise, but I tendered my resignation there and then and at the end of the week I left what turned out to be the only full-time job of my career.

Dysfunctional though this agency was, I did actually learn a lot about basic presentation, dealing with typesetters, print markups and so on that I still find useful to this day. Specifying colours, for example, was achieved by referring to a colour chart which showed each of the four print colours – cyan, magenta, yellow and black – overprinting in 10% increments. If the piece was to be printed in two or three colours, these were sometimes added on overlays: a sheet of acetate was hinged from the top edge of the board and the area in question masked out with Rubylith, a photo-opaque film. The Pantone or CMYK breakdown was then indicated on a tracing paper overlay for the printer to (sometimes) follow.

Today, working live in colour on-screen, I sometimes forget that camera-ready artwork used to be in black and white; the colour was only added at the printing stage. If you were lucky and the client obliged, you'd see a proof called a Cromalin which was made directly from the film separations before the printing plates were exposed, and this would be your last chance to make corrections. However, changes at this late stage were expensive so you often had to let them slide. As you had to be pretty sure about the final result from the outset, mock-ups using coloured paper and gouache were created – these were sometimes works of art in themselves. I have included a few examples of surviving camera-ready artwork in this volume.

After leaving, I freelanced at Da Gama, a record sleeve design company run by John Warwicker and Alex McDowell, where I designed sleeves for forgotten bands like Ellery Bop and Thomas Leer, and storyboarded pop videos for Strawberry Switchblade, Killing Joke, Modern Romance, Jimmy Page, Evelyn 'Champagne' King and Robert Plant. Da Gama had evolved out of a previous design outfit called Rocking Russian, and would go on to change names and staff many times – x=x, Vivid ID – in the manner of one of those 'Rock Family Trees' before eventually becoming Tomato. They were based in a converted terraced house off Upper Street in Islington, decorated inside in gold and pastels. I was an arch rationalist in my design thinking and John Warwicker was more of an intuitive image-maker, but again I learned a lot about the practical business of producing viable ideas under tight deadlines, and more about the art of explaining them in unpretentious layman's terms.

Unfortunately I joined a few months before they went under, the reason for which was never clear, but I think had something to do with the use of non-union staff on a video shoot, which meant that no broadcaster would air it. It was the *Smash Hits* union stamp situation all over again.

After the demise of Da Gama, John moved to A+M Records, where he would pass me work when he found something which he thought would suit me. I designed logos and mascots for **Bad Boys Inc**, a British boy band, and Stock Aitken Waterman's **Roadblock** and **Packjammed with the Party Posse**.

That summer I briefly worked as a designer for the fashion and style magazine *i-D* and at Condé Nast on a variety of titles from *House and Garden* to *Tatler* and *Brides and Setting Up Home*. Stephen Male was the art director at *i-D*, and on the side worked as an illustrator for many of the same magazines as me. *i-D*'s headlines were created on an early dot-matrix typewriter, which provided a dozen or so variations on a basic bitmap font. *i-D* didn't have a PMT camera, so the type was enlarged, waved around on the copier as the scanning head went past, cut and pasted together. This was style by necessity, but it gave the magazine a suitably post-punk aesthetic. I always felt like a bit of a pretender in the world of high fashion; I simply didn't know that much about shoes.

Condé Nast seemed to be staffed by more than its fair share of predatory middle-aged homosexuals and aristocratic debutantes for whom a job was a diversion that presented interesting social opportunities. Based in Vogue House, just off the junction of Oxford Street and Regent Street, it had the slightly worn elegance and charm of an earlier age, a contrast to the more innovative johnny-come-lately Emap. I was shuffled between magazines, designing spreads for bathroom fittings, home decor and lighting. Lunch was dispensed from a little hatch on the floor below, or a selection of ornamental cakes from a shoot would be shared around with champagne. A laid-back, unhurried atmosphere of polite gentility prevailed.

It looked like I might be taken on full-time. This being before mobile phones and email, I'd begun to field more and more calls at work for freelance illustration. I could tell this was becoming something of an annoyance to the art directors, one of whom pointedly dropped the phone on my desk with a clatter.

Somehow (the exact timeline is foggy in my memory) I also managed several months at another music design agency, Mainartery. Based on Oxford Street in offices above a shop, they worked for artists the calibre of James Brown, Motown and Paul McCartney. I produced sleeves for **General Kane**, The New Jersey Mass Choir and **Perry Como**. For McCartney I pitched several designs for *Only Love Remains*, the first single taken from his *Press to Play* album. None were used. Eleven years later, while sharing studio space with Rob O'Connor's music design agency Stylorouge, I was asked to come up with ideas for McCartney's **Flaming Pie** album. None of these would be used either.

Around 1986 I saw an advertisement for a designer in the window of **Forbidden Planet**. The owner, one-time 2000AD editor Nick Landau, was expanding **Titan Books**, the publishing arm that had begun with a reprint of Brian Bolland's *Judge Dredd* strips.

Leigh Baulch and Mark Cox soon had me designing covers for their range of TV tie-in and comic book collections, T-shirts, posters and magazines. I would produce roughs using marker pens, card and gouache, just as I had when working at the design agency. These would then be artworked by their in-house studio.

It was a joy to be let loose on books that featured material that had fired up my early interest in design and illustration: **Gerry Anderson**, **The Man From U.N.C.L.E.**, **Batman**, **Love and Rockets**. There were Neal Adams' *Batman* collections, Alan Moore's **Superman**, and best of all, Jaime and Beto Hernandez's **Love and Rockets**, a masterpiece of the form that is now in its thirtieth year and has lost none of its power to impress.

From a cramped basement below Forbidden Planet 2 in St Giles High Street, London, where the only ventilation was a

Focus Photosetting
Typesetting company
College project
c1984

544
Menswear shop
College project
1984

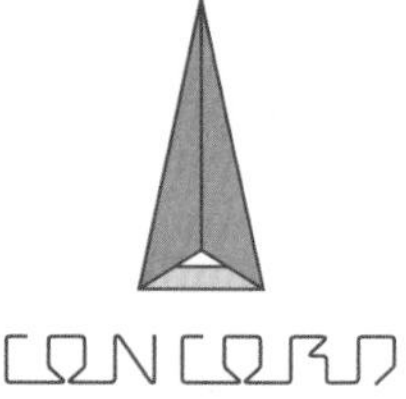

Concord
Track-mounted lighting manufacturer
College project
1984

DIY Records
Record label
College project
1984

grille to the alley behind the shop through which tramps would occasionally urinate, Titan has grown into a powerhouse publisher of books, magazines and comics with a sideline in toys and merchandise, and now has a staff of 150 over five floors in a building near the Tate Modern.

I still occasionally work for them. I recently illustrated the covers of writer Robbie Morrison's *Doctor Who* comic, and designed a 'facts and stats' book for the **Batman** TV show. I researched, edited and designed a collection of **Chris Foss**' SF cover art, whose paintings had graced the covers of the Isaac Asimov and Arthur C. Clarke novels I'd read as a teenager.

I sent the early comic strips I'd had published in Paul Gravett's seminal comic magazine *Escape* to a Belgian publisher called Magic Strip. Under the 'Atomium 58' imprint, they had been producing a beautiful series of small two-colour albums by some of the artists I most admired – Serge Clerc, Yves Chaland, Dupuy et Berberian and Daniel Torres. I was asked to draw a volume in the series – a chance to draw a European album with high production values! I couldn't believe it.

I travelled to Brussels to meet the editors, identical twins Didier and Daniel Pasamonik. We went for dinner at the Falsaff, a beautiful fin de siècle restaurant, and later had drinks in the 1930s surroundings of L'Archiduc; the Pasamoniks always did things with a certain sense of style. Didier took me to visit Ever Meulen at his studio, another illustrator whose work I admired enormously. Working for Magic Strip was a young Tierry Tinlot, who would go on to be editor of *Pilote* and later *Fluide Glacial*. I recently bumped into him at the Angoulême comics festival; he was carrying a huge leg of ham he'd just won in a 'guess the weight' competition.

Publication of **The Science Service**, written by John Freeman, was delayed for a year or so as Magic Strip was bought out by another comic publisher, Loempia. This meant that the English edition, published by Dick Hansom and Cefn Ridout of Acme Press (in association with Eclipse Comics in the US), was the first to see print. *i-D* praised its "stylised 1950s sensibility and gritty 80s realism". "Slick, thrifty and effectively told – in which content matches style" said **Speakeasy** magazine. Roger Sabin in his *City Limits* review called it "the ultimate designer comic", a quote that Acme used widely in publicity. In the interests of full disclosure, the quote in full read "the ultimate designer comic – beautiful to look at, but utterly vacuous".

The Science Service would act as my calling card at **Fleetway** and lead directly to my being offered the **Dan Dare** strip in their new title **Revolver**, which was to be scripted by rising newcomer Grant Morrison. We were introduced by Grant's sister, Leigh, in a café opposite the original **Forbidden Planet** in Denmark Street. He was quiet and serious, as most likely was I, which is probably why we got on. I went on to draw **Really and Truly**, **Robo-Hunter** (with *Resident Alien*'s Peter Hogan) and **Tales from Beyond Science** for the Galaxy's Greatest, all of which have been reprinted in the last few years by Image or **Knockabout**.

Every reader vividly remembers their first encounter with thrill-power – mine was Brian Bolland's cover for Prog 224, showing **Judge Death** escaping from **Judge Anderson**'s body, which has been entombed in Boing™. Many years later, Brian would be drawing the covers for **The Invisibles**, using my logo.

Grant and I have continued to collaborate, most recently on a strip for the BBC called *The Key* and a short for *Heavy Metal* magazine, of which he is the guest editor. *Heavy Metal* began as an American edition of the seminal French magazine *Metal Hurlant*, and was instrumental in introducing an entire generation of English speakers (myself amongst them) to Mœbius, Caza, Tardi and their contemporaries. In 2014, I designed Grant's huge **Multiversity** event for **DC Comics**, central to which is the Map of the Multiverse, probably the single most complex piece of design/illustration I have ever produced.

Steve Cook was the art director at *2000AD*, and for a while we felt like the only designers in British comics. I assume there must have been many more, because there were many more comics being published, but almost all of them looked just like comics had always looked, their slow evolution always a good decade behind the curve. Mark Cox was doing interesting work on the collections at **Titan**, but the weeklies and monthlies were another matter.

Steve and I agreed that, for a vital visual medium, this was absurd. Steve set out to reinvent the look of *2000AD*, injecting some much needed cultural savvy, and between us we handled almost all of **Fleetway**'s new wave of comics that rode the post-*Watchmen*/*Dark Knight* boom: **Revolver**, **Crisis**, **Xpresso** and many of the books in their new graphic novel range. These titles are discussed in more detail on their own pages. Somehow I also found time to draw **Dan Dare** for **Revolver** and go clubbing twice a week.

The early 1990s comics boom and subsequent bust came as little surprise when viewed from the inside. Built on the back of a handful of standout titles that genuinely pushed the medium forwards, publishers followed up with a slew of very average titles in fancy formats that completely misunderstood the very reasons for this spike in interest. The structural storytelling innovations of *Watchmen* or Frank Miller or Jamie Hernandez were completely overlooked, and instead of opening up an artform dominated by superheroes it gave them a new lease of life – as nihilistic antiheroes. The general public, having read articles about how comics "aren't just for kids anymore", must have been hugely disappointed. Comics' incipient maturation had been traded for a protracted adolescence.

Though I continued to design comics and logos for comics throughout the 1990s, I only read a couple that were written or drawn by friends. I couldn't make any sense of the slew of new titles epitomised by Image Comics. Today, Image is a powerhouse of creator-driven left-field experimentation, but in their early days they seemed to brashly ignore every tenet of clear storytelling. Backgrounds were secondary to dramatic poses, and it was impossible to tell if the scowling characters who filled the frames with an excess of overhatched muscle were indoors or outdoors, in a secret base or having dinner at home with the kids. It took Grant Morrison and Frank Quitely's run on the **X-Men** and Mark Millar's **Ultimates** in the early 2000s to bring mainstream comics back onto my radar.

In the early 1990s, Steve Cook and I shared a studio above a Chinese bakery between The Brain Club and The Wag on London's Wardour Street. We recruited Kev Hopgood, Pauline Doyle, Kim Dalziel, John Tomlinson, Brian Williamson, Andy Lanning and Lucy Madison to fill out the space and share the rent. The atmosphere was one of enthusiastic hard work during the day, while after hours we'd explore the local bars and dives.

But it was all about to go horribly wrong. One afternoon some intimidating thugs turned up looking for our landlord. He apparently owed these Triad types several tens of thousands of pounds in rent, and they had come to collect. We pleaded honest ignorance, and they eventually left. When confronted, our 'landlord' swore innocence and then, that night, changed the studio's locks. Coming in on Saturday morning to collect material for a

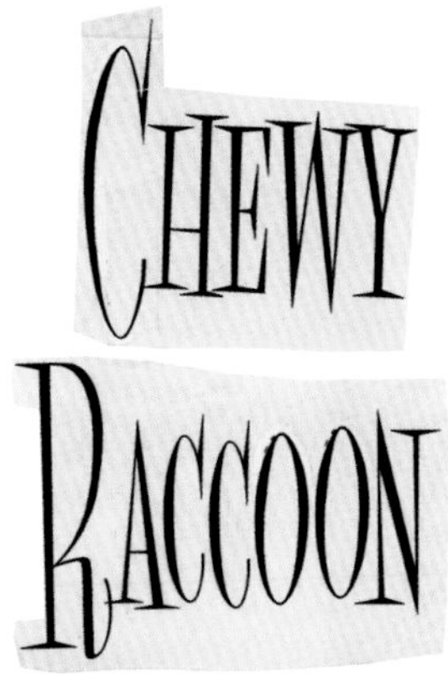

Posing for a fake band photo to promote a Sony Tape competition
1985

Chewy Raccoon
Da Gama/Phonogram
Band
1985
Original logo artwork

Star System
Britains
Toy range
1985

Tundra Comics launch, I was faced with a new heavy-duty steel lock and a note demanding advance rent money in return for the keys. A few calls later, the other studio members and I convened in the Falcon pub opposite.

An ask-no-questions locksmith was quickly found. "It's a drillproof lock," he observed. My hopes evaporated. He opened a large plastic case and pulled out a pneumatic demolition drill that looked like something Sigourney Weaver would wield in *Aliens*. "Should take me ten minutes."

We hired a van and, in relays, during the height of the Saturday rush when we couldn't park outside for more than three minutes without blocking the street back to Leicester Square, managed to move all our stuff to the cavernous Tundra Comics studio in Brixton. I got off lightly – the 'landlord' had just taken my airbrush and the cover for the first issue of Fantagraphics' **Dare** reprint. Kev Hopgood lost an entire issue of **Iron Man** pencils and John Tomlinson a *Mighty World of Marvel* **Captain Britain** cover that had been a gift from Steve Dillon.

There have been more than a few studio moves since then. For eight months I rented space in The Coach House, Ealing Green, next door to Ealing Film Studios; the Red Lion pub opposite has a 'Stage 5' sign mounted by the door. Here ex-Brody studio member Tony 'TC' Campbell taught me Photoshop for *2000AD*'s 17th anniversary cover ("See that icon like a wanking hand? That's the burn tool . . .") and I held my 30th birthday party, at which Mark Millar played naked Twister. Next, I moved to Salem Road, Bayswater, where for six years I had an office on the same floor as Rob O'Connor's music design agency Stylorouge. When the lease came up, I briefly moved to Westbourne Studios, a new development built under the Westway, a flyover on the main route west into London and coincidentally very close to **Knockabout**'s old offices. Jamie Hewlett's production company had the largest space, which overlooked the atrium and the bar. I decided to move after a fellow tenant had a gun pulled on him late one night as he crossed the nearby footbridge over the Hammersmith and City Line.

The studio is now located in a quiet mews in Kew, very close to the botanical gardens. Here, the only place you'll be mugged is in the overpriced artisan wholefood store.

Included in this volume are examples of logos designed before I moved to the Mac. There were several methods of creating sharp, clean lines with the analogue tools of the trade, most of which were prone to smudge or fade or discolour. For the best results I'd use Rubylith, the red photo-opaque film on a transparent backing that I'd seen type designer Alan Meeks use during an inspirational trip to the offices of Letraset when I was 16. He adeptly cut intricate curves from this material with a razorblade attached to a weighted piece of wood. This is how the typefaces from the Letraset studio were prepared, each letter cut at a cap height of around 150mm.

For fine keyline work I'd use a drawing board with a parallel motion, an adjustable set-square and a Rotring pen. The pens used India ink and came in a variety of widths; their fine nibs were prone to clogging and their upkeep was an art in itself. The drawing surface was smooth CS10 board (now discontinued), which had a chalky surface that could be scraped away with a scalpel to create sharp corners. A pre-digital designer would become intimately familiar with the idiosyncrasies of their chosen tools.

In 1993 Steve Cook and I decided we would invest in this new computer technology we'd heard about. We both bought the exact same kit, a Mac IICi with a whopping 8MB of RAM and a cathode-ray tube monitor that was as deep as it was wide and took two people to lift. We figured we could operate as mutual support, and call each other for advice on the intricacies of Quark Express or when it crashed – which, back then, it did often. Despite the early programs' limitations, the results were immediately seductive. Every line was perfect, every corner sharp, every curve free from splatter and fluff.

It takes a while to master any new tool, and in the early days the computer's signature fell heavily over much of graphic design. There was an excessive use of stretched type, drop shadows and textured Photoshop effects just because you *could* (and usually when you *shouldn't*).

For design archaeologists, I've included some original pre-digital logo artwork. These were never intended to be seen, a clean PMT copy mounted on board being the presentable end result. Today, they are interesting artefacts in their own right. I am of the generation that has one foot in the pre-digital, one foot in the post: a seismic change not just in graphic design but across almost every industry, and in our social and cultural lives as well. This will only happen once in human history.

Wherever I could, I used custom fonts of my own design in my work. Originally these were laboriously drawn letter by letter, then photocopied, rearranged into words and reduced on a PMT to crisp them up for the final artwork. The Mac, and specifically Altsys Fontographer, allowed me at long last to create fully functional fonts that I could type directly from a keyboard.

To be able to use a font of your own in running text is something that designers have longed for since Gutenberg. If you happened to be Eric Gill and knew someone at Monotype or Linotype who might indulge you it may have been possible, but even then you'd need to wait months for the punches to be cut and the type to be cast. With the new font creation tools, I could produce a fully functioning typeface in a matter of days.

My hand-drawn headlines for **Revolver** and **Speakeasy** were among the first to be digitised. I sent printouts of my early efforts to FontShop, care of Neville Brody, and he called me up a few days later; I spent an afternoon at his studio in Islington, where young intern Tobias Frere-Jones ran through the basics of producing a publishable font. I still use the kerning tables he gave me.

Those first fonts – FF Crash Bang Wallop, FF Outlander, FF Identification and others – were released through Erik Spiekermann and Neville's Berlin-based company FontShop, who had been among the first to see the potential of the digital font market. I very quickly accumulated such a backlog that the only sensible course of action was to release them through my own foundry. Device Fonts was launched in 1997, and has now published over 600 fonts across 170 families, available direct through the Device site, MyFonts, and more recently, Adobe Typekit.

Several logos have been the starting point for successful font releases – the **Yellow Boots** logo became Blackcurrant, and the **Teenage Mutant Ninja Turtles** logo spawned a font that is used for the localisations of the show and merchandise. The ability graphic designers now have to control every last aspect, like a particle physicist drilling down into the subatomic realm, is a wondrous thing.

Steve Cook commissioned the fonts Scrotnig and Judgement for *2000AD*. Scrotnig was used for the launch of the notorious 'Summer Offensive', one of the semi-regular *2000AD* reboots designed to entice new readers on board, which featured Grant Morrison and my strip **Really and Truly** as well as Grant and Mark Millar's *Big Dave*. Judgement was designed the year after.

My font designs have been catalogued in the books *Ten Year Itch* (2004) and the forthcoming *Typodiscography*, both

ORCHESTRAL MANŒUVRES IN THE DARK

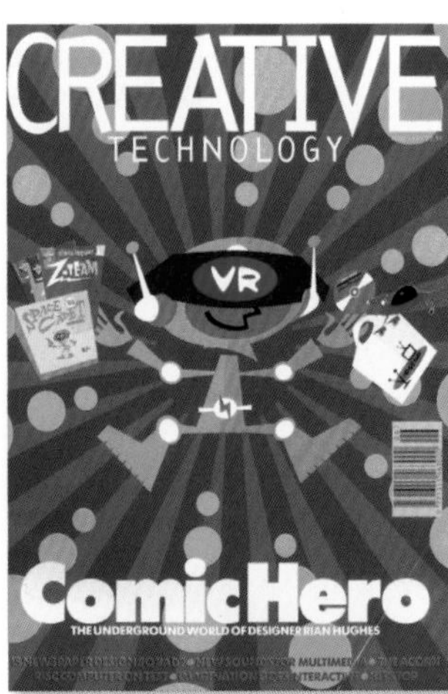

Nemesis
Fleetway
2000AD comic series
1990
Original logo artwork

Torpedo
Fleetway
Graphic novel (unpublished)
c1990
Original logo artwork

Orchestral Manoeuvres In The Dark
Starship Enterprises
1985
Unused logo for tour programme

2000AD
Prog 876, 9 February 1994
Possibly 2000AD's first all-digital cover

Creative Technology
June 1995

of which feature lengthier essays on the design and application of type.

As many of the UK's new crop of writers and artists began to be offered work at **DC Comics** and **Marvel**, I was asked to design some of the logos for their new titles: **The Invisibles**, **Kid Eternity**, **Shade the Changing Man**. American editors began to fly over for the annual UK Comic Art Convention (UKCAC) to scout for talent, and there was some cultural adjustment as British sarcasm and the ability to drink superhuman quantities of beer rubbed up against the more polite and enthusiastic US approach. At the DC Comics parties, generally held in a Soho club or bar, several well-known figures could be counted upon to either pass out or pick a fight.

Mutual understanding was quickly arrived at, and I have to thank Richard Bruning, Karen Berger, Tom Peyer, Mark Chiarello, Shelly Bond and Curtis King for opening the door, especially when up till that point US comics had either been designed in-house or by a small cadre of local New York-based designers. I have now been creating logos for American comics for over twenty-five years, many of which are showcased here.

Around 1996 I was offered the chance to draw a new series at DC to be written by Dean Motter, the talented designer behind the **Mr. X** comic whose strong, graphic covers had stood out so well on the racks. Mark Chiarello also asked me to draw a *Batman: Black and White* strip. I was then in the process of developing a new approach to my illustration using the Mac, and was completely burned out on the weekly deadlines for *2000AD*. After much soul-searching I declined Mark's offer, admitting at the time that I knew I'd regret my decision. I was turning down the chance to draw **Batman** – was I *mad?* – but I was seriously overworked.

Through the late 1990s, though I was still designing comic book logos I worked primarily as a designer and illustrator for magazines, book covers, advertising and the music industry. The graphic brush and ink illustration style I had developed, inspired by those early *Huckleberry Hound* comics and the Franco-Belgian 'ligne claire' (clear line) style of Yves Chaland and Serge Clerc, quickly found a new means of expression through Adobe Illustrator. I dropped the outlines and laid down angular shapes in flat, vibrant colours, and tried to close the gap between design and illustration even further.

This style, which was dubbed "sans ligne" by Will Kane, proved to be hugely popular. It was picked up by certain magazines that were ahead of the curve, and featured on the cover of industry magazines such as *MacUser* and *Creative Technology*. There would be periods at the studio in Bayswater when I would draw three, four or even more illustrations per day, sometimes working seven days a week, from 10am till the last train back to Ealing left around midnight. I'd then lie in bed with my arm hanging over the side, my neck and arm muscles throbbing.

One day I couldn't hold the mouse – the muscles in my hand had gone limp. I worked for a few days using my left hand, then bought an early Wacom Bamboo. My hand recovered, though I still have a bump on my wrist where I'd scoot it over my desk. A pen is a more natural tool to wield than a mouse, and I have used Cintiqs ever since, even when designing fonts.

As with all fashions, my illustration style was very quickly appropriated by others. (I dislike the word 'style', implying as it does that illustration is more about superficial appearances than underlying concepts, but it was the style that proved so popular.) I was again courted by an agent – when I declined, one of the illustrators already on his books filled the gap by aping me under the name "Roman Grey". This was reported to the Ethics Committee of the Association of Illustrator's Agents, who absolved the agency of any wrongdoing – possibly because the person who ran the agency also sat on the Ethics Committee of the Association of Illustrator's Agents.

Around 1998-2000 you could open an illustration annual such as *Contact Illustrators* or the American equivalent and find a half-dozen or so copyists busily cutting and pasting heads or hairstyles or pot plants from one of my greetings cards or CD covers. Published by Die Gestalten Verlag, my 2002 monograph *Art, Commercial,* which collected much of my illustration and design work up to that point, proved to be something of a cribsheet. An apotheosis was reached when I fielded a call one day: "We want someone who can draw like Rian Hughes – can you draw like Rian Hughes?" I told them I hoped I could, because I *was* Rian Hughes. There was a pause, and then they hung up. When the copyists become more employable than you, maybe it's time to move on.

Opportunities arose for exhibitions of my work - a small show of original illustrations at Café Casbar in Covent Garden, London, in 1988; 'Toybox', a show of limited edition prints at the Coningsby Gallery,

The Madness
Illustration by Dave Gibbons
1988

The model taxi that was stolen from the Power::house UK exhibition
1999

Frank Wynne at the offices of *Deadline*
Orinoco Studios, South London
1995

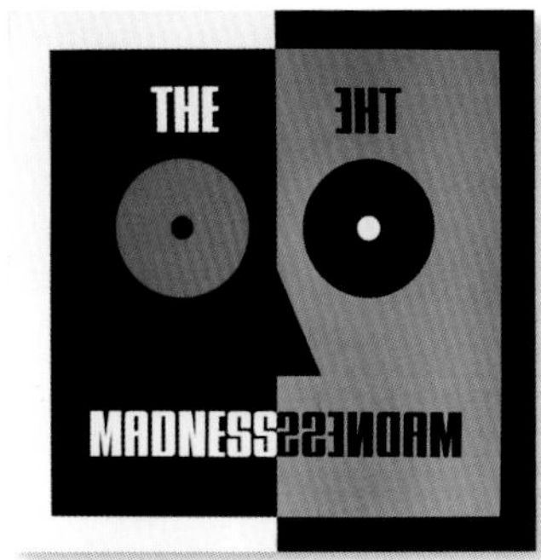

London, in 2003. In 1999 I was part of 'Powerhouse::uk', a government initiative that showcased the creative industries. Sited on the central axis of Horse Guards Parade, it was an eclectic exhibition housed in four inflatable domes. Along with other designers, I was asked to customise a model of a London black cab that would run around a Scalextric circuit set in a diorama of London. Before the official opening night, most of them, including mine, had been stolen. The remainder had to be tied with wire, immobile, to the track.

In 2009 Paul Gravett asked Woodrow Phoenix and myself to be part of 'In Search of the Atom Style', a group exhibition held in the iconic Atomium in Brussels. This featured many of the artists who had inspired me when I was starting out – Serge Clerc, Ever Meulen, Joost Swarte and others – and it was a great honour to be included.

I also began to be invited to lecture at design conferences. Nerves meant that I overprepared for my first major presentation at a conference in Stockholm, reading out my talk word for word from prepared notes. My delivery must have been dreadful – but not as bad as the person before me, who didn't even know what slides were in her carousel. Evenings were spent at a kebab restaurant talking to type designer Lucas DeGroot and The Designers Republic's Ian Anderson. Ian, I don't think it's hyperbolic to claim, must be one of the most influential – certainly one of the most copied – designers of the 1990s.

At the hotel bar during the Typo Berlin conference in Germany in 2003 I was introduced to Syd Mead. His book *Sentinel* had blown my mind, and Ridley Scott's masterpiece *Blade Runner,* for which he designed sets and vehicles, is probably my all-time favourite film. We spoke for several hours; he was full of stories of his film design work, and I wish I'd recorded him.

Compared to design conferences, comic conventions have traditionally been more casual affairs. The long-running UKCAC (United Kingdom Comic Art Convention) was a fan-run event, and guests would be interviewed on stage or take part in panels rather than deliver prepared talks. In the early 1990s there was usually a "Future of Comics" round-table in which the superhero was given a premature burial, the assumption being that a new dawn of European-style comics for grown-ups was just around the corner. In the bar, Alan Moore might tell you about this new project for DC he was working on with Dave Gibbons, and the costumes in the 'masquerade' looked hilariously homespun compared to today's cosplay.

The American conventions were enormous by contrast, held in convention centres the size of aircraft hangers instead of threadbare hotels. I first went to the San Diego Comic-Con in 2002, staying with my uncle who lived a few miles up the coast in La Jolla. It was possible to dip into the convention and escape again without bodily harm. I was pleasantly surprised to be able to meet, and be invited to dinner with, Shane Glines, Bruce Timm and Glen Murakami, sit on the roof of the beach house Cameron Stewart had rented in Mission Bay with Darwyn Cooke and Michael Cho, go to lunch with Scott Dunbier and Jim Lee at Wildstorm, and have gravy accidentally spilt down my back at a Wildstorm dinner. I smelled like reheated school meals for the rest of the night.

Glen asked me to design the logo for his new **Teen Titans** animated show, and though in the end it wasn't used I was invited up to visit Warners Animation in LA. The doors of the lift opened to reveal an enormous display of bright pink *Powerpuff Girls* merchandise. The animators sat in little booths; one of them was the son of Harvey Eisenberg, the uncredited artist on those *Huckleberry Hound* and *Tom and Jerry* annuals I had read as a child, and whose angular, dynamic style had been such an inspiration.

The French comics festival held in Angoulême was very different.The Brits were the guests of honour around the time of **Deadline**'s ascendancy, just before **Revolver** was published. An entire French town given over to comics, it boasts a dedicated exhibition space, library and museum, and was opened by the French culture minister. Brett Ewins behaved in a suitably punk rock fashion on stage, and the exhibition of the work of architectural fantasist Francois Schuiten was one of the best I have ever seen. Grant and I wandered around town in the evening looking for a restaurant, but ended up eating French fries in 'Quick'.

On another visit some years later, writer and artist Dave Hine, illustrator Vikki Liogier, Steve Cook and I were stopped at French customs as we drove off the ferry. I made the mistake of asking to use the toilet, and everyone was strip-searched for drugs as a consequence. This they have never let me forget.

In 2011 Maria Cabardo, who I had met when she was working as an editor at DC, was over in the UK filming **Better Things**: *The Life and Choices of Jeffrey Catherine Jones*. We went to Paris to interview Jean 'Mœbius' Giraud, legendary figure of the 1970s French comics renaissance, in his studio. I had read his *Airtight Garage* strips when they were translated in *Heavy Metal,* and his art had featured on the cover of the second *Tales from The Forbidden Planet* collection I had designed. He had just had a major retrospective exhibition, and the open-plan ground floor was full of original art, including many key pages from early in his career. I asked if he worked here, in the room we were in. He enthusiastically leapt up the stairs, several at a time, beckoning for me to follow. Upstairs, in what was effectively a tiny spare room, he had an unpretentious setup just like a budding teenage artist: art books on wonky shelves, a trestle table covered in paints, brushes, pens and inks, and a tablet and basic Mac setup precariously balanced on more books. He immediately started working on a drawing in Photoshop, oblivious to the repeated calls of "Jean? Jean?" from downstairs. On his desk was the prop revolver he had used to draw *Blueberry*. I picked it up, and he took a photo of me.

He died just a few months later.

Roy Lichtenstein is a divisive figure in comics. I remember being impressed by the sheer scale of *Whaam!* as an art student, but it has become apparent through the detective work of David Barsalou that practically every one of his comic book paintings is a direct enlargement of someone else's work – Russ Heath, Tony Abruzzo, Ross Andru and many other uncredited artists. Unfortunately this is not an uncommon practice: certain 'fine artists', enabled by the dealers and gallery system that supports them, steal from comics, illustration or design, presumably seeing it simply as authorless raw material that can be freely appropriated – a form of cultural detritus that they can magically turn into Art with a capital 'A'. This transmutation generally takes the form of enlargement – make it BIG – and recontextualization – hang it in a white-walled gallery space. This somehow elevates these scraps of ephemera to something of value, measured in millions of dollars, and a coveted place in art history.

To try and rebalance the situation, Dave Gibbons, long a vocal critic, Jason Atomic and I organised a show in Orbital Comics, London, timed to coincide with the Tate Modern's 2013 Lichtenstein retrospective. Contributors from illustration, comics, fine art and modelmaking went back to the original panels and "re-reinterpreted" them with wit, scathing social satire, skill

Sheldon checks out the Batman and Robin logo. Leonard prefers Casper
The Big Bang Theory
c2015

Batmobile
Eaglemoss
2016

Paul Gravett, Peter Stanbury, Woodrow Phoenix, Serge Clerc, Rian Hughes
Brussels, Belgium 2009

Holding Blueberry's revolver
2011
Photo: Mœbius

and originality. After the show they were auctioned, with proceeds going to the Hero Initiative, a charity set up to help ageing comics creators who didn't benefit from the exploitation of their work.

Seventeen years after he had first asked, Mark Chiarello emailed me out of the blue – *Batman: Black and White* was returning for a fourth volume, and could I stop playing hard to get and write and draw a story for him this time around? A second chance! Of course I said yes.

It featured Tal-Dar, an alien with triangular eyes that appeared in the very first **Batman** story I ever read, a reprint in a British annual. The Batmobile I designed for the strip was subsequently produced as a die-cast model – this could be my career high-water mark.

The authorial creative control comics permit is in contrast to much of mainstream graphic design and illustration, which, however beautiful or inspired it may be, is ultimately in the service of something other than itself. This realisation has led me to make a concerted effort to produce more comics. *I Am A Number,* published in 2017, is the first graphic novel I have both written and drawn. *XX*, a 'novel, graphic', I hope will open up new ways in which designers can also become the authors of their own content.

During the preparation of this book, there was some discussion as to exactly what criteria should be used when deciding what to include and what to leave out. There are more than a few designs that border on illustration, or could be better described as one-off pieces of custom lettering. There are others that are logos only in context: when isolated, they become a simple line of type. I have erred on the side of inclusion if it was a comic book logo, and tended not to include it if it was part of a CD sleeve or a book cover, where it would make more sense to show it in context. To meaningfully showcase such examples I would need a volume twice the size, and this one is all about the logos.

I make no claims that all the roughs included here are what might be deemed 'good' designs. They are here to throw light on the process, the route to the final version. Where my favourite wasn't chosen by the client, this is an opportunity to show the proposed logos that got away. Some I thought were the perfect solution to a difficult brief, but for some unfathomable reason the client didn't agree. In retrospect, I can see that sometimes they were right.

Though this volume concentrates on my logo designs, because I have always worked in parallel as a graphic designer, type designer, comics artist and illustrator these often feed in. I see them very much as part of a continuum anyway; there are no hard and fast divisions, and the most interesting results often happen when two or more disciplines collide. I justify this by reference to the artists who inspired me: Cassandre, the Stenberg Brothers, Jean Carlu, Ever Meulen, Fortunato Depero, Barney Bubbles and others who straddle design and illustration.

The division of graphic design into ever-finer specialisations was a product of the corporatisation of the field in the 1960s and 1970s. It was not easy to set up shop – equipment was pricy, darkrooms were cumbersome, and the range of type very limited. The Mac changed all that forever, and put the means of production back in the hands of the skilled individual. Steve Jobs and Steve Wozniak (who I had the pleasure of talking to over drinks at Soho House after a D&AD judging session) have democratised the field, confounded those unionised printers with their special stamps, and in the process unshackled creativity. Good ideas, as illustrator Brian Grimwood once advised me, never go out of style. I'd add that they do, however, occasionally need a new suit.

More prosaically, the versatility of a 'commercial artist' is also a prerequisite of continual employment – in some years the illustration has been in the ascendant, in others the type design or logo design seemed to take up most of my time. These arcs seem to rise and fall on seven-year cycles, and I'm sure some grand and sublime truth about the way certain memes propagate through culture could be deduced from this. I don't think it's possible to engineer such twists and turns in advance: sometimes I've accidentally found myself at the vanguard of a new style or technology, evolving as fast as I can produce work; at other times I feel like I might be swimming in a completely different direction to the prevailing currents.

I was asked at a talk recently if I had any advice for students. I'm afraid I'd have been lying if I'd pretended that I had some grand plan from the outset. The best I can offer is to take it all in your stride, as you learn as much from the jobs that go horribly wrong as the jobs that breeze through. Be passionate, be dedicated, be original. Work hard. You'll meet chancers and saviours, people who try and rip you off and people who push you on to do your best work. Learn to recognise them. They may even be the same person.

Stay interested by stepping outside your bubble to look in afresh on a regular basis. Be professional. Meet deadlines. Be articulate and engaged. Read the brief. Listen to criticism. Stick up for what you think is best for the job, without being a prima donna. It's not a zero-sum game – if you win, the client wins, and vice versa.

Don't forget to invoice.

I have to mention the support I've received over the years from the art directors at the companies I've worked for, and especially those at **DC Comics**, **Marvel**, **Valiant** and **Image**, plus those at the record companies, advertising agencies and publishers. Your willingness to let me experiment and your professionalism in seeing work through to the final printed article has been invaluable.

One of the great pleasures of designing logos is working with artists, writers and musicians, and I'm happy to have had the opportunity to work with some of the most talented, inspirational and creative people in the field. My designs would be very much diminished without your genius to support them.

I'm just the window dressing.

Rian Hughes
Kew Gardens

Device
My company logo
2005

The original Device logo was a hand – the appendage by which ideas become materialised. It had a 'D' in a circle above the middle finger. When the company had been in existence for a decade, I added a second hand, ten fingers in all.

I've been told it looks like two swans kissing. This is unintentional.

Shadowman
Valiant Comics
Comic book series
2012

Shadowman: End Times
Valiant Comics
Comic book series
2013

SHADOWMAN

SHADOWMAN END TIMES

Created by Jim Shooter, Steve Englehart and David Lapham, **Shadowman** originally debuted in 1992 during **Valiant Comics**' first incarnation. As part of the newly relaunched company's line, the character and logo got a contemporary makeover.

Shadowman – Jack Boniface – inherits his voodoo powers from his father, and becomes caught between two warring groups, both of whom want to enlist him in a battle of good versus evil.

I felt that the striking 'Man in Doorway' motif was the only part that could be salvaged from the original logo.

Early ideas reference the 'spooky' curved shapes from the very first logo **3** or play with shadow-like solidity by knocking out the counters **10**, **11**. I attempted to evoke the character's New Orleans setting by using split-serif Tuscan type of the kind familiar from carnival freak show hoardings **12**, **13**. Worn, distressed American wooden type with inky imperfections featured in **14**, while I used Gothic spiky serifs reminiscent of cast-iron railings in **8** and **9**. Others have a wonky imperfection, like listing gravestones in a Hammer Horror graveyard **15**, **19** or rotting slats on a decaying building **20**. **1** and **5** feature tendril flourishes for a touch of the Gothic macabre.

In the final analysis the client chose a very straightforward condensed sans, which captures little of the character but possibly has a broader appeal outside of the horror genre.

The more interesting version with spiked serifs **7** that I favoured was resurrected for the later **Shadowman: End Times** series, with an additional perspective to allow the subtitle to sit directly below.

All my **Valiant** logos are designed so that they occupy a rectangle of specific dimensions in order to sit neatly on the standard **Valiant** cover design and the trade paperback collections I designed. They are almost always in white, with an element picked out in colour that keys to the art – here the doorway. (The **Valiant** logo and trade dress are discussed separately.)

I drew the mask cover for issue 11, which was printed on perforated card.

19

1 SHADOWMAN

2 SHADOWMAN

3 SHADOWMAN

4 SHADOWMAN

5 Shadowman

6 SHADOWMAN

7 Shadowman

8 SHADOWMAN

9 SHADOWMAN

10 SHADOW MAN

11 SHADOW MAN

12 SHADOWMAN

13 SHADOWMAN

14 SHADOWMAN

15 SHADOWMAN

16 Shadowman

17 SHADOWMAN

18 SHADOWMAN

19 shadowman

20 SHADOWMAN

Liberty Rocket
Matt Haley
Computer game and comic book
2007

Fraktur type, WWII aircraft livery and V2 missile silhouettes were explored for this game and comic book property featuring an 'alternate history' rocketeer. The final type style owes something to the 'Firestone' logo, an American classic which has remained pretty much unchanged since 1900.

1

2

3

4

5

6

7

8

Royal Holloway
Proposed logo update
Brand Remedy/Royal Holloway
2013

Royal Holloway is one of the UK's leading research universities. Founded in 1879, it was officially opened in 1886 by Queen Victoria as an all-women college.

A silhouette of the iconic Founder's Building is combined with elements of the current coat of arms **4**, the colour taken from the red brick. My aim was to communicate tradition but without stuffiness. The logo was not used.

1

2

3

4

The Burlesque Space
The Life Drawing Society
Burlesque themed events
2014

A brand for a series of life drawing classes and events.

My own portraits of London's burlesque performers are collected in the book *Soho Dives, Soho Divas,* published by Image Comics in 2013.

1

2

The Spirit
DC Comics
Comic book series
2006

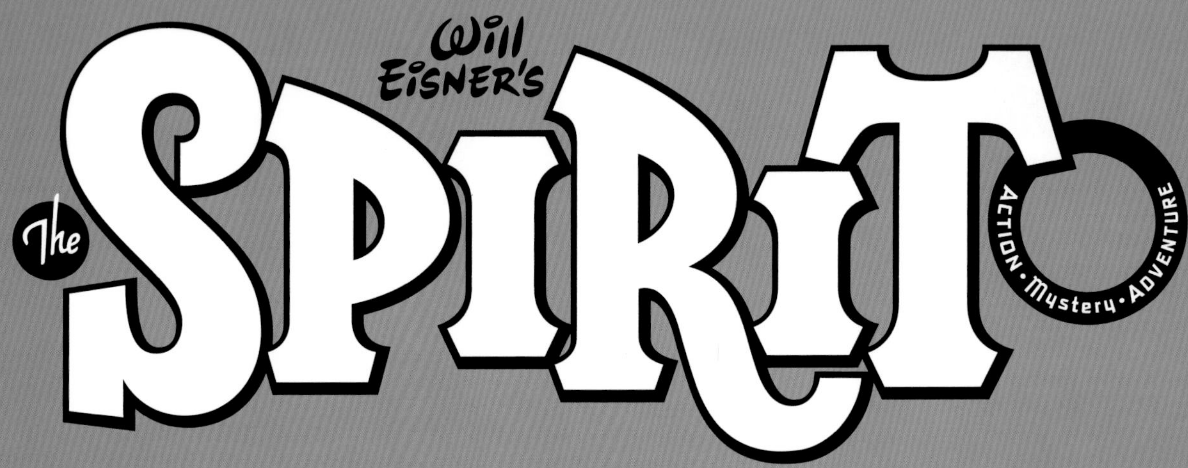

1

2

3

4

5

6

Darwyn Cook's ongoing **The Spirit** series followed on from the **Batman/Spirit** one-shot. I wanted to honour the history of the character and Will Eisner's legacy – the 'Eisners', the most prestigious awards in the field, are given out at the San Diego Comic-Con each year in his memory.

Denis Kitchen, Eisner's publisher at Kitchen Sink from the 1970s to the 1990s, had a lot of useful advice for the redesign of this classic logo: "What Will and I both discovered over thirty years is that his three-dimensional logos for Harvey **4**, Warren **5**, Ken Pierce and early Kitchen Sink Press **1** had the least sales impact on store shelves. That's why he modified it, using the essential shape but dropping the dimensional portion for the later long-running Kitchen Sink reprint series **3**. What we finally concluded is that his very first comic book logo from the 1940s **2** had the most impact, and so we revived that on *The Spirit: The New Adventures*. Will came to see [the more complex designs] as decorative logos best suited to splash pages, but not covers."

Keeping the playful bounce of the chosen original version **3**, I beefed it up, made it a little less tall so that it wouldn't cover too much of the artwork, and generally rationalised it. Updating a vintage logo is a delicate affair, as sometimes its charm lies in the idiosyncrasies (the reversed-stress of the 'A's in **Batman**, for example), and it's easy to go too far and lose the essential character.

The somewhat uneven gaps between the letters – note the large space between the second 'I' and the 'T' – were evened out by tucking the 'I' under the crossbar of the 'T' and respacing. The characterful curl on the 'S' was taken across to the tail of the 'R', and the slopes on the sides of the serifs, as seen on the top and bottom of the 'I' were added to the 'R' and 'P', which originally sloped in the opposite direction. I decided that similar serifs on the top of the 'T' would also be a nice consistent touch.

The outline was treated as a subtle shadow rather than a monoline, to impart just a little of the three-dimensional quality of the more outré logos. The 'The' was tucked into the 'S' in a small circle so it would read clearly over the art, and Will's signature was also tidied up.

I liked the versions with the sweeping cape and head, but as with the **Batman/Spirit** book, in situ these often clash with the actual characters in the art, so they were not used.

The 'Action, Mystery, Adventure' tagline **7**, **11** was redrawn from a scan of an original Sunday page **6**, keeping the mix of upper and lower case but replacing the script-form 's' with a roman version. Each issue, Darwyn would drop a vignette of a different character into the circle. The barcode, DC logo and credits were added in-house.

7

ACTION
Mystery
ADVENTURE

8

The SPIRIT

9

The SPIRIT

10

Will Eisner
Will Eisner's

11

12

The SPIRIT

13

Ray Death
Death Ray magazine
Blackfish Publishing
Mascot
2007

Matt Bielby, who launched Future Publishing's leading SF magazine *SFX*, and for whom I had drawn numerous illustrations since the very first issue, was launching *Death Ray* magazine, the first title from his own company **Blackfish Publishing**.

The magazine covered a similar range of film, book and TV SF and fantasy, and Ray Death was to be the magazine's mascot. Matt suggested he look like "the little face of someone who's just been zapped by a death ray, so his head is sort of lit up from the inside, like a Halloween pumpkin".

I added some 'Kirby Krackle', a cigar and a ray gun.

Batman Incorporated
DC Comics
Comic book series
Proposed logo
2010

Written by Grant Morrison and illustrated by Chris Burnham, **Batman Incorporated** told how Bruce Wayne took the **Batman** 'franchise' and expanded it into a global team of heroes, each inspired by and modelled on his example.

I misunderstood the direction of the series, taking a much more militaristic and aggressive line for this first round of designs than Grant intended. Although not appropriate, there are some interesting and unusual Bat-related shapes here that combine the warning stripes seen on the back of trucks and heavy machinery, a glowering, simplified Bat cowl and angular, stripped-down stencil letters.

The correct direction for the logo, shown on the following pages, was a slicker, more polished corporate brand: a Porsche emblem, perhaps, something Bruce would have on the hood of his Batmobile or private jet, or the logo for an international tech brand.

There was some discussion around whether the comic was to use 'Inc.' or 'Incorporated', the final version settling on 'Incorporated'.

1

2

3

4

5

6

BATMAN

7

8

1

BATMAN
INC.

2

3

4

5

6

BATMAN
INCORPORATED

7

8

9

10

11

12

14

15

16

Batman Incorporated
DC Comics
Comic book series
2010

The minimalist treatment of the Bat outline and the way the wings sweep down to describe the sides of the two symmetrical 'A's **4** was, I felt, a particularly elegant solution, but it was not chosen.

Grant suggested incorporating the yellow oval Bat symbol that Jim Lee's 'New 52' costume designs had reintroduced. The lettering is clean and elegant, again reminiscent of an automobile marque, and much simpler than the heavier, militaristic first pass shown on the previous page. I usually shy away from Photoshop effects, but here a subtle reflection and emboss seemed conceptually appropriate. Though yellow matched the costume, different colourways were provided to key with the art on each issue **14**, **15**, **16**.

13 are some of my experimental extrapolations of the Bat silhouette.

The final trade dress used here is the 'New 52' line-wide branding created in-house, though it does use the Device font Quagmire top right.

13

BATMAN
INCORPORATED

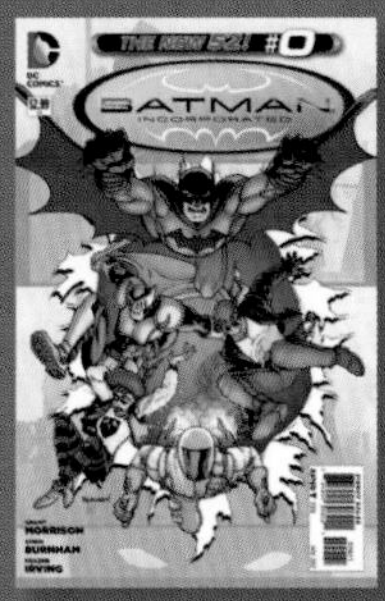
THE NEW 52! #0
BATMAN
INCORPORATED

THE NEW 52!
BATMAN
INCORPORATED
MORRISON
BURNHAM

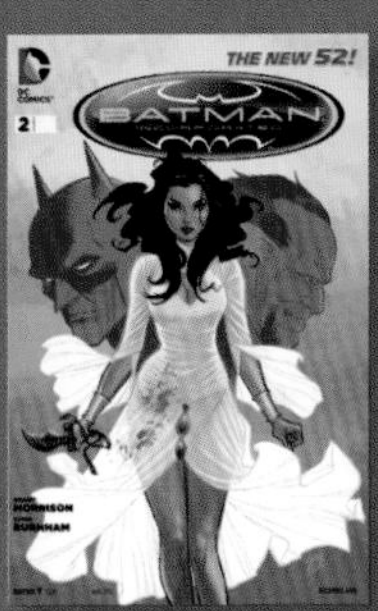
THE NEW 52!
BATMAN

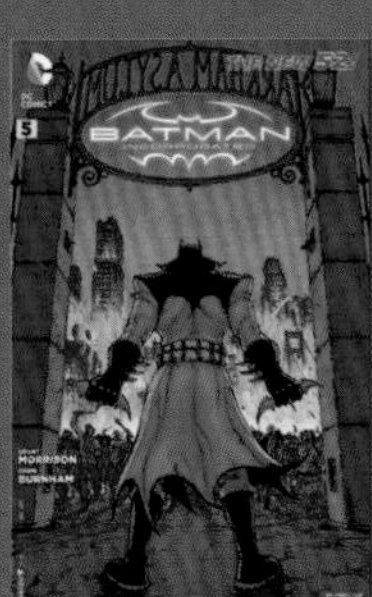
BATMAN

THE NEW 52!
BATMAN
INCORPORATED
MORRISON
BURNHAM
MASTERS
R.I.P.

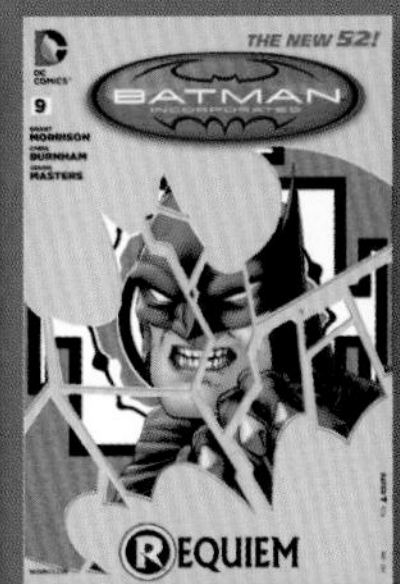
THE NEW 52!
BATMAN
INCORPORATED
MORRISON
BURNHAM
MASTERS
REQUIEM

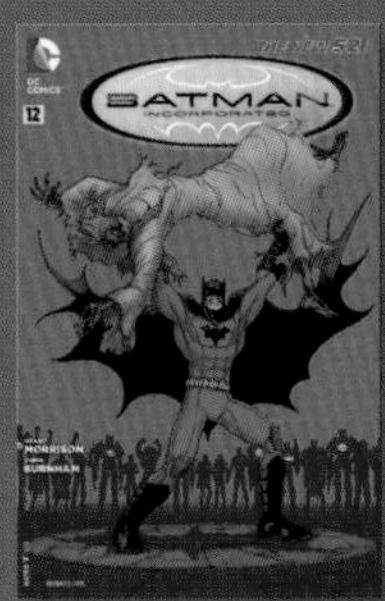
BATMAN
INCORPORATED

Teenage Mutant Ninja Turtles
Nickelodeon
TV show and merchandise
2010

Nickelodeon had recently acquired the **Teenage Mutant Ninja Turtles** and planned a new CGI animated show to air in 2012. Donatello, Raphael, Michelangelo and Leonardo were to be spruced up for a new generation, and It was felt that most of the earlier logos were now too old-fashioned or lacked a certain typographic finesse.

My designs moved away from the previous overtly cartoony style, aiming for a more contemporary, slightly older market. Graffiti, spray paint stencilling and weathering conjure up the show's gritty urban and sewer locations, and the classic Turtle-green colour served as a visual link to the original design. I preferred a less fussy treatment without the 3D rendering that many CGI shows and films favour, but during the design process I did submit some concepts along those lines **10, 15**.

The final logo was used for the titles of the TV show **3** and across all the merchandise and advertising **1, 2**. It was also extended into a custom typeface: the full 'Teenage Mutant Ninja' font **5** incorporated all the necessary accented characters, ligatures and other glyphs required for the localisation of an international TV series **4**.

Turtle power!

1

2

3

4

5

ABCDEFGHIJKLMNOPQRSTUVWXYZ

ABCDEFGHIJKLMNOPQRSTUVWXYZ

#0123456789 £$¢ƒ¥%‰.&(/)[\]

AA AC AE Æ Æ AF AG AM AW AV CE CF CG

CW CG CV DA DC DE DG DG DM DM DN DT

DV DW EE EF EG EV EW EC EG FA FG FI FL JE

JM JA JE JG JN MA MA MC ME MF MG

MM MV MV MW NA NA NAG NC NE NF NG

NN NV NW Œ DN SS TF TG TC TE VA VC VE VG

VM VN WA WC WC WE WE WG WM WN

6

7

TEENAGE MUTANT NINJA
TURTLES

8

9

10

11

TEENAGE MUTANT NINJA
TURTLES

12

13

14

15

16

17

18

19

The Seal of the Grand Hermetic Order of the Ascended Gentleman
Image Comics
Graphic novel incidental logo
2011

A logo for a spoof advertisement in **Tales from Beyond Science**, a collection of my comic strips reprinted from *2000AD*.

Third Person
Third Person Productions
Publisher
2011

Third Person was a graphic novel imprint publishing adventure, horror and SF.

They requested a "graphic symbol as our logo, with the text subservient, that feels mysterious, even noirish. The 'third person' refers to an omniscient narrator, perceiving all things at once with a clarity of vision. Who is the third person?"

The two figures with the negative space suggesting the third central figure - a person described by an absence rather than a presence - was the immediate choice. The hands of the figure on an early version **4** were moved to the hips to avoid any possible crotch-grabbing misinterpretations, something the client had to point out to me. A case where a second opinion is vital.

The reverse of the business cards used cropped close-ups of the three figures, one for each of the directors **1**.

1

2

THIRD
P3RSON

3

4

Archaia
Graphic novel publisher
2009

Archaia is an American comic book and graphic novel publisher, home to the Eisner Award-winning *The Realist* and numerous Jim Henson Company properties. I was asked to look at updating their existing logo, designed by the company's founder, Mark Smilie **1**.

The basics were there. I suggested a general simplification of the design that would make the linework thicker and more robust for use at smaller sizes, a more attractive face, and shortening the snakes to give a more compact design that could work horizontally as well as vertically **8**, **9**.

I also implemented a bolder, simpler type treatment that had enough presence to be used as the main element supported by a smaller face or even on its own, for example on the spines of thin books **10**.

It was suggested that we keep the orange as a visual link to the original, but in order to lift the face out of the background and introduce more definition I added white keylights either side, an outline around the snakes, and picked out **Archaia** in white type.

1

2

3

4

Archaia Black Label
Graphic novel publisher
2010

Archaia is primarily a creator-owned publisher, but it had also been entering into licensing deals with Hollywood production companies. A new sub-brand was therefore required to differentiate these 'partnership' books.

The new logo needed to have a visual link to the original so they were recognizably related. I felt that the obvious pairing would be a male face drawn in a similar style. Several ideas were floated which extended the mythical themes of the Queen design, including fire, a ram's horn, a fire-haired man **5** and an oak tree.

The 'Green Man' of myth was also explored **6**, though it was felt his facial leaves looked more like a bushy moustache. The oak tree idea morphed into the intertwined vines which replaced the snakes, and the Green Man into a King. The surrounding rectangle is, by necessity, slightly taller to accommodate the extra 'Black Label' line. A masculine silver was chosen to counterpoint the Queen's bronze.

7 uses a more ornate Art Nouveau-influenced type style, based on the Device font Absinthe. **2** are the foil-blocked business cards.

5

6

7

8

9

10

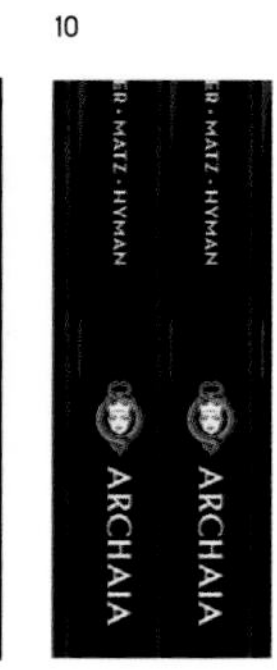

Blogstar
Blog and website content and marketing services
2013

1

Established in London in 2011, **BlogStar** was one of the first dedicated content marketing agencies, providing blog and social media content for all manner of organisations who wanted to reach out to a new demographic.

The logo works as a stand-alone type treatment and as the 'Blogstar Tomato', which can be used with or without the identifying text underneath.

Bleeding Monk
Valiant Comics
Comic book one-shot
2000

A stand-alone issue spinning out of the ongoing **Harbinger** title. The final version as used on the comic cover tucks the Harbinger logo over 'Monk', shortening the ascender of the 'k' and italicising it to match.

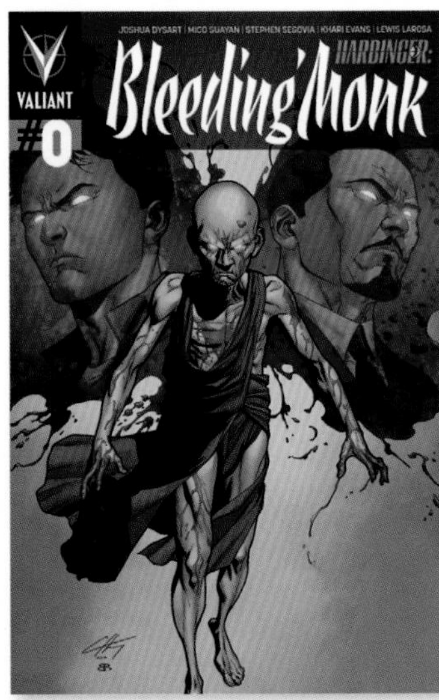

1

adrian mole

2

3

YES, M'LADY

4

5

JUDGE DEATH

6

7

8

9

MASSACRE

10

1 **Adrian Mole: The Adulterous Years**
Penguin Books
Book cover incidental logo
1998
Writer: Sue Townsend
The book was later renamed *The Cappuccino Years*. This logo is from an unused cover illustration/design I created for the first paperback edition

2 **Yellow Boots**
Yellow Boots
Women's clothing store, Tokyo
1997
The Device font Blackcurrant is derived from this logo

3 **Yes, M'Lady**
Forbidden Planet
T-shirt
1987
T-shirt featuring Thunderbirds' Parker

4 **Midnight's Children**
Fleetway/Judge Dredd Megazine
Judge Dredd serial
1990
Writer: Alan Grant
Artist: Jim Baikie

5 **Judge Death**
Fleetway/Judge Dredd Megazine
Judge Dredd serial
1990
Writer: Brian Skuter (John Wagner)
Artist: Peter Doherty

6 **A Sound of Thunder**
Valiant Comics
Album
2015
Shadowman band tie-in

7 **Emily Fairweather**
Photographer
2012

8 **Northern Lights**
BBC
CD cover
Proposed logo
2002
Philip Pullman audio dramatisation

9 **Massacre**
Valiant Comics
2016
Harbinger: Renegades comic book arc

10 **Labyrinth**
Valiant Comics
2016
Eternal Warrior comic book arc

Armor Hunters
Valiant Comics
Comic book mini-series/crossover
2014

Armor Hunters was a **Valiant** crossover event that tied together the **Unity**, **Bloodshot** and **Harbinger** titles. As well as a brand that would sit above the existing logos and set the tie-in books apart, there was also the trade dress for the four-issue stand-alone mini-series to consider, which needed to sport the same logo but be sufficiently different to avoid confusion across all the variant covers.

The requirement was for a logo that looked 'battle-damaged'. Early designs played with the shapes of the X-O armour's overlapping plates **1-3**. The favoured approach featured **X-O Manowar**'s helmet impaled on a sword, a kind of 'mission patch' for the **Armor Hunters** themselves **main image**, **5**, **6**, **8**. This appeared on the teaser ads, but proved to be overly complex for the comic covers themselves, so a simpler, stripped-back version **4** was used. The trade dress design for the stand-alone series included a strip of silhouettes that ran along the bottom of each cover. I also drew a special die-cut mask cover for issue 2.

The white cover is a blank 'sketch' variant. The logo continued into the one-shot follow-up, **Armor Hunters: Aftermath.**

1

ARMOR HUNTER

2

ARMOR HUNTERS

3

ARMOR

4

ARMOR HUNTERS

5

6

7

8

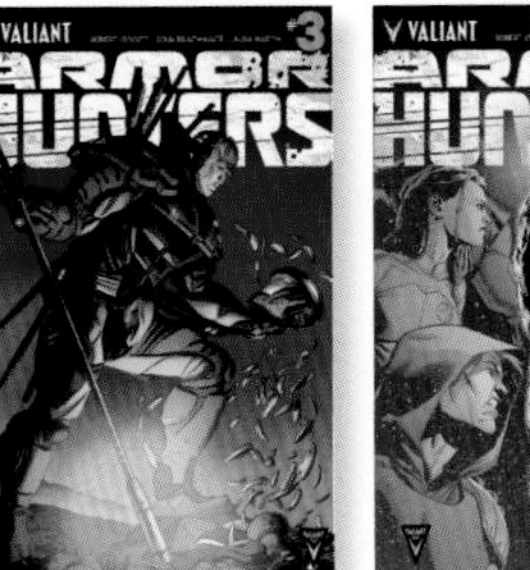

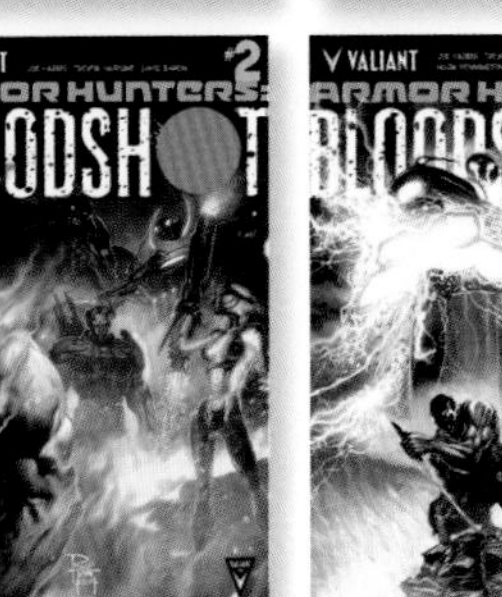

Nameless
Image/Supergods
Comic book series
2014

For his Image Comics horror/SF collaboration with **Batman** artist Nathan Fairbarn, Grant Morrison requested a logo that evoked The Misfits' logo or Skywald Comics' *Nightmare* magazine from the early 1970s. I felt that a direct pastiche might look a bit cartoony next to Nathan's detailed art, so I attempted a more modern interpretation. I kept the rough edges and 'bounce', but dropped the heavy outlines and shadows, then added a distressed texture. There's also a touch of the original craggy **Judge Dredd** logo in the way the letters interlock.

The inside front covers **1** set all of the credits in one point size, interspersed with the enigmatic glyphs that can also be seen on the back covers, as if it were an alien signal with no differentiation.

The back covers were mandalas I created by mirroring and duplicating photographs of decaying machinery I took in the Science Museum, London. The insides of V2 rockets, Gypsy Moth engines and jet turbines, each the science fiction technology of its day, are made strange and alien once again. I produced dozens of these images, only a few of which I used. The rest I collected in an issue of my occasional magazine, **Misc.**

The graphic novel collection was designed by Nathan using my elements.

1

Mighty Love
DC Comics
Graphic novel
2004

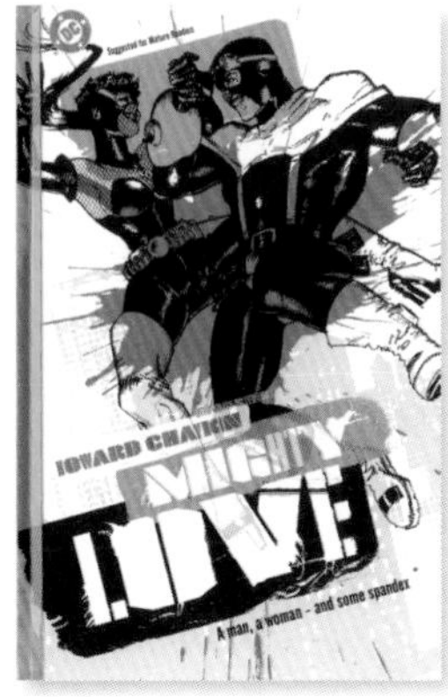

Being an avid follower of Howard Chaykin's graphically inventive series *American Flagg!*, I was very happy to be asked to design his first graphic novel in years. **Mighty Love** is the story of two masked vigilantes who get it on in their secret identities while being arch rivals in civilian life. Howard permitted me to play fast and loose with his cover art, cropping and overlaying colour.

1

2

3

4

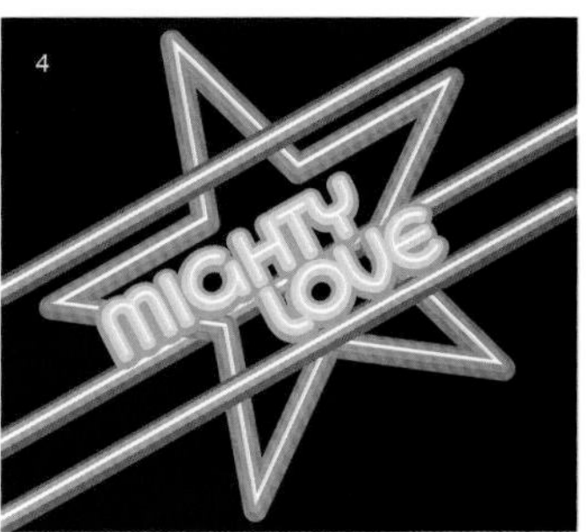

Avengers: Endless Wartime
Marvel Comics
Original graphic novel
2013

Written by Warren Ellis and drawn by Mike McKone with colours by Jason Keith, **Endless Wartime** launched a new series of self-contained original graphic novels.

The finale of the book was set in the Nordic snows, so in close collaboration with Warren, Mike (who provided endless sketches to indulge my suggestions) and editor Tom Brevoort, I designed the cover with a cool, subdued colour scheme and a clean expanse of white across the lower part of the cover to frame the title.

I redrew The **Avengers** 'A' **1** with a three-line enclosing circle so that the 'A' was more prominent, then I ran the credits around this device and added a perspective. This image was repeated across the half-title and title pages inside **3**, **4**, slowly being covered over in snow.

The back cover continues the circular type arrangement and places all the small intrusive logos in a line along the bottom to try and keep the clutter to a minimum **2**. **5** is laid out like a page from an imagined **Avengers** corporate manual.

The endpapers (opposite) used a tessellated 'A', and the final cover was printed in silver, black and red on a pearlescent paper that sparkled like frost.

1

2

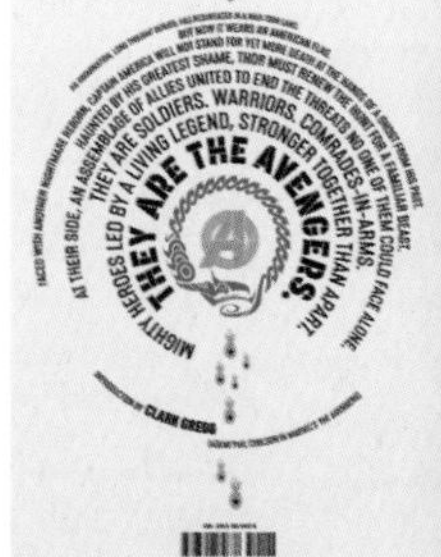

3

4

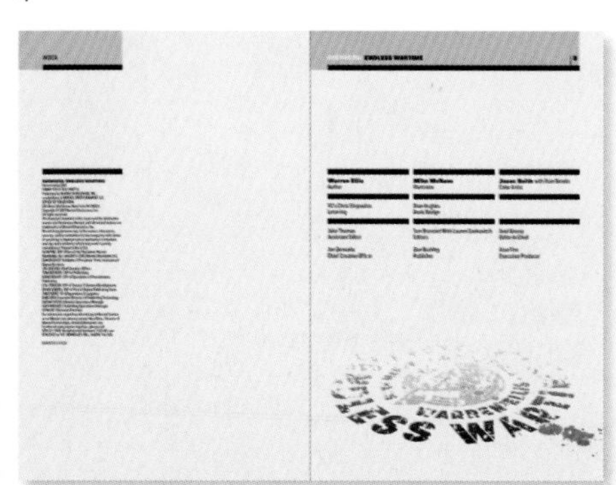

5

Actua BD
L'Agence BD
Website
2016

Actua BD is a European comics website featuring news, interviews and articles, and is considered to be one of the foremost reference sources of its kind on the internet.

The logo needed to be long and horizontal to work as a website banner and on the spines of books, where it runs vertically. The reliable (or perhaps clichéd) convention of the speech bubble was pressed into use, arranged in a circle **6**, **10**, **11** as a metaphor for interviews and to suggest a round-table forum where discussions about comics take place.

The final logo uses the bubbles as quotation marks. In isolation, these are used as page identifiers and buttons **7**. Some options used a clean sans serif, either Korolev **6** or Paralucent **10**, **11**; the final version uses my take on the *Tintin/ Blake and Mortimer* lettering style, which is intrinsically linked to the history of Franco-Belgian comics.

Vintage colours were sampled from classic albums **4**; a simple cyan was used for the final version, which exists in boxed **3** and unboxed variants.

1

2

3

4

5

6

7

8

9

10

11

1

2

3

Sect Civil War
Valiant Comics
Comic book arc
2013

This **Archer & Armstrong** story arc is a head-to-head battle between all the secret societies you've ever heard of – the Illuminati, Skull and Bones, the Stonemasons, the Catholic Church, and even aliens.

The logo is the ultimate occult sigil mashup: the eye in the pyramid, Masonic dividers, and a skull with almond-shaped alien eyes.

The umlaut over the a, a *Spinal Tap* reference, was dropped for the final printed version.

Music Factory
MFEG
Music company
2003

Music Factory is a small independent music company based in Yorkshire, UK, with interests ranging from hard house labels to aerobics fitness clubs. Director Amadeus Mozart [sic] felt that their old logo **1** was, to quote, "shite". The full company name was sometimes shortened to MFEG, but this "sounded like a bad foot disease".

Often an update of a logo consists of lifting the best ideas from the original and simplifying and clarifying them, discarding any extraneous details. This was one such case.

Other directions included speakers made from records and CDs **4**, cogwheels crossed with speakers **6**, **7**, industrial noise warning signs **5** and musical note/cog hybrids **8**.

1

2

3

4

5

6

7

8

9

Kaliphz
London Records
Band
Proposed logo
1993

Kaliphz were a British hip hop crew formed in Rochdale, Greater Manchester by 2-Phaan and Jabba da Hype. They began as part of the breakdancing scene in the early 1980s before branching out into spoken word and rap.

My proposed logo for the band references spray paint, the arrow on the nozzle of the spray paint tin, stencils and the collaborative nature of the rotating roster of band members.

1

2

3

4

5

6

7

8

Black Panther
Marvel Comics
Comic book series
2016

T'Challa the **Black Panther,** created by Stan Lee and Jack Kirby, first appeared in **Fantastic Four** #52 back in 1966. He was the first black superhero in mainstream American comics.

For his 50th anniversary and 2016 relaunch by writer Ta-Nehisi Coates and artist Brian Stelfreeze, an updated logo that kept some of the angularity and proportions of the previous design was requested. The blocky 1970s logo was ignored entirely.

I offered a few alternatives that endeavoured to made it stronger and more refined, while keeping a hint of the character's trademark claw necklace. For versatility on the cover, the final logo was supplied in both stacked and one-line versions.

Logos for the spin-off titles *World of Wakanda* and *Rise of the Black Panther* were created in-house by inexpertly cutting and pasting parts of my letters.

BLACK PANTHER

1

BLACK PANTHER

2

BLACK
PANTHER

3

BLACK
PANTHER

4

BLACK PANTHER

Manowar
10 Records
Band logo and record sleeve design
1984

Sign of the Hammer was **Manowar**'s first album with 10 Records, and one of my very first professional jobs after graduating from art college.

I designed the hammer, the updated logo, and the sleeve. Previous **Manowar** sleeves looked like Frank Frazetta *Conan the Barbarian* book covers, so this was something of a departure.

The background is a shot of the top of an old metal filing cabinet which photographer Simon Fowler (who later had an office in the Salem Road studio) and I hit with hammers, scratched and splashed with paint stripper, then sprayed with water to make it look like it was sweating. It's an unsophisticated and direct reference to heavy metal – but then I reasoned heavy metal is often unsophisticated and direct. I was looking for something tough, evocative and abstract; some fans apparently thought it was a birch tree. The 12" single sleeve for *All Men Play in 10* is an amp flightcase. *Spinal Tap* was coincidentally released the same year.

I only met the band once, at the offices of the record company. They were unsure about the line above the logo, because "you can't put a ceiling on **Manowar**!" I was concerned that it might look a bit Third Reich, but no-one seemed to notice. The logo has become a popular tattoo with fans.

The 'Sign of the Hammer' type is a font called Glenlake, to which I added a stencil effect. It has recently been revived as part of type designer Stuart Sandler's Filmotype digitisation project.

Channel 52
DC Comics
News column
2012

Channel 52 was a feature that ran in the back pages throughout **DC Comics**' titles, promoting new series and events in a reportage format.

The logos reference satellite uplinks and microphones. **3** and **7** show a Clark Kent-style reporter with a press pass tucked in the band of his hat. **6** is pretty hard to decipher.

1

2

3

4

5

6

7

8

Ealing
London Borough of Ealing
Unsolicited logo proposal
2011

1 

2 

I came back late at night from a trip abroad to find the trains from Heathrow to London were not stopping at Ealing Broadway due to "rioting". Rioting? In **Ealing**? Could Waitrose have run out of organic taramasalata, I wondered? Stepping out at West Ealing, the station before, I found myself in the middle of the **Ealing** riots.

Cars sped by without their lights on, and a group of wannabe gangstas were swaggering up The Avenue towards me. The jobsworth in the minicab office wouldn't let me in behind the toughened glass screen, so fearing for my safety, I ducked into the Drayton Arms, where a bizarre normality reigned. I told the barman that the bikes outside were all being stolen, and three or four punters went out to remonstrate – and came right back in again, bolting the doors behind them. I called up a friend who drove by as slowly as he dared, opening his car door so I could run out, jump in and get away.

Gangs of thugs roamed unchallenged through the borough, setting cars alight and looting into the early hours. Unbeknownst to me, riots had been spreading across London for several days. Type "**Ealing** Riots" into YouTube, and you'll see some of the cameraphone footage.

The next day, walking from Acton to Hanwell, I could see that almost every shop had been broken into, every car window smashed. A bus had been hijacked and driven into a lamppost on Ealing Common, a car driven through the window of a supermarket, and a local shopkeeper who stepped out to remonstrate was killed on Haven Green. I have lived in **Ealing** all my life, and didn't think I'd ever see burning cars outside my old school.

The borough's existing logo **1** is ugly and utilitarian, incorporating a cartoonish oak tree paired with Frutiger. It communicates none of the tradition, elegance or charm of the 'Queen of the Suburbs', instead conjuring up stern demands for council tax arrears or road cleaning services. Who designs these monstrosities?

I took it upon myself to design a new one. I arranged oak leaves into a Queen's crown, and drew up custom lettering based on the old Walpole Picture Theatre fascia that is an **Ealing** architectural icon.

I hoped that a more attractive logo might be popular on T-shirts, mugs, enamel badges and other merchandise that locals could buy to show their support and to raise funds. Small help, but what's a designer to do?

I sent my proposal to **Ealing** Council. They replied: "Replacing our logo would, of course, be an extremely expensive undertaking given the massive number of applications including vehicles, buildings and uniforms. In these tough financial times, when councils are having to reduce their budgets by millions of pounds, you will appreciate that isn't realistic, even if it was desirable."

OK, thanks for missing the point entirely. One more try. "Perhaps it could be used alongside it. Rather than a borough-wide rebrand, it could co-exist as a 'heritage' marque for projects where the current logo might look too utilitarian and have the wrong tone of voice."

I didn't hear back, so I had some shirts printed up myself **2** and handed them out to friends.

Last Gang in Town
Vertigo/DC Comics
Comic book series
2015

Simon Oliver and Rufus Dayglo's **Last Gang in Town** is a six-issue mini-series from Vertigo. Something of a nostalgic punk paean to misspent youth by a bunch of men bordering on middle age, the blurb announces "it's time for a new generation of criminals to rise: a band of snotty-nosed heroes driven by destiny and cheap cider, who will strike fear into the establishment, put art back into crime and crime back into art."

A few years ago the Sex Pistols reissued the digitally remastered *Never Mind The Bollocks*. It was advertised with the strapline 'A Present for Father's Day.' Soon, it'll be a 'Perfect Gift for Grandad.'

For the logo I attempted to evoke a scrappy photocopied DIY fanzine aesthetic, printing out type, screwing it up then scanning it back in to introduce some analogue grit, then overlaying it to mimic out-of-register cheap printing effects. The crossed guitars were suggested by a band member's leather jacket **7-11**, while **1** is a cleaner, more post-punk 'new wave' approach. **6** was cut from black paper with scissors then scanned in. The version with the map of London behind it **3** was an early favourite that was incorporated on many of the rough cover sketches, but proved to be less versatile.

The final logo is a mashup of Franklin Gothic, Dom Diagonal, an extended Clarendon and Cooper Black, all typefaces that have found themselves on the wrong side of the font fashion police at some time or other. It was supplied in a range of suitably flouro punk colours.

Cover artist Rob Davis incorporated the logo in unusual and creative ways each issue. The final covers were laid out in-house.

1

2

3

4

5

6

7

8

9

10

11

12

LAST
GANG
IN
TOWN

LAST
GANG
IN
TOWN

LAST
GANG
IN
TOWN

LAST
GANG
IN
TOWN

LAST
GANG
IN
TOWN

LAST
GANG
IN
TOWN

LAST
GANG
IN
TOWN
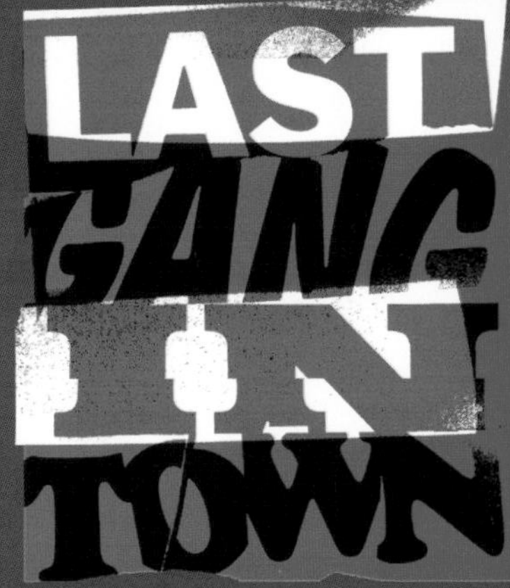
LAST
GANG
IN
TOWN

LAST
GANG
IN
TOWN

Zuda
DC Comics
Digital comic site
Proposed logo
2007

Zuda was **DC Comics**' webcomics imprint from 2007 until 2010.

Though **Zuda** comics series won plaudits and nominations from the industry's Glyph Comics Awards and Harvey Awards, it was eventually folded into DC's new mainstream digital publishing arm.

My favoured logo designs explore the similarity of a computer monitor and a speech balloon **5**, **20**, **main image**, and use colours that are very vibrant on the Web in RGB but are not reproducible in print, and so would normally be avoided – a logo needs to look consistent across different media.

11 and **12** combine computer screens and comic panels, while **14** and **15** illustrate the collaborative nature of the site: **Zuda** hosted competitions, open to all comic creators, who could submit their own eight-page stories. Each month ten were selected by the editorial team and visitors could vote for their favourites, the winner receiving a contract to continue their series.

None of my ideas were used.

I have no idea what, if anything, **Zuda** means, other than being a memorable four-letter Web address.

1

2

3

4

5

6

7

8

9

10

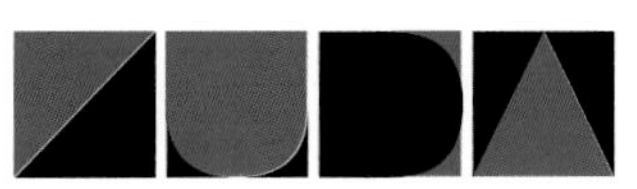

11

12

13

14

15

16

17

18

19

20

Batman and Robin
DC Comics
Comic book series
2009

For Grant Morrison and Frank Quitely's ongoing **Batman and Robin** title, Grant sent me scans of late 1950s and early 1960s Batman covers that had the strong, flat pop-art look that he was after.

Some of my early type treatments bordered on the psychedelic **7**, while others were too minimalist **3**, **4**, **5**, **6**.

I settled on heavy block capitals with a curved baseline. The angled 'B' and 'N' were achieved by sloping the mirrored 'A's while keeping the 'T' and 'M' upright. This enabled me to elegantly fit the type within the Bat shape without arbitrary distortions.

Grant's original cover sketch **1** included the circular **Robin** 'R' monogram (as featured on his costume) centred below. As this was italic and the rest of the logo was upright, it proved hard to integrate elegantly **8**, **9**, **10**. For the final logo, 'Robin' is set in a matching heavy sans with a serif on the last 'N' to mirror the extended stroke at the top of the 'R'.

I supplied a number of colourways that used the limited palette that 1960s printing allowed: CMYK values that mix 100%, 50% or 25% values of each ink with no gradations and few tertiary colours. The art also used bold, flat colours to great effect, the first issue being reprinted in several different colourways.

The final covers were laid out in-house by Kenny Lopez and also bear his then-current *Batman: Reborn* branding that ran across all the Bat-related titles.

1

2

3

4

5

6

7

8

9

10

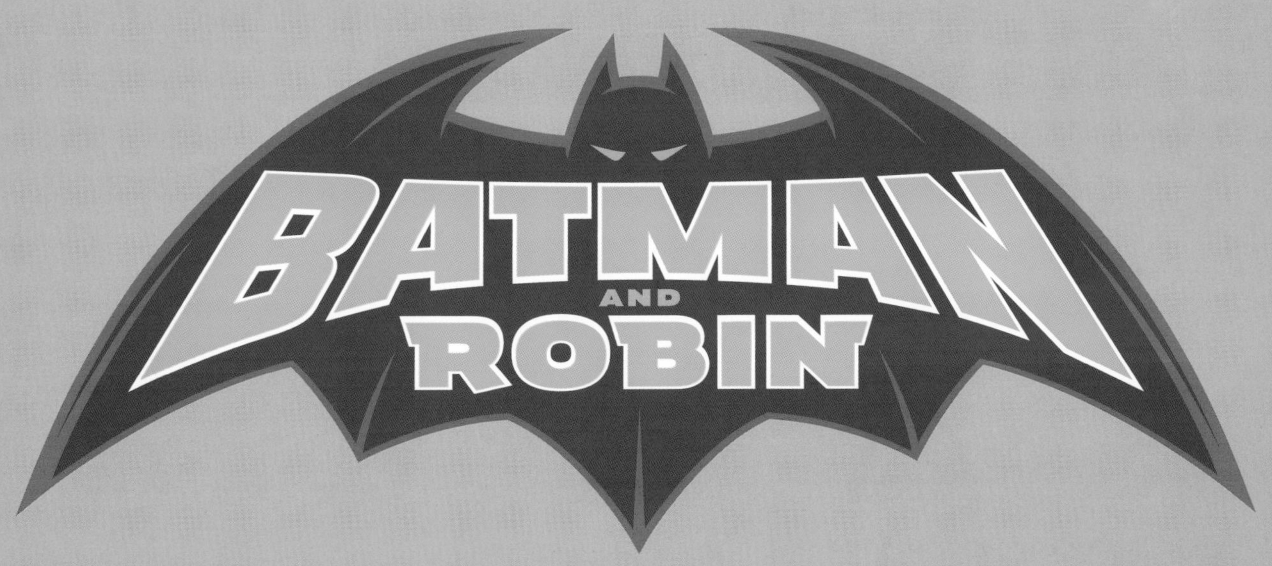
BATMAN
AND
ROBIN

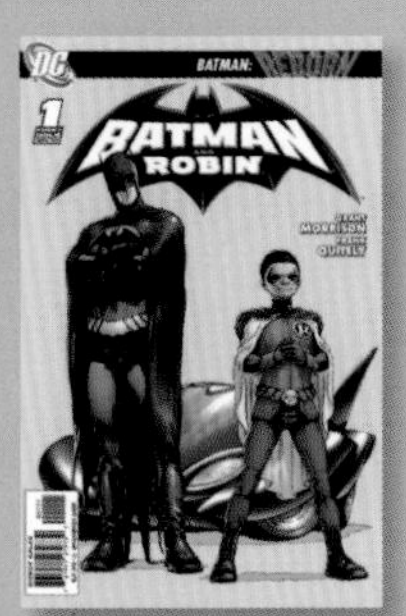
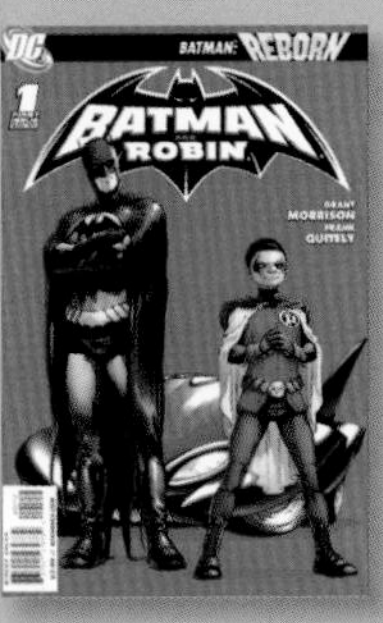
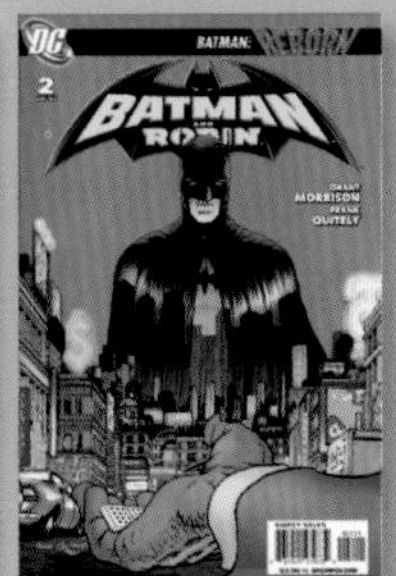

Infestation 2
IDW Publishing
Comic book arc
2012

Infestation was a crossover event in which the rugose, squamous and unspeakable creatures of H. P. Lovecraft's Cthulhu Mythos encroach into the worlds of San Diego comic publisher IDW's licensed properties *G .I. Joe, Dungeons and Dragons, 30 Days of Night, Transformers, Ghostbusters, Teenage Mutant Ninja Turtles* and *Star Trek*.

The design is a banner that runs above the existing logos of each comic for the duration; as the licensed logos were a given, it wasn't feasible to try and pull them together stylistically.

Fantastic Lesbian
MacCab Films
Promotional T-shirt
2000

T-shirt motifs for Maria Cabardo's documentary **Better Things**, which explores the life of artist Jeff Jones. After gender reassignment in later life, Jones would describe herself as "a **fantastic lesbian**".

1

2

Sam Williams
Music producer
Personal mark
2000

Sam Williams is a music producer who has worked with Supergrass, The Noisettes, Gaz Coombes and The Go Team.

1

2

3

4

Knackerman
Sub Rosa
Theatre production
2008

Designed to promote a limited-run stage production for which I also drew the posters and flyers. The letters were taken from a vintage American wood type catalogue, and extra knackering added in Photoshop. It was subsequently digitised and released as the Device font Wormwood Gothic.

Jonny Double
DC Comics/Vertigo
Comic book series
1998

Jonathan Sebastian **'Jonny' Double** was created by Len Wein and Marv Wolfman in 1968. He was reintroduced as an aging private investigator in San Francisco with a fascination for 1960s counterculture in *Two Finger Discount,* a 1998 four-issue mini-series written by Brian Azzarello with art by Eduardo Risso. The graphic covers were by **DC Comics**' art director Mark Chiarello, a talented illustrator as well as DC Comics' art director.

The logo plays on the obvious doubling of the character's name and draws on the dramatic typographic language of vintage pulp detective paperbacks, right down to the evocative straplines. The Vertigo logo and trade dress are by Richard Bruning.

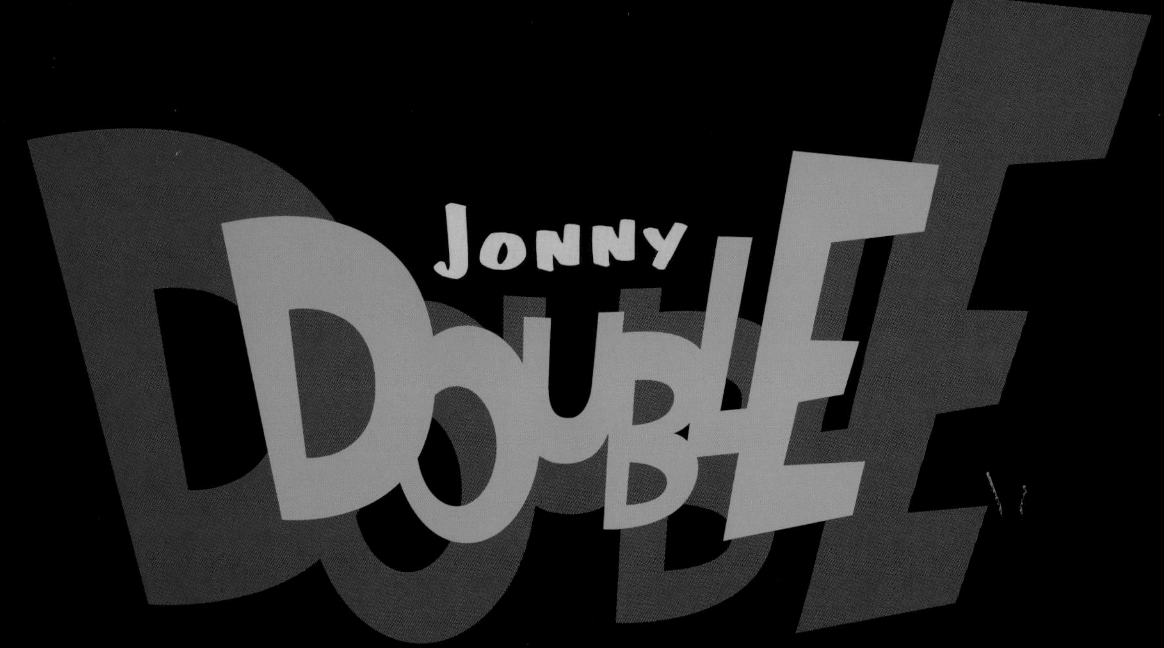

1

2

JONNY
DOUBLE

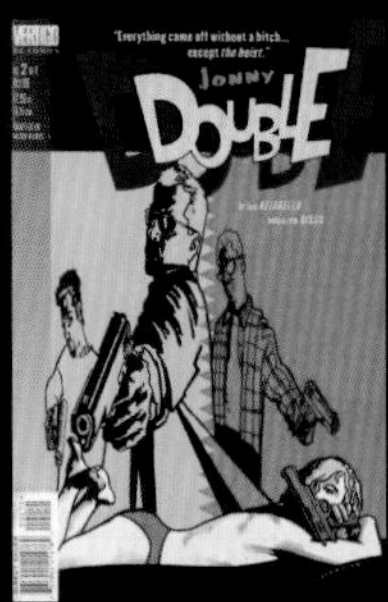

1 **Device**
Device
Company logo
First iteration
1995

2 **Copperknob**
Copperknob
Website/entrepreneur
2000

3 **Memetic Footprint**
Incidental logo from the book
Cult-ure: Ideas Can Be Dangerous
Fiell
2011
Author: Rian Hughes

4 **Bad Tune Men**
Nonchalant Records
Jail Head Rack 12″
1984

5 **98**
Matrixmedia
Desk diary cover
1997

6 **Garrod Beckett and Co.**
Solicitors
1987

7 **Safe**
Matt Haley/Outsider Films
Motion picture
2008

8 **Batman Classics**
Titan Books
Book series
Logo proposal
1988

9 **Blue Angel**
Blue Angel
Record Label
1998

10 **Zit**
Device
Personal stamp
1984

11 **Chidge**
Actress' personal mark
1998

12 **Dunce**
Incidental logo from the book
Cult-ure: Ideas Can Be Dangerous
Fiell
2011
Author: Rian Hughes

1

2

3

4

5

6
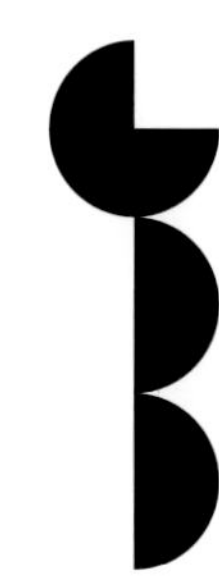

7

8

9

10

11

12

X-0 Manowar
Valiant Comics
Comic book series
2012

X-0 Manowar is perhaps **Valiant**'s flagship character from the company's first 1980s run. The logo needed to be punchy, evoke the blocky design of the original and foreground the 'X-0' element.

I took the seams and curves from the segmented armour plates of the X-0 suit and ran them through the type, suggesting futuristic military stencilling. The suit also has a little triangular motif on the chest, which was placed in the '0' and highlighted with a colour, keyed to the art each issue.

I favoured versions with a more unusual construction for the 'X' that flowed into the '0', and enabled the hyphen to elegantly sit directly above the '0' in '**Manowar**' and echo the same shape, and the 'X' and '0' to be the same width as each other **1**, **11**, **12**.

The final version uses a less outré 'X' in which the hyphen tucks into the vertex, and the 'X' has been widened for visual balance. The logo occupies the same area all **Valiant** logos adopt in order to fit neatly and consistently into the trade dress and the subsequent collected editions (bottom row, overleaf) that I also designed.

Later issues use a redesigned trade dress in which the logo extends full-width across the cover and the **Valiant** branding, having now been firmly established, is reduced in size to run in a black stripe along the top, which also houses the credits and issue number. Keeping this information in the same position issue to issue and not having to free-float it over the art means that inelegant additions such as outlines and drop shadows, often seen on comic covers to lift small text out of a busy image, never become necessary.

The *Dead Hand* arc features a narrow 'half-wrap', a two-colour sheet that folds over the front cover.

Shown at left is the logo applied to the packaging of a vinyl toy.

1

2

3

4

5

6

7

8

9

10

11

12

X-O
MANOWAR

Vertigo Pop!
DC Comics
Comic book line
2002

Edited by the always modishly attired anglophile Shelly Bond, **Vertigo Pop!** was a line of three mini-series, each set in a different city around the globe: Tokyo, London and Bangkok.

With Karen Berger, Shelly oversaw many famous Vertigo series during her two decades at DC Comics. In 2017 she launched Black Crown, a new imprint at IDW, named after the fictional English pub around which the stories revolve.

1

2

3

4

5

6

7

1

2

3

4

5

6

7

8

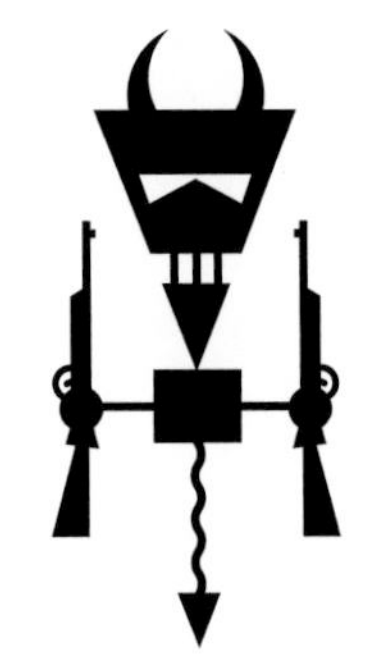

9

10

wire

11

wire

12

1 **Children's CDs**
MacUser magazine
Review icon
1995

2 **Bull Doze**
Construction and design company
1996

3 **Doc Chaos**
Vortex Comics
Comic book
Incidental logo
1990

4 **Coffee Hut**
Wall/Serpent's Tail
Book cover
Incidental logo
2002

5 **Mask Noir**
Serpent's Tail
Crime book imprint
Proposed logo
1993

6 **Gothette**
Device
T-shirt motif
2006

7 **Coms Regulatory Consulting Limited**
Telecom consultancy
2008
Note the hidden 'crc'

8 **Armed Devil**
Fleetway/Crisis Magazine
Incidental logo
1989

9 **Chris Foss**
Titan Books
Book cover
Based on artist's personal mark
2011

10 11 **Furlongwire**
Marketing news service
Proposed logos
2007

12 **Mambo de la Luna**
Stylorouge/Kirsty MacColl
Single
Proposed logo
1999

Juicy Musical Creations
Juicy Recordings
Record label
2006

Britannia
Valiant Comics
Comic book series
2016

Written by Peter Milligan and set during the Roman occupation of Britain, **Britannia** features the world's first detective, or 'detectorist'.

Trajan-style Roman inscriptional lettering seemed too obvious, and had already been used on another recent **Valiant** project, so I based the logo on the unique British runic writing that was around at the same time. A sharper graphic edge prevented it looking too 'Middle Earth'. **3** derives from Roman pen-script initials.

The trade dress incudes a semi-transparent Roman maze border, which the art 'pops over' where appropriate. Strong art from Cary Nord and Dave Johnson feature on the variant covers. **4** is an unused treatment for the sequel.

1

2

3

4

1 Brad and Ange
Alison Jackson
Proposed magazine article header
2008
Part of a series of designs for artist Alison Jackson's unrealised spoof celebrity magazine

2 Demon
Internet service provider
Advertisements
2001

3 Commonwealth Bee
BBC
Mascot
1998
Proposed mascot for the Commonwealth Games coverage

4 Brat
Million Dollar
T-shirt motif
1996

5 Titan Books
Titan Entertainment Group
Publisher
1986
Titan, moon of Saturn, seen edge on against the rings

6 Sadie Rocks!
Scholastic
Book cover
2009
Karen McCombie's series of young adult novels, for which I also drew the covers

7 Goatsucker
Fortean Times magazine
T-shirt motif
2000

8 Dead Hand
Valiant Comics
Comic book arc
Proposed logo
2014

9 Lion Forge
Lion Forge Comics
Proposed update of existing logo
2017

10 11 Baby Cow
Cowshed/Soho House
Private members club toiletries range
2004
Floyd the cow was produced as a soft toy.

12 E-Christmas
Christmas-themed online retailer
1999

1

2

3

4

5

6

7

8

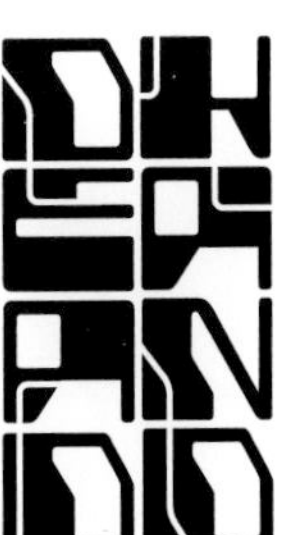

9

10

11

12

Mythic
Image Comics
Comic book series
2015

I'd designed John McCrea's very first graphic novel, **Troubled Souls** (written by a newcomer called Garth Ennis), so it was nice to be collaborating again on **Mythic**, his first series for Image with writer Phil Hester.

The pitch: "Science is a lie. The truth is, magic makes the world go round. And when magic breaks, **Mythic** fixes it. The crack field team is assigned with keeping the gears of the supernatural world turning, and more importantly, keeping you from ever knowing about it. When magic gets messy, we clean it up."

Early concepts used an inky quill pen lettering style **2**, but I felt this had been seen many times before. The final logo (main image) is based on sigil – a pictorial representation of a demon's name, or a focus for an Austin Osman Spare-style magical act of will.

The gauntlets grasp a bolt of lightning and a spanner, symbolising magical power and fixing things. It is surmounted by an all-seeing eye, and at the bottom a pointed demon's tail. A second logo, the team badge for Mythic Lore Services themselves, features on the back cover **1**, and John worked it into his art on team uniforms, calling cards and vehicles.

I used an existing teaser image John had created on the first cover. The design presents a difficult canvas, but each artist rose to the challenge, working behind, in front and around the centrally placed logo, while undoubtedly cursing me under their breath.

5-7 are the cover and opening spreads of the graphic novel collection.

1

2

3

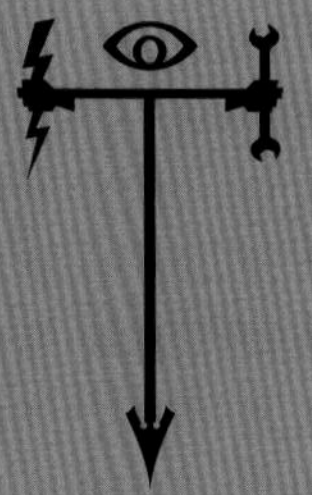

4

PHIL HESTER
JOHN McCREA
WHEN MAGIC GETS MESSY, WE CLEAN IT UP.
HESTER AND McCREA

5

6

7

1 **Pearson Low Carter**
Financial advisors
1994

2 **Ugenia Lavender**
Pan Macmillan
Book series
2008
Writer: Geri Halliwell
A series of six children's books by the ex-Spice Girl, for which I also drew the covers and interior illustrations

3 **Shift Recordings**
Record label
1996

4 5 **Bag of Destiny**
Maxim magazine (US)
Game icons
2001

6 **Black Dog**
The Designers Republic
Depression awareness charity
2017

7 **Camden Live**
Music event
1995

8 9 **Camden Live**
Camden Live
Music event
Proposed logos
1995

10 **Gossip's VIP Nightclub**
Ethos
Mug
2007
A design that purports to be merchandise from an insalubrious 1970s nightclub

11 12 **Telica**
Eve
Record label
2007
Logo and incidental logos from the generic 12″ bag I designed

1

2

3

4

5

6

7

8

9

10

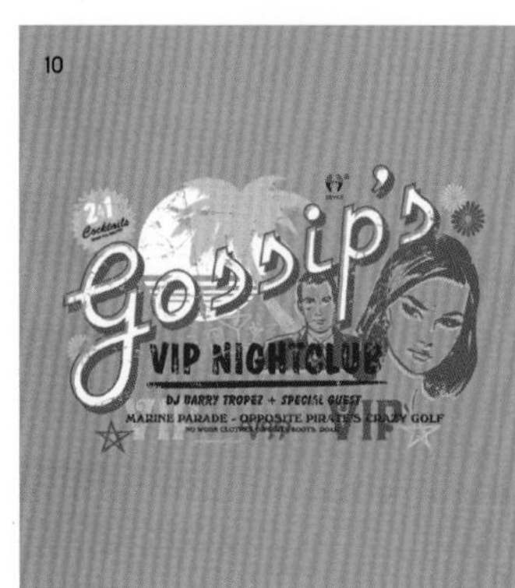

11

12

Joker: Last Laugh
DC Comics
Comic book crossover
2001

The **Joker** discovers he has an inoperable brain tumour, and decides to go out in style.

This crossover event required a top banner to run above the existing logos of the tie-ins, and a stand-alone version for the titular six-issue mini-series. The design references medical packaging – a single colour on white, with tear-off strips and other functional information in a clean, rational sans serif, incorporating a laughing skull motif that resembles a 'poison' or 'danger of death' warning label.

'Johnny Artist' and 'Fred Writer' (and 'Alice Colourist') are names I often use as placeholders when the actual creators have not yet been agreed or announced.

The design was undercut somewhat by the inclusion of traditional comic-style slogans and straplines on the final covers, one reason why a trade dress in which every element coheres in a single vision can be more successful than just a stand-alone logo design.

1

2

3

1

CHRIS KERR

1960 BESPOKE TAILORS SOHO

2

chris kerr

BESPOKE TAILORS SOHO
CLOTHING THE ECCENTRIC AND UNHINGED SINCE 1960

3

CHRIS KERR

BESPOKE TAILORS SOHO
CLOTHING THE ECCENTRIC AND UNHINGED SINCE 1960

4

CHRIS KERR

5

6

CHRIS KERR

7

CHRIS KERR

CLOTHING THE ECCENTRIC AND UNHINGED SINCE 1960

8

CHRIS KERR

Bespoke Tailors Soho

CLOTHING THE ECCENTRIC AND UNHINGED SINCE 1960

9

10

11

Chris Kerr
Bespoke Tailors
2015

Soho's longest-established bespoke tailor, **Chris Kerr** was founded on Berwick Street in 1960 by Chris's father, the legendary 'Mr Eddie', tailor to many show business stars of the swinging sixties. Chris continues the tradition, catering to those who prefer a more individualistic style of dress. He has made suits forJared Leto's **Joker**, Meryl Streep, Tom Hingston in *High Rise,* the Pythons and Harry Hill.

A dog's head mounted on a tailor's dummy in Chris' window **13** had become his unofficial mascot, and seemed a natural choice for a logo. I gave him various expressions, from quizzical to aloof, and a bowler hat. Quizzical without the hat was chosen.

My first instinct was to subtly reference the history of English menswear, and I particularly liked **1**, which sports pin-stripe moderne geometric lettering and manages to make 'Chris' and 'Kerr' the same width, thus allowing the name to be neatly centred below the dog.

Other options included English Grotesque, a signwriter's exaggeration of the quintessentially English typeface Gill Sans **4** and type derived from the kind of condensed capitals found on vintage WWII 'Caress Talk Costs Lives' posters **7**. An overtly 1960s bold condensed lowercase design in which the ascender of the 'k' joins the 'h' above was an early favourite **11**, but Chris settled on clean, elegantly letterspaced Korolev, a Device font based on lettering photographed at the Red Square parade of 1937 by Alexander Rodchenko. This was applied to labels **16**, bags, accessories, gift certificates **12** and the shopfront **10**.

The suit Mr Eddie made me for my sister Saron's wedding has a silk lining patterned with Jack Kirby romance comics **15**.

12

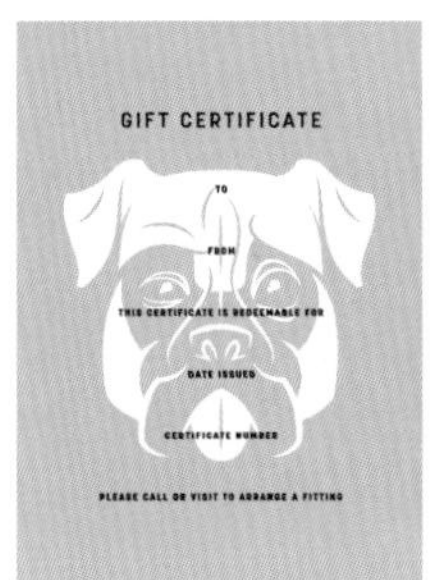

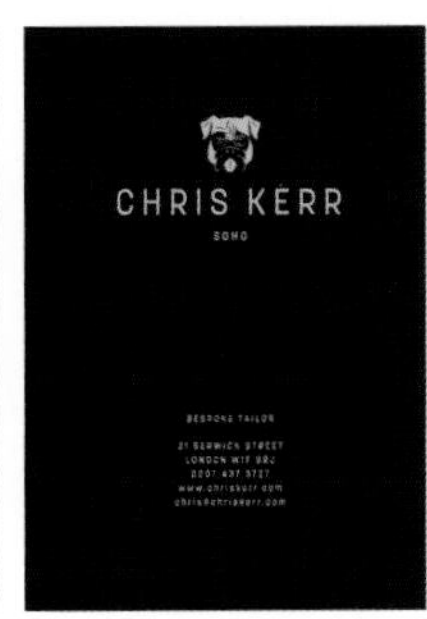

13

14

15

16

Giant Generator
Rick Remender
2000

Giant Generator is the umbrella company of US comic book writer and artist Rick Remender, creator of *Fear Agent, Low, Deadly Class, Tokyo Ghost* and *Black Science*. Early versions of the logo explored dials, batteries, cogs, giants and electrical generators; the final version is inspired by Nikola Tesla's famous experimental transmitter Wardenclyffe Tower, built in Shoreham, New York, in 1901-2.

GIANT GENERATOR

1

2

GIANT
GENERATOR

3

4

5

6

7

8

GIANT
GENERATOR

9

10

11

GIANT
GENERATOR

12

13

14

15

GIANT
GENERATOR

Marvel
Comic book publisher
Logo rationalisation
2006/2016

My original critique of the existing **Marvel** logo was done in 2006 when I was working on the **X-Men** logos. I'd been sent a digitised version which was in obvious need of a polish. Though my suggestions were appreciated by the editor, it was too daunting a prospect to replace the existing design throughout the company.

Ten years later, **Marvel** Studios adopted my version. Now I'm very happy to see it in use across both print and film.

Annotations:
1 Lumpy 'R'
2 Optically heavy spots
3 Sides of 'V' and 'A' not optically parallel
4 Letter overlap not consistent
5 'E'-'L' gap too wide
6 Registered ® is in a different font and close to the edge of the box
7 Widths of strokes differ
8 Horizontal strokes wider than vertical strokes, indicating type has been squashed
9 Line segment too small

Original logo

Original logo: annotated

Revised logo

Get>Go
H & T Pawnbrokers/Inovus (agency)
Cheque cashing and loans
2005

Get>Go is a cheque-cashing and payday loan high-street chain. The alliterative gecko mascot forms a capital 'G', and the 'E' and 'G' below are made from the same shape, simply flipped. The forward-facing arrow suggests an advance, while also evoking the missing 'K'.

The colours in the logo were taken through to interior of the shop itself.

Vital Steel
Benno Schoberth
Interior designer
2010

New York designer Benno Schoberth creates hand-blown glass and laser-cut steel screens under the name **Vital Steel**. Early versions of his logo featured a looping script that drew on his ruler-and-compass style **7** for inspiration. The final version (main image) resembles a signature - expressive and free-flowing.

1

2

3

4

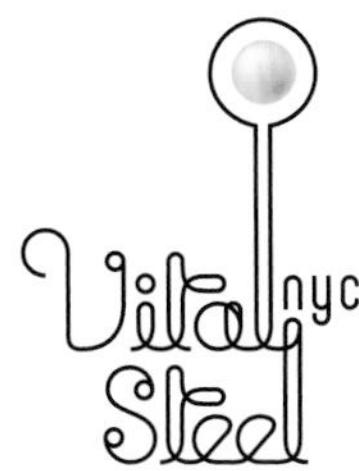

5

6

7

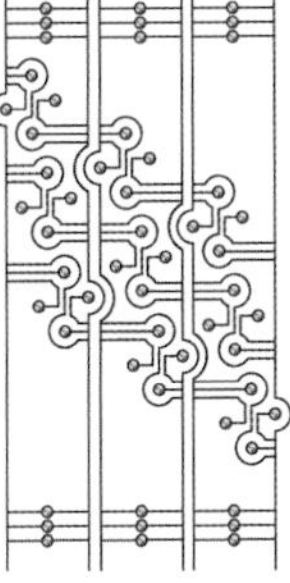

Bootleg Boys
Clarks Shoes
In-store display
2003

This logo accompanied a series of posters and in-store cutouts and displays that I designed and illustrated for Clark's over several seasons.

The British shoe manufacturer was founded in 1825 in Street, Somerset, where it still has its headquarters. It's been a mainstay of the British high street for generations; my school shoes came from my local branch, which was stacked floor to ceiling with their green and black shoeboxes.

Accompanying the posters (which lie outside the remit of this book) there were numerous small point-of-sale display cards which advertised the fit and the range of sizes. The rounded logo and water-drop logo, loosely based on Clark's existing Bootleg logo design **1**, **2**, promoted the girl's range.

1

2

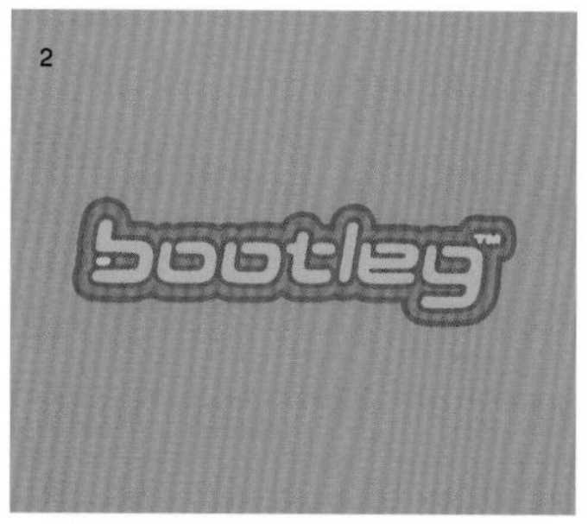

3

Millarworld
Mark Millar
Films and graphic novels
2013

Glaswegian Mark Millar is set on world domination with his very successful line of comic-to-movie adaptations that began with *Wanted* and *Kick-Ass*.

He needed a new logo to use on the retrospective I was designing, *The Art of Millarworld,* that would be a bit more distinctive than the straight block sans he was currently using. This would then be rolled out across his line of titles.

Early designs use an angular 'M' with a mirrored 'W' below, made from overlapping chevrons that echo the dividers used by William Blake's god in *Ancient of Days* to carve up the world. Mark has simple, puritan tastes when it comes to logos and wanted an unadorned block sans, so it took some time for him to come around to the final iteration with the globe. I see it hanging on the wall behind him in his Ken Adam-designed supervillain lair as he strokes an albino cat.

6 is a vertical version for use on graphic novel spines.

For the title page of *The Art of Millarworld*, character portraits were dropped into each section of the globe **2**. The cover of the limited edition **1** has a die-cut silver and spot-varnish dustjacket, designed to resemble the suitcase in *Kick-Ass* in which Hit-Girl's father, Big Daddy (Nicholas Cage) keeps his valuable stash of collectable comics. Jock's cover art can be seen through the circular hole.

Way back when Mark was still in shorts we collaborated on the strip **Tales from Beyond Science** for *2000AD,* now collected in one volume by Image.

1

2

3

4

5

6

MILLARWORLD

Comics Without Borders
Comic book organisation
2014

Run by Igor Goldkind, **Comics Without Borders** is an "initiative to start a conversation with professionals in the comics and related industries about cross-cultural consensus".

The logo uses CMYK print colours and the borders of the comic book frame, opening them out to the rest of the page.

1

2

3

4

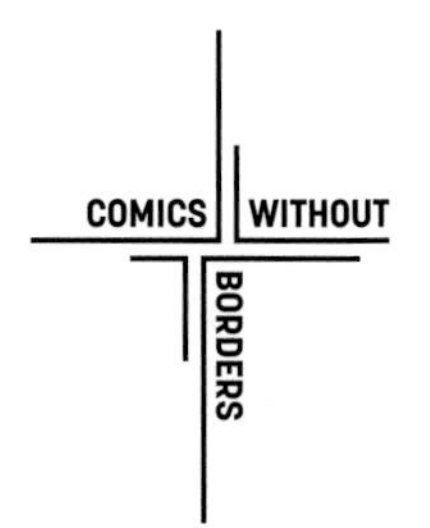

5

6

7

8

Tangent Comics
DC Comics/Tangent Comics
Comic book line
1997/1998

Tangent Comics consisted of nine one-shots that shared a common fictional universe that diverged from the **DC Comics** mainstream following the events of the Cuban Missile Crisis. Developed by Dan Jurgens, the series featured characters with the same names as their familiar DC counterparts, but who were otherwise unrelated.

The logo directly illustrates this 'going off at a tangent' concept, with added 3D perspective. In addition to the logos, I created an overarching trade dress in which the art was laid out in a similar fashion across all the titles, placing the characters against graphic backgrounds and with the logo at the centre or bottom rather than at the top.

As the line was intended to look like it came from a near-future alternate world in which superheroes have influenced technology and politics, I used a plethora of corporate marks, logos and slogans and a Pantone silver to set them apart from the regular DC range. It was a complex logistical job in which the different artists on each comic worked very closely from my mock-ups. I provided the complete print-ready covers, and DC's able art director Curtis King shepherded the whole thing through.

The colouring was flat, rather than the airbrushed Photoshop style then popular, and the linework was also rendered in a colour rather than black. It was a huge team effort that came together beautifully, and remains one of my favourite comic designs.

The font used here is Quagmire, one of my Device Fonts releases.

1

2

3

4

5

6

7

8

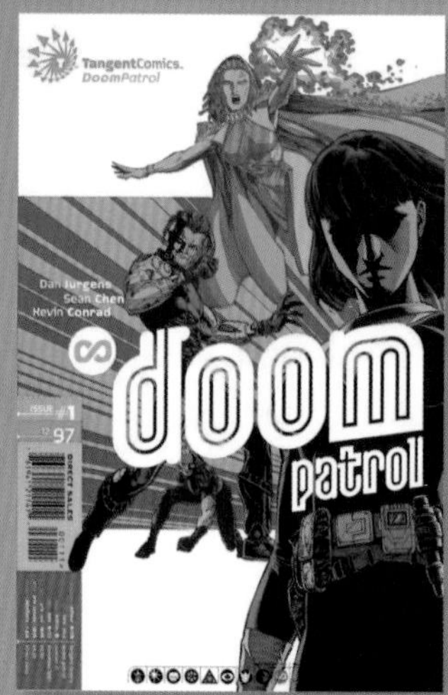

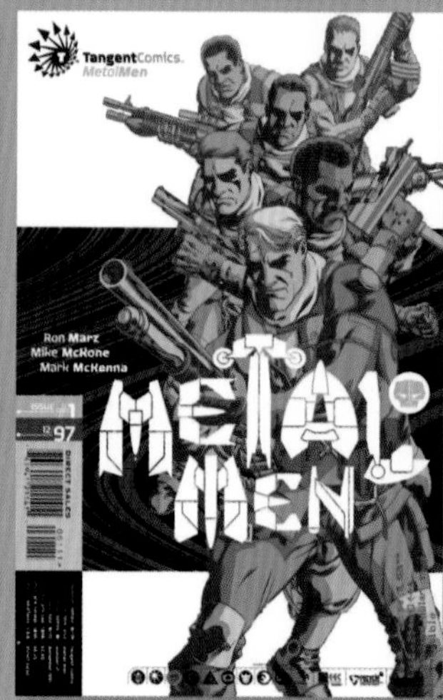

The 1997 titles

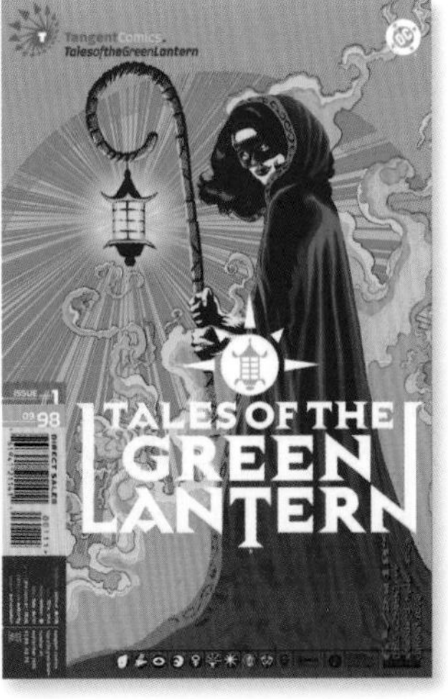

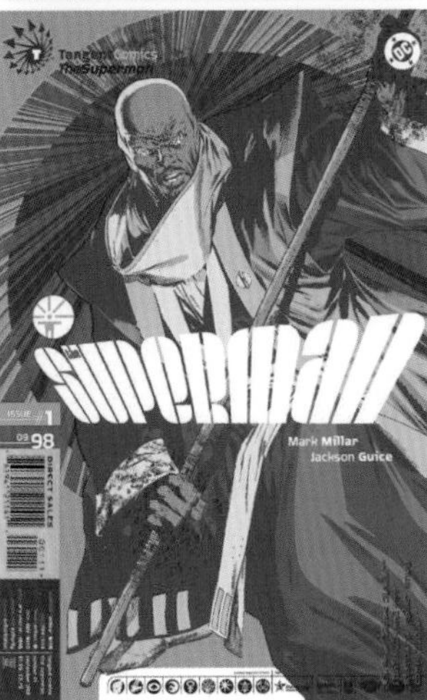

The 1998 titles

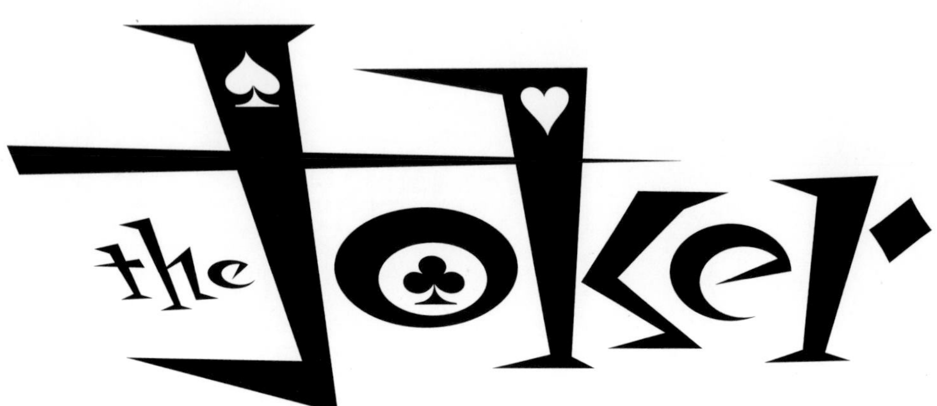

The Joker
DC Comics/Tangent Comics
Comic book
1997

From the first year's series, the **Tangent** version of **The Joker** is a costumed vigilante in the city of New Atlantis, using her tricks to highlight the hypocrisy of those in power. It was written by Karl Kesel with art by Matt Haley.

The logo takes cues from the character's costume, her anarchic attitude, and playing card suits.

The Joker's Wild
DC Comics/Tangent Comics
Comic book
1998

The second year's set of **Tangent** titles again featured **The Joker**, this time in **The Joker's Wild.**

Written by Karl Kesel and Tom Simmons with art by Joe Phillips, the story focussed on three superheroines, Madame Xanadu, Mary Marvel and Lori Lemaris, each masquerading as **The Joker.**

The logo is closely related to the previous year's, with the playing card suits repurposed as an apostrophe or an i-dot.

JLA
DC Comics/Tangent Comics
Comic book series
1997

The **Tangent Comics** series featured characters with the same names as mainstream DC characters, but who were otherwise unrelated to them. The concept was later integrated into the DC Multiverse (see **Multiversity**) as Earth-9.

The covers sported numerous tiny incidental logos **1**, designed to resemble sponsorship branding, corporate legalese or health and safety information from a parallel world.

The **Tangent JLA**, written by Dan Jurgens with art by Darryl Banks and Norm Rapmund, is a covert group of operatives formed to counter the **Tangent** superhumans **Batman**, **Wonder Woman**, **Green Lantern** and **Superman**. The logo references an American eagle in profile with stylised wings, and was also worked into the costumes of the characters inside the comic – a nice piece of continuity that should happen more often.

1

6 1/2 x 10"
[165x254mm] <<<
standard mylar snug
compatible

Metal Men
DC Comics/Tangent Comics
Comic book
1997

Another logo for the first **Tangent Comics** series, **Metal Men** was written by Ron Marz with art by Mike McKone. It featured Hawkman, Lobo, Gravedigger and Black Lightning as a covert military group who earn their nickname because they came back from every mission unscathed.

The logo is built from sections of airplane wings, fuselage and undercarriage. Each **Tangent** logo featured an inset pictorial element, here a metal skull.

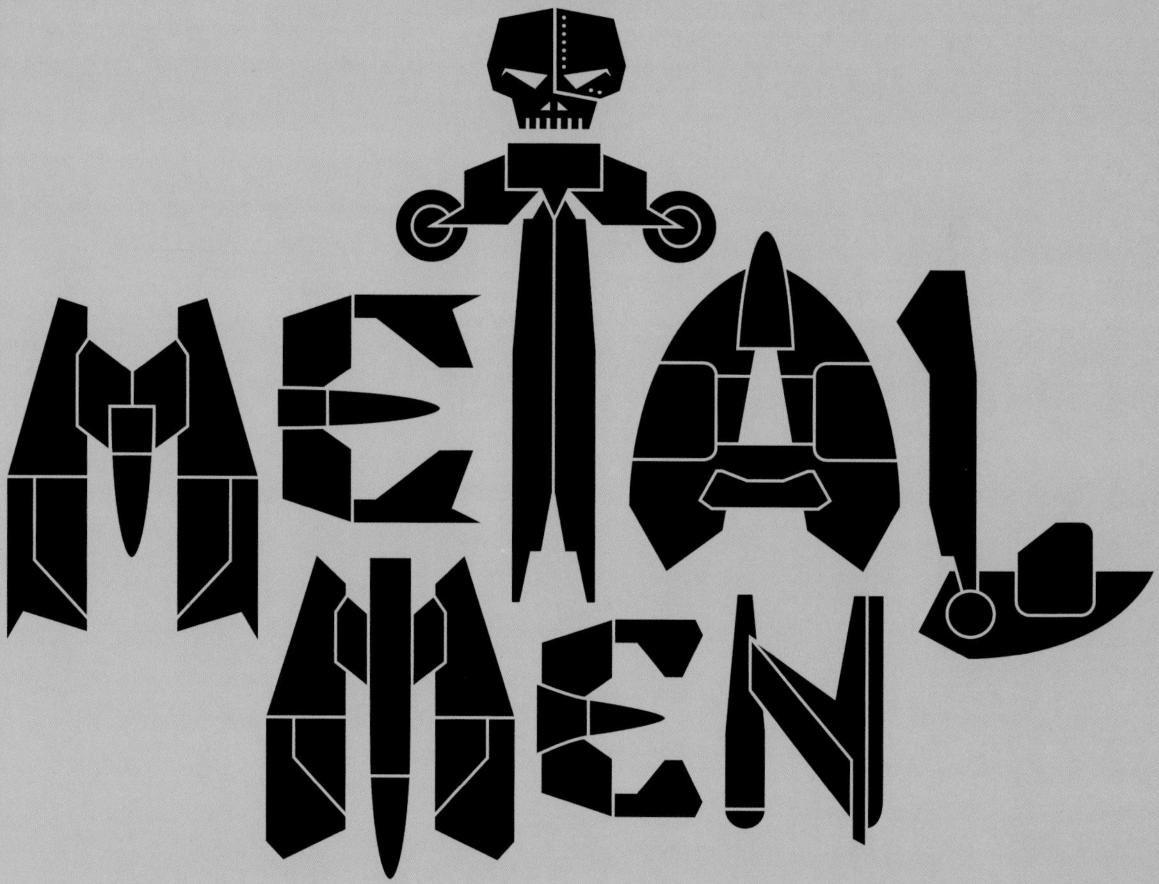

Nightwing
DC Comics/Tangent Comics
Comic book
1997

Written by John Ostrander with art by Jan Duursema, **Nightwing** is a group of agents belonging to a mystical secret society that controls much of the world.

The crescent motif was also worked into the characters' costumes.

1

NIGHT-
WING

2

3

4

Nightwing: Night Force
DC Comics/Tangent Comics
Comic book
1998

The rogue **Nightwing** agents Jade, Obsidian, Black Orchid and Wildcat attempt to rescue the **Doom Patrol** from the Soviet Union, only to unleash the Ultra-Humanite. Written by John Ostrander, art by Jan Duursema.

The logo for the second year's issue incorporates the **Night Force** tagline, the almost calligraphic letter shapes again derived from the crescent motif.

The Batman
DC Comics/Tangent Comics
Comic book
1998

The **Tangent Batman** is reimagined as a knight who once fought King Arthur, and is now forced to atone for his sins by seeking justice through the agency of an empty suit of armour.

Earlier logo designs **2** used elements of the more familiar **Batman** iconography, the cape and cowl; though I was pleased with these, they didn't reflect the angular, pointed appearance of his medieval outfit.

An unused design **1** was later developed into the font Gargoyle and released as part of the Device Fonts range.

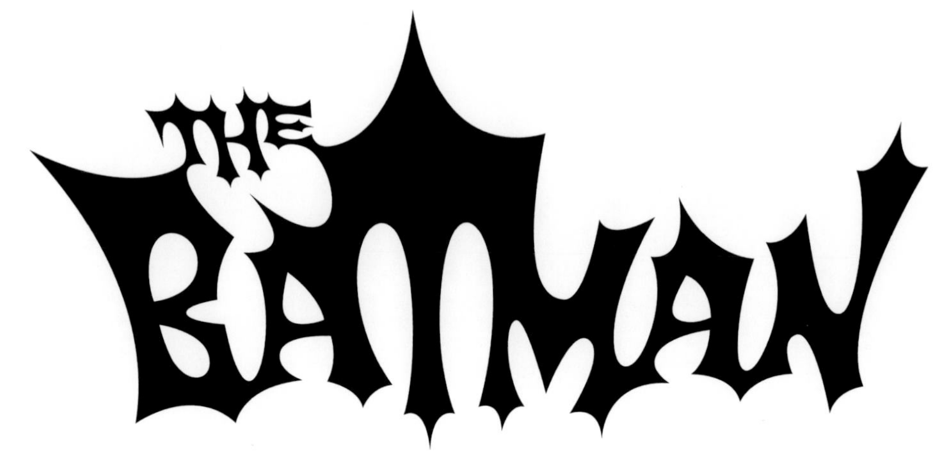

1

2

1

SUPERMAN

2

The Superman
DC Comics/Tangent Comics
Comic book
1998

Dan Jurgens' re-imagining of **Superman** went through many permutations. Writer Mark Millar wanted to echo "Kafka's metamorphosis, where we actually see this likeable, regular guy transform into a superhuman."

3

Sea Devils
DC Comics/Tangent Comics
Comic book
1997

A race of mer-people are created by the fallout from the nuclear exchange that destroys Cuba and Florida in the **Tangent** universe's version of 1962. Written by Kurt Busiek, with art by Vince Giarrano.

The logo is a gene-splice of waves and devil's horns, and incorporates a portrait in a circle.

Wonder Woman
DC Comics/Tangent Comics
Comic book series
1997

Written by Peter David with art by Gene Ha, the original character designs featured a bearded woman; this metamorphosed into an alien.

The shapes of the letters in the logo mimic the character's ribbed headdress, but also have a passing resemblance to the flowing script of the original **Wonder Woman** logo and its characteristic looped script 'W's.

1

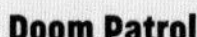

Doom Patrol
DC Comics/Tangent Comics
Comic book
1997

The series included a one-shot **Doom Patrol** title. Written by Dan Jurgens and pencilled by Sean Chen, it featured the characters Doomsday, Star Sapphire, Firehawk and Rampage.

The final logo takes its sinuous linework from the seams of the character's uniforms. The dot matrix type from one of the earlier proposals **1** was later extended into my Doom Platoon family of fonts.

1

Powergirl
DC Comics/Tangent Comics
Comic book
2000

Written by Ron Marz with art by Dusty Abell, **Powergirl** tells how US agents attempt to kidnap China's first genetically engineered superhuman. The logo owes a debt to the lettering-covered, information-heavy costume the character wears.

1

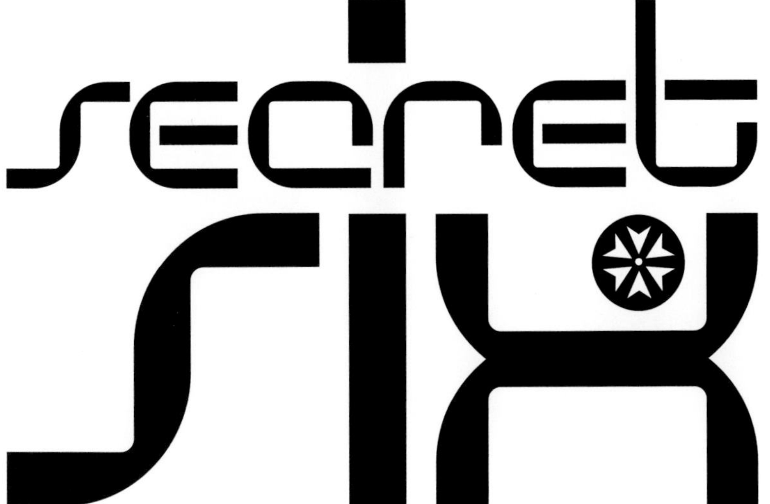

Secret Six
DC Comics/Tangent Comics
Comic book
2000

A team book written by Chuck Dixon with art by Tom Grummett., the **Secret Six** are formed when **Flash**, **The Atom**, **The Joker**, The Spectre, Plastic Man and Manhunter join forces to combat Dr. Aquadus, a living ocean. The circular icon represents the coming together of the six members.

1

Flash
DC Comics/Tangent Comics
Comic book
1997

The first baby born in space grows up to become a teenage superhero with light-based powers, able to create holographic constructs and move at the speed of light. Written by Todd Dezago, with art by Gary Frank.

The logo features a spark of light at its centre and a dramatic perspective to evoke speed.

1

The Trials of the Flash
DC Comics/Tangent Comics
Comic book
1998

In the second year's **Flash** title, the heroine teams up with the **Secret Six** to rescue one of their own from **Nightwing**. The logo incorporates the new strapline by shortening the left limb of the central spark. Written by Todd Dezago with art by Paul Pelletier.

Green Lantern
DC Comics/Tangent Comics
Comic book
1997

The retooled **Tangent** version of the **Green Lantern**, a woman with a mask covering her eyes, served as the comic anthology's host. Her mysterious lantern, when placed upon a grave, can bring the dead back to life just long enough for them to complete any unfinished business. The final logo features a graphic rendition of her Japanese-styled lantern.

Written by James Robinson, with art by J. H. Williams III.

Tales of the Green Lantern
DC Comics/Tangent Comics
Comic book
1998

The second year's **Tangent** releases also featured a **Green Lantern** title, renamed **Tales of the Green Lantern**, a reference to the mainstream **DC Comics** title *Tales of the Green Lantern Corps.*

Green Lantern tells three possible and contradictory stories of the character's origin. The framing sequence was again written by James Robinson and drawn by J. H. Williams III and Mick Gray.

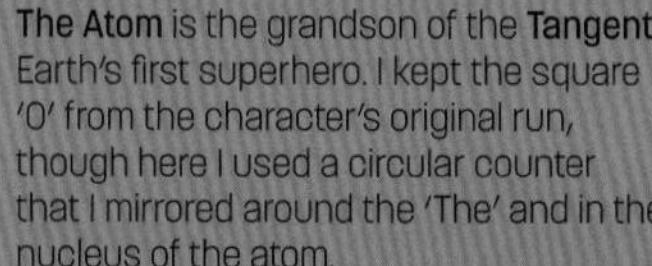

The Atom
DC Comics/Tangent Comics
Comic book
1997

The Atom is the grandson of the **Tangent** Earth's first superhero. I kept the square 'O' from the character's original run, though here I used a circular counter that I mirrored around the 'The' and in the nucleus of the atom.

Perhaps the letters shrinking left to right is an obvious way to illustrate the character's powers, but sometimes it's possible to successfully whip a cliché back into use. Written and penciled by Dan Jurgens, with finishes by Paul Ryan.

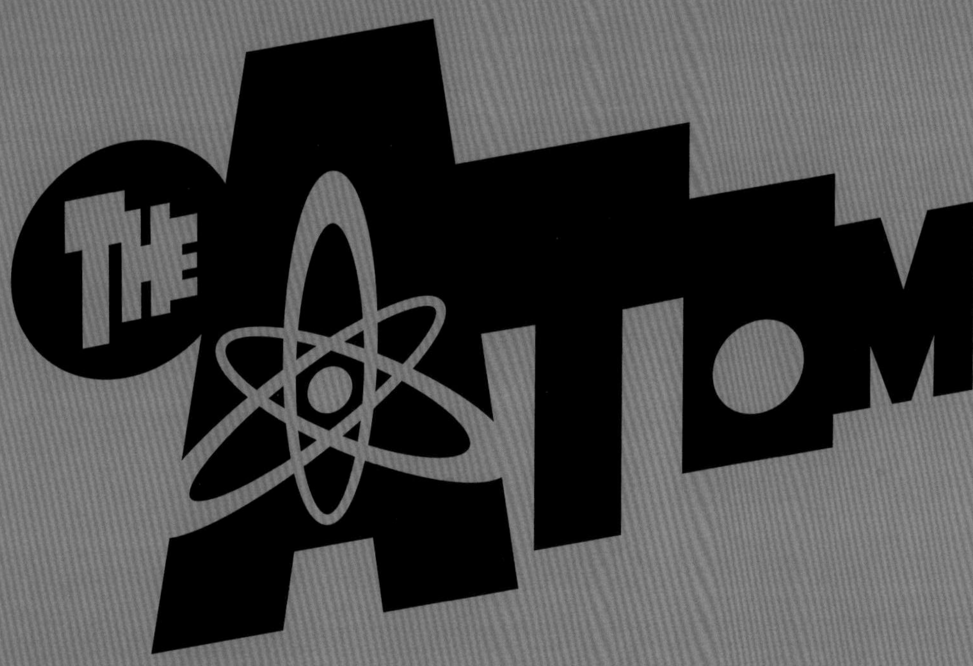

1

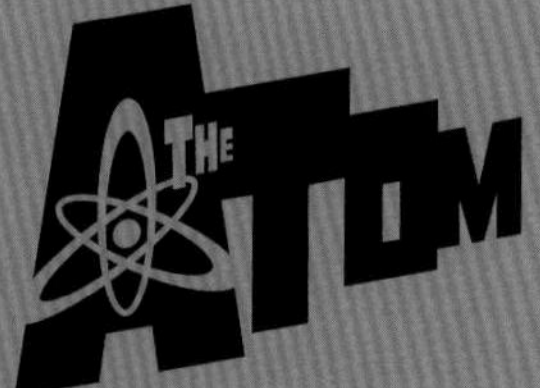

2

3

4

1

2

3

4

5

6

7

8

Superman's Reign
DC Comics/Tangent Comics
Comic book series
2009

Written by Dan Jurgens with art by Carlos Magno, this twelve-issue series revisited the **Tangent** Universe ten years on.

I designed the **Superman's Reign** logo to stylistically fit with the previous **Tangent** logos; this time around, the covers were laid out in-house at **DC Comics** using elements from my original trade dress design.

Book View Café
Publisher
2016

Book View Café began in 2008 as an offshoot of a women's SF and fantasy writers' email list that was dedicated to making out-of-print and orphaned books available again as e-books.

From there it expanded to include printed books as well, and now the imprint sells to libraries worldwide and has scored *New York Times* and *USA Today* bestsellers.

The logo needed to communicate 'bookstore' to a general viewer, but also emphasise the e-reader aspect. The button mirrors the handle on a blind hung in a café window. Previous versions of the website had also included a cup of coffee, a detail they requested I keep.

Practical concerns meant that the logo also had to work in black and white as a small colophon on a book's title page.

1

2

3

4

Bizarro and Bizarro World
DC Comics
Graphic novels
2001/2005

Bizarro World is ruled by the **Bizarro** Code: "Us do opposite of all Earthly things! Us hate beauty! Us love ugliness! Is big crime to make anything perfect on Bizarro World!" Created by writer Otto Binder and artist George Papp in 1958, **Bizarro** provides a surreal foil for the Man Of Steel.

In this hardcover anthology, some of the best-known alternative cartoonists were given free reign to run rampant through the DC Universe. Winner of the Eisner and Harvey awards, **Bizarro** returned four years later for an encore with **Bizarro World**. Here, **Bizarro**'s cube-shaped Earth stands in for the O. The DC Bullet is also given a square makeover, an intervention that in most cases would not be permitted.

The cover of **Bizarro** is by *The Simpsons'* Matt Groening, **Bizarro World** by *Love and Rockets'* Jamie Hernandez.

1

2

Spiral Sketch
Chad Valley
Game
1995

One of a series of travel games for the long-established British company Chad Valley, 'Toymakers to H.M. The Queen', for whom I also illustrated the packaging **1**, **2**.

1

2

Wilderlands
Fleetway
2000AD/Judge Dredd Megazine
1994

A Miro-inspired psychedelic rendering of the hallucinatory trip **Judge Dredd** and his cohorts take at the climax of the story. **2** was made from cut paper.

1

2

Kill a Bad Idea
T-shirt slogan
From the novel *XX*
2017
Author: Rian Hughes

The best way to
KILL A BAD IDEA
is to have a
BETTER ONE

RBEL
Rothman Brecher Erich Livingston
Literary agent
2017

RBEL

ROTHMAN BRECHER
EHRICH LIVINGSTON

Illustration Art Gallery
The Book Palace
Original comic art dealers
Proposed logo
2008

The **Illustration Art Gallery** is run by Geoff West and deals in original illustration art, with a focus on British comic strips.

4 uses letters from the mastheads of three well-known titles from the 1960s, including Faber and Faber cover designer Berthold Wolpe's 'A' from **Eagle**. **5** inadvertently resembles a female body.

1

2

3

4

5

6

7

8

Boom! Studios
Comic and graphic novel publisher
2012

Based in Los Angeles, **Boom! Studios** is an American comic and graphic novel publisher with a line of original and licensed all-ages titles that include *Peanuts* and *Adventure Time*.

I was asked to revamp the existing logo. The original brief was to not stray too far from the design as it stood, which incorporated a condensed sans and a stylised explosion. The all-ages remit suggested a less corporate and more dramatic, punchy and playful design might be appropriate **3-11.**

Subsequent rounds (there were many) focussed on the exclamation mark as it evolved from an overtly pop aesthetic to a cleaner, stripped-down design. Some of these also include a reference to the explosion motif. The client was enamoured of the **Marvel** and Vertigo logos, though I'm inclined to think a company's branding should set it apart from the competition rather than mimic it.

After I'd submitted a few rounds of ideas which grappled with a boxed condensed sans *a la* **Marvel** but attempted to inject a bit of personality **16**, **20**, it was requested that I use a specific font, Impact. Useful feedback generally revolves around concepts rather than the details of the shapes of certain letters; when this micro-management does happen, it tends to be because the bigger conceptual concerns are not being properly addressed. When a strong idea is articulated well, the font choice will naturally follow.

My favoured solution was the exclamation mark within the 'B' **1**, **2**, which worked well both in colour and black and white, and could be used with or without the text below. Without, it's a memorable and iconic marque that would prove very versatile in use, especially on merchandise or the spines of books.

Sadly, shifting editorial goals eventually scuppered the project. I did a final presentation with my favoured solution (main image); the final logo, which I didn't design (not shown) resembles the then-current **Marvel** Studios logo, a condensed sans in a rectangle with 'Studios' letterspaced below – the solution I think they were after all along.

1

BOOM
STUDIOS

2

3

4

5

6

7

8

9

10

11

12

13

14

15

16

17

18

BOOM!STUDIOS

19

20

21

22

Harbinger Wars
Valiant Comics
Comic book series
2012

Spinning out of the regular **Harbinger** title, **Harbinger Wars** echoes the design of the original logo but drops the italic to allow a centred symmetry. For the sequel, I also centred the II.

Harbinger: Omegas
Valiant Comics
Comic book series
2014

The **Harbinger: Omegas** mini-series again follows the main **Harbinger** logo closely. The emphasis in the final version is on **Harbinger**, rather than **Omegas** as originally intended.

1

2

1

2

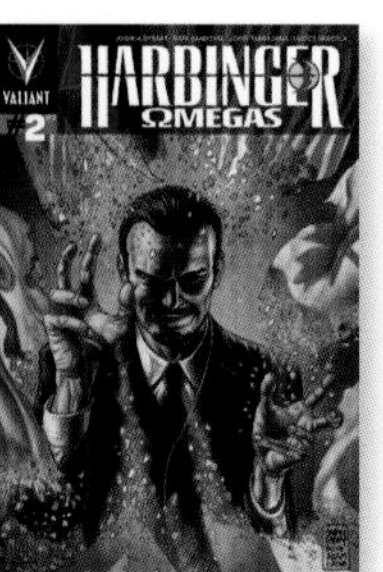

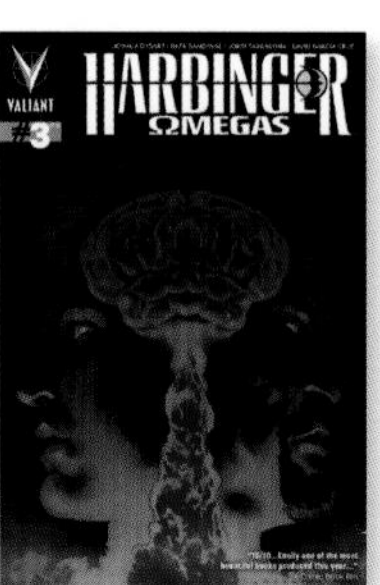

The Dark and Bloody
DC Comics/Vertigo
Comic book series
2016

1

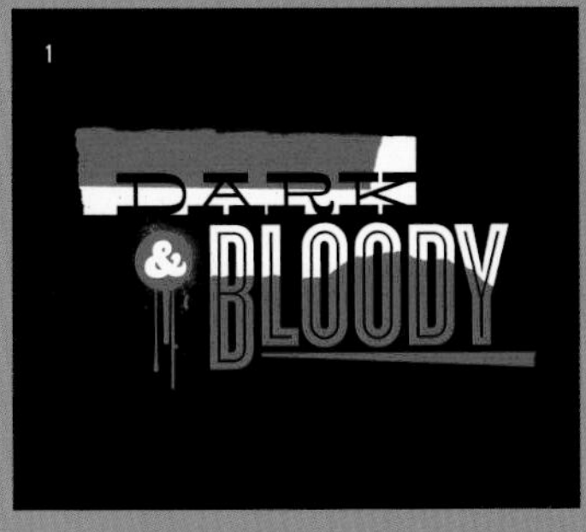

2

Edited by veteran Vertigo editor Shelly Bond, **The Dark and Bloody** is a horror series set in Kentucky by writer Shawn Aldridge and artist Scott Godlewski, with covers by Tyler Crook.

As the blurb has it: "Guns, moonshine, monsters – there's a lot going on in the backwoods of Kentucky. Iris Gentry is a war veteran who returned from Iraq to find his options for supporting his family limited, so he turned to running moonshine for his former ranking officer – meaning the two now share crimes at home and abroad."

Shawn suggested labels from vintage bourbon bottles as a visual starting point. Americana latin-seriffed wood type was given the once-over by printing it out, screwing it up then scanning it back in again. The contrast was then adjusted in Photoshop before exporting as a vector file for ease of colouring.

3

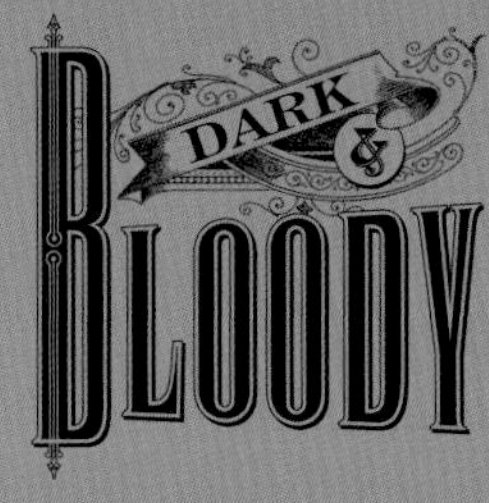

4

5

DARK&
BLOODY

6

The Marvels Project
Marvel Comics
Comic book series
2009

1

EXTRA! Daily Bugle EXTRA!
MAN ON FIRE TERRIFIES BROOKLYN RESIDENTS!
REPORTS DEFY EXPLANATION, SAYS MAYOR

2 3

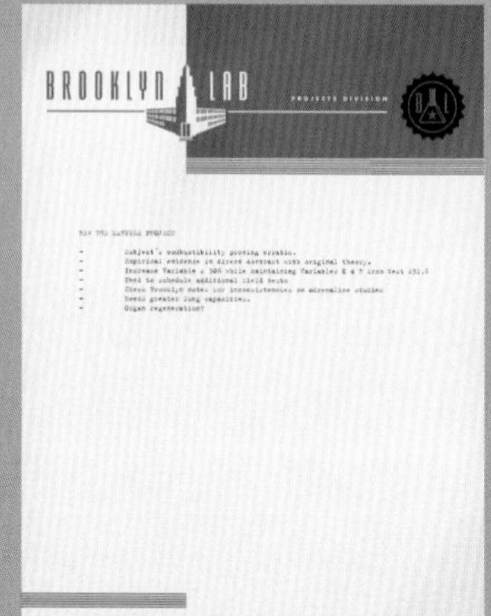

It's WWII, and the race is on to create the next generation of human beings capable of waging war across the globe. Planned as the centrepiece of **Marvel**'s 70th Anniversary, **The Marvels Project** by Ed Brubaker and Steve Epting explored the origins of the earliest Timely-era superheroes in the **Marvel** pantheon and the hidden connections between them.

My designs began as a marketing campaign to entice those who may not be that familiar with the history of the Human Torch or Namor **4-6**, and were subsequently taken across to a set of wrap-around variant covers (each had the same back cover **7**) that ran alongside the in-house designed versions.

There were three slightly different teaser ads, named Air, Ground and Sea, each showing the secret files relating to the development of an enhanced infantryman (**Captain America**), an aquatic officer (Sub-Mariner) and a flying soldier (The Human Torch). The sketches in each were not intended to resemble the actual characters, but to suggest exploratory experiments in increased muscle strength, underwater respiration, and so on.

I photographed some original government files at the National Archives, which happen to be near my studio in Kew, West London, adding American seals, rubber stamps, red diagonal stripes and other details.

Signatures, slides and yellowing newspaper clippings from *The Daily Bugle* were also added for verisimilitude.

A top secret lab would probably not risk exposure by printing up letterheads, but I couldn't resist designing Brooklyn Lab's logo and stationery **1**, **3**. I was concurrently working on the book *Custom Lettering of the '40s and '50s* so was immersed in the typography of the period. The beautiful pulp-flavoured, fully painted art is by Gerald Parel, and the back cover and teaser pencil sketches are by Paolo Rivera.

I designed then printed out the fingerprint sheet **8** and let documentary filmmaker Martin Hollywood, a Cap aficionado who was then sharing our studio, add his prints, then scanned it back in. He framed the original.

4 5 6

7

8

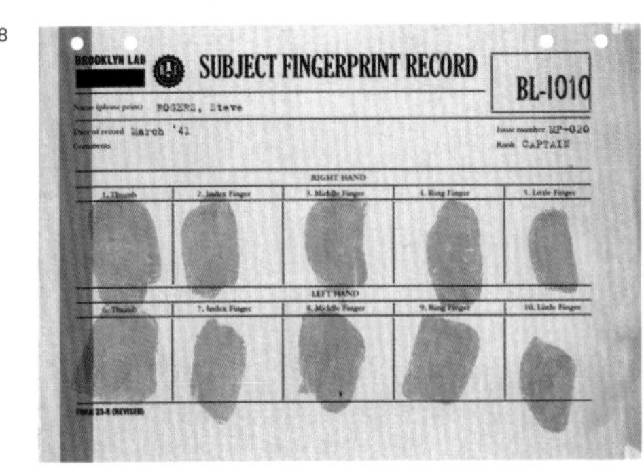

BROOKLYN LAB

SUBJECT FINGERPRINT RECORD

BL-1010

Name (please print) ROGERS, Steve

Date of record March '41

Issue number MP-020

Rank CAPTAIN

RIGHT HAND

1. Thumb	2. Index Finger	3. Middle Finger	4. Ring Finger	5. Little Finger

LEFT HAND

6. Thumb	7. Index Finger	8. Middle Finger	9. Ring Finger	10. Little Finger

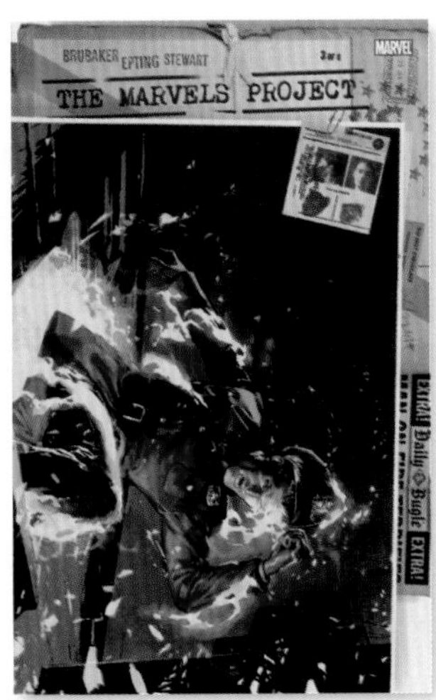

The Invisibles
Vertigo/DC Comics
Comic book series
1994

Grant Morrison's epic tale of the inter-dimensional battle between the forces of order and chaos spanned three volumes. I designed the logo, and for the first volume, the trade dress – the cover layout and typography.

The logo was intended to look as if it had been cut out of the cover art, leaving a subtle shadow on the background behind – an absence of logo, a logo visible by the hole it leaves. Invisible, perhaps. For the first issue I posterised a photograph of a real hand grenade, giving it a pop-art treatment in magenta and fluorescent Pantone orange. The remainder of the first volume's covers were drawn by the great Sean Phillips, who I knew from our collaborations on **Crisis** at *2000AD*. His art always has a strong sense of design and colour, making it a gift to work with as a designer; I could always easily pull colours out of the art to use.

The covers were laid out on the Mac in Aldus Freehand, but as broadband delivery was still some years away, Sean's art was sent to me in London and the final covers sent back to New York on Syquest disks via FedEx. Syquests are temperamental at best, and several issues had to be sent twice due to disk errors. Now digital delivery is all but instantaneous, the world having collapsed to a village.

Issue 5 came in four variants **1**, printed on brown paper in two colours. It was becoming the norm to use foil, embossing, die-cuts or other enhancements to boost sales; as I imagined **The Invisibles** would eschew such manipulative ploys, a 'dehanced' cover seemed appropriate. I also designed a poster to advertise the new arc.

I got the I-Ching hexagram on issue 9 wrong. My apologies, Grant. I blame an unclear fax.

The initial layout mutated as the series went on. I introduced different colours from issue 6 onwards, and textures such as leather, scanned from from my jacket, and hair, which I scanned my forearm, for the Sheman arc that ran through issues 13-15. For 18, which resurrects Grant's Gideon Stargrave character from his early *Near Myths* stories, I bought a fractal generator to use in the background. Issue 19 uses an op art chequerboard, a reference to DC's 1960s 'go-go' cover design. Sean painted the penultimate three issues as one triptych.

For the second and third volumes, the covers of which were designed in-house at DC, I tweaked the logo so it could sit over the art as a free-floating unit to give them more flexibility. This time the shadow was placed on the inside, to keep the illusion that it was cut out of the cover.

The first collection **2** features shadows of the team falling down across the cover and the grenade. Based on the original character designs by Steve Yeowell, I had to point out that they weren't in fact upside-down, and that it wouldn't make much sense to flip them. King Mob's hair was made more hairy to avoid phallic misinterpretations, which flipping the image might have only exaggerated.

The second collection, *Counting to None* **3**-**5**, has a *With the Beatles* style cover by Brian Bolland. For the title page I

1

ran dot-matrix numbers across the faces. The text throughout was repeated in a paler offset, in which random letters were replaced by numbers to suggest that everyday language is subject to hidden manipulation.

6 is a cover bullet for Volume 2.

6

2 3

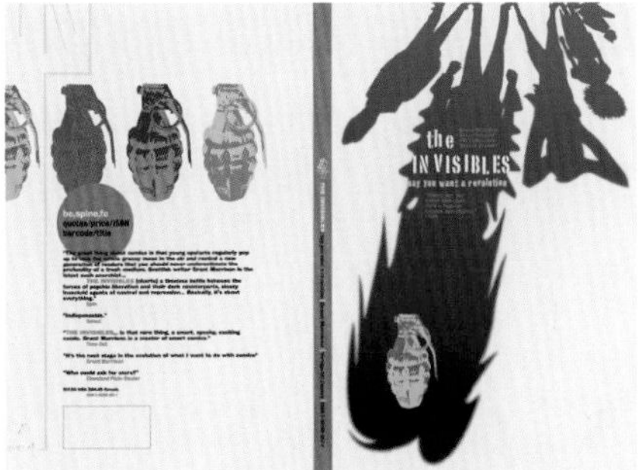

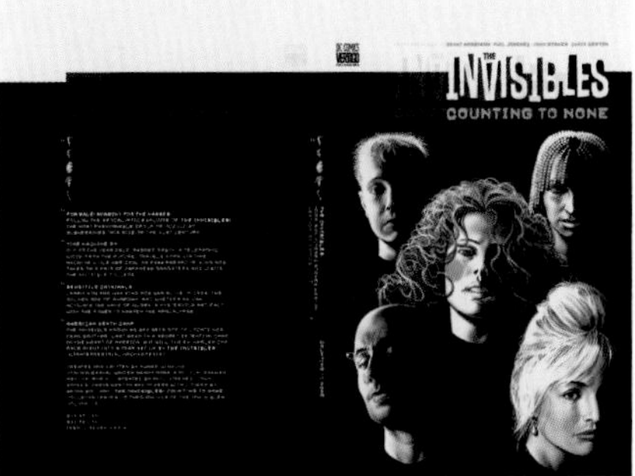

4 5

THE INVISIBLES
GRANT MORRISON

THE INVISIBLES
GRANT MORRISON

THE INVISIBLES

THE INVISIBLES

THE INVISIBLES
JILL THOMPSON
DENNIS CRAMER

THE INVISIBLES
THOMPSON
DENNIS CRAMER

THE INVISIBLES

THE INVISIBLES
DENNIS CRAMER

THE INVISIBLES

THE INVISIBLES

THE INVISIBLES
BEST MAN FAL

THE INVISIBLES
SHE-MAN
GRANT MORRISON
JILL THOMPSON

THE INVISIBLES
SHEMAN
GRANT MORRISON
JILL THOMPSON

THE INVISIBLES
SHEMAN
APOCALIPSTICK

THE INVISIBLES
LONDON

THE INVISIBLES
GIDEON
STARGRAVE

THE INVISIBLES

THE INVISIBLES
KING
MOB

THE INVISIBLES
HOW I BECAME
INVISIBLE

THE INVISIBLES
Liverpool

THE INVISIBLES
HOUSE OF FUN

THE INVISIBLES
THE LAST
TEMPTATION
OF JACK

THE INVISIBLES
GOOD-BYE
BABY
RABBITS

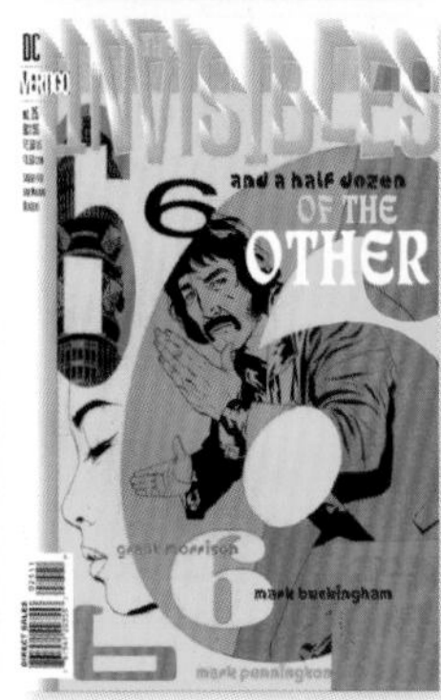
THE INVISIBLES
and a half dozen
OF THE
OTHER
mark buckingham

Mambo
Fleetway/2000AD
Comic book series
1994

Written and illustrated by David Hine, **Mambo** ('Spiritual Leader') ran for two series in the 'Galaxy's Greatest'. An alien species called the New Flesh have implanted a parasite within Rachel Verlaine's mind which allows her to mutate at will, shoot deadly tentacles from her skin and manipulate non-organic matter.

The logo explores a manga-influenced bubble gum futurism, the differing lettering styles reflecting Rachel's ever-changing form.

The Delinquents
Valiant Comics
Comic book series
2014

Quantum and Woody meet **Archer & Armstrong** in this **Valiant** team-up series. Arrows, anarchy, drunken brawls and broken bones ensue. **4** has a dose of Saul Bass' *West Side Story* poster lettering.

1

2

3

4

Sons of Asgard
Comic book/animation property
Matt Haley
2007

Designs based on mythological Norse symbols for Matt Haley's gang of child gods, **Sons of Asgard**.

1 owes something to the lettering found on covers of vintage *Commando Picture Library* comics.

1

2

3

4

Strange Tales
Marvel Comics
Comic book series
2009

The original run of **Marvel** Comics' **Strange Tales** is remembered for Stan Lee, Jack Kirby and Steve Ditko's monster tales, and later the introduction of Doctor Strange and Nick Fury, Agent of S.H.I.E.L.D. It has been revived several times since as an anthology title. This 2009 iteration showcased **Marvel** characters re-imagined by independent comics creators such as Peter Bagge, Ivan Brunetti and Jaime Hernandez.

"It should certainly look professional, but also sort of DIY at the same time", said editor Jody LeHeup in his brief. Thinking that the original logo had much to recommend it, I kept the 'jelly wobble' effect and the faded colours of vintage **Marvel** comics, including that unique eau-de-Nil green. 'Tales' is set in a Device brush capitals font called Appointment with Danger that evokes Artie Simek's signature style. The overhanging 'S' and the amorphous shape that serves as a framing device are lifted from *Tales of Suspense,* another anthology title which had very similar content (and where **Iron Man** first appeared). Simple black outlines evoke the pen-drawn logo design techniques of the period.

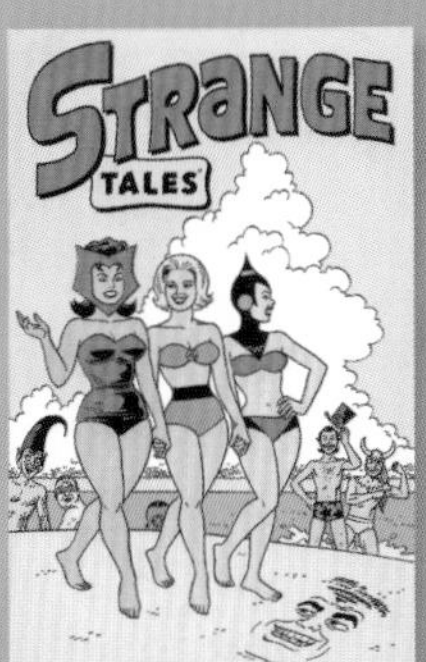

1

2

3

4

Eternal Warrior
Valiant Comics
Comic book series
2013

Wrath of the Eternal Warrior
Valiant Comics
Comic book series
2015

ETERNAL
WARRIOR

WRATH OF THE ETERNAL
WARRIOR

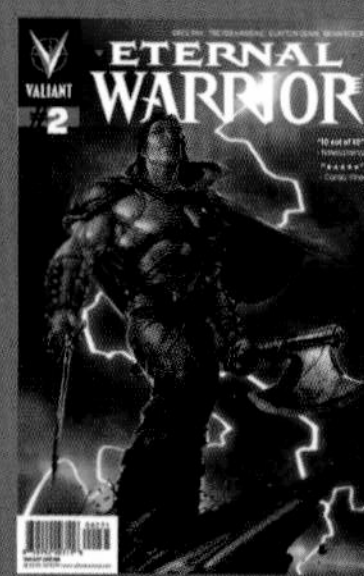

Gilad Anni-Padda, the immortal **Eternal Warrior**, lives for battle. He has a comprehensive understanding of combat and battlefield tactics amassed over 6,000 years, and now fights to protect the Earth and the mysterious Geomancers.

He has two accoutrements that are his trademarks: a spiked glove and an armoured sleeve. "A legendary figure, a larger than life badass who will hunt people down and fuck shit up," as editor Warren Simmons succinctly put it.

The final logo incorporates classical pointed serifs and a spiked 'R', a reference to his glove and also the original 1990s logo, and sits within the consistent line-wide trade dress I designed for all the **Valiant** titles.

Wrath Of The Eternal Warrior is a 2015 retitling and relaunch by writer Robert Venditti and artist Raul Allen. The logo is bolder, with the 'Wrath Of' subtitle tucked into the space top left, and is intended to be less evocative of a specific historical milieu. The trade dress for this second series departs from my design, and was put together in-house.

1

ETERNAL WARRIOR

2

ETERNAL WARRIOR

3

ETERNAL WARRIOR

4

ETERNAL WARRIOR

5

ETERNAL WARRIOR

6

ETERNAL WARRIOR

7

ETERNAL WARRIOR

8

ETERNAL WARRIOR

9

ETERNAL WARRIOR

10

ETERNAL WARRIOR

11

ETERNAL WARRIOR

12

ETERNAL WARRIOR

13

ETERNAL WARRIOR

14

ETERNAL WARRIOR

15

ETERNAL WARRIOR

Magicdrive
Mercury Records
1997

Logo and design for **Magicdrive**, a 'Jock Rock' Edinburgh-based band whose influences include the Rezillos.

I designed and illustrated three single sleeves for them before they were dropped by their record company, Mercury. The one shown here is for *On The Soft*.

1 **Smile! It's Meant to be Fun**
2 **Deep Joy, or Something Like It**
3 **Happiness, and All That Stuff**
4 **It's All Good, In Your Dreams**
Scholastic
Book covers
2009
Writer: Karen McCombie
Custom lettering for a series of four books for which I also illustrated the covers

5 **Hyper-Pop**
The Barbican
Event
2013
An event at the Barbican Centre, London that was an extension of the Image Duplicator show I co-curated at Orbital Comics as a riposte to the Tate Modern's Roy Lichtenstein retrospective. Participants reworked comic panels that Lichtenstein had appropriated, adding a new narrative before and after the single image.

6 **Sub Rosa**
Sub Rosa
Film production company
2004
Sub Rosa, meaning 'under the rose', denotes secrecy or confidentiality. 'Rose' is also director Rosanna Negrotti, whose short films tour the independent festival circuit. The logo is a literal interpretation of the name, pairing a photograph of a toy submarine and a rose taken from a vintage Italian postcard.

7 **TV Preview**
Maxim magazine (US)
Column header
2003

8 **Better Things: The Life and Choices of Jeffrey Jones**
Macab Films
Documentary
2011

9 **Galaxy 5**
WDPA Design Agency
2001

10 **Missed Deadline**
Magazine masthead
2016
Revival of Steve Dillon and Brett Ewins' **Deadline** magazine under the stewardship of Jessica Kemp

1

2

3

4

5

6

7

8

9

10

Psybadek
Psygnosis
PlayStation game
1998

Psybadek is a video game for the PlayStation console, designed and released by Psygnosis, home of *Wipeout*. The game was sponsored by shoe company Vans, whose branding appears throughout. I was commissioned to design and illustrate the cover and the accompanying posters and advertisements that ran in the gaming and style press. The logo was very loosely adapted for the in-game titles.

Psygnosis sent me a PlayStation 1 to play the game on. I'd avoided buying myself a console in the knowledge that I'd get sucked in . . . and that's exactly what happened. In a matter of weeks I'd played through every *Tomb Raider* game, plus *Soul Reaver, Half Life* and several other titles.

Though **Psybadek** boasted a soundtrack from Bentley Rhythm Ace and David Holmes, I didn't manage to get past even the most basic level. It was rated eighth by *Gamer Revolution* in their '50 Worst Game Names of All Time' list.

The Batman/The Spirit
DC Comics
Comic book one-shot
2000

Will Eisner's legendary hero **The Spirit** was folded into the DC Universe in this one-shot by Jeph Loeb and Darwyn Cooke. I approached this with some trepidation – I had read many of **The Spirit** collections as a teenager, and from both a story-telling and design perspective it's rightly considered to be a high-water mark in the artform.

Here, **The Spirit's** iconic cyan suit is treated as a graphic silhouette, the mask and hat band in black, while **Batman** is in black with his lower face in blue shadow, his eyes in white..

The design, though one of my favourites, didn't work so well in context on the actual cover, for which Darwyn had drawn the two butting heads. In the end, a simplified treatment using just the type was used.

1

2

BatMan SPIRIT

3

Robotboy
Cartoon Network
Animated TV show
Proposed logo
2005

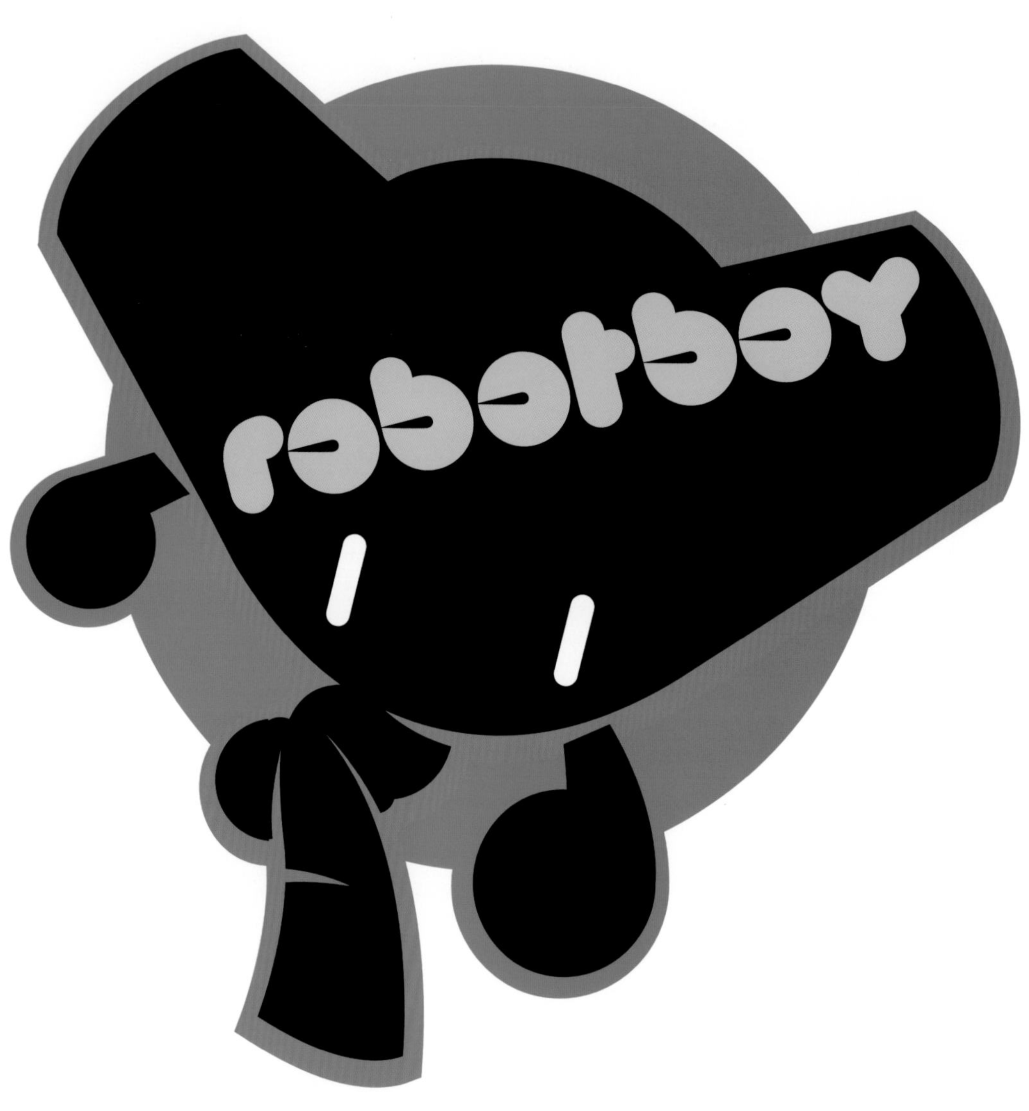

Robotboy is an American-British-French animated television series produced by Alphanim for France 3 and Cartoon Network Europe. It was created and designed by Jan Van Rijsselberge and directed in Alphanim's studio in Paris by Charlie Bean, who worked on *Dexter's Laboratory*, *The Powerpuff Girls* and *Samurai Jack*. It shares the strong stylistic heritage of those shows: a kind of contemporary mid-century modern that very much appeals to my sense of design, raised as I was on Serge Clerc's drawings and Hanna-Barbera cartoons and comics.

The logo is a simplified iconic drawing of **Robotboy**, paired with either manga-influenced type **1**, **3**, or type that echoes the shapes of the character **6**, **9**, **11**.

I was loathe to design something too obvious, steering away from printed circuits and square corners and instead focussing on the kind of cleaner, more contemporary branding a Honda 'Asimo' robot might sport: smooth curves and ergonomic shapes.

This may not have been what the client had in mind, as the final logo (which I didn't design) looks like a cross between **9** and **13**: angular, and with extra circuitry. Another case, possibly, of me trying too hard and not going for the obvious choice.

1

robotboy

2

3

4

5

6

7

ROBOTBOY

8

9

10

11

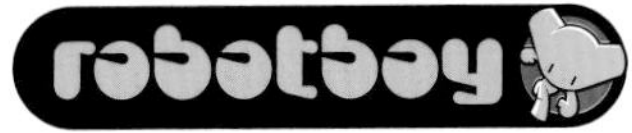

12

Lucy Skye
Mercury Records
Recording artist
2000

For **Lucy Skye**'s *Feel of Fire* single, I found a manufacturer who could take a digital file of the logo and turn it into a real sew-on patch. I combined this with a repeat 'I ❤ Lucy' motif, silkscreened on denim and suede, which was then scanned in for the sleeve artwork **1**, **2**. A second patch was used on the CD on-body **3**.

1

2

3

Mathers and Wallsgrove
Marketing/design agency
2017

John Mathers, previously the Chair of the Design Council, and Bill Wallsgrove of brand strategy consultancy Brand Voice were starting up a new partnership with a focus on charities and corporate and social responsibility.

Bill and John are characters, and their new venture's strength is their positive attitude and personal expertise, so it was a natural choice to make them into the logo. There is a subtle 'M' and 'W' on their shirts, with a '+' between them. John's smirk **2** was changed to a smile.

The font is Urbane, a Device design.

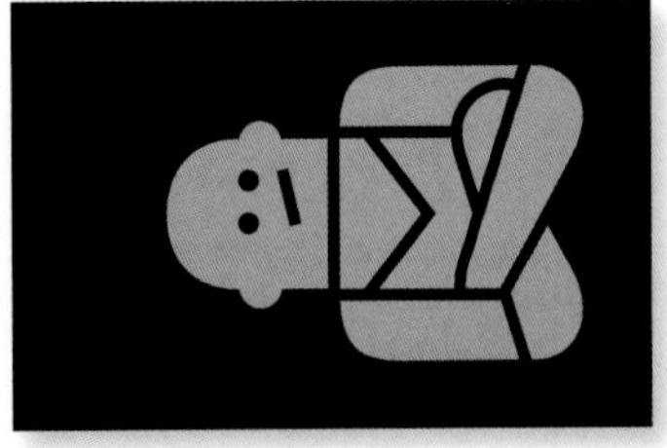

MATHERS+
WALLSGROVE

1

2

3

4

1 Device
Rian Hughes
Proposed company logo
1995

2 Furlongwire
Marketing news service
2007

3 Bang the Drum
Design agency
1997

4 Football Mad
Marks and Spencer
World Cup-themed snack range
1997

5 Klass Komic
Image Comics
Incidental logo
2013
From my Tales from Beyond Science graphic novel

6 Mondo Erotika
Book cover
Korero Press
2016
From my *The Art of Roberto Baldazzini* cover design

7 Sing
Sony
Proposed logo
2003
The best-selling karaoke game was released under the name 'Singstar'.

8 Geek Chic Socials
Dating/social website
2014

9 Letter O
The Typographic Circle
Magazine cover
1998

10 Gentleman George
Device
Shot glass
2013
Reused as an incidental logo on the cover of my book *Custom Lettering of the '20s and '30s*

11 Haddrell, Window and Co.
Accountants
2001

12 Ride the Tiger
EBP Creative
Creative agency
2000

1

2

3

4

5

6

7

8

9

10

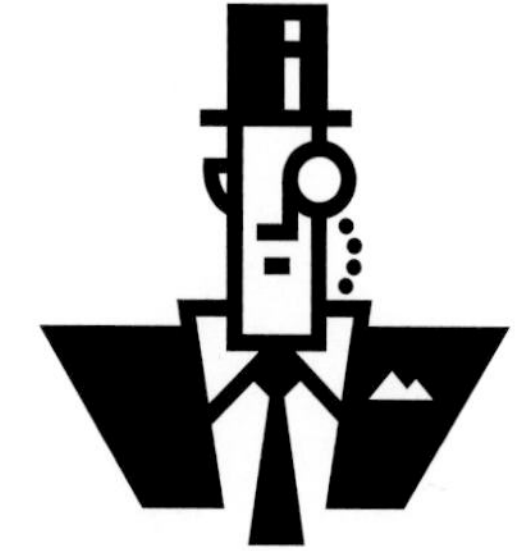

11

12

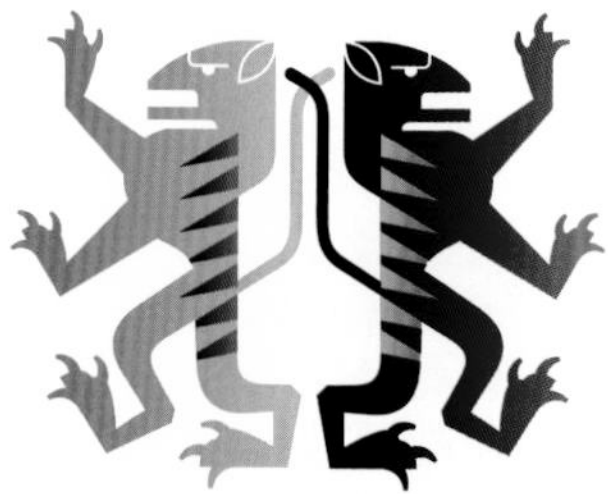

Fiell
Publisher
Proposed logo
2008

I had met Charlotte and Peter **Fiell** many years previously, when I designed their eponymous mid-century modern furniture shop and gallery on London's King's Road.

Having produced many best-selling books for Taschen and other publishers, they set up their own imprint in 2008, going on to publish four of my books: *Lifestyle Illustration of the '60s, Custom Lettering of the '60s and '70s, Custom Lettering of the '40s and '50s,* and probably my most personal work, *Cult-ure: Ideas Can be Dangerous.*

This proposed logo is a three-dimensional tubular steel frame, drawing on the Fiell's fascination with furniture design – their bestselling book is *1000 Chairs*. It was intended to be built as a large sculptural logo for use at trade shows.

Their final logo is by Farrow.

1

2

Dora and Friends
Nickelodeon
Animated TV series
Proposed logo
2012

The hugely successful animated series **Dora the Explorer** is Nickelodeon's longest-running show. A new 2003 spin-off series, **Dora and Friends**, was set to reinterpret the characters as older 'tweens'.

I tried to create a strong and versatile brand that could be used across merchandise as well as on-screen. I was asked to incorporate iconic elements from Dora and her world, and suggest the key themes of adventure, exploration and friendship (assuming such themes are graphically expressible without imagery).

Some iterations updated the style of lettering from the previous logo **2**, **6**. The colours are fresh and bright throughout, suggesting the lush tropical setting, and the bouncing baseline keeps everything positive and upbeat. The 'Nick' logo also had to be neatly incorporated into the final 'lock-up'.

I favoured the patterned type, natural textures and the hand-made, cut-paper style of the version shown to the left. In the end, the new show relocated to the city; that may be why none of my designs were used.

1

2

3

4

5

6

7

8

Collard and Trolart
Water heating appliances
2007

The logo needed to be straightforward and unfussy, easily adaptable to branding the company's appliances.

Earlier ideas tried to graphically illustrate the heat exchange process. The final logo (main image) plays on the visual similarity of the heating element in the tank and the ampersand in the name.

1

2

3

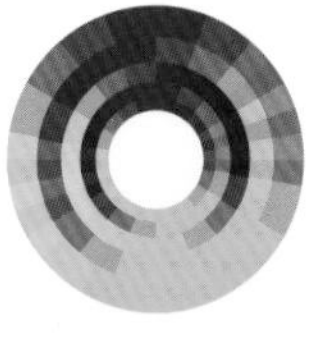

4

5

6

7

James Bond
Dynamite Comics/Ian Fleming Publications Limited
Comic book series
2015

In a deal set in motion by Mike Lake, Dynamite commissioned Warren Ellis to pen a new **James Bond** comic series based on the novels – the Bond of literature, rather than the Bond of the movies. Mike asked if I would like to create the logo, cover template and interior page templates that would be used each issue by Dynamite's in-house designers.

I felt the logo needed to be elegant, sleek and masculine, like a bespoke gentleman's outfitter or high-end automobile livery. Early roughs (not shown) played around with a Bond signature.

Having emailed over the concepts, Mike and I had a meeting with the Fleming Estate at The Society Club, a bookshop/café in Soho. We spoke for an hour about the films, the books – in fact, everything except my designs. Then, in passing, it was mentioned that they liked the logo, and that it was approved. And then we didn't talk about it again.

The chosen design manages to be sophisticated without being feminine, hard-edged without looking like a *Fast and Furious* franchise. Understated but self-assured, just like Bond.

The art was intended to occupy a square area below the logo; unfortunately, as several covers for the first issue had already been commissioned before the design was approved, I had to crop and extend some of them to fit. Where I could, I involved the artists concerned to make the process as painless for them as possible. The colour touch in the logo serves to differentiate '007' from the name, and was keyed to the art each time. The credits, 'Ian Fleming' strapline and indicia are all set in Clique, one of my own Device designs.

The first issue of **James Bond**: *Vargr* had more than twenty variant 'retailer incentive' covers. Warren Ellis followed up with a sequel, *Eidolon,* and Andy Diggle with the four-issue mini-series *Hammerhead* for which the logo was reversed, white on black.

I also designed the inside front cover and inside back cover (usually given over to advertisements in **Marvel** and **DC Comics** titles) which enabled me to make sure the design was consistently applied throughout the whole package, and drew some dramatic black and white silhouettes that served to frame the comic itself. Note the removal of the gun and bow tie for the final printed version (overleaf).

1

2

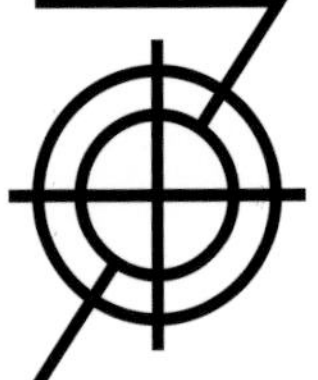

3

JAMES
BOND

4

IAN FLEMING'S

James Bond
Dynamite Comics/Ian Fleming Publications Limited
Comic book series
2015

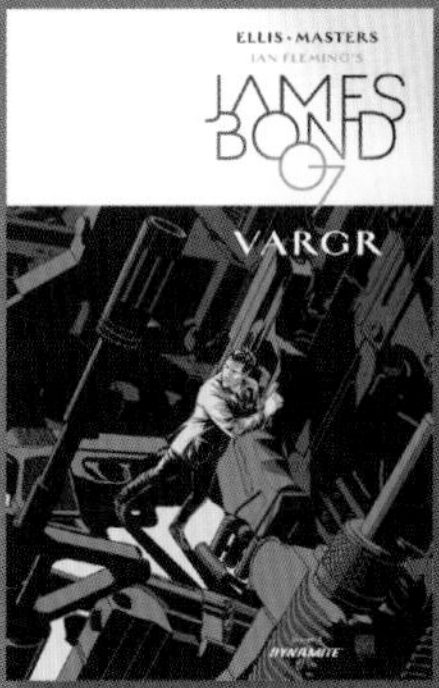

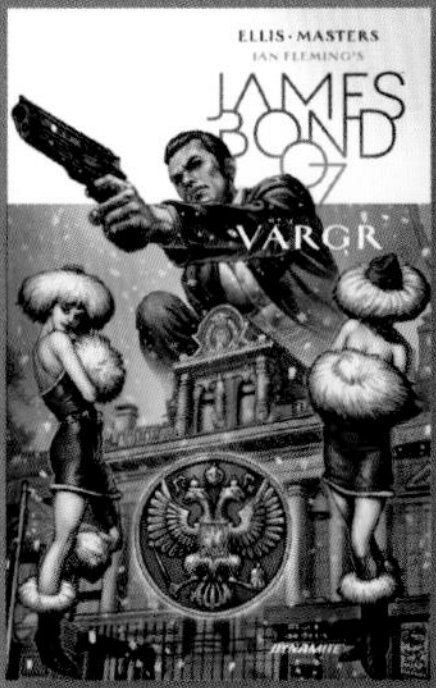

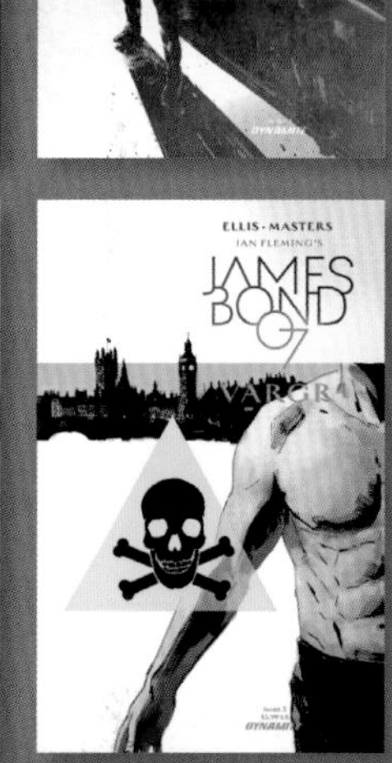

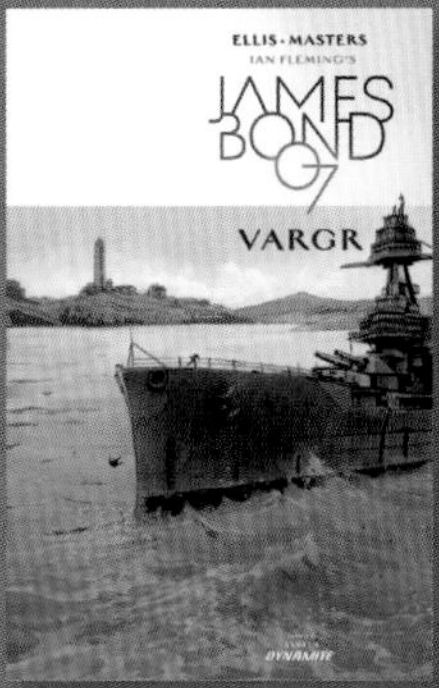

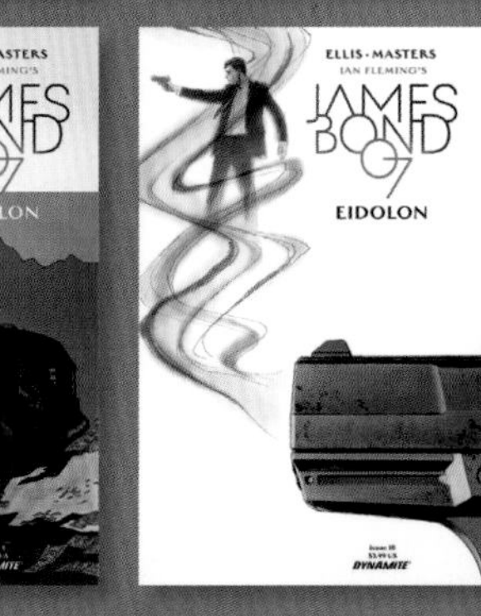
ELLIS · MASTERS
IAN FLEMING'S
JAMES BOND 007
EIDOLON

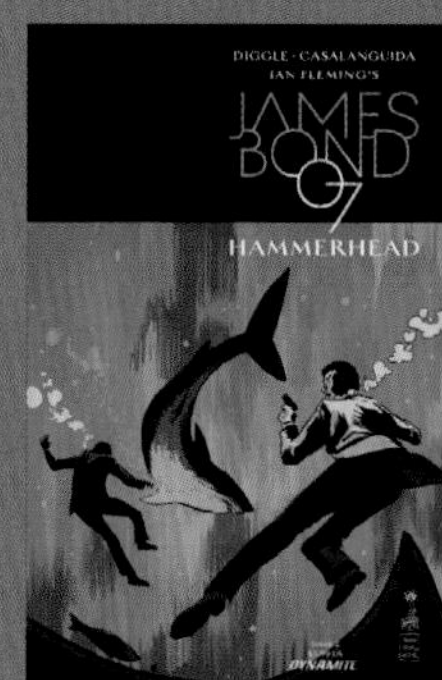
DIGGLE · CASALANGUIDA
IAN FLEMING'S
JAMES BOND 007
HAMMERHEAD
DYNAMITE

PERCY · LOBOSCO
IAN FLEMING'S
JAMES BOND 007
BLACK BOX
DYNAMITE

PERCY · LOBOSCO
IAN FLEMING'S
JAMES BOND 007
BLACK BOX
DYNAMITE

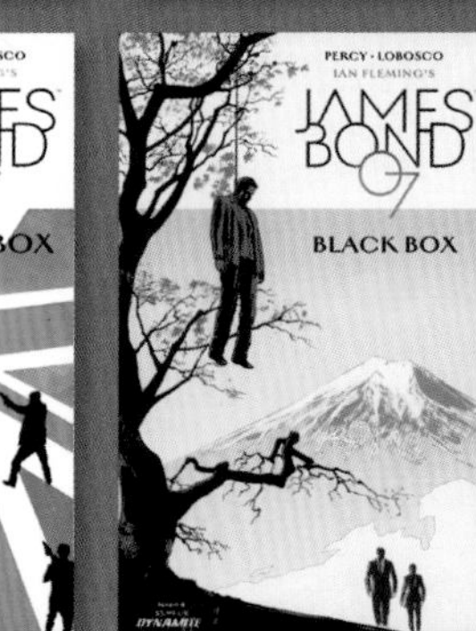
PERCY · LOBOSCO
IAN FLEMING'S
JAMES BOND 007
BLACK BOX
DYNAMITE

DIGGLE · CASALANGUIDA
IAN FLEMING'S
JAMES BOND 007
KILL CHAIN
DYNAMITE

DIGGLE · CASALANGUIDA
IAN FLEMING'S
JAMES BOND 007
KILL CHAIN
DYNAMITE

Hungry Eye
Korero Press
Book imprint
2015

Korero Press launched their **Hungry Eye** imprint with DJ Jay Strongman's Tiki-themed gangster novel **Ritual of the Savage** in 2016.

Days Missing
Roddenberry Entertainment, Inc.
Comic book series
2009

Roddenberry Entertainment, Inc. is run by Eugene Wesley 'Rod' Roddenberry Jr., *Star Trek* creator Gene Roddenberry' son.

The **Days Missing** comic book series tells of crucial tipping points in history where, with the help of a mysterious protagonist, events were nudged in one direction or another. I designed both the logo and trade dress for the first series – the logo itself is a grid of dates and letters, which flow across to the back covers. The 'S' and 'I' in Missing are numbers, and with this clue, certain hidden messages could be decoded. Shown are Frazer Irving's covers, which were drawn as one long image. There were numerous variant covers as well.

2851212DAYS145225
3112151 4MIS51NG71

1

DAYS MISSING

2

3

4

1

motion pixels

2

KANDI KRUNCH
LOVE COMMANDO

3

THE strontium
bitch

4

WALKING IN
ETERNITY

5

6

7

8

9

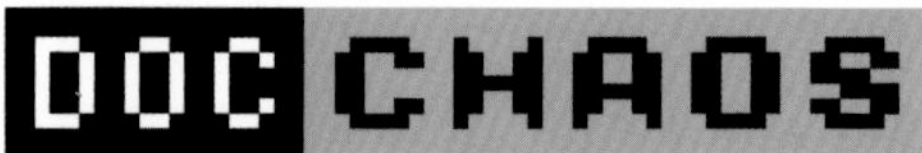

10

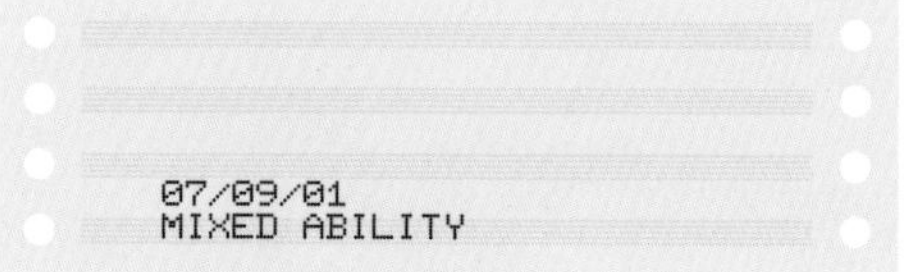

1 **Motion Pixels**
Web design agency
1999

2 **Kandi Krunch, Love Commando**
Device/Stephen Dalton
Comic series proposal
1990

3 **The Strontium Bitch**
Fleetway/2000AD
Comic series
1987
Writer: Alan Grant
Artist: Carlos Ezquerra

4 **Walking in Eternity**
Factor Fiction
Doctor Who short story compilation
2001

5 **Fantasia**
Tomato/Chrysalis Records
Single
1988

6 **Rocketship into Space**
Image Comics
2013
Incidental logo from the
Tales from Beyond Science
graphic novel

7 **Net Directory**
The Net magazine
Supplement
1998

8 **Raptaur**
Fleetway/Judge Dredd Megazine
Comic series
1991
Writer: Alan Grant
Artist: Dean Ormston

9 **Doc Chaos**
Vortex Comics
Comic book series
1990
Writer: Dave Thorpe
Artist: Steve Sampson

10 **Mixed Ability**
Uncle Grey Presents
Gallery show
2001

Psi-Lords
Valiant Comics
Comic book
2016

The **Psi-Lords** are superbeings from **Valiant Comics**' 41st century. The characters were first featured in a short-lived eponymous series of ten issues between 1994 and 1995 during **Valiant**'s original run.

At the time of designing the logo, story proposals were still being considered and the book had yet to be written, so there was very little to hang the design on conceptually. "Futuristic, sleek and clean", was editor Tom Brennan's one-line brief.

1

2

3

4

5

6

7

8

Eternity
Valiant Comics
Comic book series
2017

The logo for this series from **Valiant** was first presented on a teaser poster, shown left. The 'T's loop around, echoing the circular anomaly in space through which a whole new universe may be lurking. The logo is placed centre bottom on the covers themselves.

Marvel Universe vs The Punisher
Marvel Comics
Comic book series
2010

Marvel hardman Frank Castle is the last man left on Earth after a virus has turned most people – including the super heroes – into violent cannibals. For this hero/horror mashup, the main design problem was the surfeit of words, each requiring a similar level of importance. I used one font, Korolev, aggressively sliced and stacked, with colour keyed to the art each issue to help separate the elements.

The franchise was later extended to *Marvel Universe vs The Avengers* and *Marvel Universe vs Wolverine*, both of which sport logos adapted in-house from this design. For reasons which remain opaque, these freely mix Gill Sans Condensed and Impact with the original font, Korolev.

Professor Elemental Comics
Professor Elemental
Comic book series
2013

Professor Elemental, "Chap Hop's leading exponent" (so says the *Wall Street Journal*) first came to the attention of the tea-sipping public with *Cup Of Brown Joy*, which notched up over two million hits.

This led to a scuffle with another rapper, Mr B the Gentleman Rhymer, the result of which is the musical stand-off *Fighting Trousers*.

This logo was designed for the comic-book adventures of Steampunk's finest and his assistant Geoffrey, whose portraits were dropped into the circles either side of the type each issue. I imagined an engraved design that might appear on a tin of snuff or the label of a vintage bottle of absinthe.

Eagle Awards
London Film and Comic Con
Comic award
2014

Named after the classic British comic, celebrated for Frank Hampson's **Dan Dare**, the **Eagle Awards** are Britain's comics oscars. For 2014, **Marvel** supremo Stan Lee was set to present them on what was billed as his last visit to the UK.

The original **Eagle** comic was designed by Ruari McLean; the title was suggested by Frank Hampson's wife, and the actual masthead was drawn by Berthold Wolpe, who is celebrated for his Faber and Faber covers. The **Eagle** was modelled on a brass inkwell editor Reverend Marcus Morris bought at a vicarage garden party.

My version of the logo hews closely to the original in its general outline, but I quickly moved away from a more literal update **1**, **2**, simplifying the feathers considerably and swapping the signal red for a deep blue. The tail overlaps the type so it holds together as a unit, and a subtle brushed chrome effect (like the hull of the *Anastasia*, perhaps) has been added to the upper surfaces.

1

2

3

The Death-Defying Doctor Mirage
Valiant Comics
Comic book series
2014

Doctor Mirage is a Valiant Comics character originally created by writer/artist Bob Layton and artist Bernard Chang in 1993; the series was rebooted with a change of gender in 2014 as part of the relaunched Valiant line. This logo is based heavily on lettering Dave Johnson had incorporated into his first issue cover art.

THE DEATH-DEFYING
DOCTOR
MIRAGE

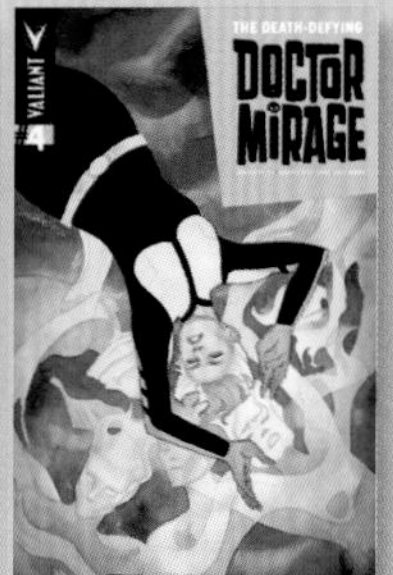

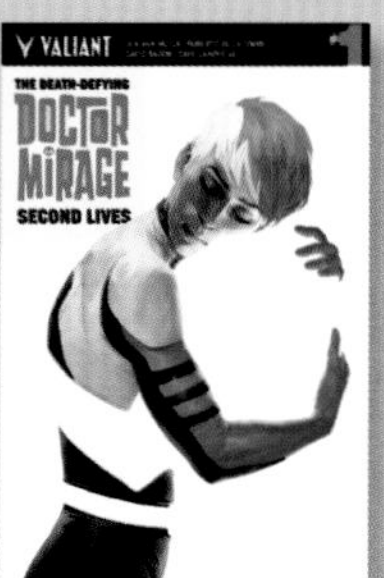

Journey into the Improbable
Image Comics
Tales from Beyond Science graphic novel
2013

Peculiar Encounters
Image Comics
Tales from Beyond Science graphic novel
2013

It's a Way-Out Love In
Image Comics
Tales from Beyond Science graphic novel
2013

Appointment with Weirdness
Image Comics
Tales from Beyond Science graphic novel
2013

Bizarre Art Mystery Tales
Image Comics
Tales from Beyond Science graphic novel
2013

Odd Stories
Image Comics
Tales from Beyond Science graphic novel
2013

Shocking Suspense
Image Comics
Tales from Beyond Science graphic novel
2013

Tales to Flabbergast
Image Comics
Tales from Beyond Science graphic novel
2013

Tales of the Anomalistic Observer
Image Comics
Tales from Beyond Science graphic novel
2013

Science Amok!
Image Comics
Tales from Beyond Science graphic novel
2013

Stranger Than You Think
Image Comics
Tales from Beyond Science graphic novel
2013

Preposterous Stories
Image Comics
Tales from Beyond Science graphic novel
2013

Gotham Academy
DC Comics
Comic book series
2014

Writers Becky Cloonan and Brenden Fletcher and artist Karl Kerschl's **Gotham Academy** was pitched to me as "a sort of **Batman** meets Nancy Drew meets Harry Potter". The creators asked for a logo resembling a school crest or coat of arms, and passed me a sketch to which **1** adheres fairly closely.

The four sections illustrate various subjects on the curriculum, while the ribbons were extended out to the side so the actual title could be made larger. Looking at this design in context on the cover, it was probably too complex to be read easily. In the end a simple Futura was substituted, with the crest appearing as a small inset.

1

2

3

4

Maximum Ride
Marvel Comics
Comic book series
Proposed logo
2014

James Patterson's **Maximum Ride** is a series of popular young adult fantasy novels that had previously had a manga-style comics adaptation. The story follows Maximum 'Max' Ride and his five winged friends as they flee 'The School', a mysterious establishment where they have been subjected to medical experiments.

For **Marvel**'s licensed adaptation, I was asked to ignore the previous logos and design something with a bit more edge to it, while still staying within the parameters of a young adult series.

I delved into wings, tattoos, and Gothic teen angst. Unfortunately, no feedback from the licensor was forthcoming and none of my designs were used.

1

2

3

4

Milkfed Criminal Masterminds
Kelly Sue DeConnick/Matt Fraction
Comic book writers
2014

Comic book writers Kelly Sue DeConnick and Matt Fraction, for whom I had designed **Iron Man** and **Bitch Planet**, asked me to design their personal company logo. They were using a simple line drawing I'd assumed was a monocled woman with a moustache, but which actually turned out to be their baby son in costume. I thought this was a striking idea that could be developed.

Matt wanted to satirically play up to the 'global domination' idea, so the one-eyed monocled lady now has a glass of milk in one hand and a bag of cash in the other. Two more hands grasp for the globe below. On the reverse of the business cards is the disclaimer: "Not actual criminal. Not actual mastermind."

The original logo was in brown and gold, which coincidentally were Kelly Sue's high school colours: "UPS brown and babyshit yellow", as she put it. To avoid bad flashbacks, a more appropriate banknote teal was substituted. The logo's detailed finish suggests an intricate engraving, another banknote reference, and the cards and stationery were printed letterpress for a tactile embossed finish **1-3**.

1

2

3

Top 10 Videogame Goddesses
Maxim magazine (US)
Magazine supplement masthead
and section headers
2004

The type is my Device font Glitterati, which is influenced by Tom Carnase's geometric all-capitals font Busorama, designed for ITC in 1970.

1

2

3

4

5

6

7

8

9

I Hate Fairyland
Image Comics
Comic book series
2015

1

The premise behind Skottie Young's Image comic is brilliantly simple: a little girl goes to Fairyland – and gets stuck there for thirty years. She's now forty years old, in an eight-year-old's body, and she hates the place. Cue hilarious, over-the-top cartoon ultraviolence.

A special retailers' incentive variant changed the title to **Fuck Fairyland**, which Forbidden Planet stickered over to protect their customer's delicate sensibilities.

Cut+Run
Film editing and production
Logo update proposal
2007

I was asked to update editing house **Cut+Run**'s logo. Their existing 'running scissors' motif was very strong, so I suggested a polish rather than a complete redesign. I imparted more speed by skewing and flipping it so that it moved to the right rather than the left, and made it generally sleeker and less like a paper cutout. Versions **3** and **4** included a Tintin-style quiff. The font is Ministry, one of my Device designs.

None of my ideas were used.

1

2

3

4

Week-ends.be
Patrick Pinchart
Website branding
2017

Week-ends.be is an online magazine dedicated to culture and leisure in Belgium. Covering books, movies, theatre and tourism, it sees itself as critical, objective and eclectic.

Early ideas **1**, **2** emphasised the fun aspects of the site's content, using festive bunting or a loose, hand-drawn style. These were deemed too juvenile, so for the next round I turned to elegant serifs and photographic insets **3** in an attempt to address a more mature demographic. Unfortunately these didn't work very well at small sizes and low resolutions, and the client wondered if a simpler and more iconic logo would be more appropriate.

A colourful butterfly was the solution, suggesting a lighthearted flitting around from event to event, but treated in a reasonably sober style. This could easily be used without the type for events, badges and T-shirts .

A rainbow of colourways **8** was provided for use in the navigation menu to differentiate each section of the site.

1

2

3

4

5

6

7

8

Accel
Lion Forge
Comic book series
Proposed logo
2016

1

Accel is Joe Casey, Damion Scott and Robert Campanella's speedster from **Lion Forge**'s **Catalyst Prime** universe. The byline ran: "Jose Santiago is a young man trying to make his way in the world. Can fun and responsibility co-exist?"

This more playful approach is reflected in a logo that riffs on speedlines and racing livery. The fireball in **7** was thought to resemble eyelashes, while I advised against **8** (a requested iteration) as the fireball and lettering should ideally move in the same direction.

Each hero was to have an icon or emblem that related both to the logo and to their costume or powers. Here, the fireball and double 'L' was isolated and pressed into service **1**.

Sadly none of these ideas were used, and the final logo was designed in-house.

2

3

4

5

6

7

8

9

Superb
Lion Forge
Comic book series
Proposed logo
2016

Kayla Leigh is a high-school sophomore, a black ex-nerd. Her only friend is Jonah, a white high-functioning teenager with Down's Syndrome.

Written by David Walker and Dr. Sheena Howard with art by Chuck Collins, the main character's partnership in **Superb** is intended to explore misconceptions about disabled people, and the real-world dynamics of cliques and social hierarchies that are prevalent within their communities.

The logo is bold, powerful and optimistic, and has an intrinsic duality, playing with positive/negative space to illustrate the union of the two complementary characters.

The final printed logo was designed in-house, but does bear certain stylistic similarities to my proposals.

SUPERB

1 SUPERB

2 SUPERB

3 SUPERB

4 SUPERB

5 SUPERB

6 SUPERB

7 SUPERB

8 SUPERB

Incidentals
Lion Forge
Comic book series
Proposed logo
2016

Created by Ramon Govea and written by Joe Casey, **Incidentals** revolves around Industrialist Bo Vincent Chen, who is haunted by visions of a future war. Compelled to prepare for battle, he assembles a team of special operatives, each of whom was endowed with unique abilities by the meteor crash that is the source of many of the **Catalyst Prime** characters' powers.

The logo attempts to suggest this coming together of a bunch of misfits from wildly different backgrounds, each ill-suited and ill-prepared for the job ahead. There are no sleek team costumes, and the characters need to surmount their personality clashes as well as the coming catastrophe.

As with most of the **Catalyst Prime** logos the final version was designed in-house, but resembles **6**.

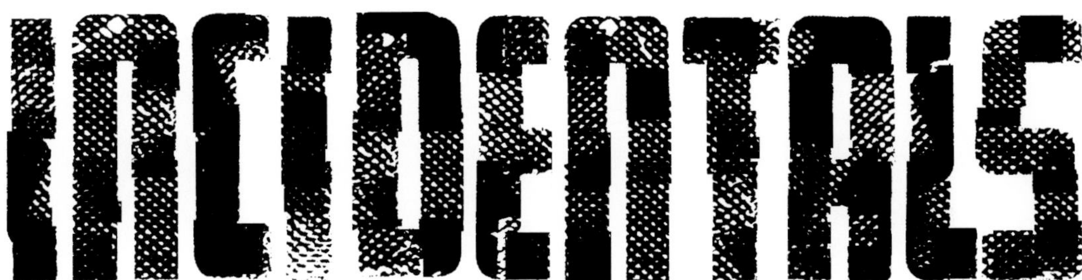

1

2

3

4

5

6

7

8

Noble
Lion Forge
Comic book series
Proposed logo
2016

Part of the **Catalyst Prime** series of interlinked titles, the **Noble** logo went through several iterations. I was attempting to capture the strength and (of course!) nobility of the character with a solid, muscular type treatment perhaps reminiscent of an ironfounder's marque or a wrestling belt.

The logo was approved, but subsequently an emblem for the character's costume quite different from the one I had designed was chosen, necessitating a rethink as the two did not share the same aesthetic.

Ultimately my ideas were not used, and the printed version of the logo was designed in-house.

1

2

3

4

Catalyst Prime
Lion Forge
Comic book series
2016

Catalyst Prime is the overarching book that sets out the events that lead to the creation of all the superpowered characters in **Lion Forge**'s **Catalyst Prime** universe.

The design incorporates a meteor, a central part of the origin story.

1

2

3

4

5

6

7

8

Summit
Lion Forge
Comic book series
Proposed logo
2016

Written by Amy Chu with art by veteran DC artist Jan Duursema, **Summit** is part of **Lion Forge**'s **Catalyst Prime** series of interrelated titles.

5 had been chosen from my first round of ideas, but the subsequent introduction of the circular symbol designed in-house necessitated a reworking. **2** suggests a series of mountain peaks rising to the right, as does **4**, though they possibly look more like logos for hiking gear. Placing the symbol between the 'M's reminded me of sunlight shining through a gap.

The final logo resembled **6**.

1

2

3

4

5

6

7

8

Kino
Lion Forge
Comic book series
Proposed logo
2016

Another hero from the new **Catalyst Prime** stable, **Kino** is written by Joe Casey with art by Jefte Palo.

After surviving an abortive space mission intended to save the human race, Major Alistair Meath was acquired by MI6, who subjected him to a virtual reality programme in which he relives Silver Age-style superhero adventures. Meath is a 'Kinetic Impulse Neoterrestrial Operative'.

The logo borrows from **Kino's** retro-styled virtual world with a nod to a NASA 'N' and a 1970s gaming aesthetic, and also incorporates his chest emblem.

The final logo was designed in-house.

1

2

3

4

5

6

7

8

Beat FM
Radio station
Proposed logo
1997

The identity for this youth-oriented dance music radio station went through several name changes, each requiring me to start afresh (see **The Source**). Here, the heart has a repeated Op Art outline, suggesting a pulse.

In the end none of my designs were used, and as far as I'm aware the station was not launched.

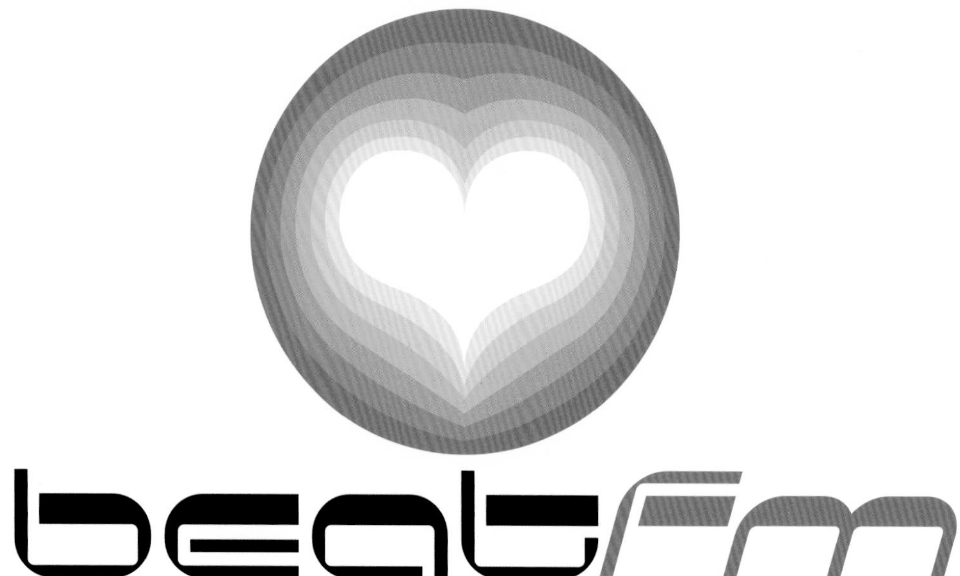

1

2

3

4

Infinity Man and the Forever People
DC Comics
Comic book series
2014

Part of **DC Comics**' New 52 company-wide reboot, **Infinity Man and the Forever People** is Dan Didio, Keith Giffen and Scott Koblish's reboot of Jack Kirby's **Forever People**, part of his epic 'Fourth World' mythology created from 1971 onwards that also included *Mister Miracle* and *The New Gods*.

1 reworks Gaspar Saladino's original design, with its extended pointed crossbars. The final logo has an unusual weight distribution that evokes a 1970s science fiction modernism.

4 was to be used on a lenticular cover, so the logo would twist as it was viewed from different angles. Sadly, cost factors meant that this didn't happen.

INFINITY MAN AND THE
FOREVER
PEOPLE

1

FOREVER
PEOPLE

2

INFINITY
MAN

3

INFINITY MAN
AND THE
FOREVER PEOPLE

4

INFINITY MAN AND THE
FOREVER
PEOPLE

Fourty Fourty
Bicycle manufacturer and importer
2000

Logos and decal designs for Fourty Bikes, an Australian bike company founded by Simon Coates that was originally set up to bring a street-savvy urban cruiser for seven- to twelve-year-olds to market.

1

FOURTY

2

FOURTY

3

4

Metropolitan Music
Record label
1997

The logo for this hard trance label references architectural shapes: two walls converging, or the corner of a building, perhaps. This theme was taken through to the design of the sleeves, for which I took a series of starkly composed black and white photographs of the Hayward Gallery, London's brutalist masterpiece/monstrosity on the South Bank.

1

2

3

METROPOLITAN
MUSIC

4

Starfire
DC Comics
Comic book series
2015

I vividly remember **Starfire** from the Marv Wolfman and George Perez **Teen Titans** run, so I was very happy to be asked to design the logo for her new solo series by Amanda Conner, Jimmy Palmiotti and Emanuela Lupacchino.

The character is something of a super-powered free-love ingénue, so early designs play with those styles of typography and her trademark big hair **3**. In the end, a more straightforward update of Todd Klein's original logo design, here seen on the *Tales from the Teen Titans* mini-series from 1982 was chosen.

Now that comic covers are more often fully painted, a simple one-colour logo often looks better than an outline or drop shadow version **7**, which were the preferred choice when they matched the style of art more closely.

1

2

3

4

5

6

7

8

Outcast
Skybound Productions
Comic book series
2014

Written by *The Walking Dead's* Robert Kirkman, **Outcast** is drawn by artist Paul Azaceta with beautiful colours by Elizabeth Breitweiser. A supernatural horror story revolving around the main character's spirit possession, it has been developed into a TV series by Fox starring *Life on Mars'* Philip Glenister. This uses a different logo that I didn't design, but which does reference the large circular 'O' of my original.

Early iterations were grittier, hand-drawn with a brush **2**, **3** or marker pen **4**, assembled letter by letter then scanned in. The final logo uses a cleaner style, still influenced by a quickly drawn brush script but with a touch of the Gothic that pays a subtle homage to the ethereal, spooky style of traditional supernatural comic and movie logos, while avoiding any direct references. Curved lines sweep from letter to letter, neatly grouping them together as a unit that is balanced by the perfectly circular 'O'. The crossbar of the 'A' mirrors the last 'T', while the tails of the 'T', 'C' and 'S' rise up like spirits.

I also provided a template for the front cover in which the credits neatly sit inside the 'O'. The supporting text is set in Korolev, a Device font.

1

2

3

4

Batman: The Return
DC Comics
Comic book
2010

For this one-shot comic taking place after the **Return of Bruce Wayne** storyline and leading directly into **Batman Incorporated**, I first revisited some unused designs **1** I had originally created for **Batwoman.**

The colon presented an unusual opportunity to place the 'M' centrally in the design, forming the lower part of the cowl. I favoured the more angular type style **5**, **6** and above, but the more readable version **4** was ultimately used.

The bat itself was subtly modelled in three dimensions to mimic the recently redesigned style of **Batman**'s chest emblem.

1

2

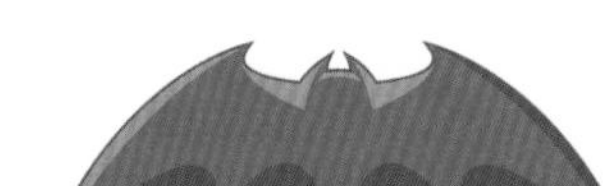

3

4

5

6

Napster
Music file-sharing site
2000

I received an email out of the blue asking me if I'd like to look at redesigning the **Napster** logo. At the time I was working for many clients in the music industry, and had heard first-hand how file-sharing had pushed bands' often slim revenues over a cliff. While some argued that greedy record companies could afford to take a hit, I saw the way in which many musicians who barely broke even lose their livelihoods almost overnight.

As someone who relies upon robust copyright laws in order to protect my own intellectual property, I felt that in all good conscience I couldn't work with them. I faxed them an article that had appeared in that week's *New Musical Express* that was strongly critical of **Napster**, Limewire and other similar file-sharing services. The cover read: "**Napster** – Game over for the music business?"

The fax shown right was waiting for me the next morning.

After a series of unsuccessful attempts to prevent copyrighted material being uploaded to its servers, legal proceedings shut the service down the following year. **Napster** agreed to pay music creators and copyright owners a $26 million settlement and $10 million as an advance against future royalties. In order to pay these fees, **Napster** attempted to convert to a subscription service. An American bankruptcy judge blocked an opportunistic buyout attempt by Bertelsmann, forcing the liquidation of its assets. The company finally announced itself bankrupt in 2002.

FAX FROM
16/06 WED 10 34 FAX 0171 611 636
15/06/ 13 58 PG 1
001

NAPSTER=GOOD

the UK.

The logo references a film I'd once seen in which the vital clue to the identity of the murderer is his typewriter, which drops a certain letter below the baseline – here, I used the lowercase 'r'. The torn paper references police jotters or newspaper clippings, and the chalk outline is a classic murder scene motif. The invitation to the opening was a bagged police report with a rubber-stamped tag **3**.

This being 1988, the roughs were drawn with a marker pen on layout paper **1**, **2**; I was still a few years away from my first Mac.

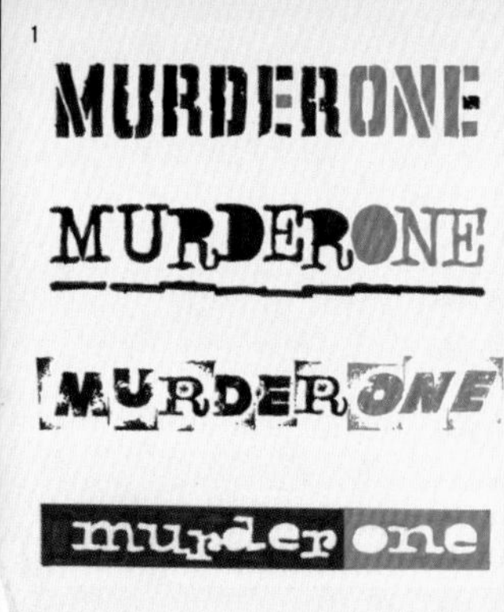

Font Pimp
Veer
T-shirt motif
2003

Promotional T-shirt for Veer, a stock photography and font reseller that is now part of Getty.

Necrosha
Marvel Comics
Comic book series
2009

X-Men villain The Black Queen plans to attain goddess-hood using **New Mutants** member Warlock's 'techno-organic virus'.

A logo was required for a **Necrosha** one-shot and to run as a banner along the top of six issues of **X-Force**, three issues of **New Mutants** and three issues of **X-Men Legacy**, all of which tied into the storyline.

1 purged the obvious horror comic cliché from my system at the outset. I favoured angular lettering constructed from a tessellated pattern based on Warlock's alien appearance. **2**–**3**, **5**–**8**.

As is often the case where a story arc crosses over several titles, the banner versions suffered from the inevitable clash of stylistically different logo designs; some of **Marvel**'s covers can have as many as ten different fonts jostling for attention. I attempted to mitigate this with a matching set of logos **6**, **7**, **8** that were stylistically related to the main **Necrosha** branding that could be used for the duration. Unfortunately they weren't used.

1

NECROSHA

2

NECROSHA

3

4

NECROSHA

5

NECROSHA

6

NEW MUTANTS

7

X·MEN LEGACY

8

X·FORCE

Hasbro Creation Studios
Hasbro
Proposed logo
2009

Hasbro Creation Studios is a US production company based in Burbank, California, that develops film and TV projects from their toy properties such as *G. I. Joe, Micronauts, M.A.S.K.* and *Rom.*

Five by Five
Production company
2010

Five by Five is a production company specialising in behind-the-scenes documentaries and 'Making of' featurettes. **Five by Five** means "I can hear you perfectly". The client suggested a "Buck Rogers/Flash Gordon type, holding a futuristic walkie talkie".

Though this was indeed the final design, I explored other less illustrative options as well.

1

2

1

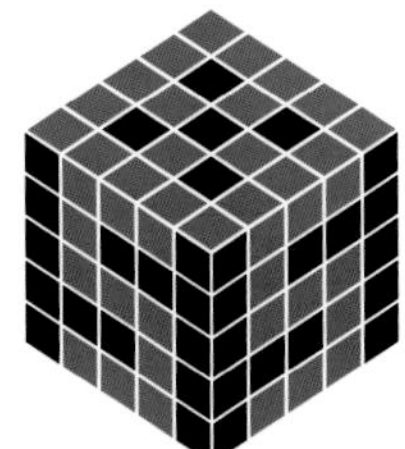

2

3

4

3

4

Pocket Superheroes
DC Comics
Toy range
2001

Pocket Superheroes was a collection of simple Lego-like figures from DC Direct, **DC Comics**' toy and merchandise division. Early versions of the logo use a silhouette of a simplified articulated figure and a pocket motif. The final logo has a gloved superhero hand – could this be **Batman** holding the little figure?

1

2

3

4

5

6

7

8

MTV Merchandise
MTV Europe
1996

A series intended for use on mugs, T-shirts and bags. As far as I am aware, none of my designs were used.

1

2

3

4

5

6

7

8

Insight Comics
Insight Editions
2016

1

2

Insight Editions launched in 2001 with titles on the Rolling Stones, Bruce Springsteen and Jerry Garcia, and are now known for their high-quality books on pop culture, comics, music, film and sports. There are several imprints under the Insight umbrella: Mandala Publishing produces books on Eastern traditions, health and ecology; Earth Aware Editions publishes leading environmentalists, photojournalists, artists and activists; Insight Collectables produces limited edition pop culture collectibles; Insight Kids focusses on children's publishing, and there was to be the launch of a new imprint – **Insight Comics**.

A suite of logos was required. Each needed to describe the remit of its specific imprint, but also share a common aesthetic so it was obvious they came from the same stable.

The existing logo is a loose brush-drawn eye. Using this as a starting point, I developed a set **3** that utilises the same basic shapes: the plinth suggests quality, while the eye above is also the dot on a lowercase 'i' for Insight. Mandala uses a lotus flower, the iris becomes a speech ballon for Comics, and so on. Differing line weights and fonts were explored; I

3

4

favoured an elegant timeless sans. Some versions feature a more obvious 'i'. I took pains to keep the line weights of both the icon and the type the same.

Unfortunately it proved difficult to get useful feedback, which tended not to engage with the big picture but to zero in on relatively minor elements like the shape of the crossbar of the 'G'. A project should really begin with a discussion of the overarching concept, and only then zero in on such details.

I dropped the pillar/i, and explored brushy type (a homage to the existing logo), thinner line weights and different motifs and fonts **4**, all the while being cognizant of the fact that any solution would need to be versatile enough to work across the set. When these didn't seem to elicit any meaningful response, I began to submit random ideas **5-9** just to see if anything would stick. I have no idea how, if these were chosen, they might have been developed into the full set.

In the end, I drew a line under the job and unilaterally delivered a set of logos based on a monoline eye (left). There is a subtle reference to the speech balloon in the Comics iteration, and a cartoon-like, kid-friendly eye for Kids, though the other two have no special meaning.

I produced both a black and a white version **1**. Note that in each the white of the eye is white and the pupil black, so they are not simply the reverse of each other. I also designed a text-only version **2** that could be used at small sizes or on a spine, or when the more detailed logo would be overwhelming.

In the end, the generic 'Editions' version (without the hidden speech bubble) was altered to read 'Comics', and is the only logo that was used. Despite its tortuous evolution, I'm pretty happy with it.

5

6

7

8

9

First Europa
Sterling Brands
Car insurer
Proposed logo
2007

1

2

First Europa was an online car insurance broker aimed at women and designed to attract a younger demographic.

I liked the Penelope Pitstop-style goggles and helmet and the Starsky and Hutch 'go faster' stripe, but the company felt that they might suggest their clients were in the habit of driving too fast.

In 2012, European judges banned risk assessment based on gender as it breached EU equality legislation.

1

2

3

TECHJACKET

4

5

"I NEED A WEAPON"

6

the learning lounge
iConnect • iLearn • iCreate

7

8

Atomic Comics

9

10

1 **Ninjak vs the Valiant Universe**
Valiant Comics
Live action web series
2016
The brief: "Like a big cheesy '80s action movie logo. Something that guarantees explosions and violence and fighting."

2 **Paradigm Project Services**
Architectural services
1994

3 **Techjacket**
Skybound/Image
Comic book
2014
An update of the previous logo

4 **Girotondo**
Eve Records
Album
1998

5 **"I Need a Weapon"**
Bungie
Incidental logo
2011
From a *Halo* limited edition poster I designed and illustrated

6 **The Learning Lounge**
Epping Forest College
2014
Multimedia library and learning resource centre

7 **Atomstile**
Limited edition print
Incidental logo
2010

8 **Atomic Comics**
Acme Press
Comic book imprint
1989

9 **For Genuine Headhunters**
DMB+B
Advertisement
Incidental type
1993

10 **The Reaper**
Magazine masthead for proposed magazine
2000

Captain America Reborn
Marvel Comics
Comic book series
2009

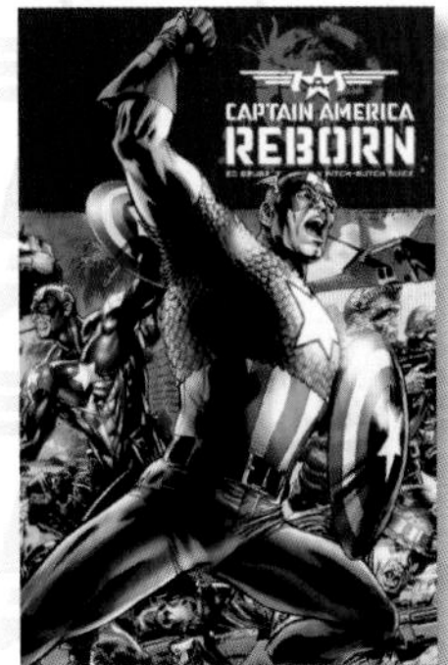

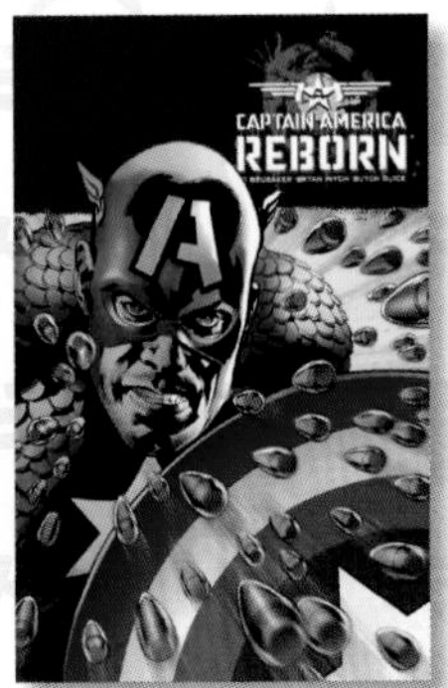

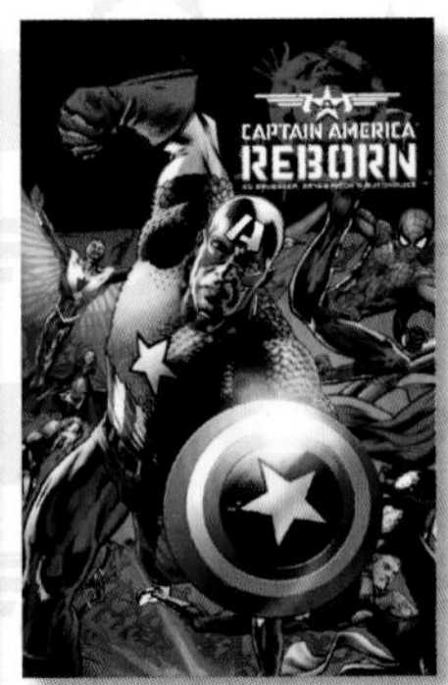

1

CAPTAIN
AMERICA
REBORN

2

3

4

5

6

7

8

9

Created by Joe Simon and Jack Kirby in 1941, **Captain America** patriotically battled the Axis powers throughout WWII.

Captain America: Reborn is a six-issue limited series written by Ed Brubaker with finely detailed art by Bryan Hitch that tells the story behind the apparent death of the original **Captain America**, Steve Rogers, and reinstates him in the **Marvel** Universe.

To design the logo I went back to Joe Simon's very first version **5**. The logo has been through many iterations since, but none have come close to improving on this basic design. The slanted horizontal stroke terminals of the 'C' and 'E' are very much features of Art Deco type of the period, so I kept them along with a 'T' that is now sloped to match and an angled leg to the 'R'. The winged 'A' is of course based on Cap's cowl, and I used it as a repeat for the endpapers of the hardback collection (background).

The whole was given a stencil treatment to evoke wartime military labelling. Cap's shield, in expressive dripping paint that also suggests blood, was used as an underprint. The trade dress, which I also designed, housed the logo in a panel that ran across the top of each issue.

To illustrate the minutiae that I fret over, for this series I redesigned the barcode box and '**Marvel** Limited Series' numbering box **8**, which between them used six fonts (not including the **Marvel** logo), each set in a different point size, orientation or tracking **8**. Combining the two, I designed one 'lock-up' that only used two weights of one font, Paralucent. The whole took up 25% less real-estate on the cover and greatly reduced clutter.

I used it throughout the run and on my **Iron Man** covers, and supplied a set of vertical and horizontal masters **9**, but it was not adopted with any consistency; a similar but somewhat inelegant version currently appears across **Marvel**'s line. I sometimes worry that I'm spending an inordinate amount of time obsessing over details that the client and public may not notice or deem relevant.

7 shows the embossed boards of the hardback collection; **6** is the title spread.

NYC Mech
Image Comics/Ivan Brandon
Comic book series
2004

"Eight million robots walk the streets, but this isn't science fiction. This is New York City, top to bottom, from a basement in the last Brooklyn ghetto to the clouds above a penthouse suite on Park Avenue. Welcome to NYC Mech."

My logo designs for writer Ivan Brandon's series explore New York City and electrical motifs – windows, sockets, eroded metal. The final design resembles an embossed foundry nameplate you'd find riveted to a piece of heavy machinery.

I incorporated one of the unused logos into the background of a splash page illustration I drew for the graphic novel collection **7**.

1

2

3

4

5

6

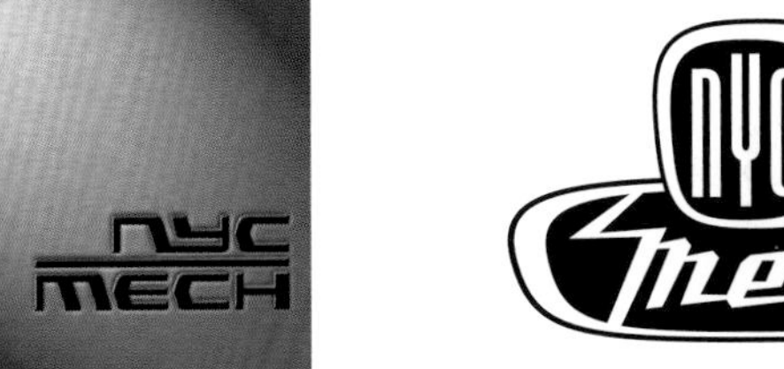

7

8

9

10

11

12

13

Young Sherlock Holmes
Macmillan Children's Books
Book cover
2010

The cover for **Young Sherlock Holmes** needed to 'position' it to compete with similar titles on the market such as *Young Bond* or *Artemis Fowl*. This is common in publishing – it can be a bit like the 'me too' world of supermarket own-brand toothpaste, where the product needs to look similar to other successful brands (but not so similar that they sue), presumably so a harried punter will pick it up without having to think too much. This can, sadly, lead to pretty generic results.

This 'outside-in', marketing led method is in complete contrast with the 'inside-out' approach I generally encounter in the music industry. I've spoken at length to almost every band or comic book team I've worked with; I've spoken to a scant handful of novelists whose jackets I've designed, and when I did (often because the author got in contact or suggested me in the first place), the publishers got a bit antsy. I suspect their preferred method of working had accidentally been circumvented, and they were wondering what they might get.

For this logo I didn't know what the rest of the cover was going to look like, so I was several stages removed from the overall design concept. In these cases, I tend to fall back on letter plays, like the magnifying glass or the Victorian enamel sign effects.

None were used.

1

2

3

4

5

6

7

8

1

2

3

4

5

Chic Geek
Device
T-shirt range
2007

Because geeky girls are best.

UZAP
Uzap/Dilemma
Online community and marketplace
2008

Uzap, an online company hosting interactive classifieds, was intended to compete with Craigslist, eBay or Loot. They promised a secure platform that would verify and protect user's identities, while ensuring a reliable service from the tradespeople who advertised on the site.

It appears they no longer exist.

1

2

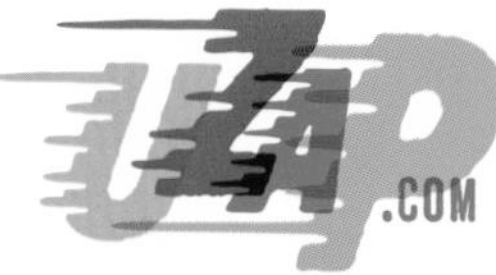

3

4

Mango Taco
John Nee
Website
2000

Mangotaco.com was a website for print on demand goods – posters, stickers and maps – featuring content from multi-player online games, with the unique feature that each was customised with the user's in-game character stats.

The font used in **2** and the final logo (main image) is Strand, one of my Device font releases, which comes in a range of decorative variants.

I'm not sure what the connection to mangos and tacos might have been.

1

2

3

4

Geri Halliwell
EMI/Stylorouge (agency)
Record sleeve and personal logo
1999

This portrait logo was used on the sleeve of the promo version of *Mi Chico Latino*, ex-Spice Girl **Geri Halliwell**'s second solo single and first number one.

It was commissioned by Rob O'Connor, head honcho of veteran music design agency Stylorouge, who are responsible for such design classics as the *Trainspotting* campaign and early Siouxie and the Banshees albums. At the time we had studio space on the same floor of a building in Salem Road, Bayswater, along with photographer Simon Fowler.

The logo began as an angel/devil hybrid 'g', but Rob wanted it to be more like a caricature of Geri herself, and found a photo which provided the basis of the final logo. It comes in two versions, one winking, here foil-blocked onto the front and back of the CD sleeve. It also appeared at a gigantic size in lights as part of Geri's stage backdrop.

Some years later, she asked me to collaborate on a series of six children's books that featured a young protagonist not unlike Geri herself: **Ugenia Lavender**, which she wrote and I illustrated. I sat in her kitchen sketching while she described the characters to me, with breaks in which she changed daughter Bluebell Madonna's nappy and showed me where she'd just had a tattoo removed.

1

2

3

4

Dolly Bird
Boutique
2000

Dolly Bird is a small vintage boutique based in San Francisco. The hair decorations are inspired by the proprietor's own personal style.

1

2

3

4

5

1

2

3

4

5

6

7

8

9

10

1 Astonisher
Lion Forge Comics
Comic book
2017

2 Superman's Nemesis: Lex Luthor
DC Comics
Comic book
1998

3 icandy
DC Comics
Comic book
2003

4 icandi
DC Comics
Comic book
Proposed logo
2003

5 Shaking Street
Lakesville
Production company
2009

6 Tranceformer
Transient Records
Album cover proposal
2001

7 The Fist and The Steel
Valiant Comics
Comic book arc
2016
An **Eternal Warrior** and **Ninjak** teamup

8 Unknown Host
Peter Hogan
Comic book
Logo proposal
2005

9 Hurricane
Wetsuit manufacturer
1984

10 Roadblock
A+M Records/Stock Aitken Waterman
Single
1987
I also illustrated the sleeve **11**. This was lifted by Mark Doyle for his club, and led to me designing the **Hed Kandi** logo

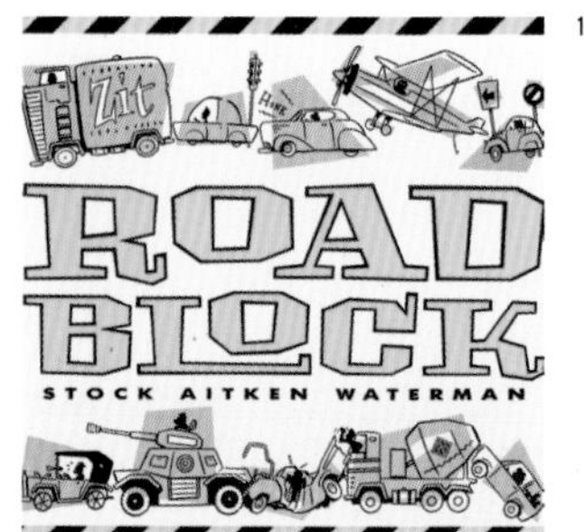

11

Shade, the Changing Man
Vertigo/DC Comcis
Comic book series
1993

Shade, the Changing Man was one of the earliest logos I designed on my first Mac, a IIci that packed a massive 4 MB of RAM and a 40 MB hard drive.

Written by Peter Milligan, the series was loosely based on Steve Ditko's original eight-issue run from 1977. This logo was introduced on #33, the first issue to be published under the new Vertigo banner, DC's mature comics line that was helmed by *Swamp Thing* editor Karen Berger.

The Vertigo logo and trade dress, the distinctive stripe that ran down the left side of all the titles, was designed by DC's art director Richard Bruning.

Batwoman
DC Comics
Comic book series
Logo proposal
2006

Katherine Kane, alias **Batwoman**, first appeared in *Detective Comics* in 1956. Originally created by Edmond Hamilton and Sheldon Moldoff to expand **Batman**'s cast of supporting characters, legend has it that she was introduced as a love interest to combat allegations of **Batman**'s homosexuality. These had been stoked by the publication of Fredric Wertham's infamous book *Seduction of the Innocent* (1954), which led directly to the introduction of the Comics Code.

To "diversify and better connect with DC's modern-day readership", the current **Batwoman** is recast as a lesbian, the company's highest-profile gay superhero. Her sexual orientation has drawn widespread media attention.

This logo is for a proposed 2006 series that didn't see publication. My designs for the logo place it within the same 'Bat-family' that incorporate the dramatic bat silhouette and stylised head and cowl. Some use an asymmetric cape similar to some of my unused **Batgirl** designs **5**, **7**, **8**, others the classic **Batman** font **4**, **7**, which I later digitised for my *Batman: Black and White* strip as Kane. This was deemed to be too heavy, so other, more refined serif styles were explored, as well as some Gothic blackletters. The light sans **2** I liked, but it might have become lost on the covers.

The later 'New 52' **Batwoman** comic book by J. H. Williams III and W. Haden Blackman was spun out of her appearances in *Detective Comics* and used J. H.'s own logo design, loosely derived from the monoline angularity of **11** and the zig-zag crossbars of **12**.

1

2

3

4

5

6

7

8

9

10

11

12

PCG/Kodak
PCG/Kodak/Giro (agency)
Proposed logo
1999

Designed for a joint venture between a paper manufacturer and an ink supplier, the logo is a straightforward representation of ink on paper, the colour describing the shape of the sheet with the undefined white areas acting as negative space. The colours are taken from the existing brand logos, which coincidentally were close to the three primary colours.

1

2

Box Tops
The Box
Cable channel title sequence
1996

I designed and illustrated the animated title sequence for **Box Tops**, cable channel The Box's Saturday morning TV chart show. This is the logo that appeared at the finale, and also ran along the bottom of the screen to introduce each act.

The Box was a music channel controlled by the viewer, who phoned in to request particular videos, and Box Tops showed the ten most requested.

The theme music, a loungecore masterpiece from The Ray McVay Sound called *Kinda Kinky*, suited the sequence perfectly. It wasn't intended to be high concept – just loud, bright and poppy.

1

2

3

4

Marathon
Bungie
Videogame
Logo proposal
2011

I'd been commissioned via **Smolhaus** to design a limited edition print for the anniversary of Bungie, the developers of the *Halo* and **Marathon** game franchises. Having completed the print, I was asked to look at updating the original **Marathon** logo. The game was an early first-person shooter, released in 1994 for the Macintosh; I vividly remember afternoons in the studio spent shooting aliens when I should have been drawing comics.

This project did not progress beyond this first round of concepts, which adhere quite closely to the original condensed and letterspaced design.

1

2

3

4

Auto Daisy Express Car Wash
Precision Productions + Post
Car wash
2009

This Los Angeles-based eco-friendly car wash uses a conveyor system that recycles water, uses less energy, and can wash and dry a car in five minutes. It was described in the brief as "the car wash version of In 'n' Out Burger".

The logo was required to be "very pop modern – future meets the past in a jet set, motorama sort of way, but it still needs to do all the things a corporate logo needs to do. It'll be used on signage and literature. It needs personality but shouldn't scare Mom off by being too hip."

I aimed for something that was simple, approachable and fun, and not too masculine or too feminine, as the client wanted to appeal to a broad demographic.

Including a stylised daisy was a no-brainer – here, its white petals have been shaped to resemble splashes of water (water is more explicitly referenced in **2**). The chequered flag references speed and automobilia.

The driving/diving goggles were pushed up to the forehead and the eyes given a white surround, which seemed to read more clearly – this is several years before the Minions were created. Reducing the number of petals made for a simpler, more compact design, with more emphasis on the daisy's face. In the final version (opposite) I placed one petal over the flagpole, so it appears as if the character is holding it up.

Pressing a well-worn cliché into use, the green communicates the system's eco-friendly credentials, while if you're delving deeper the daisy might also resemble the sun. As a final polish I added a subtle amount of modelling.

The type is loosely based on my Popgod font, with the strapline set in Paralucent.

1

2

3

4

5

6

7

8

9

10

Batman
DC Comics
Comic book series
2009

Designed for the **Batman** strip in **Wednesday Comics**, this iteration was a direct reworking of the logo from the first issue of **Batman**'s own title, designed by Jerry Robinson and published in 1941.

It was later given a distressed makeover for a project which teamed **Batman** with Doc Savage, a pulp action series that morphed into *First Wave* (for which my **Batman/Spirit** design was adapted in-house). Here, I explore subtle variations on the basic model, using italic, curved or arched type with colour offsets to mimic vintage print techniques. As always, I kept the traditional reversed-stress, seen most clearly on the 'A's.

The logo was also used on merchandise (above).

BATMAN
BATMAN
BATMAN
BATMAN
BATMAN
BATMAN
BATMAN
BATMAN

Rick Random, Space Detective
IPC
Comic book collection
Proposed logo
2008

I'm a big admirer of Ron Turner's science-fiction illustrations, especially his bright, dramatic 1950s covers for Scion's Volsted Gridban and Vargo Statten (both pseudonyms for John Russel Fearn) paperbacks. **Rick Random, Space Detective** ran in the pocket-sized *Super Detective Library* comic series, starting with *Kidnappers from Space* in #44, published in December 1954.

This logo was for an omnibus volume that collected all the **Rick Random** strips for the first time. I based the lettering on Ron's own distinctive style – I hoped the design would not look out of place on the hull of one of his spaceships. The background image is taken from a piece of original Turner art.

The final book design was done in-house by the licensee, Carlton Books.

Faith
Valiant Comics
Proposed logo
2016

Faith is **Valiant**'s popular plus-sized superhero from the pages of **Harbinger**. The brief was to communicate her personality and powers: "We'd like something that's fun, poppy, and modern. **Faith**'s power is flight. Perhaps **Faith** zipping around the logo? Is that crazy?"

Not crazy at all. I used lowercase rounded shapes with a playful bounce. In my favoured solution (below), the figure leaves a line through the crossbars.

The logo that was used - not designed by me - was thinner. Some of mine possibly foregrounded her plus-size too much – it's not her only defining feature.

1

FAITH

2

Faith

3

faith

4

faith

5

faith

6

Faith

7

FAITH

8

FAITH

Captain Britain
Marvel Comics
Comic book series
2008

Doctor Who scriptwriter Paul Cornell was relaunching **Captain Britain**, retitled **Captain Britain and MI13**, with art by Leonard Kirk and covers by Bryan Hitch. The series centred on the fictional government agency MI13, dedicated to protecting the United Kingdom from supernatural threats.

The logos reflect the Captain's red, white and blue Union Jack costume **10**, **13** and magical Arthurian origin story - there is a subtle reference to Excalibur in **8**. I favoured the type treatment from **5** or **9**. **3** looks like the label on a tin of tourist souvenir fudge.

The series launched as a tie-in to **Marvel**'s Secret Invasion event in May 2008. Though I supplied the trade dress as well as the logo, unfortunately the covers as printed only loosely resemble my design and suffer from the usual excess of clashing logos and 'First Issue' starbursts. Best intentions . . .

1

2

3

4

5

6

7

8

9

10

11

12

13

14

15

Atheism
2014

Most movements have their symbol or flag – it provides visibility in the competing marketplace of ideas: something to congregate around, wave at demonstrations or wear as a badge or T-shirt to show your affiliation.

Atheism is not a belief system or a philosophy, just the lack of one. As Richard Dawkins points out, we don't need a name for non-astrologers. However, this hasn't stopped people trying to design an atheist logo: the red A (in Hermann Zapf's Zapfino), or the atom of American Atheists, or the Christian Ichthus with legs; more playful examples include The Invisible Pink Unicorn and the Flying Spaghetti Monster. Others represent a negation – a crossed-out religious symbol, for example.

I wanted to avoid critiquing any one religion and instead promote the positive values of secular governance, rational enquiry and the scientific method – in other words, the absence of a belief system or a fixed set of ideological tenets.

My solution: a transparent flag. A symbol that does not have any design or colour so does not reference existing meanings – it just clearly reveals what lies behind it, nature as she really is.

While attaching a sheet of cellophane to a stick proves that this concept works well in reality (though from a distance you are just waving a stick), depicting it as a logo turned out to be more difficult. It's very hard to draw transparency. The white of the page? That looks like a white flag, used for surrendering. Short diagonal lines, as on a cartoon pane of glass? Again, how many? Which direction? Designers know that very little means very little, and meaninglessness is harder to arrive at than might be imagined.

To best reflect atheism, maybe the *absence* of a logo - a 'no-logo' or a 'alogo' – is the most appropriate way to show absence of belief.

Or maybe I've just argued myself out of having to come up with a practical solution.

Boots Chemists
20/20 (agency)
In-store department icons
1997

A set of icons to signpost the different departments of the UK high-street pharmacy **Boots**, which was founded in 1849.

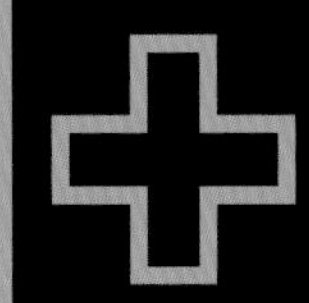

Vital
Childrens' charity
2007

Vital is a charity set up by the energetic and dedicated Yvonne Neumann to help vulnerable street children in Kolkata, India. Through a series of donations and fundraising events, it provides access to education, healthcare, protective services and sustainable community development.

India has a rich and vibrant hand-painted vernacular type tradition, and I wanted to explore that heritage; early designs evoke the style of signage seen on vans and cars on the streets of Kolkata, or the ornate design of vintage Indian matchbooks and stamps. **5-6**, main image.

1-3 use a map of India with a heart placed at the city's location. The saffron and green of the Indian flag is treated to mimic roughly applied paint on the wooden slats of makeshift housing.

Though I was fond of these, it was felt that a more clean and 'corporate' approach might give the charity better leverage as a legitimate, international fundraising organisation in the eyes of potential donors, so the final logo is a simpler, cleaner affair. It retains the heart, sliced to form the V of Vital. This is also used as a stand-alone icon for branding on shirts, caps, events **12-14**, publicity and literature **11**, **9**.

1

2

3

4

5

6

7

8

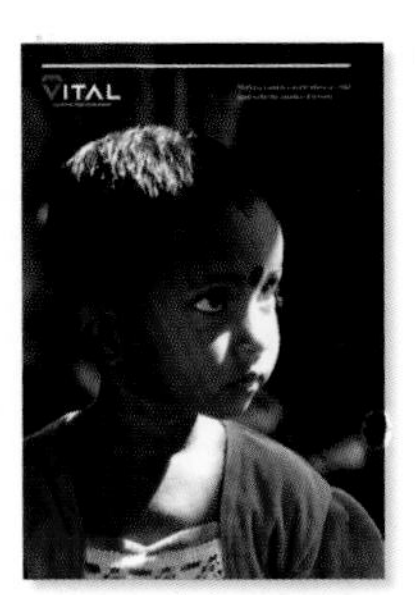

9 10

11

12

13

14

Fleetway
Fleetway
Publisher
c1991

Fleetway, publisher of *2000AD,* **Revolver** and **Crisis**, has a long and convoluted history. As with many UK magazine and newspaper publishers, the comics are but a small division in a much larger organisation.

Formed in 1959 when the Mirror Group acquired Amalgamated Press, then based at **Fleetway** House, Farringdon Street, London, it then merged into the IPC group in 1963, though the **Fleetway** banner continued to be used until 1968 when all IPC's publications were reorganised.

In 1987 the name re-emerged when IPC's comics line was sold to Robert Maxwell as **Fleetway** Publications. Egmont UK subsequently bought **Fleetway** from Maxwell in 1991, merging it with their own comics publishing operation, London Editions, to form **Fleetway** Editions, for which this logo was designed.

The winged oval of the original design **1** is fondly remembered by a generation of comics readers – it appeared on titles like *Buster, Cor! Monster Fun* and *Misty.* I paid homage by retaining the basic shapes, though reinterpreting them.

Fleetway Quality **2** was the US reprint arm. For this, the logo was adapted with the addition of an extra triangle that turned the ellipse into a 'Q'.

3, **4** and **5** are the original sketches and thumbnails.

1

2

3

4

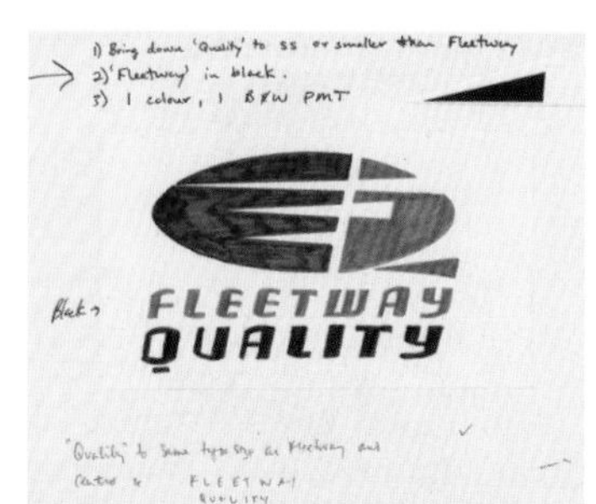

5

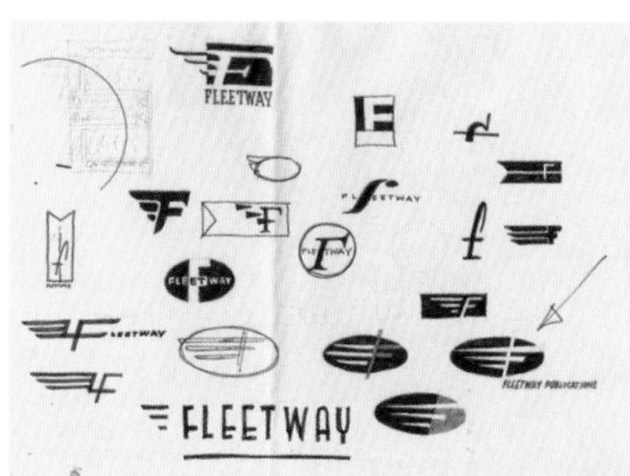

1

2

3

4

5

6

7

8

9

10

11

12

1 2 3 **Crack Up Laughing**
Carlsberg Comedy Festival
Type treatment
2001
Type treatment options as part of a series of posters and magazine advertisements for the Carlsberg Comedy Festival which I designed

4 **Sam Slade: Robo Hunter**
Fleetway/2000AD
Comic book series
1994
Writer: Peter Hogan
Artist: Rian Hughes
Designed for the series I drew for the Galaxy's Greatest

5 6 **Ultravox**
Ultravox
10″ limited edition four-track EP
2011
Logo and incidental logo for the gatefold sleeve, which I also designed

7 **Zarjazz**
Madness/Virgin Records
Logo proposal
1988
Unused logo from *The Madness* album sleeve and associated singles, which were designed in collaboration with Dave Gibbons. Zarjaz (one 'z') means 'excellent' in *2000AD* editor Tharg's Betelgeusian slang

8 **Stop That**
Blackie Children's Books
Book cover
1994

9 **Special Offer**
Incidental logo
2017
From the novel *XX*
Author: Rian Hughes

10 11 **Let's Play Capitalism**
John Brown/Citrus Publishing
Incidental logos
2006
From the book *Pick Me Up*

12 **Blue Mood**
Penny Black
Book cover
2016

Flex Mentallo
DC Comics
Comic book mini-series
1996

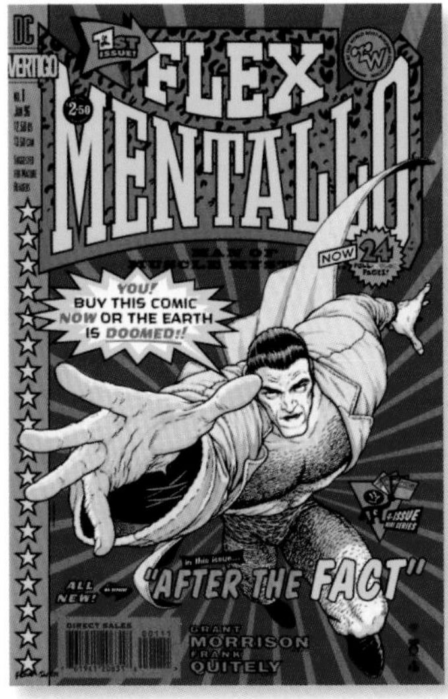

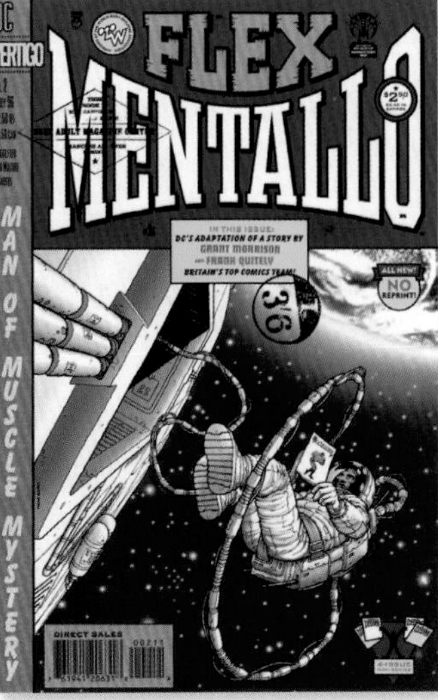

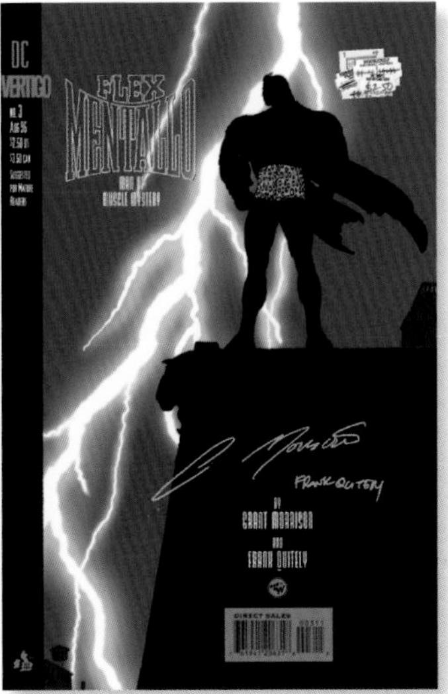

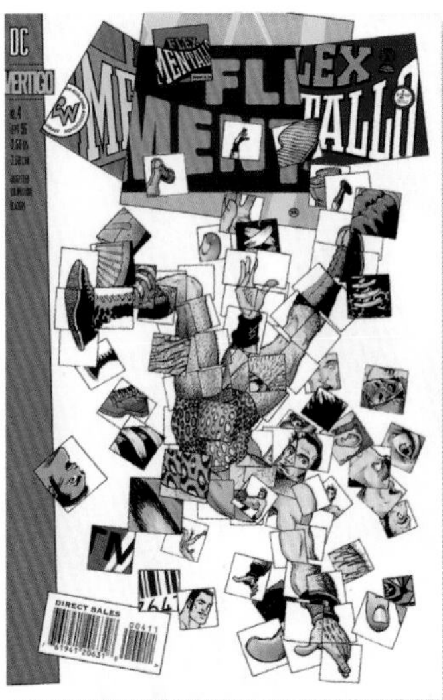

Flex Mentallo is a four-issue mini-series written by Grant Morrison and drawn by fellow Scot Frank Quitely. Based on a character from Grant's **Doom Patrol** run, **Flex** is a parody of Charles Atlas' long-running 'The Insult that made a Man out of Mac' advertisements that ran for many years in American comics.

I designed both the logos and trade dress, for which Grant and Vincent (Frank) revisit classic comic cover tropes. The first was suggested by Grant's favourite **Flash** cover, in which the hero implores the reader to buy the comic to save his life; the second spoofs the graphic language of EC Comics' famous horror and science fiction line. The third references Frank Miller's *The Dark Knight Returns*, while the last issue suggests a deconstructed narrative of falling panels, including the barcode box.

The logo has the dramatic lens-shaped distortion familiar from boxing brands like Everlast. I also designed lots of small incidental logos that pepper the covers: the first issue has endorsements from the fictitious 'World-Wide Body Building Association' and a stamp from the 'Used Adult Magazine Centre' that mimics the 'Popular Magazine Centre' stamps seen on many vintage UK comics and books. In small type up the side is the tagline 'Logo a Gogo', reused as the title of this book.

The second issue sports a 'Favourite Comic Award' from the also made-up 'Sci-Fi Boys of West Ealing Club' **2**, which I repurposed for the **Magicdrive** sleeve designs. (At the time, I was living in West Ealing, a suburb of London.) The third issue comments on the collector's boom and bust of the 1980s, with fake gold signatures and a set of price stickers from **Forbidden Planet**, Bookendz and 'Fat Tony's Comic and Taco Shack', a nonexistent comics store, that decrease in value till they match the cover price **3**. The stickers were removed from the final cover as it was thought they might confuse retailers, but reinstated for the deluxe reprint, which was designed in-house at DC.

The Charles Atlas company filed for trademark infringement, but the case was dismissed on the basis that a parody falls under fair use.

1

2

3

4

5

6

7

8

JUSTICE
LEAGUE

Justice League
DC Comics
Merchandise imagery
2006

A set of emblems and patterns designed for **DC Comics**' merchandise division. The actual applications are not specified – instead, they form a library of material that potential licensees can draw upon.

I have T-shirts, pillowcases, duvets . . .

1
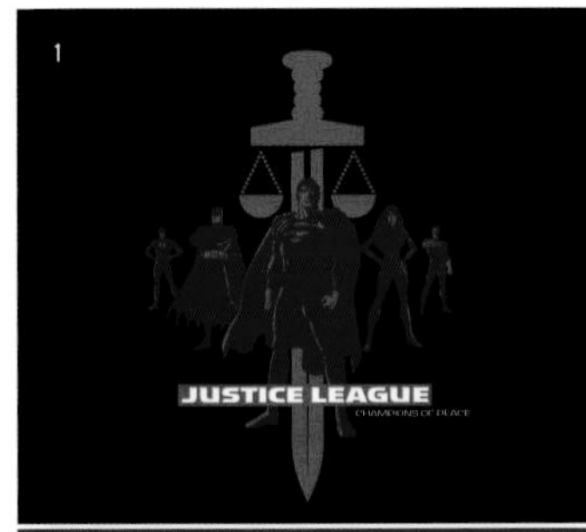

2

3

4

5

6

7

8

9

10

11

12

13

14

15

16

17

18

19

Ivar, Timewalker
Valiant Comics
Comic book
2014

Ivar, Timewalker

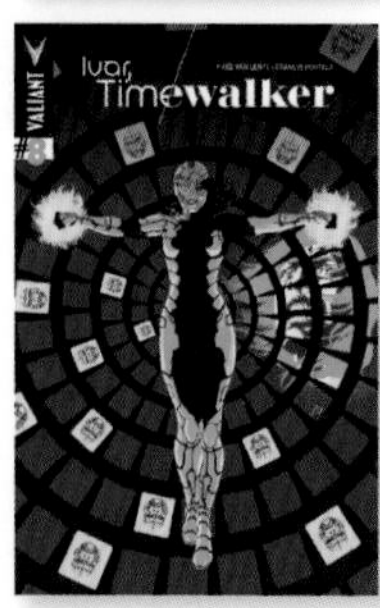

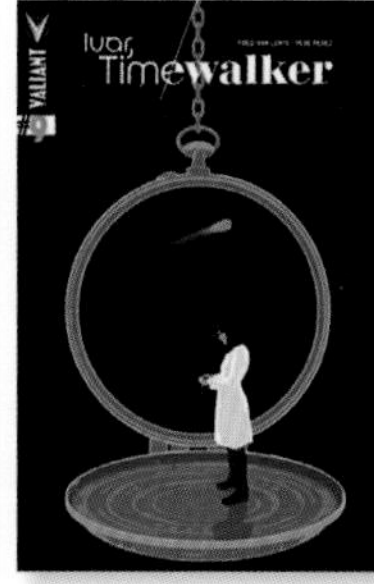

Ivar, Timewalker is Fred Van Lente and Clayton Henry's reimagining of the original 1993 character created by Barry Windsor-Smith during **Valiant Comics**' first incarnation. Ivar has the ability to sense 'time arcs' that allow him to pass from one period of history to another, though he seems to have little control over where he ends up.

The design features a door or portal, through which the logo passes into a different time period, represented by the collision of a moderne geometric sans and a traditional Bodoni serif. I confess I was inspired by the logo of an obscure 1960s science fiction digest called *Beyond Fantasy Fiction*.

The chosen version (opposite) uses a diagonal line in place of the portal. Departing from the strict dimensions I'd set for previous titles, the logo is more free-floating and dispenses with the colour band across the top that is useful for lifting it out of more complex illustrations. In a small but important touch, the usual vertical bars that separate the names in the credits were replaced by matching diagonal slashes.

The covers benefitted enormously from artist Raul Allen's strong sense of composition and limited colour palettes.

1

2

3

4

5

6

7

8

9

10

11

12

The Lipstick Melodies
White Tiger Management
Band
2001

Formed in 2011, **The Lipstick Melodies** were a five-piece band from London playing, as their Facebook page puts it, "no nonsense rock'n'roll". The line-up consisted of Alan Wass on lead vocals and guitar, Richie Stephens on keyboards, Alexi Christou on bass and Phil Clarke on drums. Diverse influences included Bob Dylan, JJ Cale, T Rex and the Stones.

Front man Alan Wass was a close friend and collaborator of The Libertines' Pete Doherty, and prior to performing with **The Lipstick Melodies** fronted Left Hand, whose song *Hired Gun* Doherty and his band Babyshambles regularly covered during live shows.

Early concepts **1**, **3**, **6** evoked gig flyers: creases, rough edges, and ink splatter combined for a DIY cut-and-paste aesthetic with a sense of thrown-together urgency. Supporting type was hand-drawn, like a photocopied fanzine.

Other ideas used a rubber-stamped logo on the back of a hand in the manner of a gig entry mark **6**; black, flouro and gold ink, with Las Vegas 'Stardust' style triangular letters for that combination of glamour and sleaze **3**; or neon **7** and a polished, lip-gloss sheen **10**.

The final design (opposite) is a linked script based on Colin Brignall's Harlow, designed for Letraset in 1977, and nods to the classic 1970s *Top of the Pops* logo, utilising a black and white 'schafline' linear-toned chrome effect.

1

HIRED GUN

2

3

4

5

6

7

8

9

10

11

12

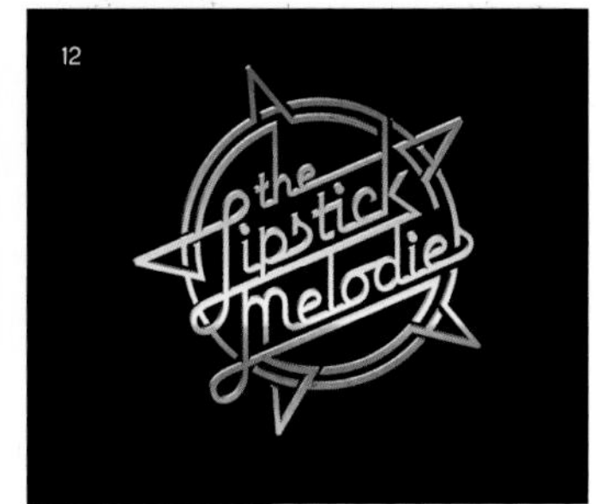

Midmoor Music
White Tiger Management
Music publisher
2012

Midmoor Music is singer/songwriter Charlie Lankester's music publishing company.

The logo uses a photograph of a tree that I have further twisted and sculpted using the Liquify tool in Photoshop. A scanned woodgrain texture has then been reversed out of the whole, suggesting wind or mist. The font is Shenzhen Industrial, taken from photographs of packing boxes I shot on a trip to Hong Kong to visit manufacturing and printing plants with colleagues from **DC Comics**.

1

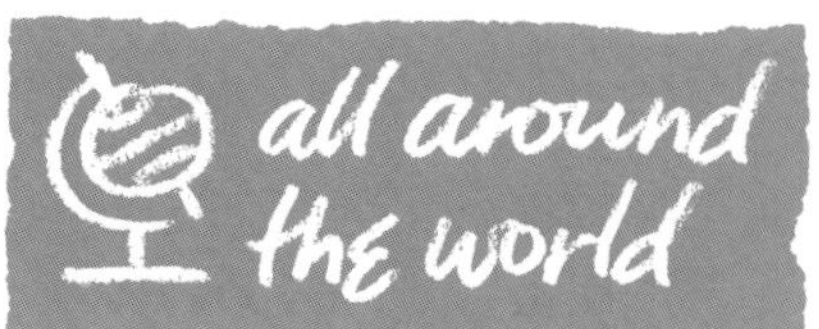

2

3

4

Poison Pink

5

PLANET DEATH

6

ORIGINAL AUDIO
vinyl
ANALOGUE

7

8

9

10

PIC
POCKET

1 **All Around the World**
Revolver/Fleetway
Comic book series
1990

2 **Mister X**
Dean Motter/Dark Horse Comics
Comic cover incidental logo
2017

3 **Cyclone Powers**
Electrolux
Vacuum cleaner brochure
2000
A spoof of the *Austin Powers* logo, which gave me the opportunity to correct everything that was wrong with the original

4 **Poison Pink**
Grant Morrison/Lady Gaga
Proposed comic character
2014

5 **Planet Death**
Valiant Comics
2014
X-O Manowar story arc

6 **Original Audio Vinyl Analogue**
Transient Records
Record bag
1996
Vinyl version of the 'Compact Disc' logo, used on merchandise

7 **Ken and Clare Cromb**
Wedding invitation
1995

8 **Lord Jim**
Fleetway/Crisis
Comic book story
1998
Writer: Igor Goldkind
Artist: Steve Sampson
A strip about the final days of Jim Morrison of The Doors

9 **Picture Pocket**
Clothing accessory
2000

10 **Pic Pocket**
Clothing accessory
Proposed logo
2000
The product name was changed to Picture Pocket

Static Shock
DC Comics
Comic book
2000

1

2

3

4

Static Shock was created in 1993 by Milestone Comics founders Dwayne McDuffie, Denys Cowan, Derek Dingle, and Michael Davis and was initially written by McDuffie and Robert L. Washington III with art by John Paul Leon.

Milestone Comics was an imprint of **DC Comics**, and after Milestone folded, **Static** was incorporated into the DC Universe, becoming a member of the **Teen Titans** and later a popular animated TV show.

This new logo was designed for the character's reintroduction as part of the second wave of DC's 'New 52' company-wide relaunch. The hexagonal element that replaces the 'O' in Shock is **Static's** 'hoverboard', and his signature lightning discharges add a crackling dynamism.

During the design process I tried to steer the client away from a more heavily rendered 3D style, which does not gel well with a flatter style of comic book art. **13**, **14**, and to a lesser extent **6**, move in this more photoreal direction. My preference was to push an otherwise flat logo into 'two-and-a-half dimensions'.

Many heavily rendered logos are typographically weak underneath all the fancy effects. While they can certainly add a final polish, a well-designed logo should first and foremost work 'bare', as it were.

The final covers were laid out in-house by the always able Kenny Lopez; I supplied a dozen colourways so that it could be easily keyed to the art each issue **1-4**.

5

6

7

8

9

10

11

12

13

14

15

16

Valiant Comics
Valiant Entertainment
Corporate logo
2011

1

2

3

4

5

Based in New York, **Valiant Comics** was originally founded in 1989 by former **Marvel** Comics editor-in-chief Jim Shooter and Steven Massarsky. It was bought by games company Acclaim in 1994, and ceased publishing a few years later. Its extensive back catalogue of characters was acquired and relaunched by Dinesh Shamdasani and Jason Kothari in 2005.

I'd been hired to design both the logos and trade dress – the whole look of the new line. Originally the plan was to use their existing 2006 logo **2**, itself an update of the original by Janet 'JayJay' Jackson **1**, but as we got deeper into plans for the line, redesigning it to work with the evolving design seemed like a better option. If it's possible to take a project back to first principles, to rethink the entire thing from the ground up, it can avoid bolting together stylistically disparate elements and makes for a more cohesive result.

Both existing logos **1**, **2** suffered from a mismatch between the lettering and the symbol. I went back to the original compass design, emphasising the hidden 'V' that had been lost in the rebrand **2**, which looks more like an estate agent. I also ditched the fine serif, which interacts awkwardly with the lowest point of the compass, and the arbitrary perspective. The new bold sans is custom-drawn, and has an angularity that matches the compass; with a bit of judicious fudging, I also managed to get the 'I' directly centred under the point of the 'V'. To throw the 'V' forward, the other elements of the compass have been knocked back to a supporting mid-grey.

Rather than a single corporate colour like **Marvel**'s bright red, which can sometimes seem obtrusive in subtler cover designs, I supplied the logo in a range of colours **12** and in use it is keyed to the art issue by issue. As well as the standard portrait version, I included a landscape version for spines, and a simpler black and white version for small sizes **3**.

Redesigning a corporate logo can be a labour-intensive process. I worked through many variants, only a few of which are shown here. In the end we came full circle, back to one of my earliest designs, but sometimes it can help to see what doesn't work in order to be sure of what does. As I said in my proposal, I wanted Valiant to "come out all guns blazing, in our best finery, looking cool as fuck and here to kick ass".

It's interesting to see how foreign licensees reinterpret my designs. Of the details of covers shown here **13**, the first five are Chinese, the sixth Korean and the seventh Russian.

6

7

8

9

10

11

12

13

1

2

3

4

5

6

7

8

9

10

11

12

13

14

15

As well as the **Valiant** logo and the logos for each title, I supplied trade dress templates for the issue-to-issue design of the comics that includes the consistent placement of credits, logo, barcode, price and so on. If overlooked, these elements tend to float around on the covers.

For the comics and trade paperback collections (shown in this volume alongside the comics themselves) a darker grey or coloured transparent panel across the top ensured that the logo and type could always be lifted out of the image without recourse to outlines or drop shadows. A limited selection of carefully chosen fonts, in this case my own designs Korolev and Rogue, also ensure unity.

It's a simpler case to make a logo or cover design work with one specific image, but an important part of designing a trade dress is that it's futureproof – that it will work with any art thrown at it, and in the case of the 'Valiant Masters' (a series that would reprint original material from the vaults) be able to accommodate **Rai** to **Eternal Warrior** without a change in point size or condensing the type. The same considerations of flexibility within a fixed format govern the design of the back covers and spines.

I also provided templates for the oversized 'Deluxe Editions', which featured foil-embossed boards (opposite). Note that all the **Valiant** logos I designed occupy the same height and width, making this across-the-board consistency possible. In practice, as other designers come on board who may not be well-versed in the internal design logic, these carefully engineered solutions can slowly unravel.

Also shown opposite, *Must Read Valiant* collected key stories at an entry-level price. To bring new readers up to date, infographics were often included on the inside front covers.

The trade dress evolved: to introduce the company, the **Valiant** branding was quite prominent for the first year or so, after which a smaller vertical logo was used. A third iteration in which it sits horizontally along the top in a black panel, along with the credits and issue number, allowed each title's logo to go the full width of the cover. This evolution can be seen on, for example, **X-O Manowar**.

Valiant's overall adherence to the original vision has given them a very strong shelf presence and helped build a solid and recognisable brand – vital attributes for a new comic publisher who wants to compete with the big guys.

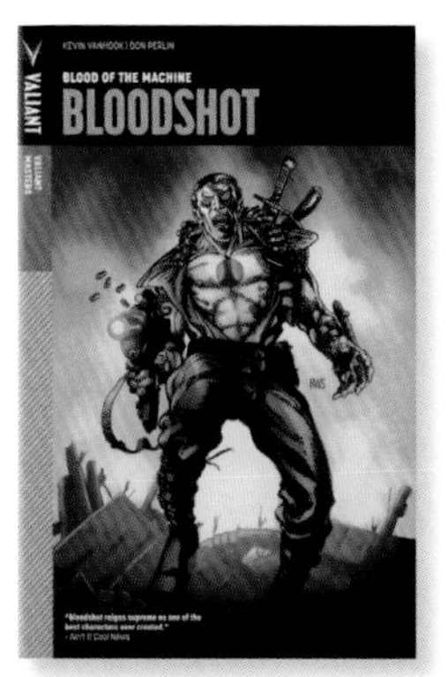
BLOOD OF THE MACHINE
BLOODSHOT
VALIANT

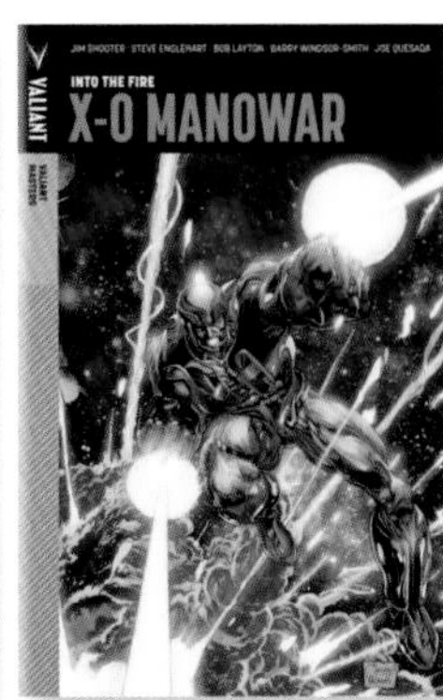
INTO THE FIRE
X-O MANOWAR
VALIANT

FROM HONOR TO STRENGTH
RAI
VALIANT

BLOODSHOT LIVES AGAIN

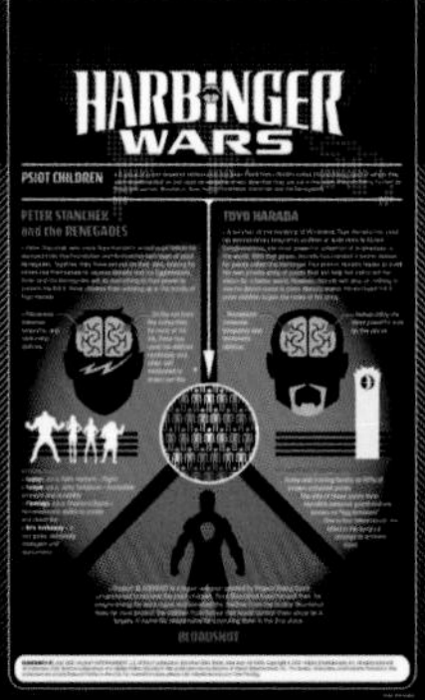
HARBINGER
WARS
PSIOT CHILDREN

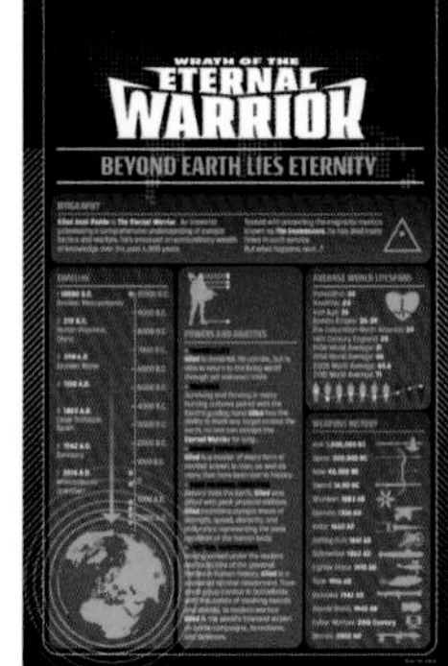
WRATH OF THE
ETERNAL
WARRIOR
BEYOND EARTH LIES ETERNITY

MUST
READ
VALIANT
GREATEST
HITS
#1
$5.99!

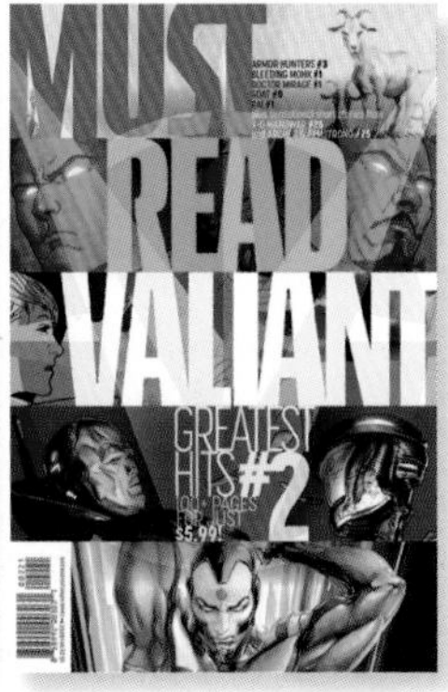
MUST
READ
VALIANT
GREATEST
HITS
#2
$5.99!

X-O
MANOWAR

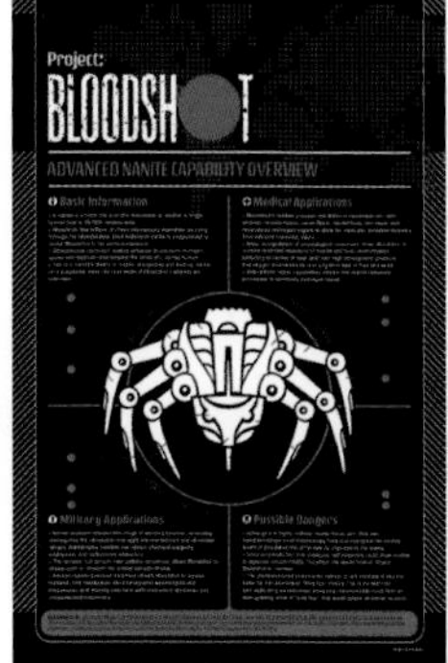
Project:
BLOODSHOT
ADVANCED NANITE CAPABILITY OVERVIEW

UNITY
402 AD TO 2013 AD: THE JOURNEY TO UNITY

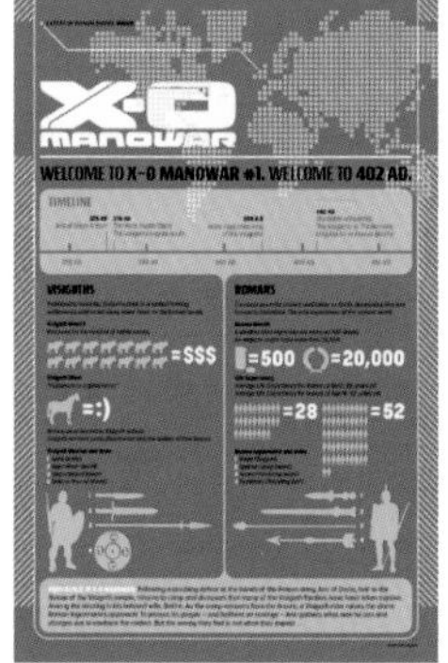
X-O
MANOWAR
WELCOME TO X-O MANOWAR #1. WELCOME TO 402 AD.

VALIANT
BLOODSHOT
REBORN
DELUXE
EDITION 1

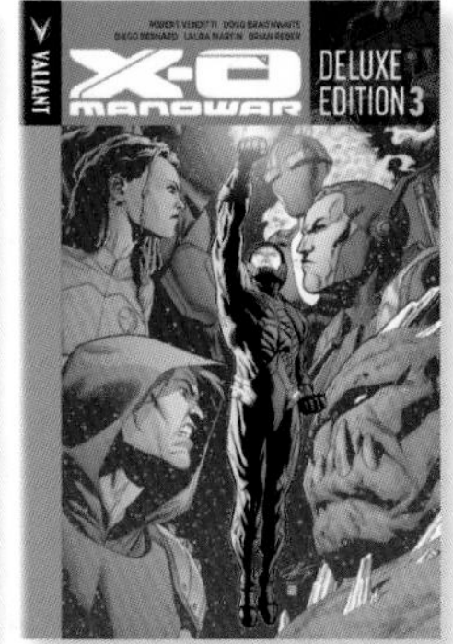
VALIANT
X-O
MANOWAR
DELUXE
EDITION 3

VALIANT
BLOODSHOT
DELUXE
EDITION 1

VALIANT
SHADOWMAN
DELUXE
EDITION 2

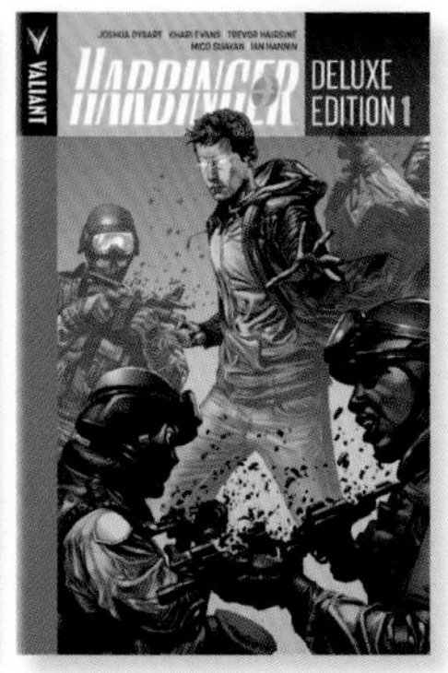
VALIANT
HARBINGER
DELUXE
EDITION 1

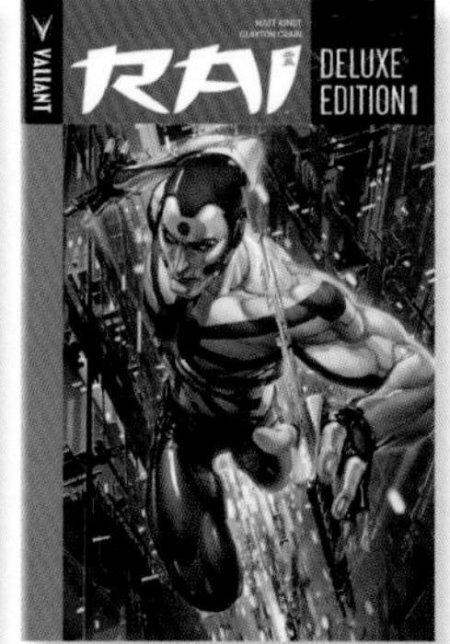
VALIANT
RAI
DELUXE
EDITION 1

BLOODSHOT
REBORN

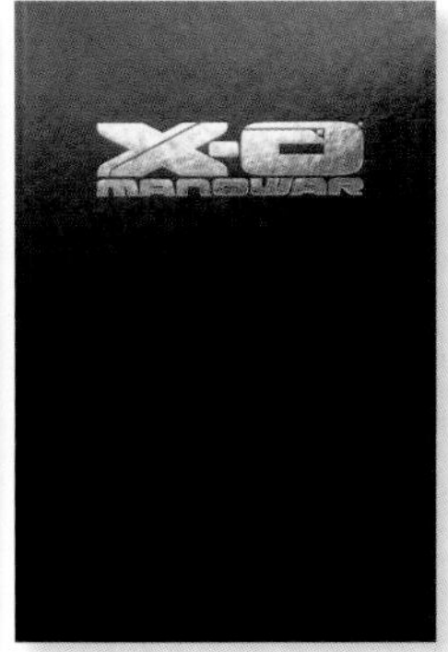
X-O
MANOWAR

THE DEATH-DEFYING
DOCTOR MIRAGE

HARBINGER
WARS

VALIANT
X-O MANOWAR
VALIANT
HARBINGER
VALIANT
HARBINGER
VALIANT
BLOODSHOT
VALIANT
ARCHER & ARMSTRONG
VALIANT
ARCHER & ARMSTRONG
VALIANT
QUANTUM AND WOODY
VALIANT
UNITY

Valiant Origins
Valiant Comics
Web-based series
2015

1

2

3

4

Valiant Origins is a series of web previews that present the background stories to many of their biggest characters. **4** uses letters taken from the individual logos; the type on the final logo is from a digitised but unreleased font that I first used on an unseen rough for **The Gerry Anderson Episode Guide,** designed back in 1989.

5

6

7

Valiant 25 Years
Valiant Comics
Anniversary branding
2014

1

2

3

4

Counting from its original inception, **Valiant** reached the 25-year milestone in 2014.

I quite liked the 'XXV' conceit **7**, but it was (rightly) considered to be too confusing. In the final logo, some of the characters have small details added in white which help to identify them.

5

6

7

1

2

3

4

5

6

7

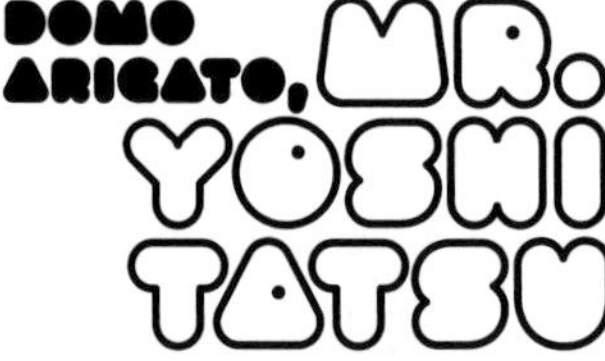

8

9

10

11

12

1 2 **Angels Unlimited**
HarperCollins
Book cover incidental logo
2000
Author: Annie Dalton
Logo and logo proposal for a series of young adult books for which I also designed and illustrated the covers

3 **The Three Eyes**
Madness/Virgin Records
Music rights
1988

4 **Club Kook**
Ethos
Mug design
2010
A mug design that purports to be merchandise from an insalubrious 1980s nightclub

5 **Astralasia**
Transient Records
Band logo
2001
For the *Something, Somewhere* album, the logo was designed to suggest crop circles

6 **London Nightrider**
Vital
Charity cycle ride
2010

7 **Domo Arigato, Mr Yoshi Tatsu**
WWF Wrestling magazine
Article heading
2010

8 **Really & Truly**
Fleetway
2000AD comic series
1993
Writer: Grant Morrison
Artist: Rian Hughes

9 **Never Ever**
Oxford University Press
Book cover
2001
Author: Helena Pielichaty

10 **Kweku: Tribal War**
Album cover
1996

11 **Ardmore International**
IT consultants
2000

12 **Pop One**
Sub Rosa Films
1999

Baby Doc
DJ/producer
Proposed logo
1998

As a UK hard house and trance producer Baby Doc (real name Quentin Franglen) was one of the pioneers of the Nu NRG sound in the mid 1990s.

Baby Doc and S-J ran Opium Records and Arriba Records, also co-owning the Dream Inn label with British hard house and trance producer Jon The Dentist.

The logo is intended to convey the punch and energy of the music in a direct fashion, and lend itself to merchandise such as T-shirts and slipmats.

1

2

3

Jacked
Vertigo/DC Comics
Comic book series
2015

In **Jacked**, by *Supernatural*'s Eric Kripke with covers by Glenn Fabry and interiors by John Higgins, a man suffering a mid-life crisis finds a performance-enhancing drug for sale in some dark corner of the internet. It gives him superpowers – while also being dangerously addictive.

Assistant editor Ellie Pyle suggested I look at energy drink branding for that "jarring and over-caffeinated" look; the logo for the comic would be the logo on the drug packaging itself.

I discovered such drinks were not particularly well designed, favouring tattoo-style lettering or italics with 'go faster' stripes **2**, **3**, **4**. I experimented with running the logo vertically to mimic cans stacked on a shelf; other concepts referenced pills or drug capsules **1**.

The favoured solution (main image) nods towards clean pharmaceutical packaging, with a strong simple sans and bars of colour that would change to suit the art each issue and the credits and issue number neatly incorporated. The final tweak was suggested by DC'c in-house designer Kenny Lopez: the first two spikes were reduced to emphasise the third '**Jacked**' spike.

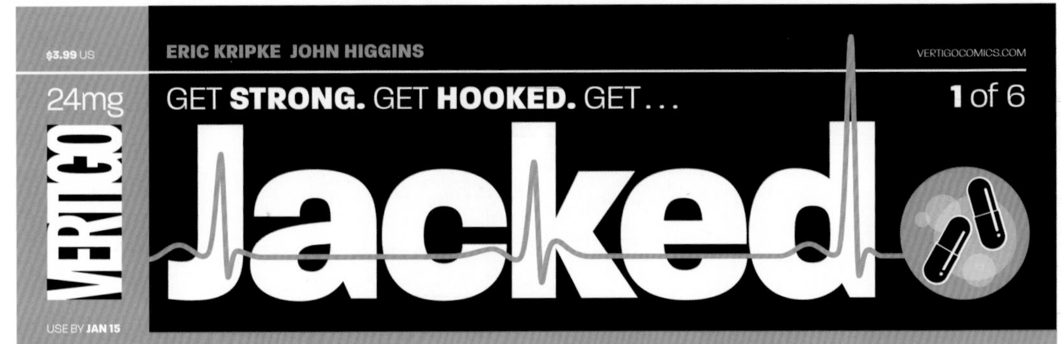

1

2

3

4

5

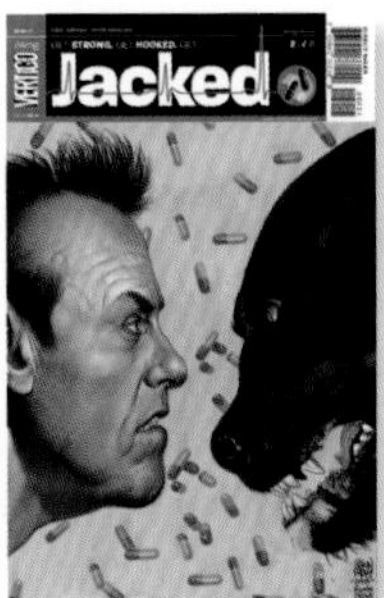

Den Trap
Fré Wollants
Music and events venue
2011

Den Trap is a youth centre in Antwerp, Belgium, a venue for gigs, sport events and parties. It is run on a not-for-profit basis by volunteers.

They had used the same logo for 25 years, which featured 'Jessica', their mascot **1**, which they requested I incorporate into the new logo somehow. It would be launched to mark the venue's reopening after a complete renovation.

The final logo exists in two versions, one with the type inside the head and one in which it sits alongside **2**.

Den Trap's punters seem to favour stonewash denim and Kagagoogoo highlights **4**.

1

2

3

4

1

2

3

4

5

6

7

8

9

10

11

12

1 **Insect**
Jeremy Banx
Publisher
1995

2 **Master Craftsman**
Device
T-shirt motif
1999

3 **Royal Automobile Club**
Private member's club
Proposed logo update
2000
Founded in 1897 the club moved to its current address, the imposing monolith that is 119 Piccadilly, in 1902 – the year they campaigned for the relaxation of the 14 m.p.h. speed limit.

4 **Iltalehti Dog**
Iltalehti newspaper (Finland)
Mascot
1999

5 **Visions of the Future**
Modern Era
Set of collectable cards
1984

6 **Shadows**
Fleetway/2000AD
Comic series
Proposed logo
1990
Writer: Peter Milligan
Artist: Richard Elson

7 **Redcoat**
Butlins Holiday Camps
Mascot
1999

8 **Mr. Thrifty**
The Idler magazine
Section header
1992

9 **Science Service Approved**
Magic Strip/Device
Personal stamp
1986

10 **Packjammed with the Party Posse**
A&M Records
Stock Aitken Waterman
7″ and 12″ single
1988

11 **Barcelona Bill**
Food retailer
2015

12 **Radio Times Travel Store**
Radio Times magazine
1995

Clairefontaine
Stationery manufacturer
Proposed logo
2008

1

I had been commissioned by long-established French stationary company **Clairefontaine**, which celebrated its 150th anniversary in 2008, to produce a series of abstract images for their 'Matris' range of pads and exercise books.

Their logo features Rebecca carrying an amphora. It has evolved over the years **2**, the amphora eventually becoming a simple circle. I proposed keeping the essential elements, but redrawing Rebecca to make her more attractive, using elegant custom-drawn lettering rather than the off-the-peg Futura, an overall rationalisation of the line thickness and the removal of the solid areas. I also suggested that the lettering be positioned at the top instead of the bottom to give a balanced triangular silhouette, as in the first two versions. I moved the circle behind the face so that it was no longer cropped on the right-hand side but mirrors the shape of the back of the head, lending the whole a more symmetrical appearance. Her hair has been redrawn to suggest the flowing water that has been lost along the way.

In the end, the existing logo was used across the new Matris range. The chosen pattern, which appeared in dozens of colourways, is shown in the background.

2

Clairefontaine

1

2

3

4

5

6

7

8

9

10

11

12

13

14

15

16

17

18

19

20

Gold Key
Dynamite Comics
Comic line
2014

For Dynamite's relaunch of the **Gold Key** heroes **Turok**, **Magnus**, **Solar** and **Doctor Spectre** a set of logos was required that, while expressing the attributes of each character, would also work cohesively as a set. A trade dress, a consistent design for cover furniture such as credits, barcode, price, etc., was also required.

For the **Gold Key** logo itself, an update of the original logo **21** was first attempted. I have a fondness for this somewhat ornate design as it appeared on many of the Hanna Barbera titles I collect. I kept the key, but updated the font and the curly shapes **1**. **2** uses a mirrored 'G' for the fob.

These didn't set the world alight, so I tried versions featuring modern styles of key **4**, **6**, **8** and less whimsical, bolder and more masculine fonts.

Though the design went though numerous rounds, many of which are omitted here, a decision was not forthcoming, and in the end the Dynamite logo was used instead. The large logo shown right was the strongest and most elegant solution, and would have worked well on badges and T-shirts.

My trade dress, in which I arranged the credits down the left-hand edge of the cover in Paralucent (a Device font), did briefly survive.

21

22

23

24

25

Turok, Dinosaur Hunter
Dynamite Entertainment
Comic book series
2013

1

2

3

4

Turok was part of Dynamite Entertainment's relaunch of the **Gold Key** heroes, a fondly remembered series of characters that were first published by Dell Comics in the 1950s and also include **Solar, Man of the Atom**, **Magnus, Robot Hunter** and **Doctor Spektor**. Both **Valiant** and Dark Horse had previously introduced their own updated versions.

His alternative strapline, 'Son of Stone', featured in early designs. **3** used a photographic element; this would have been taken through to the other logos in the series. The final design uses an offset stone texture (which was realigned in-house) and rough-hewn block capitals.

The trade dress and logos for the whole series were designed to have a continuity across the line: each was placed at the same angle and occupied a similar position on the cover, with the subhead in the same font (Paralucent, a Device design). This helped to maintain the identity of the family of titles in the absence of the **Gold Key** logo at top left.

Magnus, Robot Fighter
Dynamite Comics
Comic book
2013

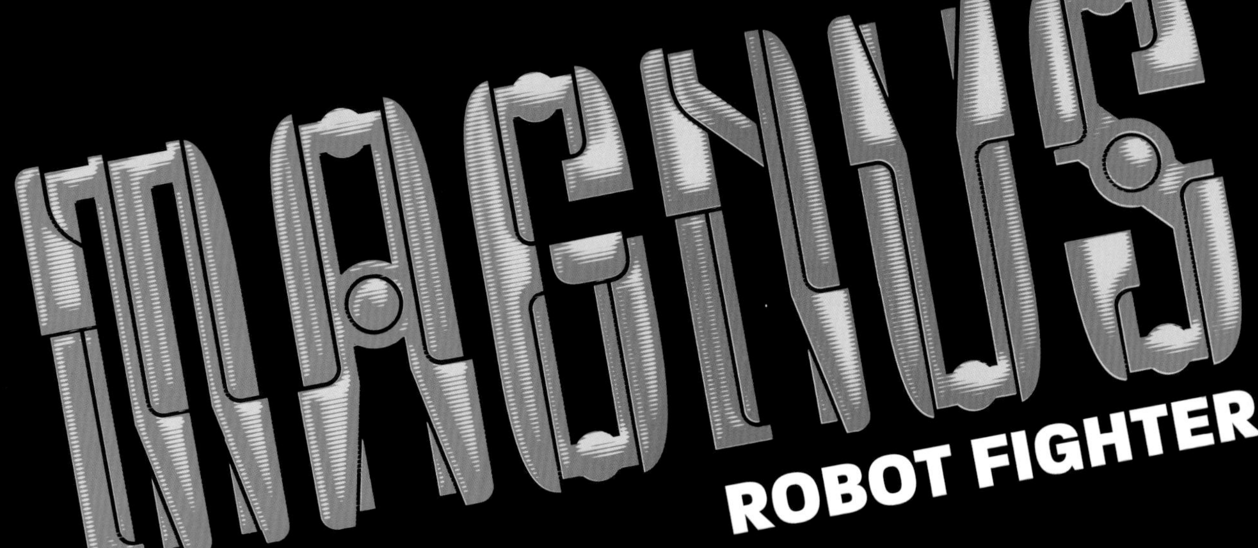

1

2

3

4

MAGNUS
ROBOT FIGHTER

5

MAGNUS
ROBOT FIGHTER

6

MAGNUS

Magnus, Robot Fighter is another title from Dynamite's **Gold Key** Heroes revamp. The logo references articulated robotic carapaces, and has a textured sheen that can be picked out in a second colour, which I intended to be a consistent feature across the line. This texture was dropped in-house for the final covers, which here have been recoloured.

Solar, Man of the Atom
Dynamite Entertainment
Comic book series
Proposed logo
2014

Solar, Man of the Atom and **Doctor Spektor** were the final two titles in Dynamite's **Gold Key** Heroes series.

For **Solar**, I again used a textured overlay and set the logo and the tagline at the same angle as **Turok** and **Magnus** to keep the overall design consistent across the series. The counter of the 'O' forms an annular eclipse, a flash of light coming from behind, while the curved letters mimic solar flares or fire.

Doctor Spektor posed a challenge in that the tagline appears above the logo rather than below it, but by keeping the same font and angle, consistency could be achieved.

Unfortunately, though **Turok** and **Magnus** were approved, after several rounds of designs **Solar** and **Spektor** couldn't be resolved. The final covers use logos that are not by me, and though interesting don't adhere to the logic of the trade dress as I originally envisaged it, shown here on mock-ups **2**, **3** with my proposed **Gold Key** logo top left.

1

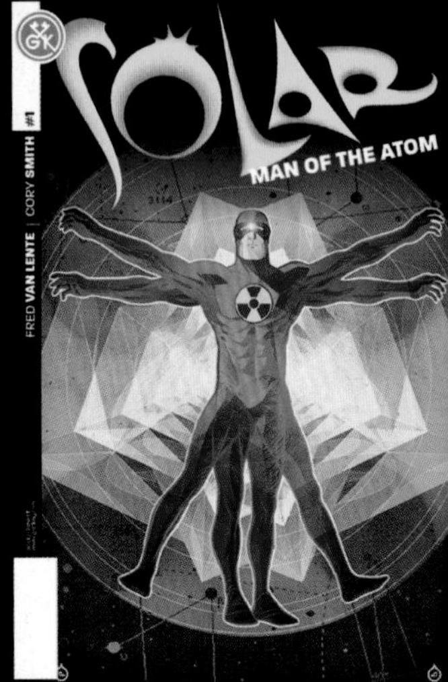

2

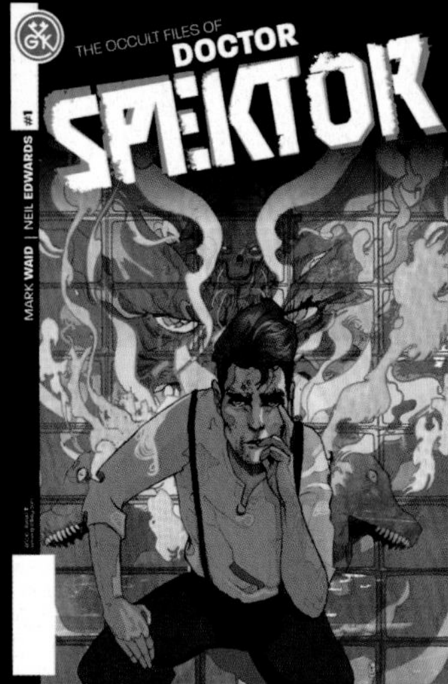

3

The Occult Files of Doctor Spektor
Dynamite Entertainment
Comic book
Proposed logo
2014

1

2

3

4

5

6

7

Yoo-Hoo
Landor/Dr Pepper Snapple Group
Proposed mascot/logo
1999

Yoo-Hoo is an American chocolate drink invented in New Jersey in 1926 and currently manufactured by the Dr Pepper Snapple Group. Neither a soda nor a milkshake, its precise ingredients have long been closely guarded.

I was asked to create a character for the brand, and came up with a stylised boy who uses inventive ways to 'Shake it' before drinking **3**, **4**.

I also tackled the logo, which was then **2** an awkward mix of references to the heritage of the brand overlaid with Photoshop shading and highlights. I endeavoured to make it cleaner and simpler, removing the profusion of outlines in varying widths and shadows falling in different directions.

The supporting text was a mix of 1920 fonts ('Drink' in Coronet), 1960s fonts ('Original, since 1920' in Helvetica Inserat) and modern revivals of 1950s brush scripts, all in several point sizes. I proposed that they reduce the fonts to one simple sans that would complement a more playful logo, saving a more illustrative font for the 'Shake it!' lettering.

A more subtle colour scheme suggestive of the chocolate flavour was also tried.

None of my ideas were used.

1

2

3

4

5

6

7

8

9

The Source
Radio station
2002

'The Source' suggested some mystical, god-like origin for the dance music that the new station was going to play. The logo features a cloud from which beams of heavenly light shine down upon us mere mortals.

1

2

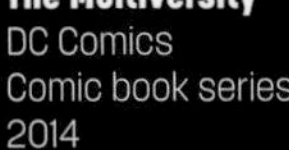

The Multiversity
DC Comics
Comic book series
2014

The Multiversity: Thunderworld Adventures
DC Comics
Comic book
2014

The Multiversity: Masterman
DC Comics
Comic book
2014

MASTERMEN

The Multiversity: Society of Super-Heroes
DC Comics
Comic book
2014

The Multiversity is a limited series of nine interrelated one-shots that sets out to chart the 'DC Multiverse', the overarching framework in which different iterations of DC's heroes and others from companies they've acquired over the years coexist.

The idea that different versions of comic characters from parallel worlds coexist dates back to the early days of comics, but was codified in **The Flash** #123 (September 1961), which introduced Earth-2, and more generally the concept of the Multiverse, to **DC Comics**. *Flash of Two Worlds* was written by Gardner Fox under the editorial guidance of Julius Schwartz. The Multiverse has been tidied away and then reintroduced several times since, starting with the 1985 series *Crisis on Infinite Earths*.

In *Flash of Two Worlds* the adventures of **The Flash** of Earth-2 were documented as a comic on Earth-1. Grant used this device in **The Multiversity** to explain how comics could be used to communicate between universes.

Each one-shot had a different logo, though later the **Multiversity** brand was incorporated above each masthead to brand the series clearly. The *Action Comics* spoof shown on the previous page is from Captain Carrot's universe; though conceptually sound from a story point of view, this was later changed to the **Multiversity** logo to avoid confusion with the regular *Action Comics* title.

There were many variant covers to design. A parallel set of variants chart the history of the DC Multiverse; there were also black and white versions and Morrison sketch versions. My cover for the Guidebook, for example, comes in three variants. (I suggested one issue could read from the back, manga style, or be entirely word-free, or written in an alien script the reader would have to decipher. Grant politely ignored me.)

The **Society of Super-Heroes** is led by Doc Fate, a kind of 1940s pulp Doc Savage-style take on superheroes set on Earth-40. The logo is a distillation of the more elegant pulp magazine mastheads of the period, a condensed Deco sans with angled serifs to the top left. An alternative somewhat awkwardly split the title (overleaf).

The Just, designed to resemble a celebrity gossip magazine, is set on Earth-16 and details the idle lives of the sons of **Superman** and **Batman**. They have incredible abilities, but as the previous generation have ushered in a utopia, they have little to do but bicker and gaze at their navels. My font family Paralucent had been used for many years in *Heat*, one such magazine, so of course I also used it here.

Pax Americana, drawn by Frank Quitely, takes place on Earth-4 and features the Charlton Comics characters. Grant described it as "if Alan Moore and Dave Gibbons had pitched *Watchmen* now, rooted in a contemporary political landscape".

Thunderworld Adventures takes place on Earth-5 and features the Captain Marvel family. It's a much more light-hearted affair, for which I referenced the original *Whiz Comics'* block sans, drop shadow and speedlines. It's not often you have a chance to legitimately use speedlines.

The sixth chapter was **The Multiversity Guidebook**, for which I also drew the cover. This issue included detailed entries on all 52 Earths, and the map of the Multiverse Grant and I designed was printed on the reverse of the dust jacket of the hardback collection **1**. A discussion of the creation of the Map falls outside the remit of this book, but suffice to say it was probably the most complicated single piece of design I've ever attempted – each Earth has a unique appearance, and is carefully arranged within a web of influences and interrelationships. **7** is Darkseid, one of many simplified characters I drew for the Map.

Mastermen, the seventh chapter, was illustrated by Jim Lee and Scott Williams and takes place on Earth-10. Here, the Freedom Fighters and Nazi versions of various heroes slug it out in a universe in which Germany won WWII. I used a Gothic blackletter which is not drawn from any particular historical source, but is what I imagine a modernised Fractur might resemble. The frame is a photo in which Jim's art, treated like a newspaper clipping, has been placed; a variant has the frame in black and white.

Ultra Comics, illustrated by Doug Mahnke and Christian Alamy, takes place on Earth-33, DC's designation for our own, 'real' world. This book is a "memetic weapon", the vector through which the villains of the piece intend to infect the Multiverse. The logo references Ultra's costume design and is intended to look less like a comic and more like a fashion or music magazine.

The series was bookended by two **Multiversity** issues. The Multiversity logo itself shows the 52 worlds in the Orrery, 51 arranged into a V with the 52nd shown as a crescent centred inside. The refined semi-serif suggests a seat of learning, but with peculiar twists in the details that tell you all is not as expected. Down the left edge of each comic ran a list of the 52 worlds, 0-51, with those featured inside highlighted in white (previous spread).

I also designed the deluxe hardback collection **1-6**, for which I drew another view of the 52 worlds for the title page **3**.

1 2 3

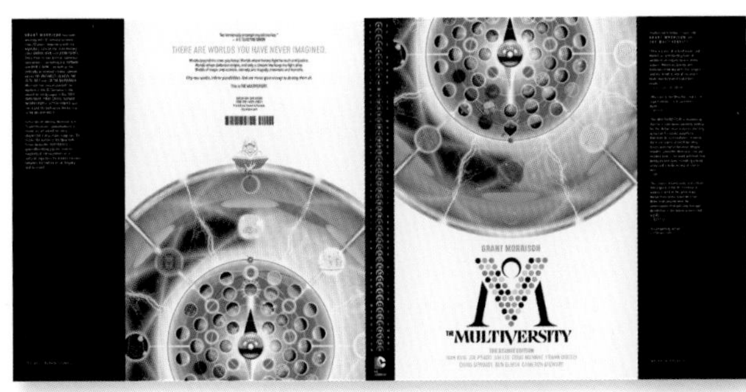

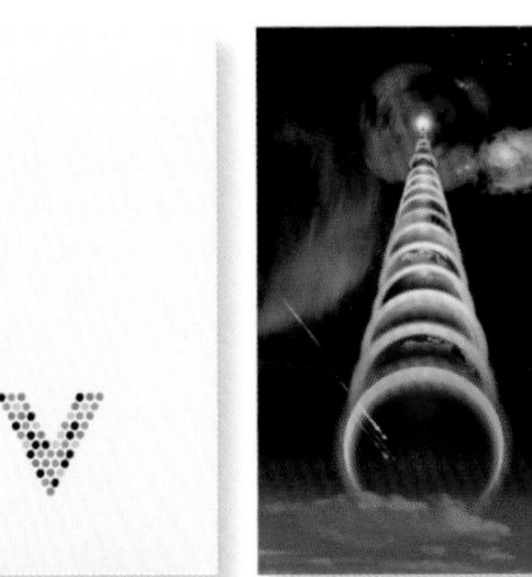

4 5 6

7

The Multiversity:
Ultra Comics
DC Comics
Comic book
2014

The Multiversity:
The Just
DC Comics
Comic book
2014

The Multiversity
Guidebook
DC Comics
Comic book
2014

The Multiversity:
Society of Super-Heroes
DC Comics
Comic book
Proposed logo
2014

The Multiversity:
Pax Americana
DC Comics
Comic book
2014

The Multiversity:
Cosmic Neighborhood Watch
DC Comics
Comic book
Cover type
2014

MULTIVERSITY
COSMIC
NEIGHBORHOOD
WATCH

Saucerheads
Fortean Times magazine
Merchandise proposal
1998

'**Saucerhead**' is a somewhat derogatory term for those on the wilder fringes of the UFO field. I decided to take the term literally for these merchandise designs for the 'journal of strange phenomena', which I have been reading since it was a small, A5 black and white quarterly.

1

2

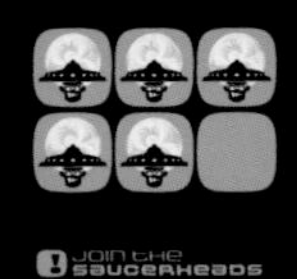

3

4

Judge Dredd: Definitive Editions
Fleetway/2000AD
Graphic novel series
1989

1

'Definitive' these books were not. Rapidly compiled from old issues of *2000AD* and coloured by adding washes to photocopies, they were put together to fill the new demand for graphic novels in the wake of the success of *Watchmen* and *The Dark Knight Returns*.

The covers were designed using analogue methods – paste-up, rapidograph and CS10 board – and the textured background was achieved by placing the top of a Hammerite-painted filing cabinet under a copy camera.

The **Definitive Editions** logo was printed in a metallic Pantone. **2** is the original hand-drawn logo.

3 is the contents page design, which uses a simplified version of a Dredd helmet icon **1**.

2

3

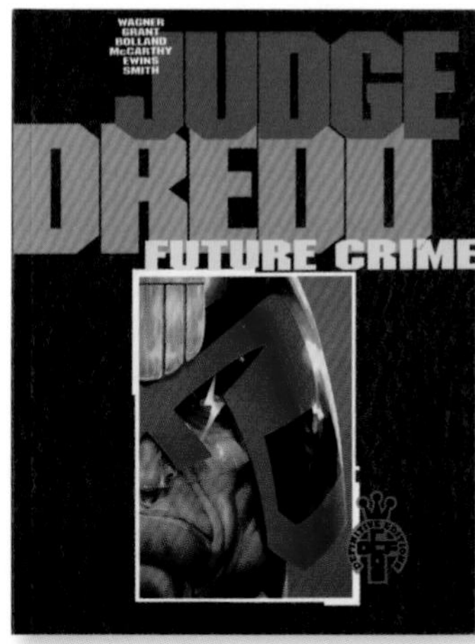

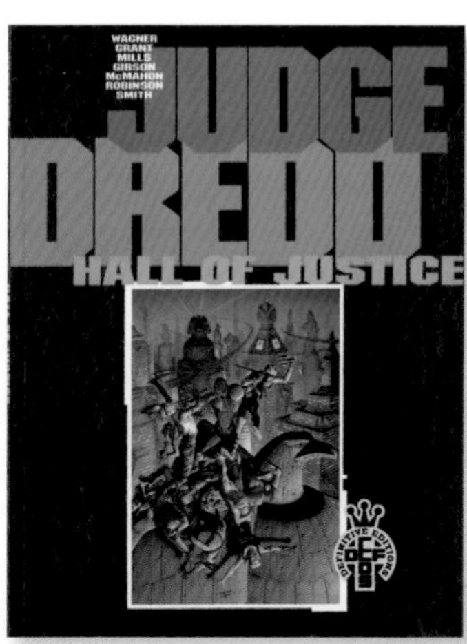

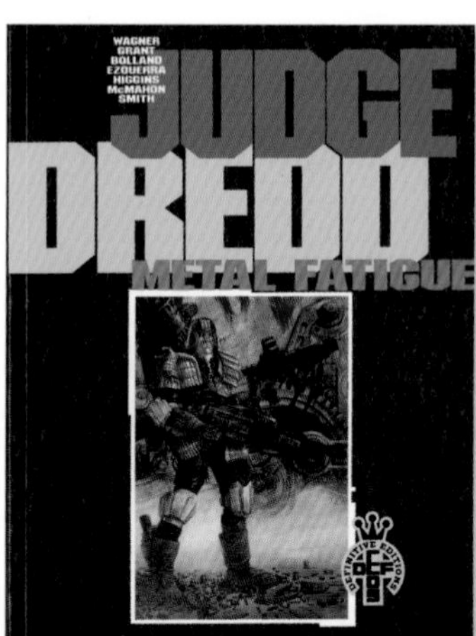

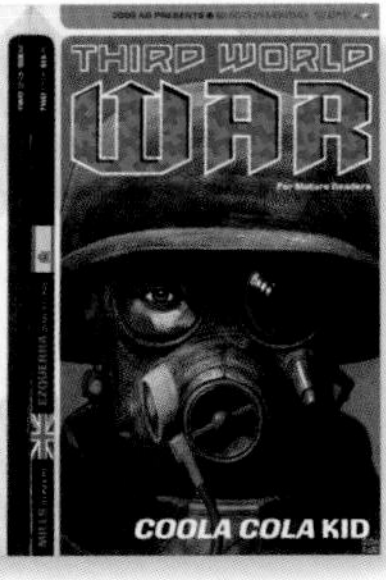

Third World War
Fleetway/2000AD
Graphic novel series
1989

Pat Mills and Carlos Ezquerra's **Third World War** series first ran in **Crisis** and was then repackaged in a smaller format for the US market. Pat's story extrapolated the effects of capitalism on the developing world through the eyes of a group of young conscript 'peace volunteers'.

As with **Crisis**, I mixed logos that suggested corporate brands with warning labels, placing them against futuristic, angular camouflage. The back cover features a dollar sign over a world map.

Produced using traditional paste-up, I'd pull colours from the art for the logo and other cover furniture, but was at the mercy of the quality of the scan (or the aptitude of the repro house) so these used to shift unpredictably. In particular, black areas in illustrations would often print a mid-grey. Now I am accustomed to the quality of modern print reproduction, it's easy to forget how poorly printed many of the comics of this period were, and how a designer's choices always had to factor in the worst-case scenario, as it was never possible to reprint if things went horribly wrong.

1 is a proof sheet for a set of six promotional button badges.

1

Section icons
PC World
Magazine section icons
1995

A series of icons that appeared throughout *PC World* magazine to differentiate each section. These were early Photoshop experiments, and perhaps show an excessive zeal for three-dimensional embossing effects.

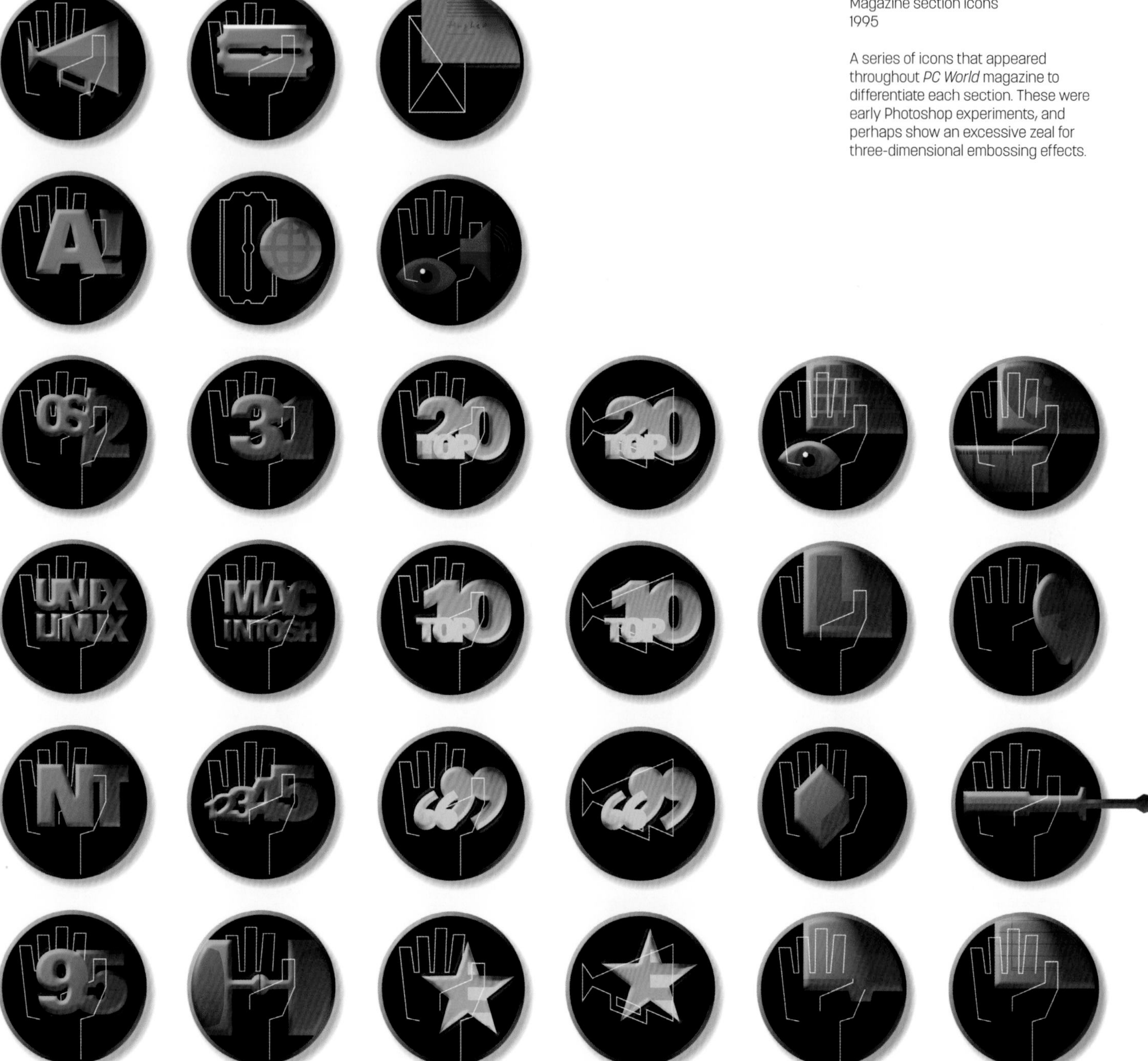

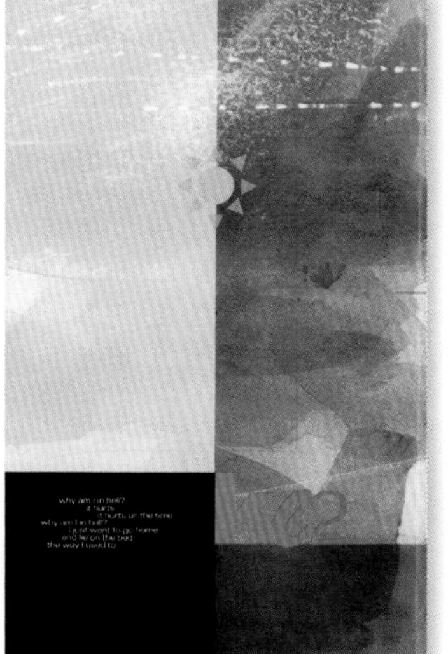
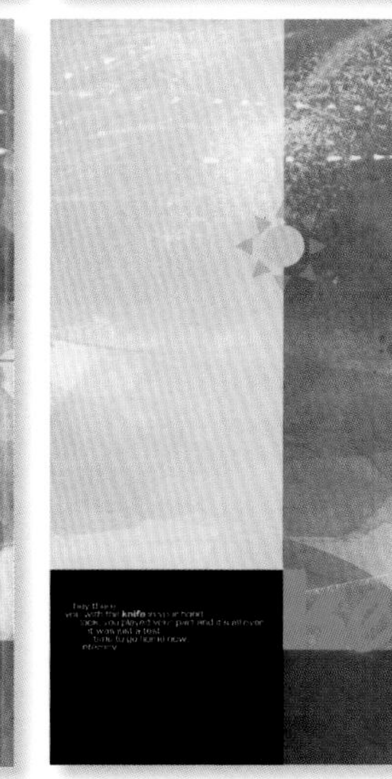

Kid Eternity
DC Comics
Prestige format comic series
1991

Kid Eternity was originally created by Otto Binder and Sheldon Moldoff for Quality Comics back in 1942.

For this darker revisionist three-issue mini-series written by Grant Morrison and with art by Duncan Fegredo, I sketched out some cover ideas **1**, **2** using coloured paper, marker pen and glue, which Duncan developed into the final triptych.

The chaos magic symbol, a major theme in the book, appears on the back covers in silver ink, and also as a silver reflection on **Kid Eternity**'s glasses on the front. These are also spot varnished to give them a reflective sheen, the rest of the cover being matt.

The logo in the original sketch used an upright and an italic; Duncan wanted more chaos in 'eternity'. "I was wrong, wrong, wrong!" he says with hindsight in the recent Deluxe Edition. I reckon it still turned out nicely, Duncan.

The title was repeated at the top in small text as it was thought a logo positioned towards the bottom of the cover was (at this point) unusual, and might prove confusing.

1

2

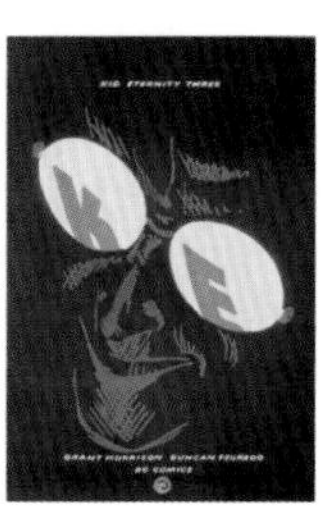

3

4

VALIANT
RATED T
4001
RAI AD
#1

VALIANT
RATED T
RAI AD
#1

4001 AD

MATT KINDT
CLAYTON CRAIN
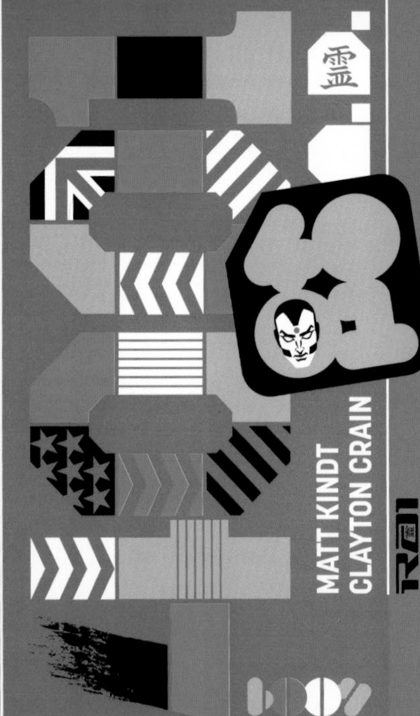
MATT KINDT
CLAYTON CRAIN

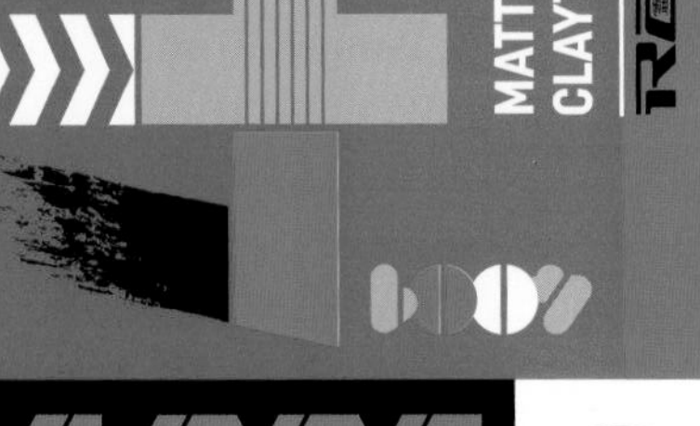

NEW
STRAPLINE
HERE!

NEW
STRAPLINE
HERE!

NEW
STRAPLINE
HERE!
00221
8 58992 00303 1
US $3.99 | RATED T+ | www.valiantuniverse.com

A.D.

00221
8 58992 00303 1
US $3.99 | RATED T+ | www.valiantuniverse.com

00221
8 58992 00303 1
US $3.99 | RATED T+ | www.valiantuniverse.com

4001 A.D.
Valiant Comics
Comic book series
2000

4001 A.D. was a summer crossover event set in **Rai**'s far-future Japan.

I wondered what an information-dense Japanese manga aesthetic taken to its logical extreme might look like. Bright neon colours, cartoon emoji representations of **Rai** and clashing type styles, all applied like overlaid stickers or windows on a tablet screen – though by 4001 I'm sure we'll all be telepathic, and written language a quaint anachronism. The rounded type was intended to evoke capsules: designer drugs, or capsule hotels, perhaps. I was asked to incorporate the vertical panel from **Rai**'s regular title for continuity.

Some were quite hard to read; **11** was considered to look too "chequered flag car race". I was asked to pull back and try a cleaner aesthetic (covers opposite) but in the end none were used.

The printed design resembles the *2001: A Space Odyssey* poster, a reference I had studiously avoided.

1

2

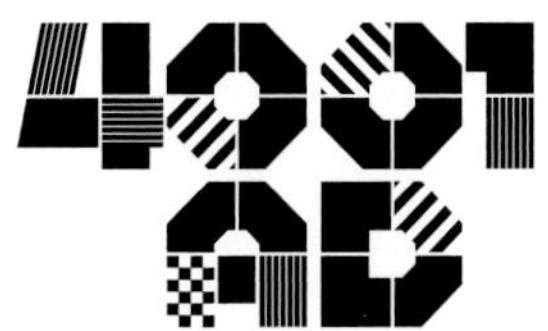

3

4

5

6

7

8

9

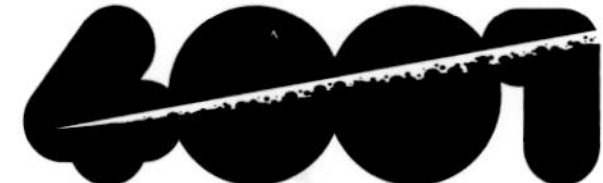

10

11

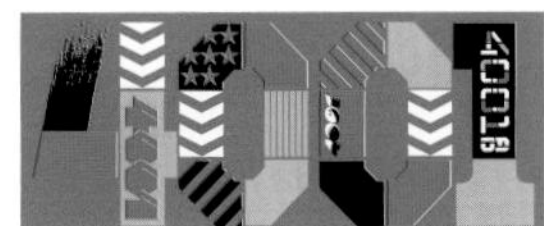

12

13

14

15

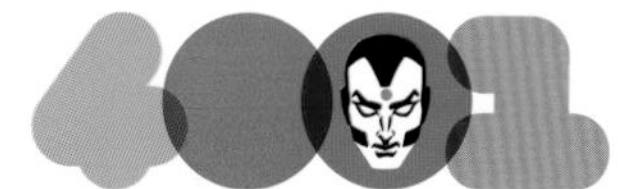

Eternal Warrior: Days of Steel
Valiant Entertainment
Comic book
2014

Veteran *2000AD*, **Hellblazer** and **Shade, the Changing Man** writer Peter Milligan was taking over the **Eternal Warrior** for this stand-alone mini-series.

I first met Peter when we toured England, Scotland and Ireland with Grant Morrison, Peter Hogan, Shaky Kane, Charles Shaar Murray and Brendan McCarthy as part of the **Revolver** signing tour in the summer of 1990, and he's a great dinner-table raconteur.

Peter and artist Cary Nord were taking the **Eternal Warrior** back to the brutality of the 10th century, and the new logo needed to convey "swords, savagery, and steel".

The working title was '**Eternal Warrior** Full Bleed'.

2

ETERNAL
WARRIOR
DAYS OF STEEL

3

ETERNAL
WARRIOR
FULL BLEED

4

ETERNAL
WARRIOR
FULL BLEED

5

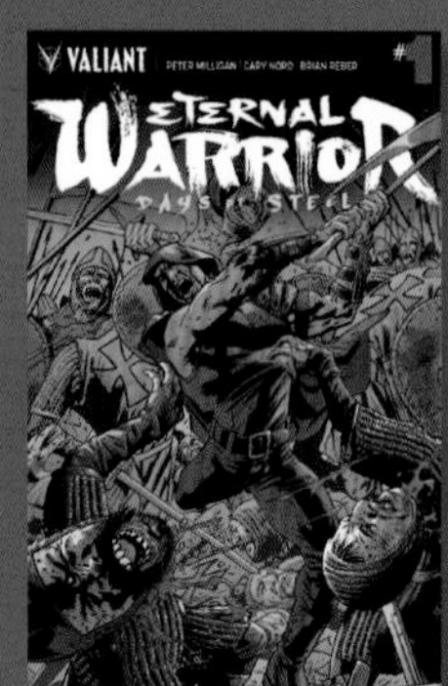

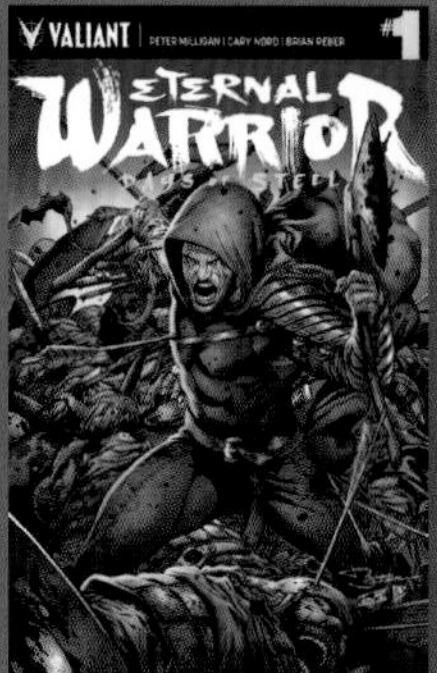

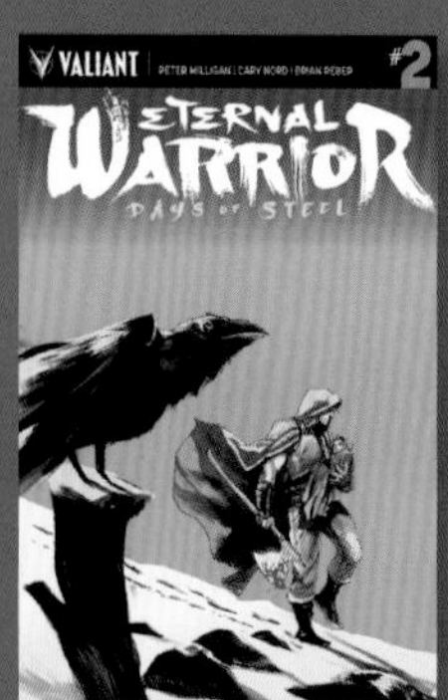

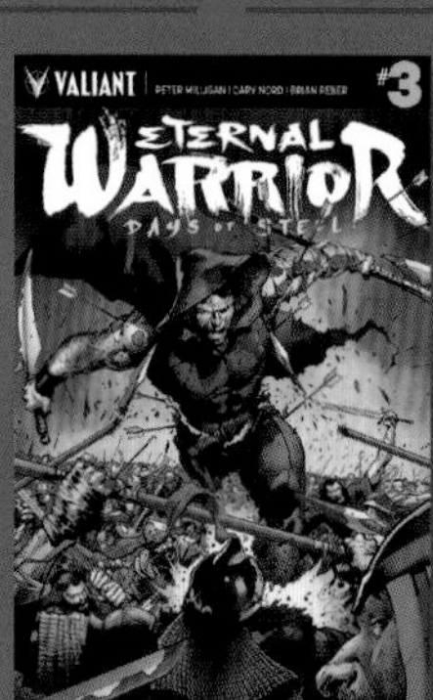

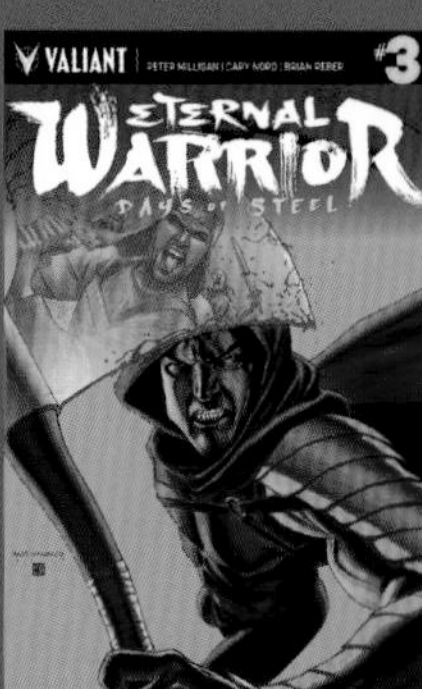

Spider-Man: The Other
Marvel Comics
Comic book crossover
2005

The Other ran from October 2005 to January 2006 across all the **Spider-Man** titles. Each comic would retain its usual logo, and **The Other** branding would run down the left-hand side of each cover.

The storyline was divided into four 'acts', and though the design could not dictate the art, I suggested that each act's issues use a different colour tint. The first has red covers, the second blue, the third grey-black, and the final act is orange-yellow.

The Spidey version of Da Vinci's *Vitruvian Man*, which had featured in Joe Quesada's promotional art, summed up the story, and was adapted for the 'O' of the logo. Construction lines and foxed parchment underlie the type.

1

2

3

4

5

6

Bloodshot
Valiant Entertainment
Comic book series
2011

Bloodshot, created by Kevin VanHook and Yvel Guichet in 1992, is a former soldier with powers of regeneration made possible through 'nanites', microscopic machines that have been injected into his blood. The logo explores military stencilling, these small creatures, and Bloodshot's iconic red chest circle.

From issue 14, the title became **Bloodshot and H.A.R.D Corps**. It was rebooted after a 25-issue run as **Bloodshot Reborn**.

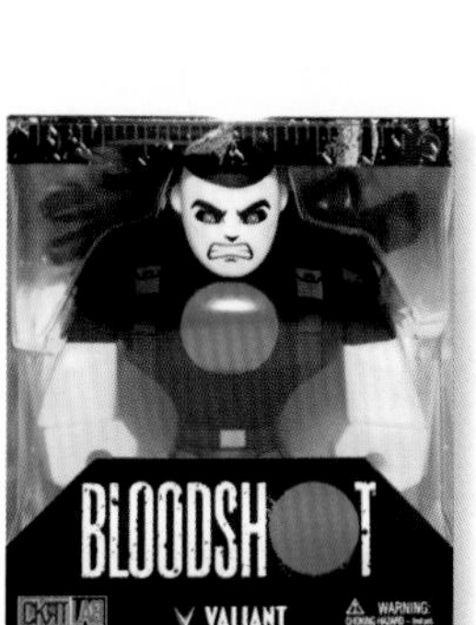

1

2

3

4

5

6

7

8

Bloodshot Reborn
Valiant Comics
Comic book
2014

Reborn told a more personal story that took place in the backwoods of middle America, a small-town setting away from the military and **H.A.R.D. Corps** in which **Bloodshot** reconnected with his basic survival skills.

The more futuristic logos **1**, **3**, **4** were passed over in favour of a subtle Americana vibe that uses a condensed octagonal serif reminiscent of vintage wood type or a picket fence. The stencil alludes to **Bloodshot**'s military origins.

1

2

3

4

5

6

7

8

Fantomah
Chapterhouse
Comic book series
2017

Fantomah is a revival of the very first comic book superheroine, created by Fletcher Hanks in 1940 under the pseudonym Barclay Flagg. Chapterhouse's contemporary iteration of the character retains her trademark blue skull and white hair.

Early designs pushed the spooky carnivalesque/freak show style of the existing logo, incorporating distressed wood textures and a stylised face. These are somewhat hard to read.

I was asked to try simpler and less decorative options that were more in keeping with the other logos in the Chapterhouse line. The final version retains a touch of Gothic blackletter, but drops the skull in the 'o'.

1

2

3

4

5

6

7

8

Agents of PACT/PACT Academy
Chapterhouse
Comic book series
2017

Team book **Agents of PACT** follows the paranormal investigations department of the Canadian Security Intelligence Service. The first designs **1-3** pressed the unusual 'P' on **Captain Canuck**'s current belt buckle into use. Full stops between the letters proved difficult to elegantly space out; versions with the inline **3** meant smaller dots could be used. In the end, they were dropped entirely.

The circular icon is a set of arrows coming together, suggesting the formation of a team – and it also subtly resembles the Canadian maple leaf.

There are two iterations of this logo. **Pact Academy** is a special school for superheroes, and the final design moves away from the hard and heavy geometric sans serif towards a more classical 'Academy of Learning'-style branding – something you might see on a university, perhaps. The stencilled serif version **6** was considered to have inappropriate military overtones.

1

2

3

4

5

6

7

8

StarRise
Chapterhouse
Comic book series
2017

A new hero in the Chapterhouse 'Chapterverse'. "Star sparks rise from young Afghan hero **StarRise**'s hands . . ."

The tall point to the star in **1** and **3** would prove difficult to use in situ on a cover, as it would push the logo lower down and create a dead space either side. Note that the logo is not perfectly symmetrical – 'STA' is naturally wider than 'ISE', necessitating some optical sleight of hand. **4** has a calligraphic bent.

Freelance
Chapterhouse
Comic book series
2017

The second Canadian superhero ever created, and now part of Canadian publisher Chapterhouse's 'Chapterverse', **Freelance** first appeared back in 1941. Created by Ed Furness and Ted McCall, **Freelance** was a guerrilla fighter and spy who worked in occupied Europe against the Nazis. Reimagined as a platinum-haired gay Superman, he travels the world with his three companions.

Attempts to model a logo from the outlined 'F' on his costume proved difficult. Keith WTS Morris, Chapterhouse's publisher, found a little drawing of the character in an old comic in which he sits astride a long lance **1**. This proved to be the solution.

1

2

1

2

3

4

3

4

The Pitiful Human-Lizard
Chapterhouse
Comic book series
2017

Jason Loo's satirical Toronto-based superhero is another of Chapterhouse's stable of characters. This design is very loosely based on the existing logo, which needed to be more compact and punchy to bring it in line with the other titles.

Captain Canuck
Chapterhouse
Comic book series
2017

Created by Ron Leishman and Richard Comely, **Captain Canuck** first appeared back in 1975. My redesign of Chapterhouse's best-selling title closely follows the original logo, itself influenced by K. Sommer's typeface Dynamo, designed for the German foundry Ludwig & Mayer in 1930. Careful alignments between the vertical strokes of the top and bottom lines create a rhythm that unites the whole.

Fallen Suns
Chapterhouse
Comic book series
2017

This SF epic by Van Jensen and Neil Collyer, is a retitling of Chapterhouse's *Northern Lights*. "The alien warrior Pharos came to our world to deliver a warning: The Borealis are coming!" The logo uses a crescent to repace the crossbars on the 'F', 'A' and 'E', with the smaller sun acting as a word spacer.

Northguard
Chapterhouse
Comic book series
2017

Early iterations **1** kept the maple leaf motif from the original logo. The final version incorporates a silhouette of the character's powered arm in the 'U'.

1

Resurrection Man
DC Comics
Comic book series
1996

Resurrection Man was created by British writers Dan Abnett and Andy Lanning with art by Butch Guice, and originally ran for 27 issues starting in 1996. It was resurrected for another 13 as part of DC's New 52 lineup.

The logo features a mysterious trilby-wearing silhouette. The rubber-stamp effect made the logo difficult to read when reversed out of busy artwork, so I created a solid underprint that could be used in a contrasting colour for clarity.

Küki
Fashion brand
Proposed logo
2007

The logo incorporates a subtle smiley face, the eyes being the umlaut.

Southernhay Gardens
Westrock
Rental apartment development
2014

Aimed at lecturers and young professionals, **Southernhay Gardens** is a Georgian terrace of small three- and four-storey red-brick buildings in Exeter, UK. The logo references these red bricks and the notion of "wherever I hang my hat, that's my home."

1

2

LPG Power
Motorboat engines
1998

The final logo design needed to convey speed, power and elegance.

1

2

3

4

5

1

2

3

4

5

6

7

8

9

10

11

12

1 **Shades of Summer**
Clarks Shoes
In-store poster
Incidental logo
2004

2 **It's the Jay Baruchel Chapterhouse Party**
Chapterhouse Comics
Web series
2017
Promotional series of short webcasts

3 **Walt Thomas**
Writer/Journalist
Personal mark
2003

4 **Thumbs Up**
What Car magazine
Haymarket Consumer Media
2003

5 **Casa 51**
Device
Limited edition print
Incidental logo
2002

6 **27 Ten Productions**
Film production company
2017

7 **Soho Dives, Soho Divas**
Image Comics
Book cover
2013
Author: Rian Hughes
From the cover of my collection of burlesque illustrations

8 **S9**
Band management/rights
Proposed logo
1998

9 **Fifty Freakin' Years**
Knockabout Comics
Incidental logo
2017
Tribute for the Freak Brothers' 50th anniversary book
Author: Gilbert Shelton

10 11 **Horror/Dracula**
Kinkajou
Incidental logos
2016
Hand-drawn lettering samples from my book *Get Lettering*
Author: Rian Hughes

12 **She's Gorgeous... But She Stinks!**
Sure/Ammirati Puras Lintas (agency)
Poster campaign
1999
Type for a poster which I illustrated promoting a range of deodorants

Fantastic Four
Marvel Comics
Comic book
2013

1

Stan Lee and Jack Kirby's original run on **Fantastic Four**, "the world's greatest comic magazine" as the hyperbolic tagline has it, has a fond place in my affections. The classic run of Silver Surfer/Galactus/Inhumans issues set a high bar for cosmic invention, and are still eminently readable. I was therefore very excited to be asked to design a new logo for one of the title's periodic reboots, this one starting the numbering again from issue 1.

I first drew a clean and rational version of the classic original logo, designed (it is believed) by Sol Brodsky and inked by letterer Artie Simek, who between them did many of **Marvel**'s logos during this period **8**, **9**. Logo historian and Eisner-winning letterer Todd Klein tells me: "We don't know who did what exactly, but Brodsky probably did either a layout or pencils, and Simek did the finish."

Though I was tempted to wallow in nostalgia, I wanted something very clean and graphic – the kind of logo that a cutting-edge tech research organisation headed by Reed Richards (Mr. Fantastic) might use. I also wanted to incorporate the 4 as a numeral, rather than a word, into the design.

13 and **14** are perhaps too corporate, though **14** does reference the 'subatomic particles' of vintage comic printing: the large CMYK dots, as appropriated by Roy Lichtenstein. These would also be difficult to use in the context of a cover without overseeing the application of the trade dress each issue, which was not a practical option. **16** is a four-fold 'unstable molecule', from which the FF's costumes are made.

I also designed a stand-alone icon that featured on early versions of the trade dress but did not make it through to the final design. Each finger on the hand represents one member of the team – a knotted finger for stretchy Mr. Fantastic, a flame for the Torch, a fading finger for the Invisible Woman and a craggy pinkie for The Thing. Earth, Air, Fire and Water, the four classical elements. I mocked up a T-shirt **1** to show how it might work on merchandise.

The final logo is intended to run edge to edge on the cover, the lower area being occupied by the cover art with the strapline and credits in the white bar above **6**, **7**.

The first issue as printed suffers from two in-house additions to bring it into line with other concurrent **Marvel** titles: a red stripe across the bottom to house a clutter of other logos and the barcode, and the addition of an enormous #1 which replaced the hand motif.

2

3

4

5

6

7

8

9

10

11

12

13

14

15

16

17

18

19

Fantastic Four
Marvel Comics
Comic book
2013

The final stand-alone logo. There is added 'bleed' left and right to allow for the trim; on the trade paperback, the logo was not run edge to edge but reduced in size and free-floated. This extra bleed was not removed, and so the 'C' is too wide and the upright on the 'F' twice as thick as it should be. There is a lesson here, though I'm not exactly sure what it is.

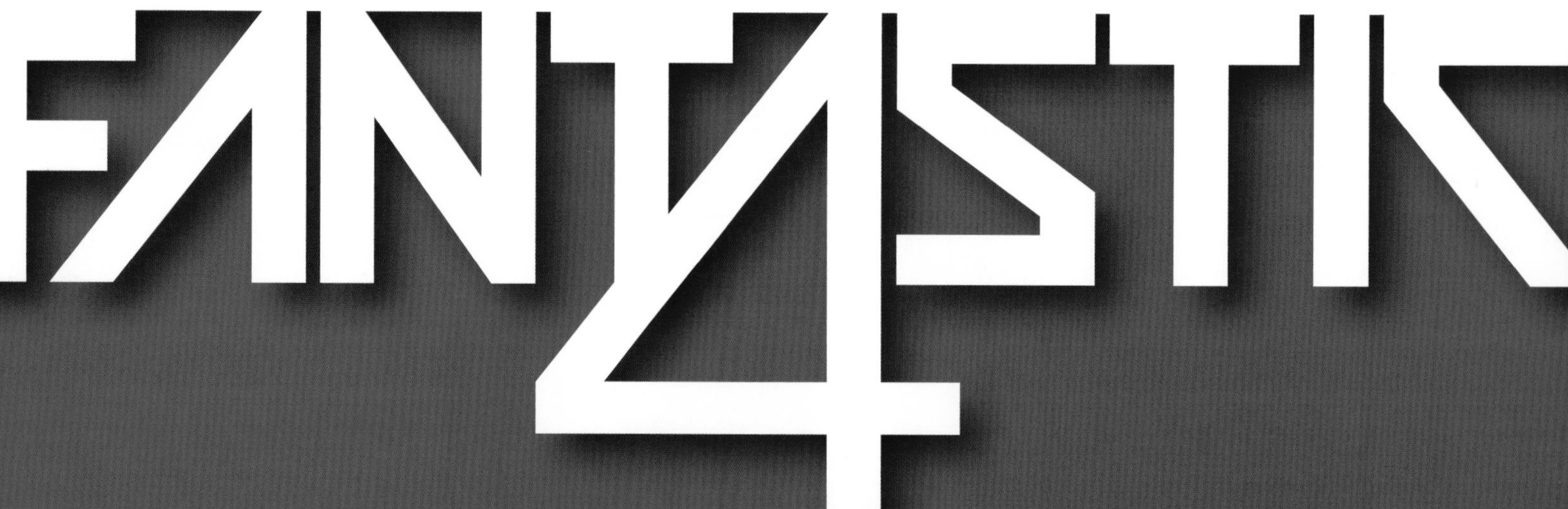

1 Chiqui Love
Burlesque artiste
Incidental logo
Image Comics
2013
From *Soho Dives, Soho Divas*, my collection of burlesque-inspired art

2 Villa Montclair
Neuman and Neuman
Private villa in Ranzo, Italy
2008

3 Astonishing Tales
Marvel Comics
Comic book
2008

4 Sam Slade, Robo Hunter
Fleetway/2000AD
Comic series
1993
Writer: Peter Hogan
Artist: Rian Hughes

5 Fiesta Flyer
Frequent flyer scheme
1985

6 Mezza Maratona di Monza
Vital
Fundraising marathon
2012

7 8 Lifestyles 2000
DMB+B Advertising Agency
Daily Mail Lifestyle 2000 exhibition
1989

9 Video Browser
Video display unit
1986

10 On the Line
Compuserve
1994
Writer: Rick Wright
Artist: Rian Hughes
Comic strip series for *The Guardian* newspaper, later collected in a small volume by Image Comics in 2010

1

2

3

4

5

6

7

8

9

10

Batwing
DC Comics
Comic book series
2011

Introduced by writer Grant Morrison in **Batman Incorporated** prior to receiving his own series, **Batwing** is one of several international superheroes modelled after **Batman**. The first **Batwing** was David Zavimbe, a Congolese police officer, later replaced by Luke Fox, the son of **Batman's** close associate Lucius Fox.

Editor Mike Marts requested that the design incorporate the bat-shape to brand it as part of the **Batman** family of titles. The character's costume features wings with struts, so I used these to divide the bat into sections. The extra letter in **Batwing** (as compared with **Batman**) meant I could centrally place the symmetrical 'W' and run the other letters out either side, subtly adjusting the line weights of 'AT' and 'IN' so that they fill out the same width.

As sometimes happens, I was asked to combine elements of two designs – the lettering from **15** and the divided bat from **9** and **2**. The final version also has a textured interior. **12** was a Photoshop indulgence at the request of the client – I tend to think these kinds of treatments are best used sparingly, and only on a logo that is already strong, and not to try and lift a bad design by (as we say in the studio) "polishing a turd".

1

2

3

4

5

6

7

8

9

10

11

12

13

14

15

16

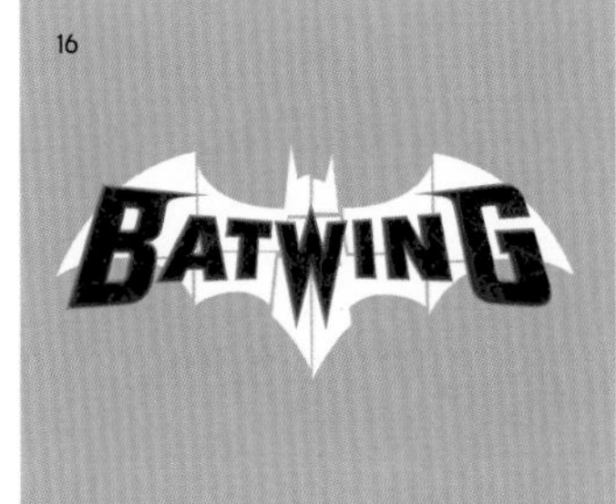

1
2
3
4
5
6
7
8
9
10
11
12
13
14
15
16
17
18
19
20

Cultureo
Patrick Pinchart
Website
2017

Cultureo is a website that covers European culture, with a focus on books and comics.

Rather than produce specific iterations of the logo for different sections, I designed a simple black and white frame into which textures suggestive of culture in the broadest sense were dropped. These were freely used as required.

21

22

cultureo

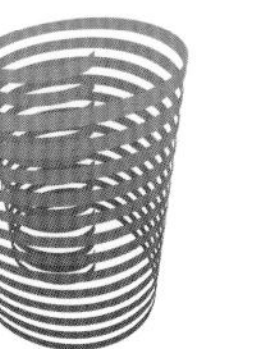

23

24

25

26

CULTUREO

27

CULTUREO

28

29

I, Joker
DC Comics
Graphic novel
1998

Written and drawn by Bob Hall with colours by Lee Loughridge, **I, Joker** was an Elseworlds tale set in 2083. **Batman** has inspired a new religion, the climax of which is an annual death race between its leader and a group of acolytes surgically altered to resemble Batman's greatest foes.

I assembled the design from Bob's line drawing of the **Joker**'s mouth, setting a bat within. The logo **2** is based on Delaware's renowned design studio House Industry's font Slawterhouse, with the supporting text **3** written out by hand in my best shaky 'mentally unhinged' style.

'HAHAHA' **1** ran down the spine.

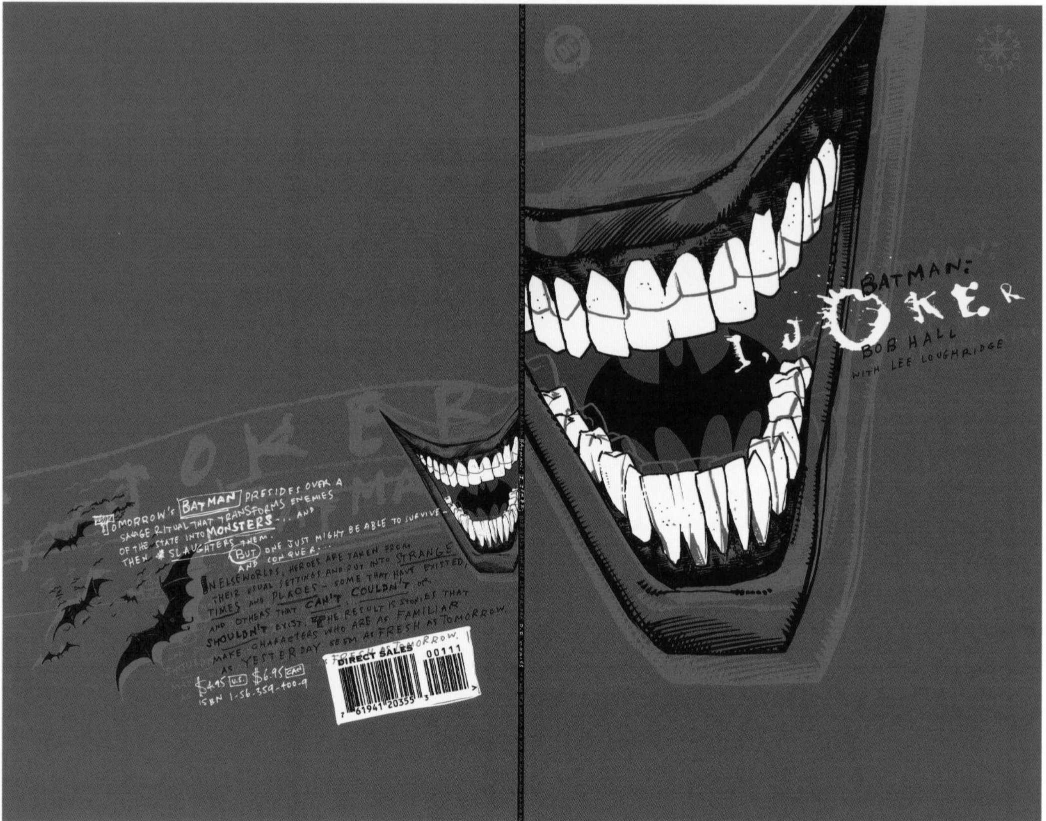

1

A HA HA HA HA HA HA HA HA HA HA HA HA HA HA HA HA HA HA HA HA HA HA HA HA HA HA HA HA HA HA HA HA HA HA HA HA HA HA HA HA HA HA

2

I, JOKER

3

TOMORROW'S BATMAN PRESIDES OVER A SAVAGE RITUAL THAT TRANSFORMS ENEMIES OF THE STATE INTO MONSTERS... AND THEN SLAUGHTERS THEM.

BUT ONE JUST MIGHT BE ABLE TO SURVIVE— AND CONQUER...

IN ELSEWORLDS, HEROES ARE TAKEN FROM THEIR USUAL SETTINGS AND PUT INTO STRANGE TIMES AND PLACES – SOME THAT HAVE EXISTED, AND OTHERS THAT CAN'T, COULDN'T OR SHOULDN'T EXIST. THE RESULT IS STORIES THAT MAKE CHARACTERS WHO ARE AS FAMILIAR AS YESTERDAY SEEM AS FRESH AS TOMORROW.

Kunoichi
New media services
Proposed logo
2010

Kunoichi is a modern term for a female ninja, derived from the three strokes in the Kanji character for 'woman'.

I began by reinterpreting the previous brushstroke logo, but wanted to push for a strong graphic interpretation of this female ninja character.

The brief had been vague: they had requested a "cool", "unique", "big brand" logo, but were unable to articulate what that might be.

After three rounds with no detailed feedback or real engagement in the back-and-forth process of thrashing out a strong concept (other than sending me a selection of company logos ranging from Google to Nike that had nothing in common other than that the company was successful), I ducked out of the job.

The logo opposite was my favourite, though their strapline 'innovating creative' does sound like an adjective is masquerading as a noun.

1

2

3

4

5

6

7

8

Human Target
DC Comics
Comic book series
1999

The modern iteration of **Human Target**, Christopher Chance, was created by Len Wein and Carmine Infantino and first appeared in *Action Comics* #419 in 1972. Featuring a private investigator and bodyguard who assumes the identities of clients targeted by assassins or other dangerous criminals, it has twice been adapted for television – in 1990, and again in 2003.

This logo is for Peter Milligan and Edvin Biukovic's Vertigo Comics revival from 1999, and incorporates the classic 'human target' silhouette seen at firing ranges, with the addition of an arm holding a gun. The type is a rough spray stencil.

The final covers were laid out in-house.

1

2

3

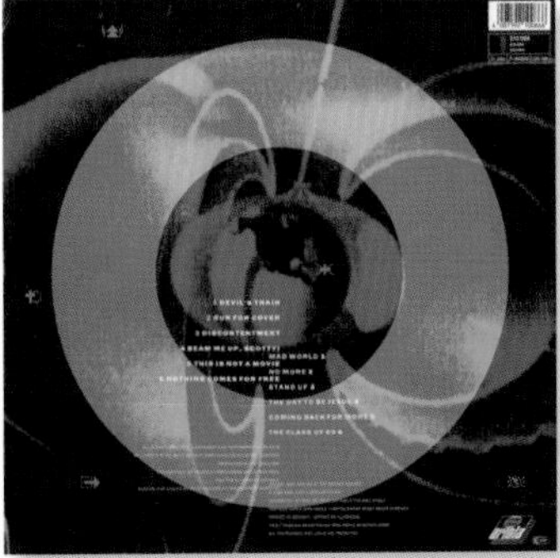

Plan B
Ariola
Band
1989/2002

The original **Plan B** logo **1** was created for the German post-punk four-piece in 1989 for their album *The Greenhouse Effect* and the single *Beam Me Up, Scotty!* which I also designed.

I presented my ideas to the band in the dressing room at the old Dingwalls in London after their live set, which must rate as one of the most insalubrious meeting venues ever.

Thirteen years later I was asked by frontman Johnny Haeusler to revisit the logo for a planned reunion (below).

1

2

3

4

Pulp Fiction Library
DC Comics
Book imprint
1999

A projected series of reprint volumes, **Pulp Fiction Library** was a brand that appeared on only one book, a collection of stories from **Mystery in Space**, DC's long-running SF title. A projected second volume, **Our Fighting Forces**, did not appear.

The design takes as inspiration classic pulp mastheads and war/SF tropes.

1

2

3

1

2

3

4

5

6

7

8

Pure Energy
Music Factory
Dance studio
Proposed logo
2003

I wasn't sure how this one should be pitched – hip workout classes for the young, or an all-ages suburban lifestyle choice. None of my ideas were used.

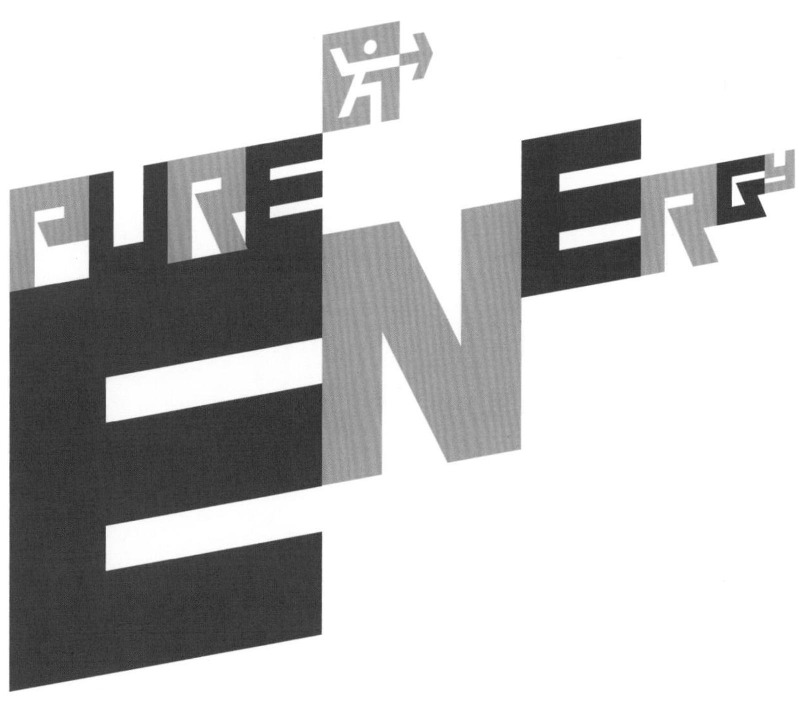

Revolver
Fleetway
Comic magazine
1990

1

2

3

4

5

6

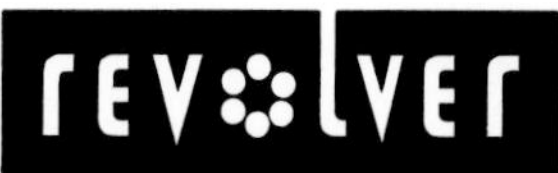

7

8

9

10

11

Revolver, from the publishers of *2000AD*, was an experiment to create a monthly comic aimed at the emerging 'mature readers' market. It featured the serialisation of **Dare**, Grant Morrison and my dystopian reinterpretation of Frank Hampson's classic British space hero **Dan Dare**.

As well as designing the logo, which was printed in a flouro or metallic each issue, I laid out the introductory pages inside. Early logo concepts **1**, **2**, **6** toyed with the chambers of a gun. The final logo was pieced together letter by letter from brush and ink drawings **11**. My preliminary rough for the first issue was assembled from cut flouro paper, marker pen and a placeholder Bill Sienkiewicz **Judge Dredd** image **9**, and is quite close to the final design. **10** is a photocopy of the camera-ready artwork as supplied to the printer. This would have had a tracing paper overlay indicating the CMYK colour breakdowns.

A trial Cromalin was produced **12** using an image I had drawn of Dan in a sombre and reflective mood in front of the decaying Space Fleet HQ, the candy-coloured spaceships of his bright but now lost future roaring overhead. Tharg (Steve MacManus) thought this was a bit of a downer for the first issue of a new magazine, so a more upbeat image was swapped in. The cover design evolved to incorporate a custom font I had drawn **16** (overleaf), also called Revolver, which was designed as a hybrid between the taut curves of a 1950s coffee table and 1960s pop psychedelia – a typographic representation of the strapline 'Where Dan Dare meets Jimi Hendrix', which publicist Igor Goldkind had come up with. This was later digitised and released as part of the FontFont range **12**.

We went on a UK signing tour to promote the first issue. Photographed outside Forbidden Planet, Dublin **13**, are (left to right) Grant Morrison, Brendan McCarthy, me, editor Peter Hogan and Charles Shaar Murray. The tour took in late-night lock-ins, cheap hotels, sub-standard curry houses, both enthusiastic and surly punters and some unrepeatable misadventures.

Revolver managed to last seven issues before lower than expected (but by today's standards, still stellar) sales forced its cancellation, after which **Dare** was completed in the pages of **Crisis**.

12

13

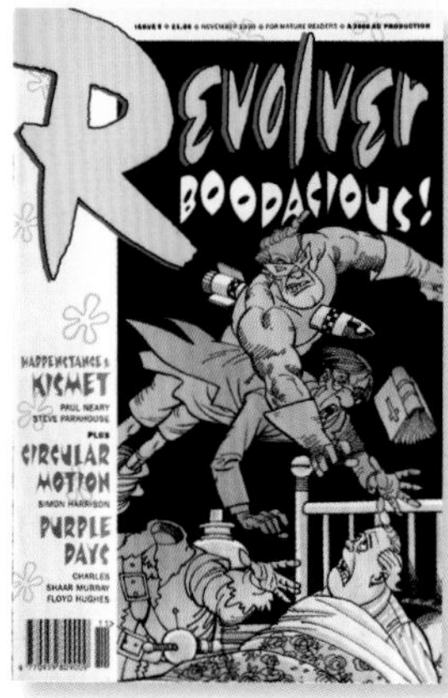

I ran Floyd Hughes' cover for issue 3 through a colour photocopier to give it a more psychedelic makeover. Issues 2 and 5 use metallic inks. The first issue shown here was signed by Peter Hogan, Shaky Kane, Grant Morrison and Peter Milligan at London's Café Casbar **14**, a venue close to **Forbidden Planet** that hosted many industry events and the infamous FP Christmas parties. Left to right: Charles Shaar Murray, Peter Hogan, Rian Hughes, Grant Morrison, unknown, Shaky Kane and Peter Milligan.

Two specials were also published: **The Horror Special 17**, **18** and the **Romance Special 19**, **20**. The latter, though put together by **Revolver** editor Peter Hogan, somehow has the **Crisis** branding as well. **The Horror Special** cover **17** is an unseen Cromalin – the cover as printed was rejigged so the emphasis was on **Horror Special** and not **Revolver**.

I had fun with the layout of the contents spreads, adding simple illustrations I'd either cut from Rubylith or drawn with a loose brush. The wavy column on **18** was achieved by slicing the galley of type line by line with a scalpel and shifting it across.

DAN DARE
ROGAN GOSH
PURPLE DAYS
FF REVOLVER

14

15

16

The Horror Special
Fleetway
Comic book themed special
1990

The Romance Special
Fleetway
Comic book themed special
1991

THE HORROR SPECIAL

17

18

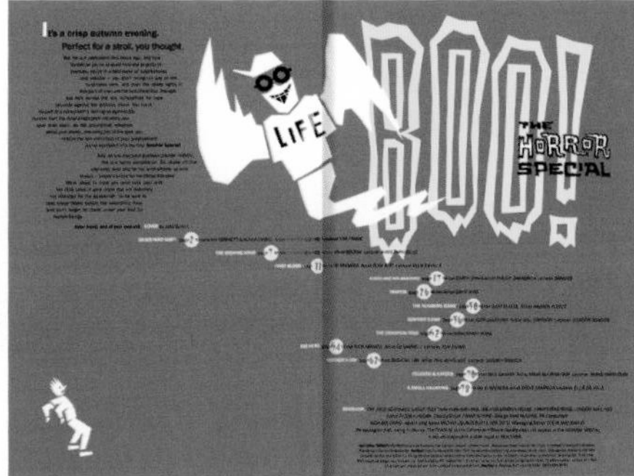

19

20

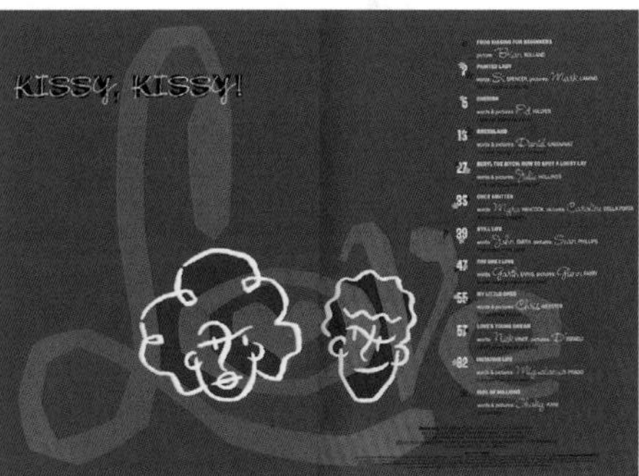

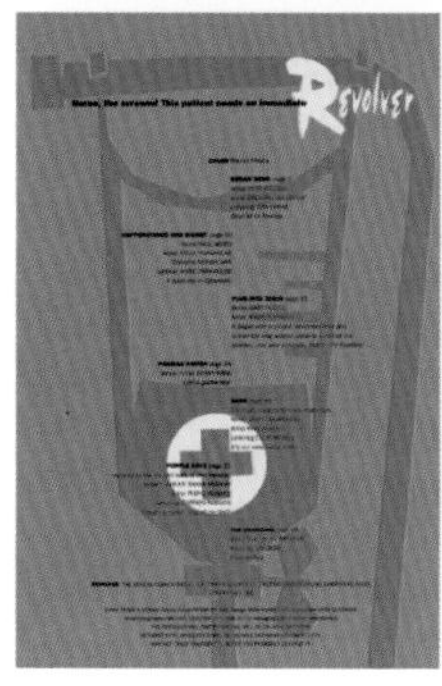

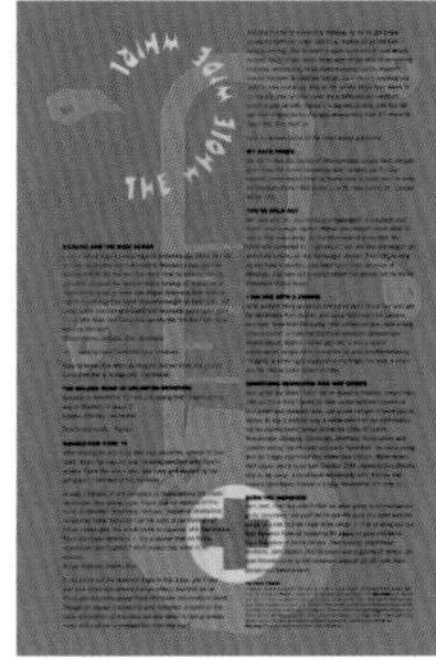

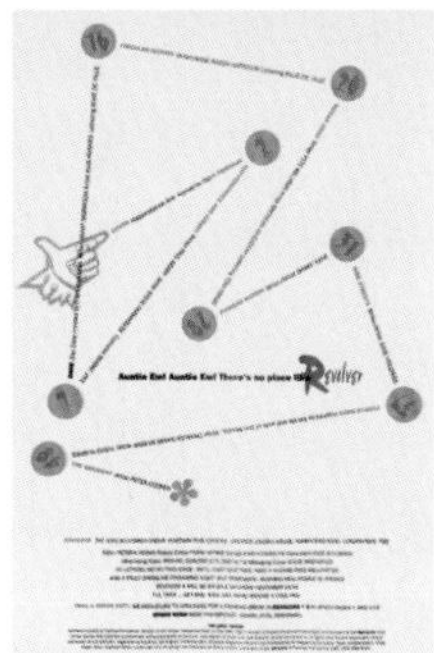

Smith & Mighty
Three Stripe/London/PolyGram
Remember Me
Band logo/record sleeve proposal
1994

Smith & Mighty are Rob Smith and Ray Mighty, a trip hop group from Bristol. Their first releases, in the late 1980s, were breakbeat covers of *Anyone Who Had a Heart* and *Walk On By*. They went on to produce Massive Attack's first single, *Any Love*.

My logo portrays them as a cartoon duo, with initials in circles on their chests in the manner of Yves Chaland's classic comic strip, *Adolphus Claar*. I did several iterations, some hand-drawn, others in Aldus Freehand **1**, a program I was just getting to grips with on my new Mac 2Ci, but either the project died or I was so far off the mark that the record label were too embarrassed to come back to me.

1

2

Scene of the Crime
DC Comics/Vertigo
Comic book mini-series
1999

Scene of the Crime is a four-issue comic book mini-series written by Ed Brubaker and pencilled and inked by Michael Lark (with inks by Sean Phillips following the first issue).

Each letter is on a little tag, an idea lifted from the boards that suspects hold up in American police mugshots. An offset underprint, taken from the same artwork, is used as a colour fill.

Other ideas feature the classic chalk outline (an idea I'd already used for the **Murder One** shop identity) and red blood – direct references to the scene of the crime. These are overly detailed, and would have been hard to use in practice. Layered designs on comic covers can be problematic – each element needs to be coloured to key to the cover, but also needs to read clearly and not get lost against it or each other, which is a difficult balance to strike. A well-defined border or edge to the type can sometimes help lift it out of the background.

1

2

3

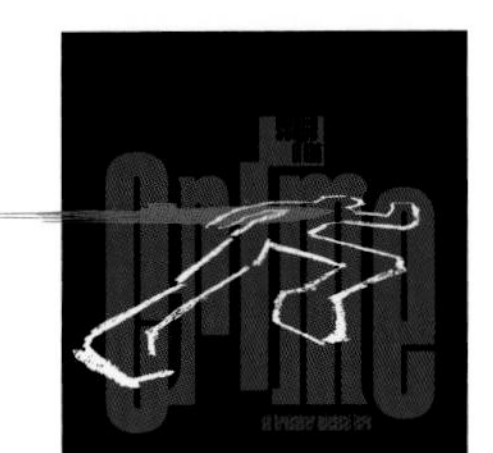

4

Mute
Record label
Proposed logo
1996

Through a connection at Rhythm King, I was asked to submit some design suggestions for the **Mute** logo. In the end, none of my ideas were used.

Mute is a force in the music industry, the home of Depeche Mode, Erasure, Fad Gadget, Moby, Nitzer Ebb, Wire and Goldfrapp.

The original logo is a Letraset architectural symbol, used on the label's first release, The Normal's J. G. Ballard-inspired *Warm Leatherette* **1**, a track later covered by Grace Jones. More recent iterations had dropped the figure; I thought it would be interesting to look at the original, and try and incorporate the type and figure into a cohesive 'lock up'.

My favourite is shown left. The line weight is consistent throughout and the whole is enclosed in a rounded rectangle, though in retrospect I may have abstracted the figure to the degree that it's not immediately obvious what it is.

Some of the versions which had small details **6** or blurred shadow effects **10**, **11** are too fussy, and as experience has taught me, would be very hard to use on sleeves where it's not always possible to guarantee a white or plain coloured background.

This being well before digital downloads or streaming, each release was a multi-format affair. **3**, **4** and **5** address this with separate vinyl, cassette and CD versions.

1

2

3

4

5

6

7

8

9

10

11

12

13

Mobfire
DC Comics/Vertigo
Comic book series
1994

For Gary Ushaw and Warren Pleece's six-issue gangster mini-series, the final logo **1** became more degraded as the issues progressed. Though I liked the more illustrative logo (main image), it didn't suit Warren's art style so well.

On the credits and indicia page, I rearranged the letters to make an image that related to the theme of each story. The covers (not shown here) were laid out in-house.

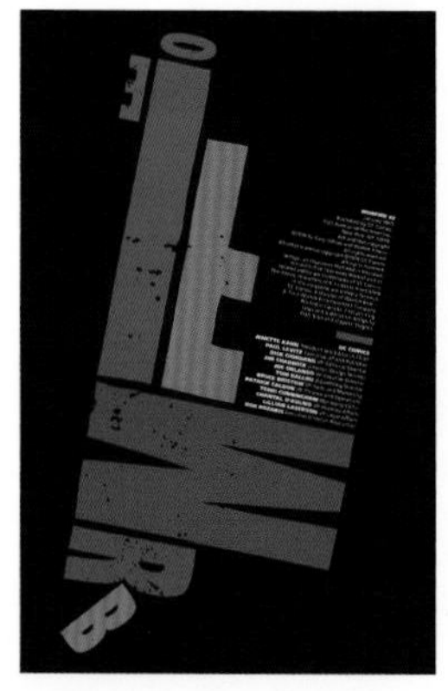

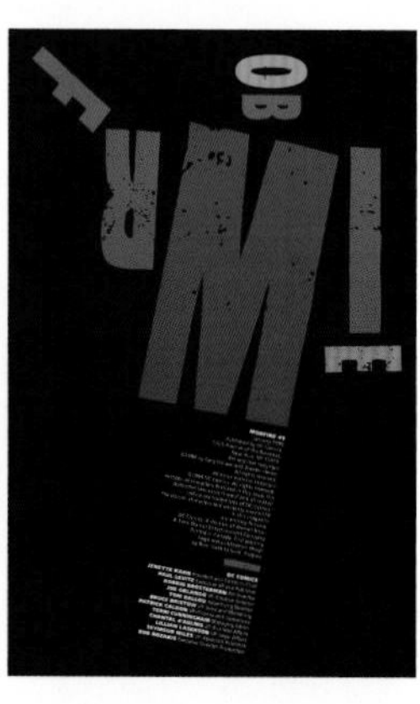

1 MOBFIRE
MOBFIRE
MOBFIRE
MOBFIRE
MOBFIRE

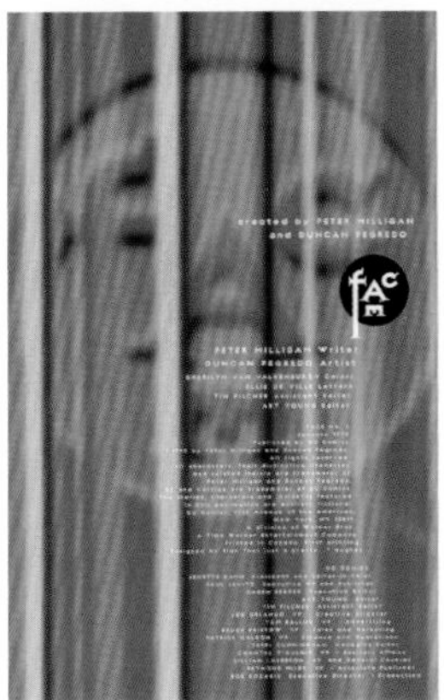

1

2

3

4

5

6

Vertigo Voices
Face
The Eaters
Kill Your Boyfriend
DC Comics
Comic book sub-imprint
1994

Put together by Art Young and Tim Pilcher from **DC Comics**' new UK office in Soho Square, **Vertigo Voices** was a short-lived run of stand-alone titles.

Kill Your Boyfriend, by Grant Morrison and Philip Bond, was a black comedy of teenage romance and rebellion with a side order of sex and violence. The logo is scrawled on lined exercise book paper.

In **Face**, by Peter Milligan and Duncan Fegredo, a cosmetic surgeon decides the human body is the ultimate canvas. The logo reflects the cubist reworking of the character's face. The indicia and credits page was an early experiment with type manipulation in Photoshop; back when I was working with 8MB of RAM, manipulating files of any size was painfully slow.

Peter Milligan and Dean Ormston's **The Eaters** revolves around a middle-class suburban family who just happen to be cannibals. The design features a framed family portrait against tasteful floral wallpaper. Shown here is the original cover illustration – it was toned down for the actual release. The credits page shows a sun-faded version, with the framed portrait removed.

Bizarre Boys, by Peter Milligan and Jamie Hewlett, failed to make it beyond a logo **6** and a series of cover roughs.

A 'sound off' poster was produced to promote the series. As the styles of each artist were very different, I used just the linework and a reduced colour scheme to pull it together.

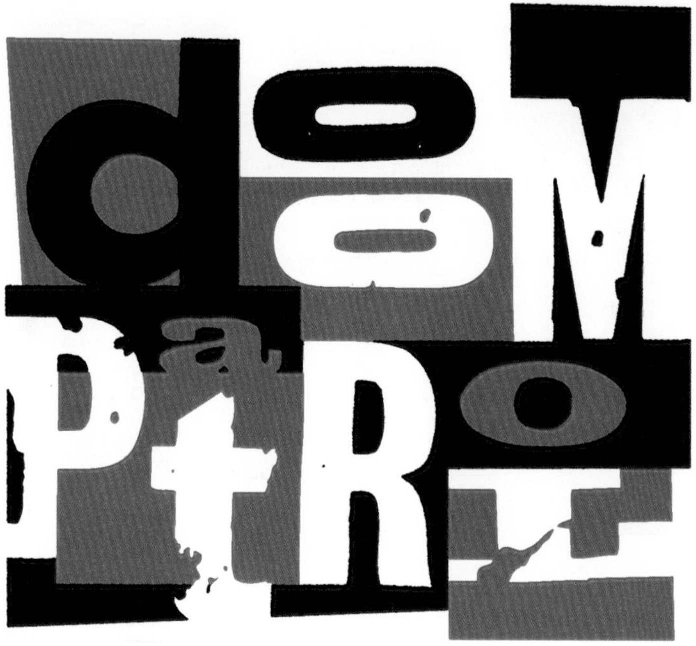

Doom Patrol
DC Comics
Comic book series
1991

The original **Doom Patrol** first appeared in *My Greatest Adventure* #80, published in June 1963. Writers Arnold Drake and Bob Haney, artist Bruno Premiani and editor Murray Boltinoff are generally credited as the team's creators.

The "world's strangest heroes" have been resurrected several times since. This Dada-inspired logo was used from #50 of the 1990s run, 32 issues into Grant Morrison's iconoclastic revamp. The issue featured a face-off between the **Doom Patrol** and their arch enemies, the New Brotherhood of Dada, for which I also drew a pin-up.

I kept the stacked 'o's, which had been a feature of the previous logo, but otherwise didn't reference the original. It was designed using pre-digital tools: a Rotring pen and ageing Letraset, which I then pulled off the board using sticky tape to roughen it up. It was later digitised and given a drop shadow.

The final covers were laid out in-house at **DC Comics**.

1

doom
patrol

2

3

4

5

Automatic Records
Record label
1996

Founded in West London by musicians and DJs Russel Coultart and Lawrence Cooke, **Automatic Records** was a sister label to their trance and psychedelic label **Transient** and focussed on dance music.

The silver and black colour scheme was applied across the single bag, label and CD inlay designs.

1

2

3

4

5

6

Tank Girl
Deadline
Magazine masthead
1995

Jamie Hewlett's beer-drinking, kangaroo-shagging Riot Grrl icon had just been made into a movie, and so Tom Astor, publisher of **Deadline** magazine, her original home, decided to spin her off into a title of her own.

I worked up a range of mastheads for the new magazine., but none were used. In the end, Jamie's own hand-drawn logo, which had been associated with the character since her inception, was thought to have the best brand recognition.

I also designed an unreleased dummy issue **1**, which was produced in order to entice advertisers and retailers; it contained a mix of blank pages and strips reprinted from **Deadline.**

The font I used is a customised version of FF Knobcheese, one of my early FontFont releases.

1

2

3

4

5

Vibe
DC Comics
Comic book series
2013

Created by Gerry Conway and Chuck Patton, **Vibe** first appeared in *Justice League of America Annual* #2 in 1984. His original costume was very much of the period, and featured 'new wave' style shoulder pads and triangular glasses, which I referenced in **1** and **8**.

This logo is for the 2013 *New 52* reboot by Andrew Kreisberg and Pete Woods, wherein he gets a revised origin and a more contemporary wardrobe.

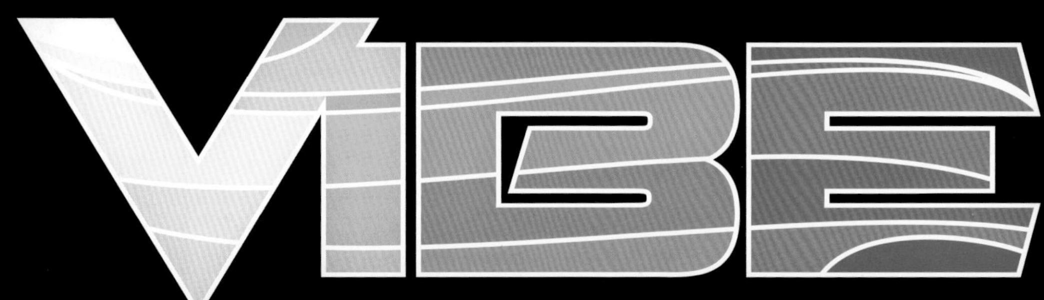

1

2

3

4

5

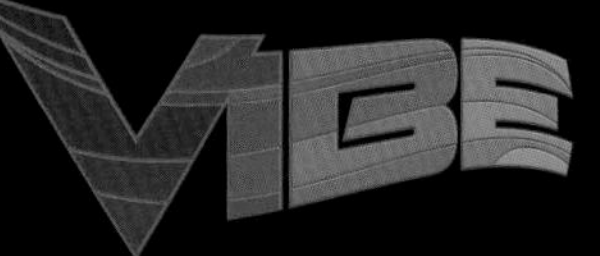

6

7

8

Thrillkiller: Batgirl and Robin
DC Comics
Comic book
1997

An Elseworlds tale from writer Howard Chaykin and artist Daniel Brereton, **Thrillkiller** posits an alternative world in which Barbara **Batgirl** Gordon and Dick **Robin** Grayson come of age against the backdrop of Gotham's 1960s counterculture.

The logo uses the condensed Compacta-style lettering of the period, with a 'unicase' mix of lower- and upper-case forms; this is given a dramatic psychedelic wave and a perspective.

1

THRILLKILLERS

Thrillkiller '62
DC Comics
Comic book
1998

The sequel to **Thrillkiller: Batgirl and Robin** tells how this particular version of Bruce Wayne becomes **Batman**. The logo follows on from the previous design, shortening the red dividing stroke to become an apostrophe.

For both volumes a silhouette icon representing the two main characters was designed, with **Batgirl** common to both. The final trade dress and the collected edition were designed in-house.

Kid Eternity
DC Comics
Comic book series
1992

Ann Nocenti and Sean Phillips took the veteran Quality Comics character **Kid Eternity** in a new direction after Grant Morrison and Duncan Fegredo's three-issue mini-series.

The circular logo, which reflects the character's chaos magic origins and glasses, is a self-contained bullet that sets off Sean's bold and graphic covers. His experimental montage techniques were here achieved entirely without Photoshop. The first issue uses metallic gold ink.

1

2

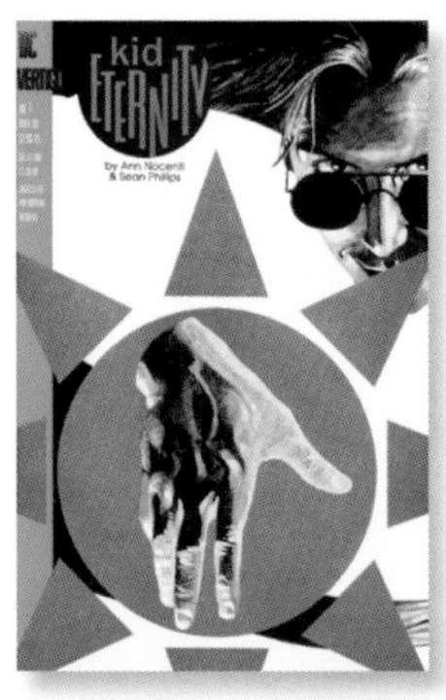

Font Aid V: Made For Japan
Font Aid
Charity font project
2011

In 2011, the 'Made For Japan' font was created to raise funds after the devastating earthquake and tsunami in Japan. Nearly 300 contributors from 45 countries sent in over 500 glyphs.

Apollo . . . Sound!
Million Dollar
Clothing brand
1994

Apollo was a brand from **Million Dollar**, a retail store in London's King's Road with its own range of clothing. I produced numerous logos and designs for them over a few years.

The **Apollo** shirt **13** was printed in black and a reflective silver; the Professor Love shirt **5** was printed in a glow-in-the-dark green. I didn't come up with the sweary slogans.

1

2

3

4

5

6

7

8

9

10

11

12

13

14

15

16

17

18

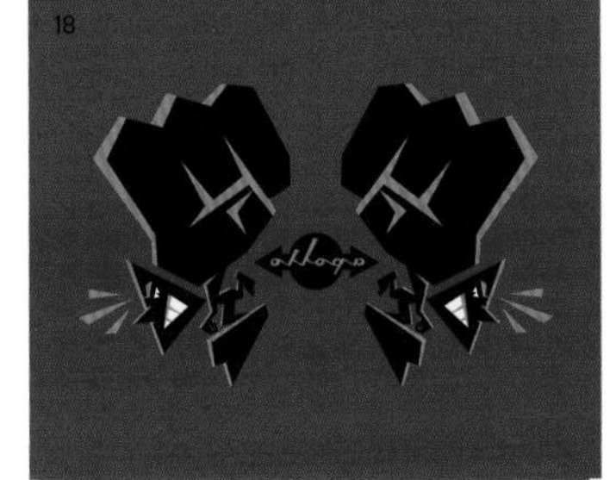

19

20

Space Cadet Battledress
Million Dollar
T-shirt motif
1993

Designed as part of the **Planet X** series for King's Road retailer and T-shirt manufacturer **Million Dollar**, the shirt was printed in a variety of colourways including a peculiar silver on off-white **2**, **3**. The font used here is Outlander, one of my early FontFont designs.

™ TRADEMARKED, ® REGISTERED AND © COPYRIGHTED, BABY!
#7 IN A SERIES. COLLECT THE SET!

1

2

3

Transatlantic Trading Company
Import/export specialist
1986

Designed pre-Mac, the logo was hand-drawn with colour separations added as an overlay. The printed version has poor ink registration that originally annoyed me, but nowadays I'm more inclined to view it as part of the vintage analogue charm.

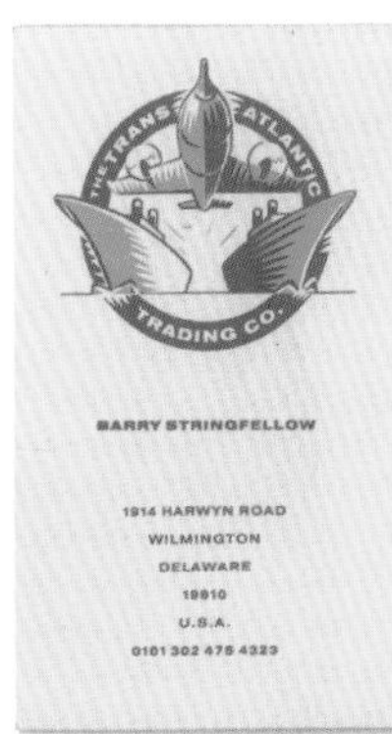

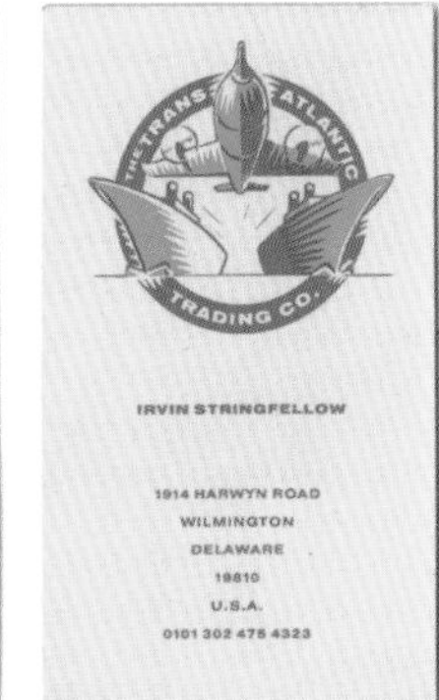

Masterplan Management
Band management
1989

Masterplan is Plan B's German management company. The logo was applied in black and a fluorescent orange to stationery: letterheads, business cards and compliment slips. These were designed to resemble architectural floor plans, and (expensively) die-cut to shape.

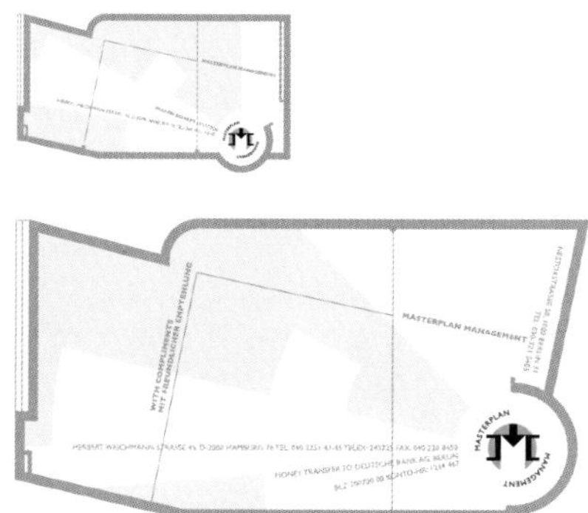

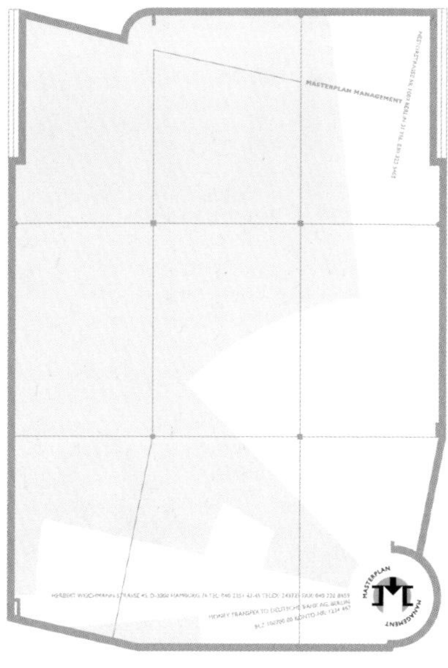

Deadline
Deadline magazine/Tom Astor
Magazine masthead and design
1995

Created by Brett Ewins and Steve Dillon, **Deadline** was an eclectic and vital independent comic magazine that ran a mix of comic strips and articles. Best-known as the birthplace of artist Jamie Hewlett and writer Alan Martin's **Tank Girl**, the magazine also regularly featured work by Phil Bond, Peter Milligan, Nick Abadzis, Ilya and Shaky Kane, as well as reprinted work by Peter Bagge and Jaime Hernandez.

Frank Wynne, who I had worked with on **Crisis**, had recently taken over as editor. The previous designer, Mark Cox, was taking a sabbatical, and so I found myself stepping in. The magazine was run out of a small office in Orinoco Studios, publisher Tom Astor's recording studio just off the Old Kent Road, which came to prominence with the release of Enya's Orinoco-produced *Orinoco Flow*. The studios were central to both the dance explosion of the late 1980s and the indie/Britpop era of the early to mid-nineties; Oasis mixed *(What's the Story) Morning Glory?* there.

Deadline was designed in-house over two or three intensive days per issue. Wrestling with the shortcomings of early Quark Express and a limited budget that meant only the cover was ever proofed, I experimented with shaped text boxes, large type, and photographs dropped inside letters. I pressed my own fonts Elektron, Regulator and Amorpheus into use, which I later released through my new Device Fonts foundry. The **Deadline** logo itself is derived from another Device font, Darkside, which itself was developed from an aborted Fleetway magazine of the same name that was to reprint Vertigo material. The little skull logos **1** were used for the letters page, 'Plug City', comic and music reviews and competitions sections, as well as general page furniture.

The photographs of Peter and Jamie that were used on the back cover of **Hewligan's Haircut** were shot by John Ward in the adjacent pool room. There were semi-regular parties where bands and DJs would play in the main space, at one of which I somehow ended up falling face down in Phil Bond's lap.

Just after I started, **Tank Girl** was spun out into her own magazine to capitalise on the new movie; sadly, without her support (and, I hope, not because of my redesign!) the magazine folded a few issues later.

1

ISSUE 69
THE STYLE MAGAZINE FOR UNDERACHIEVERS
JUNE/JULY 1995 £2.95
deadline
Summer Special!
EARTHLING
Alien Lifeforms
YOUNG GODS
Heaven on Earth?
COP OUT!
The glory of seventies Cop shows
ED WOOD
From Drag to Stitches
BURN, BABY, BURN!
Free Tank Girl Poster

ISSUE 70
THE STYLE MAGAZINE FOR UNDERACHIEVERS
AUGUST/SEPTEMBER 1995 £2.50
deadline
THROWING MUSES
Kristin Hersh on blondes and power
Suzy Wrong
Chinese New Gear
Blondes
Does peroxide lower your IQ?
plus
The Verve
Whale
Global Communication
David Singh at the Reichstag
and
Sadist
Frieda's Friends
Evan Dorkin
End of the Century
WOMEN GET LOADED!
Sex objects
Richard Kern on women and power fantasies

ISSUE 71
THE STYLE MAGAZINE FOR UNDERACHIEVERS
OCTOBER/NOVEMBER 1995 £2.50
deadline
GEEK LOVE
The love that dare not squeak its name
JARVIS COCKER
King of the Geeks?
QUENTIN TARANTINO
See above..
Plus
DOGG HOGG
Probably the best rock 'n' roll band in the world
THE FALL
Get back up again
and David 'geek basher' Singh

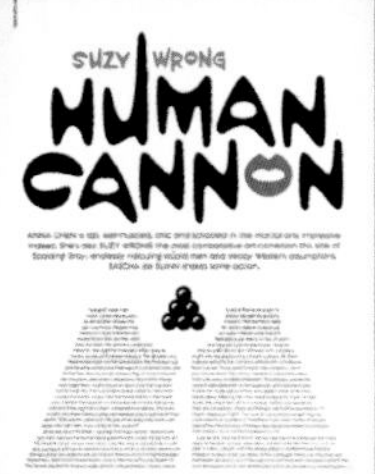
SUZY WRONG
HUMAN CANNON

INTO THE
SLOUGH
OF DESPOND

COP OUT!

COP OUT!

PLATINUM RISKS

DEATH

AND TAXES

holidays in

ooh ooh ooh
i wanna be like
you
ooh ooh

Belfast's CHIMERA have been away for two long years. One of the best bands on the planet, their records are almost impossible to find and Day Star, their brand new EP, is available only on import. DEADLINE hunts them down to find out what the fuck is going on.

PAGAN RITES AND CORPORATE WRONGS

CHIMERA

Pix: PHIL NICHOLLS

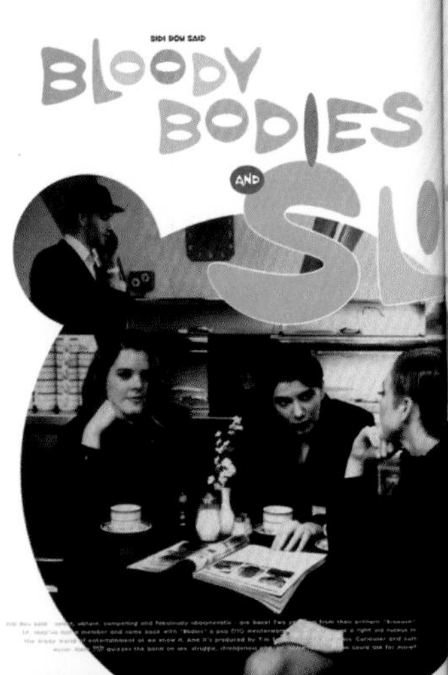

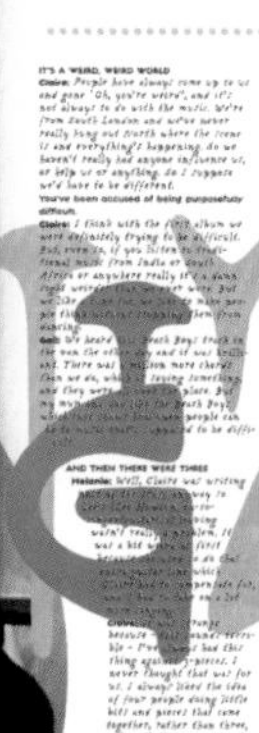

Earth calling

Earthling?

Heaven Up Here

Can You
Ross Hogg

richard kern
doing the dirty

that was smashing

PINKIE MACLURE

BACK IN THE GROOVE

Russ Meyer

mixing it with the
global communication

WE'LL CALL THAT A

1

2

3

4

5

6

7

8

9

10

11

12

1 **Unknown Host**
Comic book series
Logo proposal
2005
Writer: Peter Hogan

2 **Harley and Ivy**
DC Comics
Prestige format comic book
2001
Writer: Judd Winick
Artist: Joe Chiodo

3 **Friends Together**
Clarks Shoes
In-store promotion
2001

4 **Melissa Tricoire**
Publicist
Personal mark
2015

5 **G.I. Spy**
Boom! Studios
Comic book
2005
Writer: Andrew Cosby
Artist: Matt Haley

6 **Kaliphz**
London Records
Proposed logo
1995

7 **Getting Rid of Karenna**
Oxford University Press
Book cover
2000
Author: Helena Pielichaty
Cover type for book, for which I also illustrated the cover

8 **Keep Gotham Tidy**
Device
T-shirt motif
2009

9 **Keep Metropolis Tidy**
Device
T-shirt motif
2009

10 **Punk Mambo**
Valiant Comics
2014

11 **Exhibit Z**
Exhibition design company
2001

12 **Hurricane Sandy Relief**
The Society of Typographic Aficionados (SOTA) and Building Letters
Font Aid IV
2005

Pic Format
PC Format
Section headers
1994

This series of icons that were used throughout *PC Format* magazine as section headers and page furniture illustrate how fast technology changes – several of these are already obsolete.

The set was later released under the name Pic Format as part of the Device Fonts range.

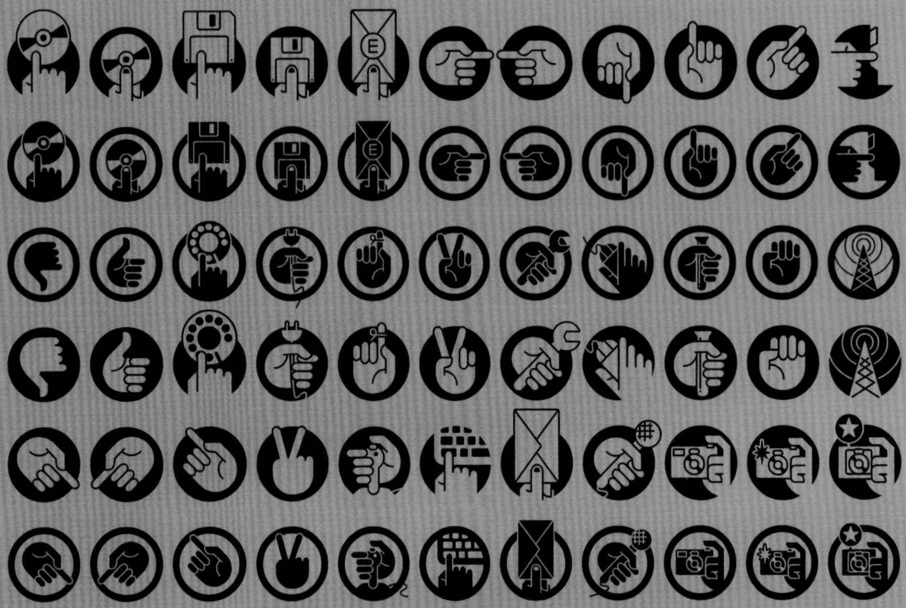

Iconics
Virgin Media/Young and Rubicam
Advertising icons
2001

Designed for Virgin's move into financial services under the Virgin Money brand, these icons appeared on a range of billboards and newspaper advertisements.

They were later released as a set of four fonts, in both positive (shown here) and negative versions.

Clouddog
Children's charity
Proposed logo
2006

Clouddog offers inner-city youngsters an intensive twelve-month programme of personal development and skills acquisition in environmental and conservation issues.

The name was coined when an inner-city child on an excursion saw a sheep for the first time. Not knowing what it was, they called it a 'cloud dog'.

Note that the feet of the cloud dog are floating a short distance above the ground.

Discoo
Fashion retailer
2004

Situated in London's fashionable Carnaby Street, **Discoo** was a women's fashion retailer carrying "cult and independent styles" that started life as an online retailer, then opened outlets in department stores such as Top Shop.

Working from the elongated format of a shop sign, I tried to evoke the international glamour of classic airline livery, which is required to work on a similarly shaped canvas. The wings suggested the speedy online delivery, the globe their international range of boutique brands, the whole the jet-setting lifestyle to which they wanted their customers to aspire.

For versatility, cut-down versions with just one wing or stacked elements were also provided **1-3**. The name is set in the Device font Popgod, with the strapline underneath in Paralucent.

1

2

3

Shadowpact
DC Comics
Comic book series
2005

Shadowpact is a group of magical heroes introduced in the *Day of Vengeance* series, a sort of **Justice League** of the supernatural. The logo presses suitably Gothic typographic ornaments into use. The rules above and below were dropped in the final version.

1

2

3

4

SHADOWPACT

1

2

Utopia/Exodus
Marvel Comics
Comic book series/crossover
2009

Written by Matt Fraction, **Utopia** was a crossover starring the **X-Men** and the Dark Avengers. It ran through both titles and was bookended by two stand-alone issues, the second titled **Exodus**. I confess that, even after designing these issues, I'm not sure of the order in which they're intended to be read.

My early pared-down designs **1**, **2** highlight the 'x' and 'a', standing for **Avengers** and **X-Men**. The final **Utopia** logo uses a combined 'X' and 'A' in the 'O' of Utopia (and Exodus, which in one of those happy design coincidences, also has an 'O' in the exact same position) that mimics an anarchy symbol. This is counterpointed by a refined serif to suggest a utopian golden age. The tension between the two – the use of violence to achieve what is thought to be a justified end – ties into the riots that kick off the series and lead to the creation of the Dark Avengers team. The art as supplied is shown here.

Unfortunately the issues as printed were marred by the in-house addition of large, intrusive barcodes and bright red number boxes. The second printings, variant issues and the trade paperback collection all freely adapt my design with varying degrees of success – and sometimes credit me as designer.

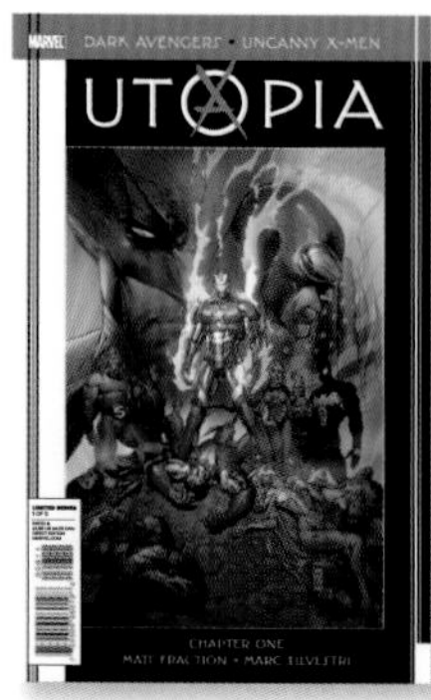

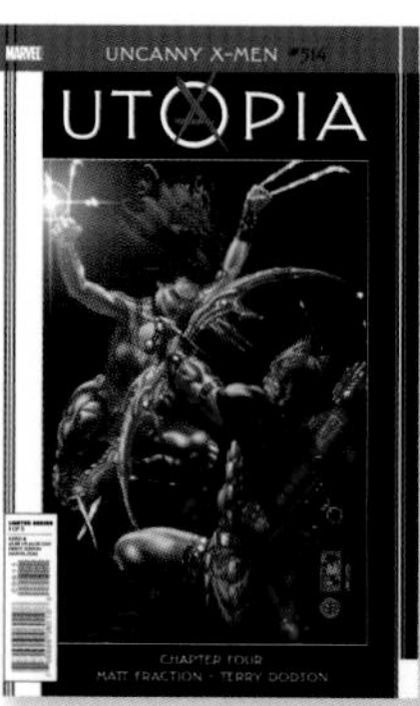

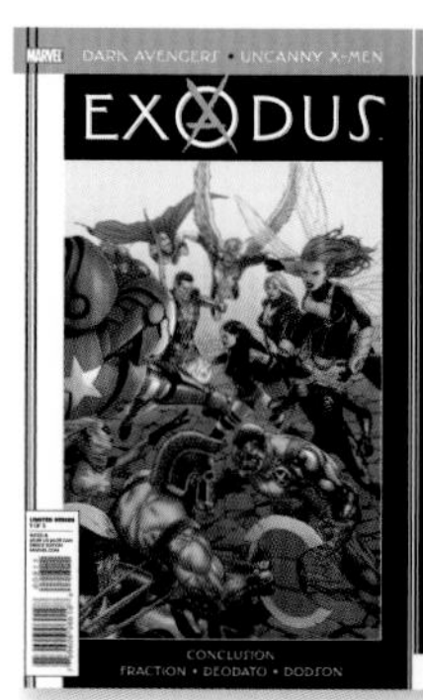

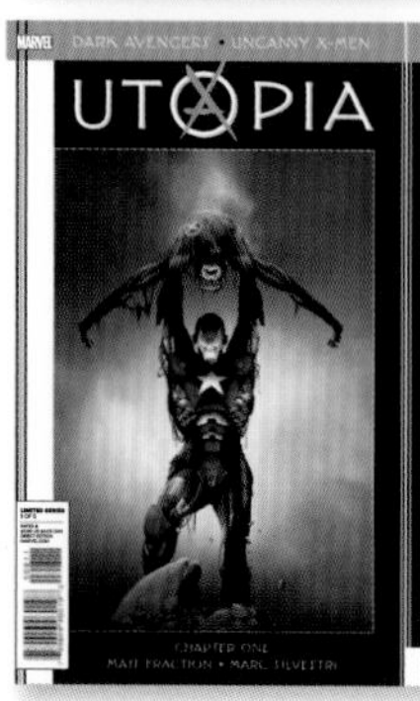

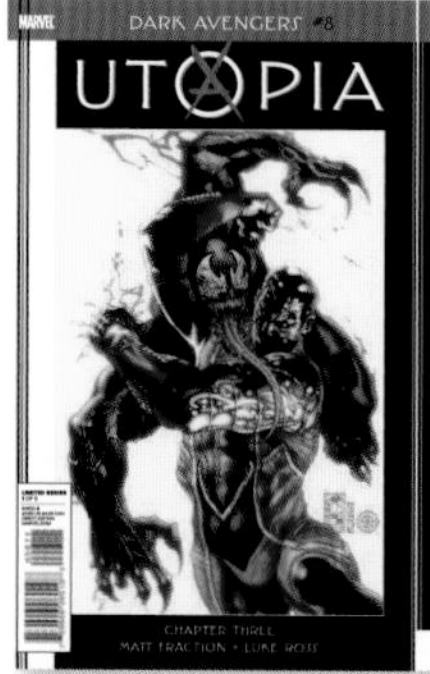

The Flash
DC Comics
Comic book series
1999

The extreme perspective of **The Flash** logo is a hoary old design cliché that imparts speed – but if ever there was an appropriate use of a cliché to impart speed, this is it.

The modular letters are intended to suggest photons, or discrete units of the Speed Force, perhaps. For consistency I attempted to use the same thickness of lines for the 'the', but even at just three tiers high it looked too large for the rest of the logo.

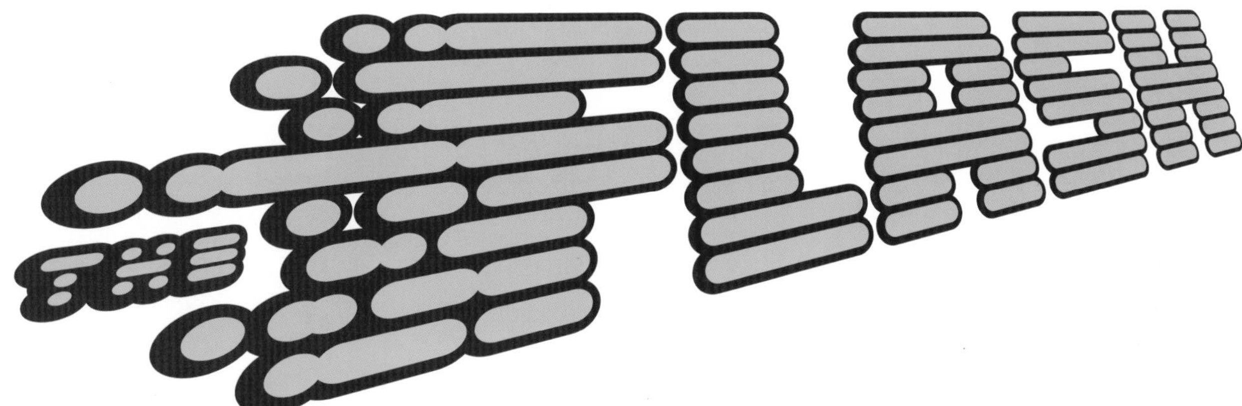

1

2

3

4

Illegal Mutant
High Risk Citizen
Juve Rehab
Citi-Def
Forbidden Planet/Fleetway
T-shirts
1987

A series of four T-shirt designs for futsie perps using **Judge Dredd**'s Mega City slang. The three on this page are silkscreened proofs, printed on a kind of porous gauze. They were designed pre-Mac, using Rotring pen and Rubylith masks.

BRIT-CIT
JUSTICE DEPARTMENT
JUVE REHAB
LONG TERM PATIENT
1
MARGARET THATCHER BLOCK
CITIDEF
COMBAT UNIT
2
MEGA-CITY ONE JUSTICE DEPARTMENT
ILLEGAL
MUTANT
3
MEGA-CITY ONE JUSTICE DEPARTMENT
HIGH RISH
PSYCHO CUBE OBSERVATION RECOMMENDED
4
MARVEL
5
6
ChicGeek
7
ChicGeek
8
CAPTAIN AMERICA
REBORN
9
mech
10
mech
11
67
12
13
14
67
15
67
16
VITAL
CASINO FOR CHILDREN
17
SHADOWMAN
18
UNITY
19
HARDINGER
20

1
THE DEATH-DEFYING
DOCTOR MIRAGE
2
FORBIDDEN PLANET
3
FORBIDDEN PLANET
4
FORBIDDEN PLANET
5
6
VALIANT
7
VALIANT
8
NOT ALL MEN ARE CREATED EQUAL
9
THE AVENGERS
10
AVENGERS
11
12
CHARLIE
13
BATMAN
14
CRISIS
15
GOVERNMENT
OFFICIAL
HOOLIGAN
16
17
MANOWAR
SIGN OF THE HAMMER
18
FIGHT BREAST CANCER
19
WAR
20
BATMAN ROBIN

T-shirts, previous spread

5 9 **Captain America Reborn**
Marvel 2009

6 **Days Missing**
Roddenberry Entertainment 2010

7 8 **Chic Geek**
Device 2007

10 11 **NYC Mech**
Ivan Brandon/Image 2004

12 15 16 **67**
Celtic football club unofficial merchandise 2007

13 14 17 **Vital**
Children's charity 2009

18 **Shadowman**
19 **Unity**
20 **Harbinger**
Valiant Entertainment 2013

This spread

1 **Doctor Mirage**
7 **Valiant**
32 **X-O Manowar**
33 **Bloodshot**
34 **Bloodshot Reborn**
Valiant Entertainment 2013-6

2-4 **Forbidden Planet**
9 10 **The Avengers**
30 **Halo Jones**
Forbidden Planet c1986

8 **Not All Men Are Created Equal**
14 **Crisis**
15 **Government Hooligan**
Fleetway/Crisis 1988

11 **Catwoman**
13 **Batman Incorporated**
16 **Harley Quinn**
20 **Batman and Robin**
DC Comics 2008-2016

12 **Charlie Lankester**
Midmoor Music 2013

17 **Manowar**
10 Records 1984

18 **Fight Breast Cancer**
Giro 2003

21 23-28 **Transient Records**
Transient 2000

22 **Speakeasy**
John Brown Publishing 1990

29 **Packjammed with the Party Posse**
A+M/Breakout 1987

31 **Stylorouge Fish**
Stylorouge 1999

21

22

23

24

25

26

27

28

29

30

31

32

33

34

35

T-shirts, this page

1 **Keep Gotham Tidy**
2 **Keep Metropolis Tidy**
Device 2009

3 **Quantum and Woody: The Goat**
6 **X-O Manowar**
Valiant Entertainment 2013

15 **Revolver**
13 **Crisis**
Fleetway 1988

4 **Fantastic Lesbian**
5 **Better Things**
MacCab Films 2010

7 **Creamy**
Million Dollar 1994

8 **Vital**
Vital for Children 2015

9 **Bizarre**
Bizarre Magazine 2006

10 **All Design is Digital**
Timing Zero/PIE Books (Japan)
1998

11 **Goatsucker**
Fortean Times magazine 2001

12 **Murder One**
Murder One
1987

14 **Bad Boys Inc.**
A+M Records 1993

Illustrators
Book Palace Books
Proposed magazine masthead
2011

Published by **The Book Palace**, **Illustrators** magazine is a quarterly featuring interviews with contemporary artists and historical career overviews. My logo designs were loose and expressive, suggesting the more traditional tools of the illustrator's trade. I also designed a set of covers to show how it might work in situ. None of my ideas were used.

Heart Throbs
Vertigo/DC Comics
Comic book series
1999

Named after the DC title that ran from 1949 to 1972 **1**, **Heart Throbs** was a four-issue Vertigo mini-series that put a modern twist on traditional love story tropes. I designed the logo and trade dress around Bruce Timm's art, alluding to the psychedelic heyday of romance comics. The final logo is grittier, to suggest the more contemporary content. The trade dress I designed was not used.

1

2

3

4

Transient Records
Record label
1995

Transient was a key player in the mid-'90s trance music and nightclub scene. It was founded in Ladbroke Grove, London in 1994 by Russel Coultart and Lawrence Cooke, who also released tracks under the Disco Volante name.

I designed their logo, singles bags and many of their artist and compilation CDs (which lie outside the remit of this book). Visually, the scene was a mix of psychedelic Photoshop montages and fractal computer imagery that owed much to the drug counterculture.

The logo has organic curves suggestive of a Fillmore West poster but with a much cleaner, more contemporary bent. Developed into the font Amorpheus (working title Capersville), it was released in 1995 as part of the first slew of fonts in the Device range and became intimately associated with the scene.

The orange sleeves featured a fleet of UFOs in formation **6**, printed in a dot-tint as if from a newswire blow-up. Being a dance label aimed at the DJ market, all Transient's releases were available on 12″ vinyl – sometimes pressed in purple or luminous green, though an attempt to mix both orange and purple on the one pressing to produce a marbled effect came out as an unattractive vomity mottled beige **1**. For the *Transient 3* compilation **2**, the numeral sprouts from the T like a Thai calligraphic flourish.

Some years down the line, the logo was redesigned with a harder edge as the music evolved away from its roots **18**, **19**. The swooping lines suggest movement across a plane or along a road, or, reflected above, perhaps cirrus clouds – a journey travelled. The accompanying 12″ single sleeve **7** was printed in a navy and a blue metallic (there is also a one-off in red). The font used here is Ritafurey, another Device design.

5 is for a series of reissues; **2** and **4** are for compilation albums. **3** was reserved for releases of overseas material. **11** and **8** are from an unused single bag design.

1

2

3

4

5

6

7

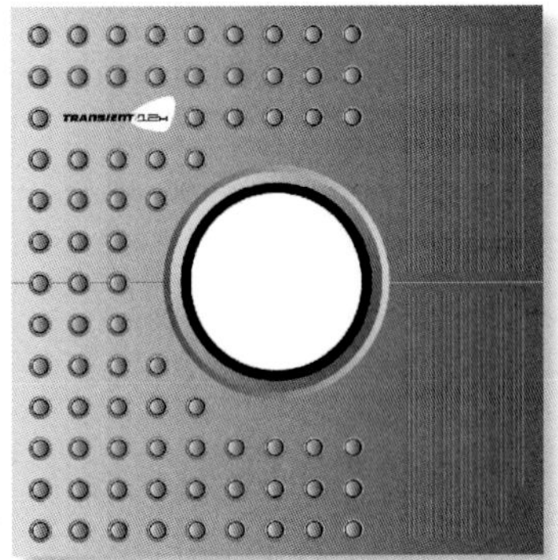

8

9

10

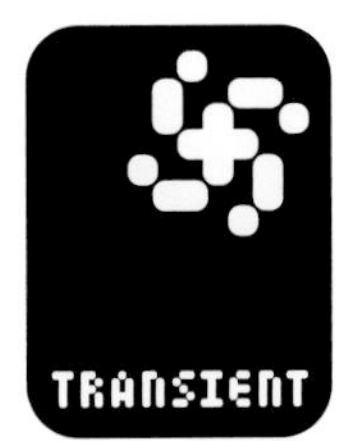

11

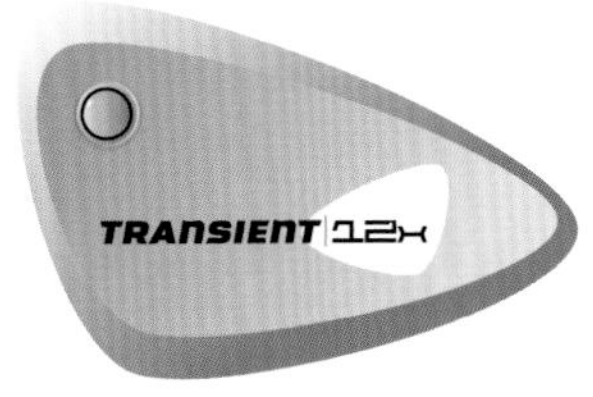

12

TRANSIENT 2
NU ENERGY AND TRANCE

13

14

15

16

17

18

19

20

We3
DC Comics
Comic book series
2004

A three-issue American comic book mini-series by Grant Morrison and Frank Quitely, **We3** tells the story of a government project to breed three prototype 'animal weapons'. Kidnapped from a nearby city, encased in robotic armour and given a limited ability to speak via skull implants, **We3** are a dog, a cat and a rabbit.

Early concepts featured 'lost pet' posters which have been placed, like a piece of evidence, in a plastic bag featuring the logo **5**. There was to be one poster for each of the animals over the three issues. The logos evoke an official governmental or corporate branding; **1** resembles the 3M logo. I was also asked to try treating them as if they were hi-tech name tags **3**, **4**, made from the same fluid metal as the armour.

None of my designs were used, and the final logo is by Vincent Deighan (Frank), with rendering by Josh Beatman.

Superman merchandise images
DC Comics
2006

A series of **Superman** type treatments and designs for **DC Comics**' merchandise division, incorporating line drawings by Jon Bogdanove and Brett Breeding. These were provided as a set on a CD to potential licensees along with a series of repeat pattern designs, logos, borders and bullets, and these elements would be freely mixed, often with additions and deletions, as the licensee saw fit.

My variations on the classic **Superman** logo riff on perspectives and hefty 3D extrusions. It's a unique case: the **Superman** logo, unlike the **Batman** logo, has remained more or less unchanged since its inception.

The flat colours and limited palette is designed to lend itself to T-shirt silkscreening.

1

2

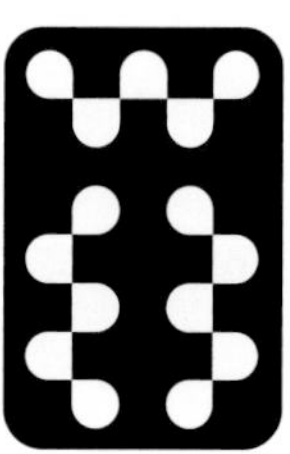

3

4

5

Edinburgh International Televison Festival
Event
1996

Medical brochure icons
Summerhouse (agency)
1997

TV Review icons
Maxim magazine
Dennis Publishing
2000

2 3 **Awards icons**
SFX Magazine
Future Publishing
2000

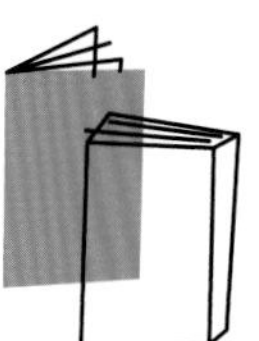
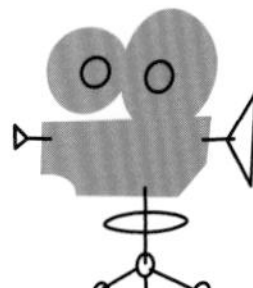

The Observer
Proposed newspaper masthead
1995

First published in 1791, **The Observer** is the world's oldest Sunday newspaper. Owned at various times by Lord Northcliffe and the Astors and employing the likes of George Orwell, since 1993 it has been part of the Guardian Media Group, which also publishes *The Guardian* daily paper. It has a politically left-leaning viewpoint.

Rick Gadsby at *The Guardian* approached several designers to submit ideas for a redesign of the masthead. I was sent a photocopy of the cover of the very first issue **1**, in which the all-seeing eye keenly observes the world's events.

My designs focussed on reimagining this eye, and ran the gamut from a tightly spaced serif to a thin geometric sans.

None were chosen.

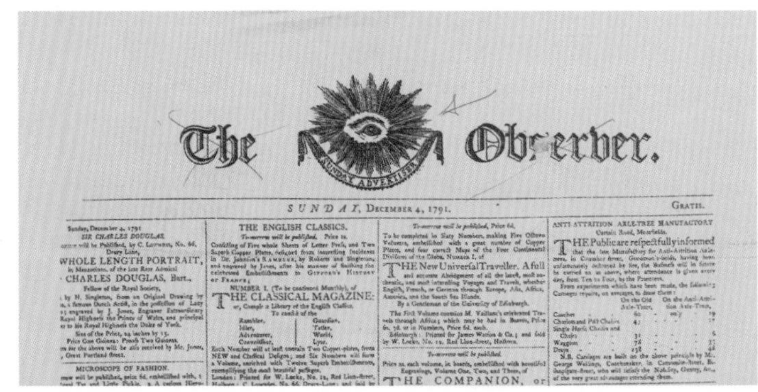

The Observer.

SUNDAY ADVERTISER

SUNDAY, December 4, 1791. GRATIS.

Sunday, December 4, 1791

SIR CHARLES DOUGLAS.

WHOLE LENGTH PORTRAIT,

CHARLES DOUGLAS, Bart.,

Fellow of the Royal Society,

Size of the Print, 24 inches by 15.

MICROSCOPE OF FASHION.

THE ENGLISH CLASSICS.

To-morrow will be published.

NUMBER I. (To be continued Monthly), of

THE CLASSICAL MAGAZINE:

or, Compleat Library of the English Classics.

To consist of the

Rambler,	Guardian,
Idler,	Tatler,
Adventurer,	World,
Connoisseur,	Lyar.

To-morrow will be published, Price 6d.

THE New Universal Traveller. A full and accurate Abridgement of all the latest, most authentic, and most interesting Voyages and Travels, whether English, French, or German through Europe, Asia, Africa, America, and the South Sea Islands.

By a Gentleman of the University of Edinburgh.

To-morrow will be published.

THE COMPANION, or

ANTI-ATTRITION AXLE-TREE MANUFACTORY

THE Public are respectfully informed

1

2

3

4

5

6

7

8

9

10

11

12

OBSERVER

13

Observer

14

15

16

Observer

17

Observer

18

19

OBSERVER

20

Million Dollar
T-shirt motif
1993

Million Dollar was a clothing brand and retail store on London's King's Road specialising in streetwear and clubbing gear. I designed numerous shirts for them, often coming up with the slogans myself.

Each was printed on a variety of different coloured shirts, including some brightly striped varieties. The designs shown here send up an aspirational materialism suggested by the label's name – wedges of notes, crowns and gold rings engraved with dollar signs.

I very much doubt that any actual millionaires wore them.

1

2

3

4

5

X-Force/Cable: Messiah War
Marvel Comics
Comic book story arc
2009

Messiah War was a crossover story running through two comic book series, **Cable** and **X-Force**, and also included an introductory one-shot titled **X-Force/ Cable: Messiah War**.

This somewhat confusing plethora of titles, each of which needed a similar logo that branded it as part of the story but still emphasised the title of the comic itself, made for an interesting design challenge.

The solution was to create an almost modular design **5**, **6**, **7**, **8** where different elements could be enlarged or reduced (or dropped altogether) to give the needed emphasis. The typeface is a Device font called Dukane, based on type taken from scuffed microfiche 'lead-ins' unearthed during research in the New York Public Library.

As sometimes happens with the logos I design for **Marvel**, it was repurposed several times in-house for other series with differing degrees of sensitivity. Stripped of the strapline and given a drop shadow (and occasionally a graduated fill), it became the regular **X-Force** logo.

1

2

JOE WRITER FRED ARTIST
MESSIAH WAR
CHAPTER 1

3

4

5

6

MESSIAH
WAR
CABLE

7

8

MacUser Awards
MacUser magazine
Dennis Publishing
1995

A graphic rendering of Maxine, the *MacUser* magazine mascot, who is based on Maria, the *Maschinenmensch* (machine-human) from Fritz Lang's 1927 science fiction movie *Metropolis*.

A much simplified version was used for small sizes. The icons were later developed into a custom font called **MacDings**, which included the mouse ratings icon.

1

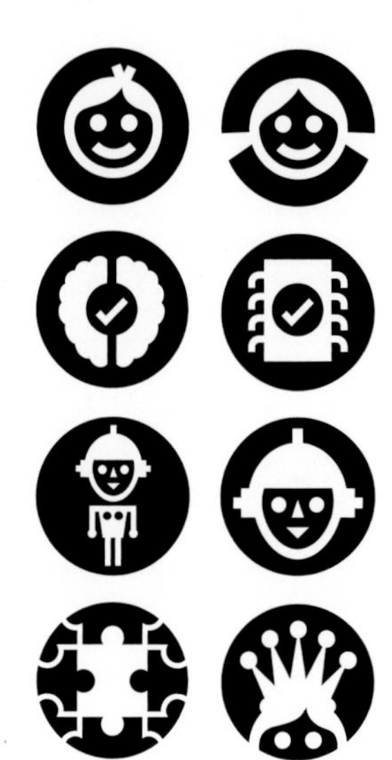

2

3

Pure FM
Radio station
Proposed logo
1997

The station's main focus was to be dance and club music, hence the reference to drug packaging and pills in **1**. Unsurprisingly this did not make it through the first round.

The final proposal (main image) featured three spotlights in a darkened space, converging at the centre to give a pure white light, perhaps on a stage or dancefloor. **5** and **6** show how one iteration of this idea might be developed for advertisements or promotions. The font is a customised version of Franz Heigemeir's Modula, designed in 1972.

1

2

3

4

5

purebrilliancefm

6

pureexcellencefm

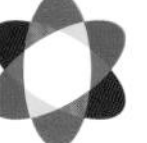

puremadnessfm

Hot Rod
Device Fonts/DGV
Symbol font
2001

Hot Rod is a set of decals inspired by the livery on vintage Matchbox toy cars. The font was made available on a CD mounted in the back of *Art, Commercial*, the retrospective book published in 2001 that collected much of my illustration and design work up to that point.

Chris Foss
Titan Books
Book cover
2011

For the cover of **Chris Foss**' monograph *Hardware*, which I researched and edited, I created a logo that mimics the artist's trademark battered spaceship livery.

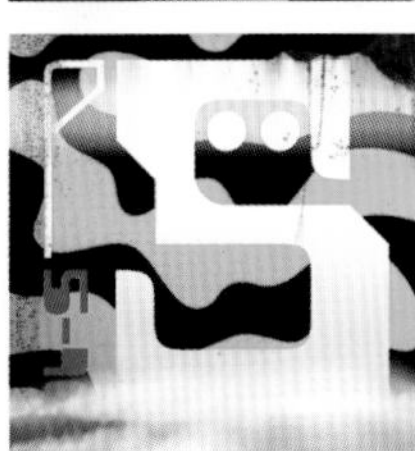

Mad Max
DC Comics
Incidental logo
2016

Part of my double-page illustration commissioned by **DC Comics** for their *Mad Max Fury Road: Artists Inspired* book.

Just Go
Maria Cabardo
Travel clothing
2014

Just Go is a range of travel clothing designed to pack into a small space for easy portability. The elements can be combined in different ways to create a variety of outfits.

I Singe the Body Electric
Fleetway
Judge Dredd Megazine story
1991

A **Judge Dredd** tale written by Alan Grant with art by Dean Ormston; this is a vintage PMT copy of the original Rubylith logo.

Mathengine
Mathengine Game Physics
Computer game resource
1998

Mathengine is a development tool designed for the PlayStation to provide natural behaviour and complex, physics-based interactive simulations. The company has offices in Oxford, San Francisco, Montreal, Chennai, Helsinki and Tokyo.

Some of the logos explore the interaction between hard and soft objects, the 'M' casting a shadow 'E'; others the notation used to denote the physical elements. I came up with the tagline, which is a pun on Einstein's famous quote in which he expressed his distaste for the uncertainties of quantum mechanics: "God does not play dice with the Universe".

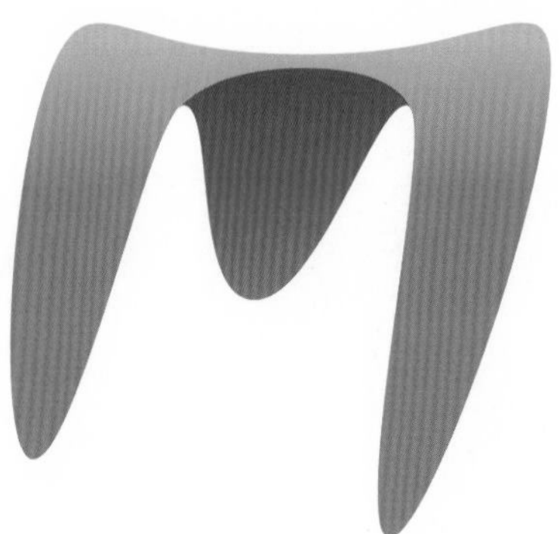

"BE GOD. PLAY DICE."
MATHENGINE
GAMEPHYSICS

1

2

3

4

5

6

7

8

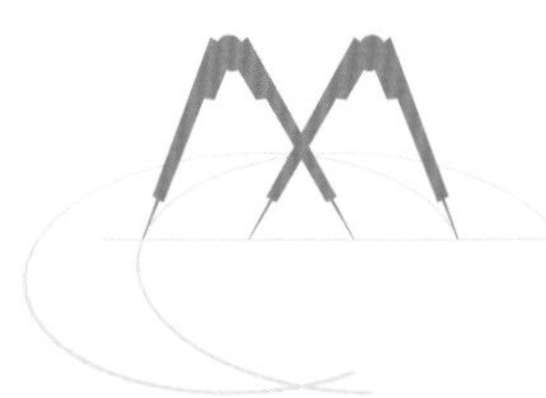

Flaming Pie
Stylorouge
Album logo proposal
1997

Designed for Paul McCartney's tenth solo studio album **Flaming Pie**, under the art direction of Stylorouge's Rob O'Connor.

The title is a reference to a story John Lennon told in an interview in *Mersey Beat* magazine in 1961 when asked about the origin of The Beatles' name: "It came in a vision – a man appeared on a flaming pie and said unto them, 'from this day on you are Beatles with an A.'"

The final album cover is a more atmospheric photographic affair.

The Unseen Hand
DC Comics
Comic book mini-series
1996

Part of Vertigo's short-lived Vertigo Vérité line, this tale of secret political elites was written by Terry LaBan with pencils by Ed Hillyer and covers by the Spanish clear-line master Daniel Torres.

1

2

3

4

Ratings icons
The Net magazine
Future Publishing
1995

Department icons
The Net magazine
Future Publishing
1995

Review icons
The Net magazine
Future Publishing
1996

Specification icons
What Car magazine
Haymarket Consumer Media
2003

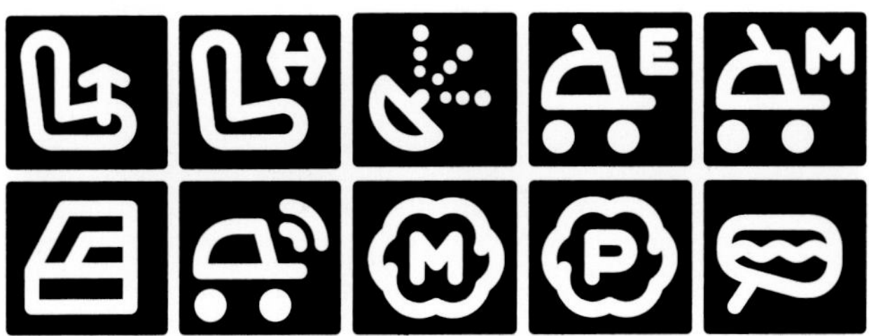

Dancemusic.com
Transient Records
Website
2000

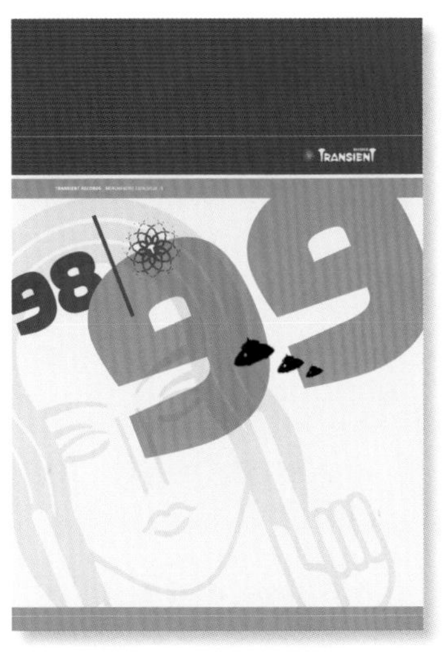

1

Dancemusic.com was **Transient Records** founders Russel Coultart and Lawrence Cooke's online retail store, through which they sold records from their own and others' labels. The site did not sell digital downloads, but catered to the club fraternity where vinyl, especially the 12″ single, was the format of choice.

The final logo features a DJ in headphones slapping a 12″ onto the turntable. Other ideas explored the shapes records make when they are pulled out of a DJ's record box and propped at an angle, ready to play. **8** features a modular robot with a record for a head. The project metamorphosed into Recordstore.com.

1-3 are the covers of the catalogues, which were printed items with a form at the back that you filled in and posted. At the time, easy and secure online ordering was still in its infancy.

2

3

4

5

DANCEMUSIC
.COM

6

7

8

9

10

11

12

13

14

15

Middle Class Hero
Device
T-shirt motif
2007

A riposte to John Lennon's *Working Class Hero*, this Device T-shirt range celebrated twee suburban middle-class stereotypes: tea **1**, embroidery samplers **3**, faux historical ornate borders **1**, **4**, and the manner in which British house names are written in brass type screwed to a log that has been sawn at an oblique angle. Bourgeois pride!

1

2

3

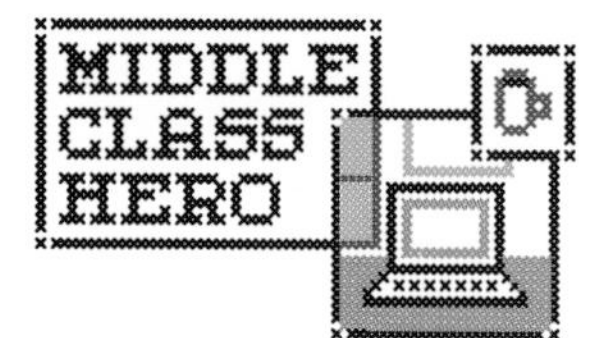

4

High Profile
Tribal
Hackney Council recruitment advertisements
2006

Nuclear families, trees and friendly animals – Hackney, an inner-city London borough, is not renowned for these things. For realism, I also snuck in a cannabis leaf and a cockroach, but they were spotted and removed.

The green 'H' is based on Hackney Council's existing logo.

1

2

3

SJ
Deep Need
Recording artist
1998

2020 Visions
DC Comics/Vertigo
Comic book series
1997

An anthology title, **2020 Visions** featured four tales set in the year 2020 and showcased mainly British talent: Jamie Delano was the writer, with Frank Quitely on the first story arc, Warren Pleece on the second, James Romberger on the third and Steve Pugh on the last.

The shrinking numbers suggest both an eye chart and the act of looking into the (now not-so-distant) future. The logo provided a 'lock up' that included the credits in the space top left.

Batman: Joker's Apprentice
DC Comics
Comic book
1999

A pretty gruesome tale by C. J. Henderson, Trevor von Eeden and Joe Rubinstein in which the **Joker** trains an apprentice to flush **Batman** out into the open.

My favoured solutions **2**, **3** reflected this gritty, frenetic atmosphere, although the chosen iteration (main image) is a much cleaner, slightly Gothic affair. The apostrophe is sometimes missed. The Batman silhouette from **2** has been repurposed from an unused **Tangent** idea. **4** was used for **I, Joker**.

1

2

3

4

1

2

3

4

Convex
Convex Records
Record label
Proposed logo
1997

Convex, a dance music label, was a stablemate of **Metropolitan** and **Shift**.

Logo concepts drew on lenses and the focussing of light, and packaging care symbols that show records being transported on trolleys. As far as I'm aware, there were no releases.

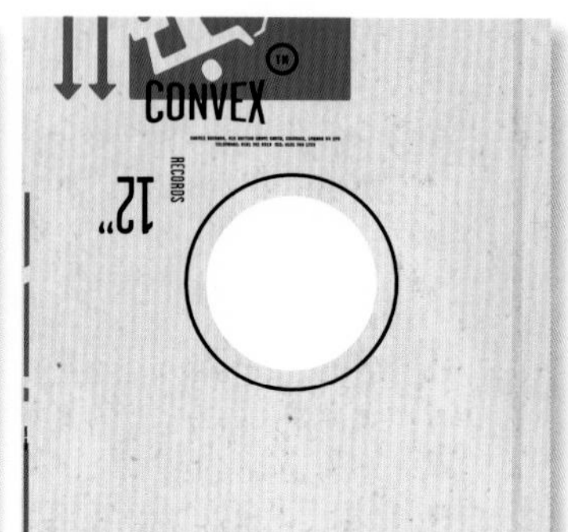

1

2

3

4

5

6

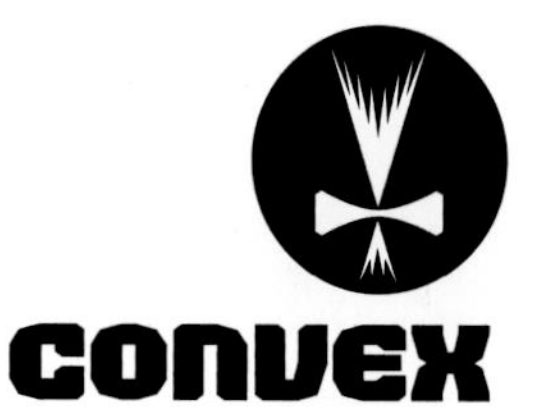

7

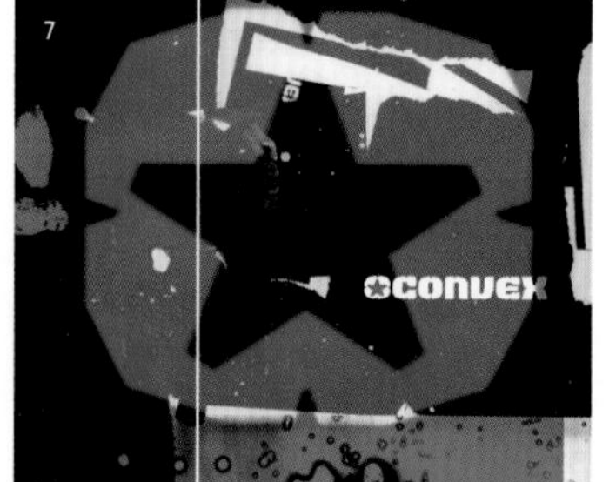

8

convex

Eve Records
Eve Nova
Record label
1996/1998

Trance label **Eve**, for which I designed many singles and albums, released much of Pablo Gargano's best work – he was fond of his trademark JV1080 pizzicato riffs and *Akira* soundtrack samples.

They kept their existing rounded **Eve** logo, but I augmented it with variations wherever I could – on the label **8**, on slipmats and on the 12″ sleeves. The definitive version is a DJ holding a sleeve and a record. Pablo nicknamed him Johnny, though I can't recall why. He was always printed in a metallic blue, which became **Eve**'s 'corporate' colour. **5** was a T-shirt design. The rounded font is Contour, one of my early Device designs.

Eve Nova 1 was a sub-label, launched in 1998. For these releases, the metallic blue was replaced by a metallic burgundy.

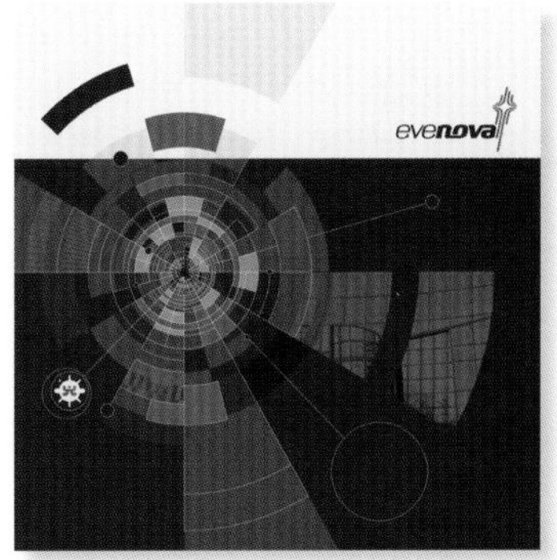

1

evenova

2

3

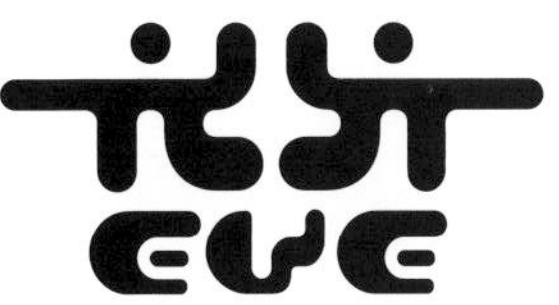

4

5

6

7

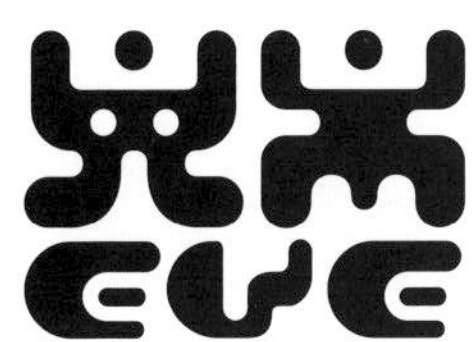

8

67
Martin Conaghan
T-shirt motifs
2006

During Celtic Football Club's 1966-67 season they won every competition they entered: the Scottish League, the Scottish Cup, the Scottish League Cup, the Glasgow Cup, and the European Cup. This range of T-shirts celebrated that miraculous year.

1

2

3

4

5

6

7

8

Good not God
Device
T-shirt
2006

Good not God is a slogan that emphasises the positive aspects of non-belief, and was designed as a counterbalance to the way religion positions itself as the arbiter of morality.

I adjusted the 'G's after I realised that the counters of the 'G', 'O' and 'D's made an inverted crucifix. Beware the unintended meaning!

The shirts are available In black and white, because that's how it is.

1

Millennium Bug
The Quentin Bell Organisation
Government public campaign
1999

These are the original concepts for the **Millennium Bug**, a UK government-funded campaign to warn the public of the global computer meltdown that would ensue when the year 2000 rolled around. In the end, of course, we all survived.

My designs were produced for the Quentin Bell Organisation, and there my involvement ended. The final **Millennium Bug**, credited to design company Smith and Milton, was used extensively in advertising, leaflets and TV commercials, for which they won several industry awards. It bears an uncanny resemblance to these designs. Convergent evolution, perhaps?

I'm reminded of a *Marketing Week* Awards dinner during which I saw two shortlisted entries, one of which reused (i. e. stole) illustrations I had done for a set of greetings cards, the other the symbols for an **Orange** brochure (included in this volume) without credit or blushing. And then there's my **Newquay Steam** type treatment, for which the agency's in-house typographer claimed a *Campaign* Press Awards Silver. When I pointed this out, a director at the agency called to tell me that "word would get around if I made a fuss". I ignored this veiled threat; *Campaign* had already offered to print a retraction, and ran a short feature on me in the next issue as recompense. Having sat as a D&AD judge, I sadly saw this kind of appropriation happening up close. It dented my belief in awards, which now seem more like a back-slapping exercise than a recognition of creativity.

1

2

3

4

5

6

7

8

The Book Palace
Book and comic wholesalers and retailers
Proposed logo
2008

The Book Palace is based in South London's Crystal Palace, near the famous TV mast. They have an extensive stock of obscure magazines and comics. Geoff West, the proprietor, kindly let me rummage in the vaults for material for my *Custom Lettering of the '40s and '50s/'60s and '70s* books.

A logo that featured the mast motif **1-3** was the first point of departure. Other ideas use palaces built from real books, which I set up and photographed – never dismiss a literal interpretation if it leads to interesting results. The silhouette was a particular favourite; the coloured versions tend to suggest a juvenile slant. Even though **The Book Palace** does deal in vintage children's comics, it was felt that their remit was much broader.

5 is a lazy cliché.

1

2

3

4

5

6

7

8

1 **Device Apparel**
Device
T-shirt label
2008

2 **Hit Mix '88**
Mainartery
Record sleeve
Incidental logo
1988

3 **Large Loader**
Device
T-shirt motif
2012

4 **Video Browser**
Video display unit
1986

5 **The Dead Set**
Lakesville
Heavy metal band/comic series
2007

6 **AIV**
AIV Limited
Proposed logo based on ATV logo
2000

7 **Ritual of the Savage**
Hungry Eye Books
Book cover
2015
Author: Jay Strongman

8 **Hello 2000**
Idée Fixe
Greetings card branding
1999

9 **B-Movie**
Goldfish Groupies
Board game
c1986

10 **Cupid**
UF6
Online dating app
2007

11 **Kingfisher**
Pan Macmillan
Book imprint
2010

12 **General Kane**
Mainartery
12″ and 7″ record sleeve
1986

1

2

3

4

5

6

7

8

9

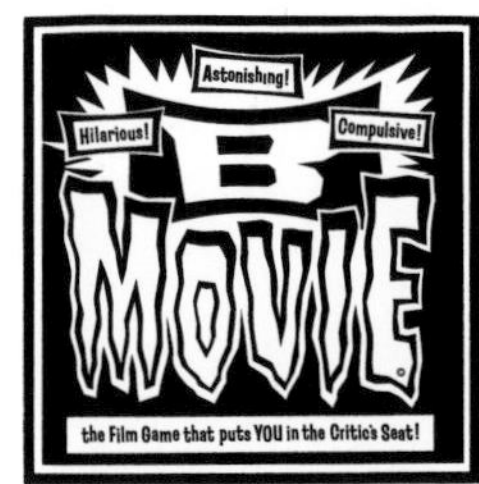

10

11

12

Autofont
Top Gear magazine
Advertising section headers
1997

Spun out of the popular TV show, *Top Gear* is the UK's best-selling car magazine. These icons were commissioned for the extensive review section and for the used car classifieds.

The categories – hatchback, 4x4, family saloon, etc. – were supplemented with the addition of other wheeled vehicles for release as Autofont, part of the Device Fonts range. Among others, I added a double-decker bus, a steamroller, a pick-up truck and a skateboarder. I also included a selection of interchangeable speedlines, puffs of exhaust smoke and traffic cones.

rinter's Devil
ontShop
-shirt motif
994

FontShop, the first reseller of digital fonts, was founded in Berlin in 1989 by Erik Spiekermann, Joan Spiekermann and Neville Brody. They published seven of my early type designs before I launched my own foundry, Device Fonts. They also run the annual Typo Berlin conference, at which I have spoken, as well as other type-centric conferences in London and San Francisco.

FontShop produced many beautiful catalogues and promotional items, including a series of 'Type Tees' for which this motif was produced..

Traditionally a 'printer's devil' refers to a print shop apprentice who performed menial tasks; they could also be blamed for typos and other mistakes.

This being the early days of digital print, many designers had a fraught relationship with printers who were still grappling with the new technology. Here, early adopters of the Mac are shown as the new digital devils working behind their screens.

The font is Contour, one of the first Device Fonts releases.

Aquaman: Sword of Atlantis
DC Comics
Comic book
2006

I have a great fondness for Ira Schnapp's **Aquaman** logo, used throughout the 1960s and 1970s, and sought to reinterpret the circular counters and curving strokes. The final version is more sharp edged and angular, as befits the **Sword of Atlantis**.

1

2

3

4

5

6

7

8

100 Bullets
DC Comics/Vertigo
Proposed logo
1999

Written by Brian Azzarello and illustrated by Eduardo Risso, **100 Bullets** is a **DC Comics** title that ran for 100 issues. It posed the question: "How far are you willing to go to seek revenge, given the means, opportunity, and 100 untraceable bullets?"

The logo was designed to complement Dave Johnson's stylishly graphic covers, using a bold drop shadow and angular stencil type. Some designs **1**, **2**, **3**, **4** evoked the 1960s and 1970s movie posters that Dave's art was inspired by.

Though I went through many iterations, in the end I think one of Dave's own logo designs was used. As an illustrator myself, I'd probably have made the same decision.

1

2

3

4

5

6

7

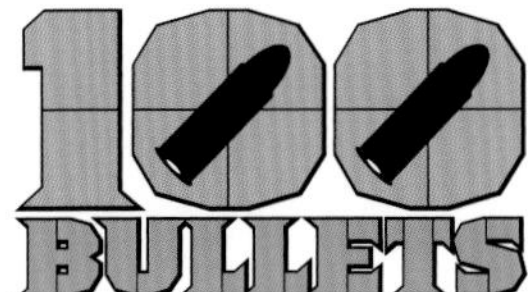

8

9

10

11

12

13

14

15

16

Our Fighting Forces
DC Comics
Proposed logo
1999

Our Fighting Forces and **Mystery in Space** were two trade collections from a projected series called **Pulp Fiction Library,** inaugurated to reprint some of **DC Comics'** classic war and SF stories.

1

2

3

4

Mystery in Space
DC Comics
1999

Mystery in Space, like **Our Fighting Forces,** was a **DC Comics** title that ran throughout the 1950s and 1960s, the former continuing with a short-lived 1980s revival I vividly remember buying.

Both titles were to be part of the planned **Pulp Fiction Library** series of reprint anthologies, but only one **Mystery in Space** volume was released. Both of the logos evoke the period of the original comics, but without direct pastiche.

Art director Amie Brockway entered it into the York Art Director's Club 79th Annual Awards and it earned a 'merit', which I presume is like a bronze star.

1

2

3

4

Challengers of the Unknown
DC Comics
Comic book mini-series
2004

A kind of proto-**Fantastic Four**, the **Challengers of the Unknown** debuted in **DC Comics**' *Showcase* #6 in 1957 in an uncredited story drawn by Jack Kirby.

For Howard Chaykin's 2004 six-issue mini-series, a new Challengers team becomes embroiled in the modern world of shadowy power politics – "the usual Chaykin mix of paranoia, geopolitics, fear and innuendo".

From the outset Howard wanted me to direct the design, rather than handing me a finished drawing that I'd then work around. Having been a fan of his stylised and stylish work since *American Flagg!*, I was more than happy to oblige.

The most conceptually sound and graphically cohesive comic covers come about when the entire package is conceived as a whole – right down to the smallest line of type – rather than the logo and art being created in isolation and then brought together.

From Howard's full-length character studies I created five silhouettes. I then arranged them for each issue, pushing the featured character to the fore and the supporting characters into the background. Each character has an icon on his or her costume that I used as a small repeat pattern. For the sixth issue, the three survivors come together in equal billing, with silhouettes replacing the two that don't make it through the story alive.

I used a very tight crop – so tight we cut off the characters' faces, which I hope suggested the undercover, black ops incognito slant to the story. As with many series where I've taken a strong design aesthetic across several issues, I differentiated them with colour, the last being a funereal black. I was apprehensive that my drastic interventions to Howard's drawings might be a step too far, but he loved the result.

The trade paperback collection, designed in-house, uses my logo but is otherwise different. A version of the lettering was released as the Device font Data 90.

HOWARD CHAYKIN
CHALLENGERS
OF THE UNKNOWN
WITH MICHELLE MADSEN

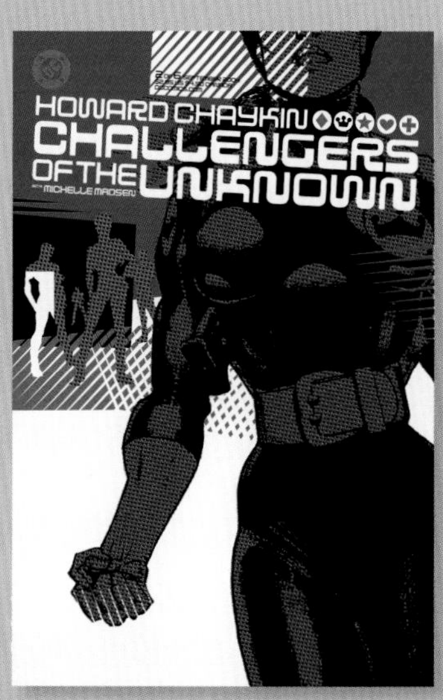

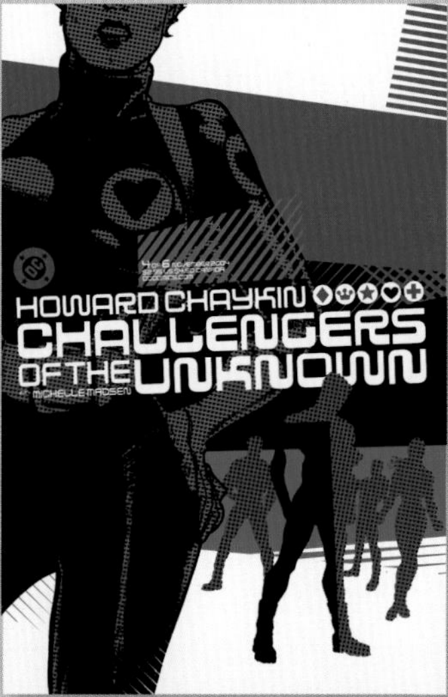

1

2

3

4

5

6

7

8

9

10

11

12

13

14

15

16

The Flash: Rebirth
DC Comics
Comic book series
Proposed logo
2009

The Flash: Rebirth was a six-issue limited series by Geoff Johns and Ethan Van Sciver that returned the Silver Age iteration of the character, Barry Allen, to DC continuity after the events of Grant Morrison's *Final Crisis*.

I was asked to keep closely to the original **Flash** logos, especially Ira Schnapp's version which was used on the long Silver Age run. Some of my designs **1, 2, 14, 15** reference the bold and chunky square capitals and the speedlines, others the lightning **10** and a very early script logo.

I updated the 1960s iteration by rationalising the inconsistent thicknesses of the letter strokes, incorporating the 'The' as neatly as I could, and keeping the unusual 'e' that references the classic Carmine Infantino era. Though something of a comic book cliché, adding a perspective to the logo does impart a sense of velocity, and I can't think of a character for whom this overused idea is more appropriate. I also designed a dimensional version of the lightning flash (overleaf) that I incorporated in some of the designs.

After the first round, the brief was revised to create a new logo without reference to the heritage of the character, an "all-new, 21st-century Flash logo". From this round, I think **13** has something going for it.

Sadly, none of my designs were chosen; in the end, the classic 1960s logo was used. My preferred version is the one above, which combines some of the best elements from the logo's heritage while imposing a modern rationalism.

Flash: Rebirth
DC Comics
Comic book series
2009

Explorations of **The Flash**'s chest emblem as part of the **The Flash: Rebirth** logo designs (previous page).

1

2

3

4

5

1

TRETCHIKOFF

2

3

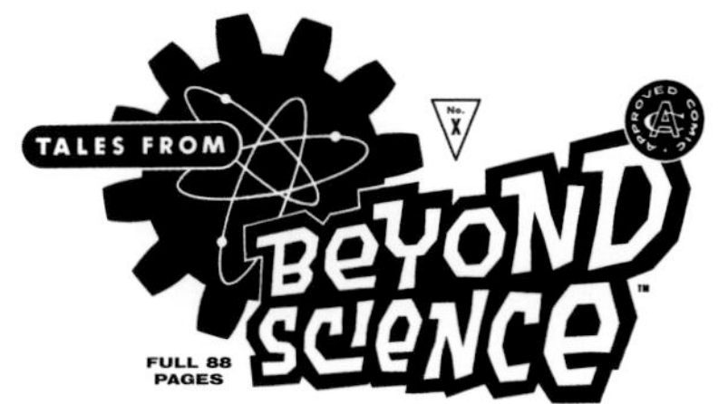

4

ANGELS UNLIMITED

5

6

7

8

9

10

1 **Tretchikoff**
Boris Gorelik
From proposed book cover
2008

2 **The Beatmasters**
Rhythm King
Band
From proposed sleeve design
1990

3 **Tales From Beyond Science**
2000AD/Fleetway
Comic book serial
1992

4 **Angels Unlimited**
HarperCollins
Book cover
2000
Author: Annie Dalton

5 **Transient Dawn**
Transient Records
Album cover
1997

6 **Atmosphere Music**
Royalty free music CDs
Incidental logo
1995

7 8 **Gotham Girls**
DC Comics
Comic book
Logo and proposed logo
2002
I also drew the cover for issue 5 **11**

9 **Hothouse**
Greenpeace
Proposed comic book
1987

10 **Igor Goldkind**
Publicity and promotions
Personal mark
1990

11

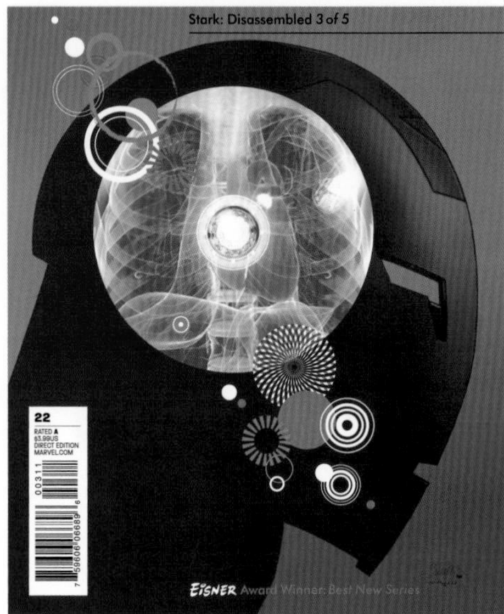

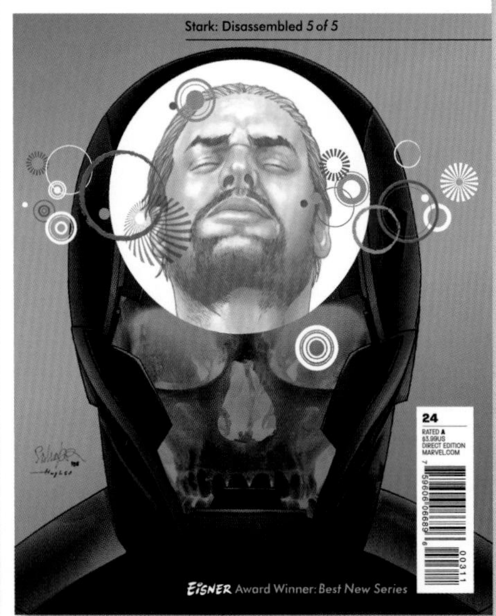

MARVEL
Matt Fraction
Salvador Larroca
Frank D'Armata
The Invincible
IRON MAN
Stark: Disassembled 4 of 5
VARIANT COVER
23
RATED A
$3.99US/CAN
DIRECT EDITION
MARVEL.COM
EISNER Award Winner: Best New Series

Iron Man
Marvel Comics
Comic book story arc
2009

1

INVINCIBLE
IRON MAN

2

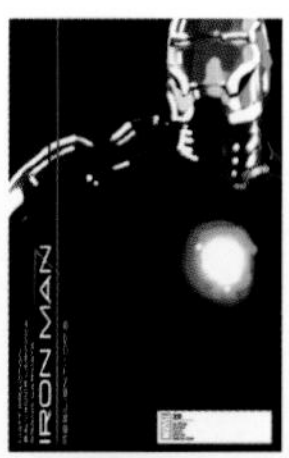

3

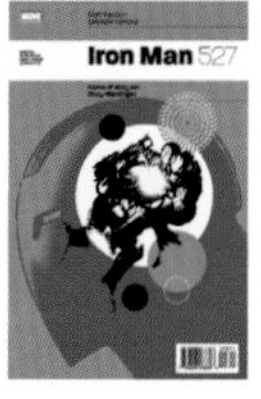

Sometimes, a 'logo' logo is not what you need. **Iron Man** writer Matt Fraction described the upcoming story arc: "Tony is deleting his brain bit by bit to destroy the data he's hidden there. He's in a vegetative state, only kept alive by machines – but he's given his associates everything they need to rebuild him. Tony Stark, lost in his own mind, embarks on a vision quest to reconnect with his true purpose. Meanwhile, in the real world, the bad guys close in."

Matt had not been too enamoured of the previous arc's overly busy design, and wanted to move as far away from it as possible. He sent me a selection of vintage J. G. Ballard and *New Worlds* covers that used a limited colour palette and clean, sans type as a starting point.

To really make a break with the previous issues' logo, which had been a riot of Photoshop drop shadows and gradations, for these five issues we would go in the opposite direction – a simple, austere sans.

I produced a series of mock-ups **3** using extant examples of artist Salvador Larocca's art. The illustrations were to be free-floating (i.e. no background), simple and graphic, laid out on white or a solid colour. As this was to be a journey into inner space, I suggested we superimpose images on **Iron Man**'s helmet, alluding to his dream-states with the overlaid concentric circles. Early designs featured a large issue number.

For the final covers Matt requested I use Paul Renner's classic moderne typeface Futura instead of Paralucent, telling me he'd "run around the house ten times in triumph" if I did. So I did.

A series of covers such as this requires the close collaboration of a very able artist to take them through to completion, and Salvador delivered in spades. I sent him my mock-ups and with very little further art direction he supplied two pieces of art for each cover: the helmet and an inset image, both in greyscale. From these I then assembled the final design, adding colour, type and the other graphic elements. For the fourth issue we also produced a Deadpool variant; the circles give the impression he's drunk.

I again rationalised the large messy **Marvel** barcode box as I had on the **Captain America: Reborn** series, corralling all the usual disparate clutter of cover text into one font. (This was not used on the early variant covers that ran alongside mine, though by the last issue in the arc a loose imitation had been adopted.)

The covers were printed as a 50/50 'split run', the variants being in a standard **Marvel** style. The editor reported that the comic shops close to **Marvel**'s New York offices had sold out of my version, and only the standard variants were left on the shelves. A rare head-to-head experiment in the impact of design on sales.

The covers were featured in *Wired* and several mainstream design magazines. *Comic Book Resources* called it "design crack – so unlike anything on the shelves, and yet perfectly evocative of the character, the mood, and the story."

For Matt's next arc, I sent him some brochures for top-of-the-range supercars. This was the aesthetic I wanted to reference, and I produced three mock-ups **2** featuring a sleek new retooled **Iron Man**. With dramatic lighting, close crops, black backgrounds and extended Porsche-style type **1**, Tony Stark was now showroom fresh. Salvador again showed his versatility by perfectly capturing the mood. Brushed chrome is something of a superhero logo cliché, but in this context it seemed conceptually sound.

This design was only used on the first issue of the arc, #25; the new **Iron Man** film was about to be released, and subsequent issues returned to the usual design.

Gosh!
Comic shop
2000

Josh Palmano has run the London comic shop **Gosh!** for more than 25 years. The shop has built a reputation for stocking an eclectic range of independent and European titles and illustrated children's books, and for hosting signings by some of comics' most high-profile creators. The superhero titles are banished to the basement.

The cartouche references the shop's original location opposite the British Museum, though the shop has now moved to more spacious premises in Soho on Brewer Street. The logo font is Citrus, supported in-store by signage in Paralucent, both Device designs.

1

2

3

4

5

6

7

8

9

GOSH

10

11

12

The Mighty
DC Comics
Comic book
2000

Alpha One is America's first and only superhero. Set outside **DC Comics'** mainstream continuity, **The Mighty** was a limited series written by Peter J. Tomasi and Keith Champagne, with art by Peter Snejbjerg.

The logo borrows from a 1930s geometric industrial aesthetic, and conveys a sense of power and weight. For the final covers, just the type without the graphic rendition of Alpha One was used. The cover art is by Dave Johnston, an artist with a fine sense of design whose covers are always a gift to work with.

1

2

3

4

5

6

7

8

9

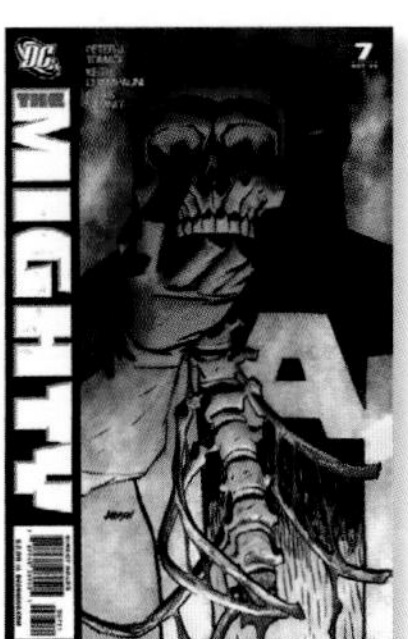

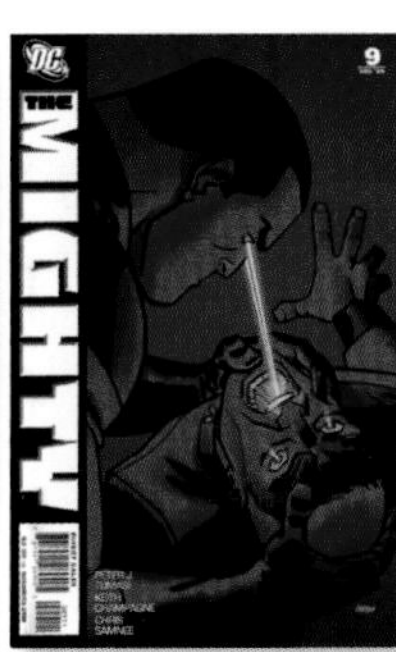

Pit Crew 2000
Fred Deakin/Airside
T-shirt motif
1999

DJ, illustrator and Lemon Jelly frontman Fred Deakin's T-shirt Club offered four designs each year from three guest designers, plus one from Fred himself. Those who signed up didn't know in advance what they'd receive.

My design draws on a memory of Bob Peak's classic *Rollerball* poster from 1975, gene-spliced with the *Death Race 2000* poster and my fascination with Matchbox Superfast toy cars. **1** appeared on the reverse of the shirt. The type is based on my Device font Bullroller.

I first met Fred when he came to show me his portfolio at the Salem Road office. He was working with Ian "Swifty" Swift, fellow Ealing resident, Gerry Anderson aficionado and co-exhibitor at 1998's Powerhouse::uk exhibition in Horse Guard's Parade. Fred's Impotent Fury club nights at 333 Old Street were a high point, with a 'Spin the Wheel' gameshow contraption dictating the next genre he would play. Where else could you dance to Motorhead, James Brown and the Carpenters in one night?

1

Fiell
Gallery and dealer in mid-century modern furniture
Shopfront and stationery
1988

Peter **Fiell** ran a showroom and gallery in London's King's Road specialising in mid-century modern furniture and contemporary art. Peter liked the Pan Am airline livery, and wanted something similarly sleek and optimistic.

The silver ellipse suggests a globe, while actually containing the Roman numeral double-x for 20; the lettering has a speedy forward slant with triangular trailing serifs. **1** is the letterhead.

Peter and his wife Charlotte subsequently wrote and edited many best-selling books on design. Many years later we would collaborate again, on the *Lifestyle Illustration, Custom Lettering* and *Cult-ure: Ideas Can Be Dangerous* books.

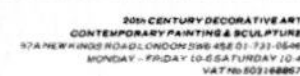

1

The Famous Five
Hachette Children's Books
Book series
2016

Enid Blyton's **The Famous Five** series is a perennial bestseller that chronicles the adventures of Julian, Dick, Anne, Georgina (George) and their dog Timmy throughout 21 books. The first, *Five on a Treasure Island*, was published in 1942 and the series has been in print ever since.

Art director Alison Padley at Hachette wanted to create two sets of covers for a reissue of the series – a vintage set and a more contemporary set designed to attract modern readers. Enid Blyton's other well-known series *The Secret Seven* was also considered during the design process to see if a similar branding would work across both. It was also suggested that the modern logo might look like an update of the vintage version, as if the brand we were creating had existed all along. Though a nice idea, this proved hard to pull off, and only one version was ultimately used.

I also cleaned up Blyton's signature **1**. The final book cover designs are by Alison, and use art from the original hardbacks.

THE FAMOUS FIVE

1

2

The Famous Five

3

4

5

6

7

Enid Blyton THE Famous Five

8

9

Enid Blyton The Famous Five

1

THE FAMOUS FIVE

2

THE FAMOUS FIVE

3

The Famous Five

4

5

6

7

8

9

10

11

Misc.
Device
Book series
2010

Impressed with the quality of the digital printing now available on the Indigo press through Blurb.com, I started **Misc.** in 2010 as an "occasional series featuring unseen design experiments, photographic essays, personal sketches, strange clippings, resampled illustrations, random doodlings, themed ephemera, visual musings, unrealised projects, curated detritus . . ."

As of 2016, there are 66 titles covering a broad range of subjects, from rayograms, Egyptian street signs, beermats and vacuum valve boxes to clip art montages, Lego tessellations and abstract Photoshop experiments.

Some of these find their way into commercial projects, but the primary object of the series is to catalogue my obsessions and inspirations.

Misc.

Wildstorm
Wildstorm
Proposed logo
2001

Originally an independent comic publisher established in 1992 in San Diego by Jim Lee, **Wildstorm**'s core titles were *WildC.A.T.S, Stormwatch, Gen13, Wetworks* and *The Authority*.

In 1999 it became an imprint of **DC Comics**, and its stable of characters were folded into the continuity of the mainstream DC Universe.

The original **Wildstorm** logo incorporated an overlapping 'W' and 'S', with a lightning strike inside the 'W' and a somewhat overcomplicated set of inlines and outlines. These were my proposals for an update, in which I dropped the 'S' and simplified the lightning inside the 'W'. I included both simpler graphic and more detailed photographic options, and a stand-alone type treatment based on the Device font Platinum that could be run vertically up the spines of the trade paperbacks.

Wildstorm also published several sub-imprints which had very different logos, including *Eye of the Storm, Signature* and *Cliffhanger,* which I suggested could be brought under a cohesive overarching identity **3**.

None were adopted.

1

2

3

4

5

6

7

8

DC Focus
DC Comics
Comic book line
2003

DC Focus was a short-lived 2003 imprint from **DC Comics** for which I designed both the logos and the trade dress. The four titles featured super-powered characters and concepts, but without the usual costumes and other genre trappings.

The **DC Focus** trade dress was designed to set the series apart from the regular DC superhero line, and so eschewed the usual language of comic covers, opting for a modular approach in which each of the logos was treated photographically. An inset panel across the top of each issue used an enlargement from the main image.

The **DC Focus** logos originally used the iris from a camera **1**; in the chosen iteration (main image) a photograph of an eye mirrors the proportions of Milton Glaser's bullet. I thought the addition of four stars, the top left one lighter than the others to suggest a highlight **4** was another nice link back to the DC logo, but the final version has just the one round highlight. The shadow underneath suggests the eye is a floating sphere.

Based on the chosen logo I designed Gravel, a font family of three weights plus italics, to be used throughout the line. Gravel was subsequently released as part of the Device Fonts range.

Steve Gerber's **Hard Time** was the most popular title, returning for a second run of seven issues under the usual **DC Comics** trade dress.

The eye belongs to fellow studio member Kim Dohm.

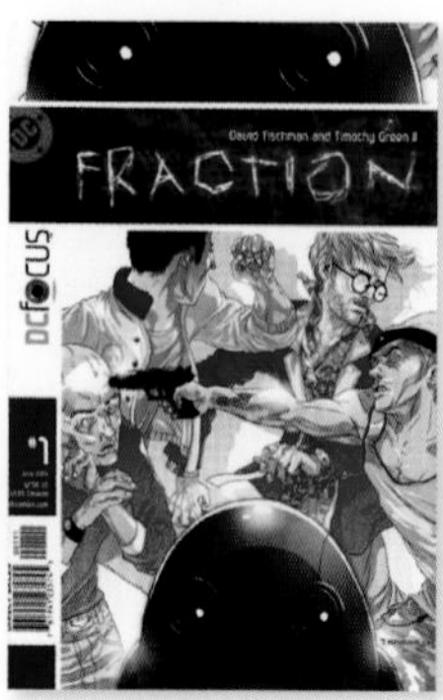

1

2

3

4

Hard Time
DC Comics
Comic book series
2003

Written by Steve Gerber and Mary Skrenes, the **DC Focus** title **Hard Time** told the story of 15-year-old Ethan Harrow, incarcerated – given **Hard Time** – for a high-school shooting in which several students lost their lives.

The logo is retouched from a scan of a fire alarm sign I have hanging in my kitchen, which seemed to have the right institutional, time-worn feel. Though logically this kind of warning sign should always be red and white, the colour was keyed to the art each issue.

1

2

3

4

Touch
DC Comics/DC Focus
Comic book series
2003

Touch by John Francis Moore, Wes Craig and Prentis Rollins explores how the less scrupulous might use a superpower to turn a profit. Cooper, the protagonist, has a mysterious tattoo on his hand which he can transfer to others, imbuing them with new abilities. Accidents are then staged, at which the 'hero' miraculously arrives just in time to save the day.

Part of the short-lived **DC Focus** line, the logo explores the hucksterish showmanship and superficiality of Las Vegas neon, tattoos and Barnum-style bill poster lettering. The final logo renders the name in lights. The transparent effect was achieved using the much-missed Kai's Vector Effects plug-in for Adobe Illustrator, though the logo used in print is a slightly simplified version **11**.

For this series I also designed the trade dress, which gave the line an identity that set it apart from DC's superhero line.

1

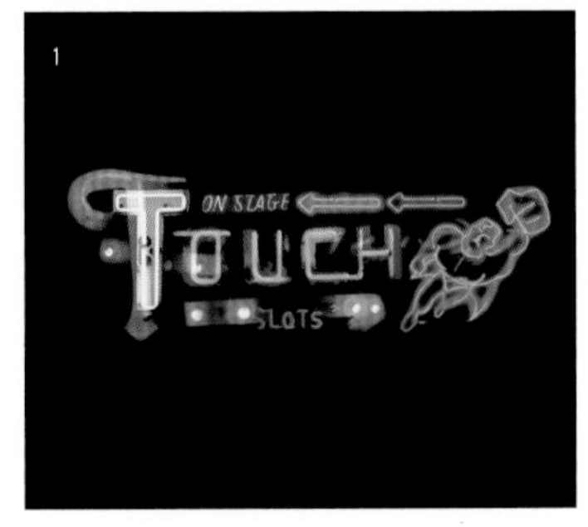

2

3

4

5

6

7

8

9

10

11

12

13

14

Kinetic
DC Comics/DC Focus
Comic book series
2003

Another title from the short-lived **DC Focus** line, **Kinetic** was described to me as "*My So Called Life* meets **Spider-Man**, if **Spider-Man** had been created today."

Created by Allan Heinberg and written by Kelley Puckett with art by Warren Pleece, the series focussed on Tom Morell, a high-school student with debilitating medical conditions who nonetheless finds he can absorb and redirect kinetic energy. Infatuated with a comic book hero named **Kinetic** (or Kenetic, in early versions of the script), Tom then sets out to emulate him.

The logos attempt to evoke this sense of fizzing kinetic energy. As with all the logos for the **DC Focus** line, I avoided clean linework and used a more photographically 'real' approach to suggest the more grounded, 'real world' nature of the stories. I supplied a variety of colourways to demonstrate how it could be keyed to the art each issue.

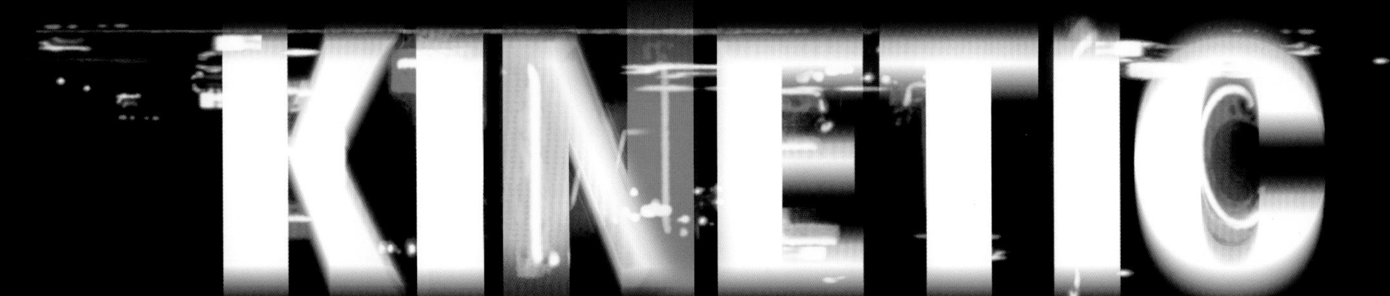

1

2

3

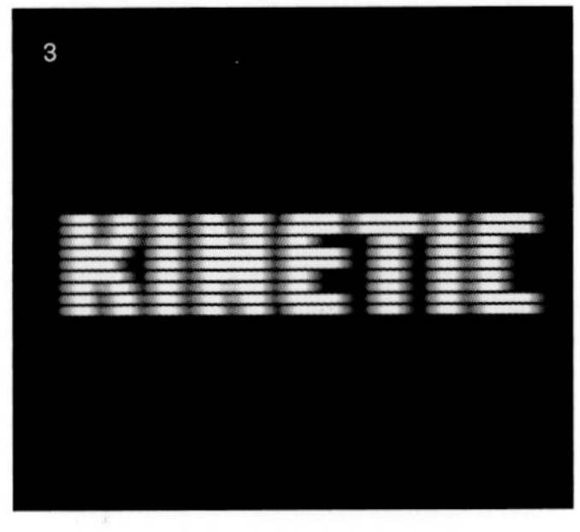

4

5

6

7

8

9

10

11

12

Fraction
DC Comics/DC Focus
Comic book series
2003

Part of the short-lived **DC Focus** line, **Fraction** by David Tischman and Timothy Green II follows four high-school friends who reunite years later to pull off a petty theft for old times' sake – and accidentally steal a powerful mechanical suit.

The logo ideas explored modular body parts, military or up-market corporate hardware branding and battle-scarred tech. The final design was scratched into a piece of board with a knife, scanned, reversed, and then further manipulated in Photoshop to lend it an electrical glow.

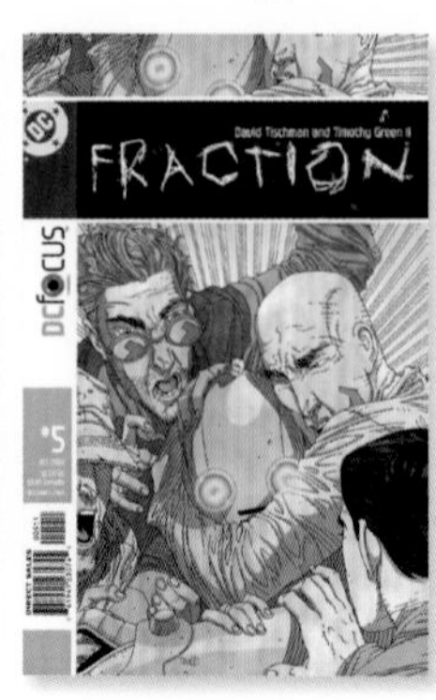

1

2

3

4

5

6

7

8

Meteoric
Internet service provider
2004

Meteoric is a specialist Internet provider whose strength is their consultancy and management services.

The logos explore spaceflight mission patches, Soviet space-age and mid-century industrial motifs.

1

2

3

4

5

6

7

METEORIC

8

Batgirl
DC Comics
Comic book series
2009

Batgirl has an illustrious career dating back to her first appearance in 1961 as the alter-ego of Betty Kane. Created by the writer/artist team of Bill Finger and Sheldon Moldoff and originally hyphenated, **Bat-Girl** was replaced in 1967 by unhyphenated **Batgirl** Barbara Gordon, daughter of Commissioner Gordon and co-star of the popular **Batman** TV show. Barbara Gordon later passed the cowl to Cassandra Cain, who put a darker spin on the character.

I was first asked to reprise the 1960s version of the logo (seen here on a Showcase collection), ideas which are explored in the first round of logos **1-3**. Though it possesses a great deal of charm, on closer examination the 'T', which is curved at the top to suggest the bat ears of the costume, is unavoidably off-centre, awkwardly necessitating two scallops on the left of the underlining cape, three in the right. Visually, this has been minimised by the italic slant.

New ideas were also explored: **4-6** incorporate a profile silhouette within a bat shape. These were considered to be too feminine. **7** evokes the Gordon era, while **9** and **10** use the classic **Batman** type with its signature reverse-stress 'A'. Here, the head is low in the cape and thus more sinister.

The design opposite was popular; however, it was felt that the bat shape should mirror the new costume, and the head might prove difficult to use in situ on the cover. A second round was requested that would better reflect Cain's less campy image.

1

2

3

4

5

6

7

8

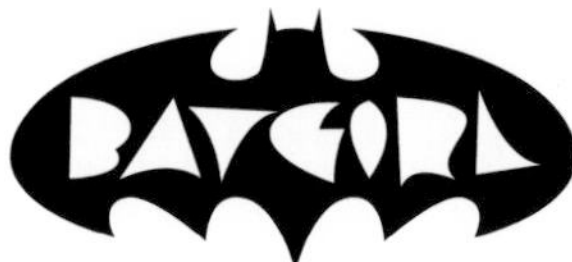

9

10

BATGIRL

Batgirl
DC Comics
Comic book series
2009

The second round of designs replaces the bat shape with a simpler face-on version without features. The more playful versions were again felt to be out of keeping with the tone of the comic; the final logo [opposite] is simpler and cleaner, with a minimum of detail on the wings.

The final layouts are by **DC Comics**' in-house team using the then-current *Batman: Reborn* trade dress. In a nice touch, the interior of the bat was often transparent to reveal the art behind.

1

2

3

4

5

6

7

8

9

10

11

12

BATGIRL

Smolhaus
Smolhaus Design + Associates
Design firm
2006

Smolhaus is a book design and publishing agency in Hoboken, New Jersey, USA. The logo takes the idea of a 'small house', and the designing and making thereof.

1

2

3

4

5

6

7

8

1 **Test**
Device
T-shirt motif
2001

2 **Approved by the Comics Code Authority**
DC Comics
Incidental logo
2013
Unofficial logo from my *Batman: Black and White* strip

3 **Elizabeth Cunliffe**
Personal mark
2003

4 **A+A** (Archer & Armstrong)
Valiant Comics
Comic book series
2015

5 **Silver Award/Gold Award**
Future Publishing
PC Format magazine
Review icons
1995

6 **Perry Como**
Mainartery
Record sleeve logo
1985

7 **Gazelle in the Woods**
Gary Harris
Clothing line
Proposed logo
2012

8 **Tik Tak Tow**
T-shirt motif
1995

9 **Tartarus**
Johnnie Christmas/Image Comics
2107
Writer: Johnnie Christmas
Artist: Jack Cole

10 **Giselle**
Proposed personal mark
2011

11 **Bad Tune Men**
Nonchalant Records
Do The Swamp
7″ single sleeve
1984

12 **The Zucchini Bros.**
T-shirt
c1986
Felt-tip pen on layout paper original

1

2

APPROVED BY THE COMICS CODE AUTHORITY
CAC

3

4

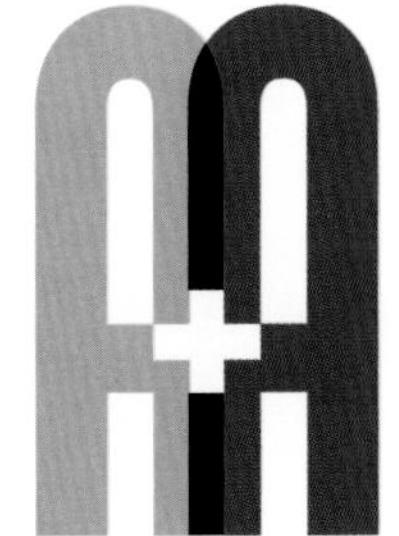

5

6

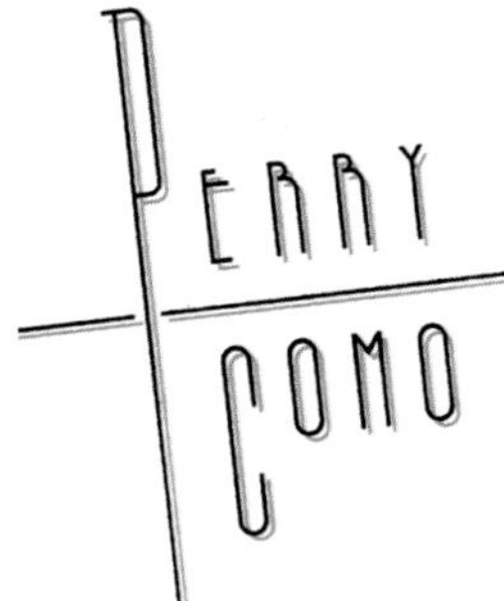

7

8

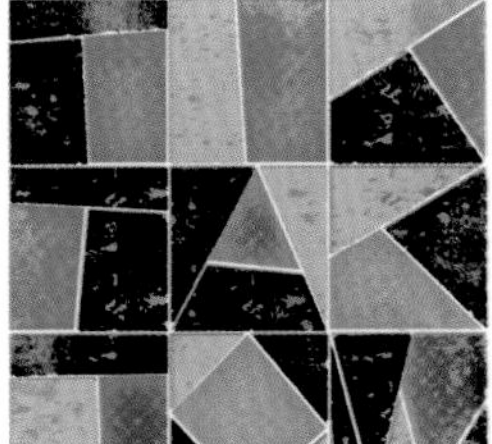

9

10

11

12

A Silent Film
The City That Sleeps
Band identity and album cover
2008

A Silent Film are an English band from Oxford consisting of Robert Stevenson on vocals, piano and guitar and Spencer Walker on drums. *The City That Sleeps* was their first album, and became a number one hit – in Portugal.

The visual language of the CD design, for which the logo was an element, was inspired by the work of architectural visualiser Hugh Ferris and his 1929 masterpiece, *The Metropolis of To-morrow*. The band were photographed dressed in utilitarian worker's garb and rendered as if they had been drawn in charcoal, then dropped into Ferris' dramatic cityscapes.

The logo draws from the cover of Ferris' book and Paul Renner's Futura Black of 1936, itself a more rational take on the lettering built from simple geometric shapes and popularised by the Italian Futurists.

1

The Next
DC Comics
Comic book series
2006

2

3

4

5

6

7

8

9

10

11

12

13

14

Quantum and Woody
Valiant Comics
Comic book series
2013

Styled as the "World's Worst Superhero Team", the original 1990s **Quantum and Woody** series lampooned the clichés of the superhero genre. The new series by James Asmus and Tom Fowler continued along the same lines, though with more emphasis on narrative and character.

The previous logo used two contrasting typefaces to illustrate the characters' different personalities, and something similar was requested for the reboot. **Quantum** is the OCD straight man – he's responsible, intense, good with money and takes everything too seriously, while sloppy and irresponsible **Woody** is the complete opposite.

The chosen logo turned out to be one of the more sober options. As with many new comics, the first issues were released with numerous variant covers. I drew one for issue 2.

A special one-shot #0 was released, **Quantum and Woody: Goat.**

1

QUANTUM AND WOODY

2

3

4

5

QUANTUM + WOODY

6

QUANTUM AND WOODY!

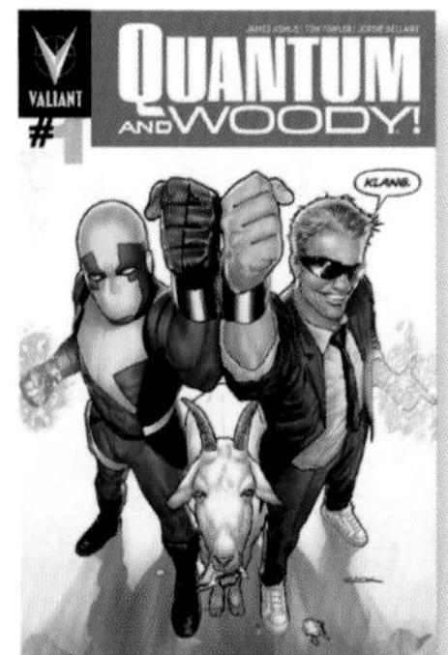

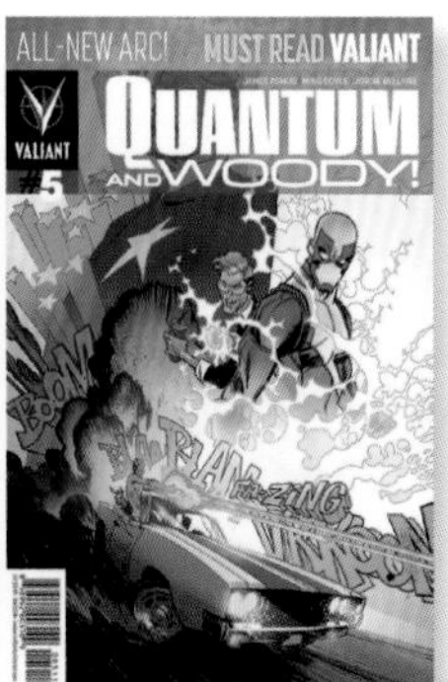

Vintage Salvation
Vintage magazine and comic shop
2009

"Saving the lost souls of pop culture", **Vintage Salvation** sells rare film posters, paperback books, comics and other collectible memorabilia from their store in Lewisville, Texas. The logo is a two-colour drawing of a female astronaut wielding a raygun.

Hepcat Events
Event promoters and organisers
Angela Diggle
2001

British comic book writer and former editor of *2000AD* Andy Diggle asked if I'd be interested in creating a logo for his wife's new venture, **Hepcat Events.**

Their target market was overworked PAs and executive assistants who struggle to organise company events. It needed to look "groovy, enticing and fun-loving" but also "reliable, dependable and trustworthy", and to work well free-floating against a white background. Andy paid me with a page of John M. Burns' **Dan Dare** comic art.

The final **Hepcat** reminds me a bit of Top Cat, in a beret and goatee.

WILDCATS Version 3.0

Wildcats Version 3.0
Wildstorm Comics
Comic book series
2002

Wild C.A.T.s first appeared in 1992 and was artist Jim Lee and writer Brandon Choi's first creator-owned comic.

Rebooted in 2002 by Joe Casey and Dustin Nguyen, **Wildcats Version 3.0** centred around Spartan's attempts to change the world not by old-fashioned superheroics but through corporate hegemony – his **Halo Corporation** sets out to develop advanced technology and clean energy with the help of veteran *Wild C.A.T.s* characters Grifter and Agent Wax.

The covers were designed to reflect this corporate theme, each of the first five featuring a leading character promoting a **Halo** product. My design incorporated a cute Babytron head **4** which was suggested by Joe.

I mocked up the first two covers using existing art by Dustin, who immediately ran with the idea and produced illustrations for the remaining covers that fitted the concept perfectly. The products I drew in Adobe Illustrator in a fully rendered style that contrasted with the flat single colour treatment of Dustin's art.

After the first arc, the design of the covers changed pretty much issue to issue, each taking their cue from Joe's stories. I responded to Dustin's varied and stylistically inventive art, and he very generously allowed me to take all manner of liberties by overlaying type and colour or by rotating and cropping.

Issue 9 is an action figure, with a kid-friendly version of the Wildcat icon **3**; issue 15 is a romance paperback. The last few issues settled into a standard layout as Joe wrapped up the final act.

My design for *Brand Building* **1**, the first of the trade paperback collections, again references the clean corporate report aesthetic and features batteries inserted into the back cover – the book itself is Halo powered. The second volume, *Full Disclosure* **2**, is a layered chaos of photocopied forms and stamps – a kind of black-and-blue bureaucratic riot.

The WS "Eye of the Storm" logo positioned top left on the covers was designed in-house.

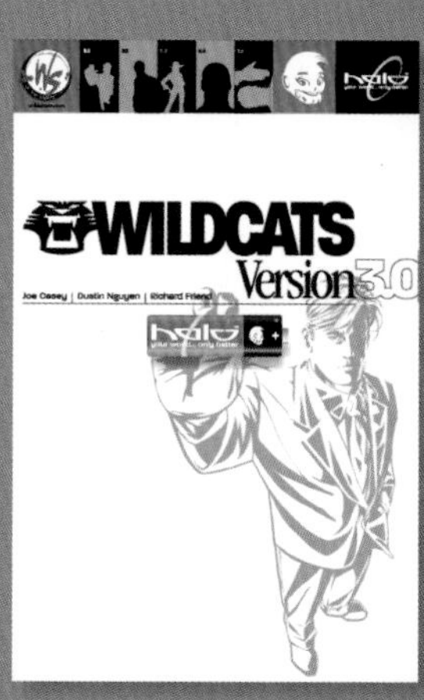

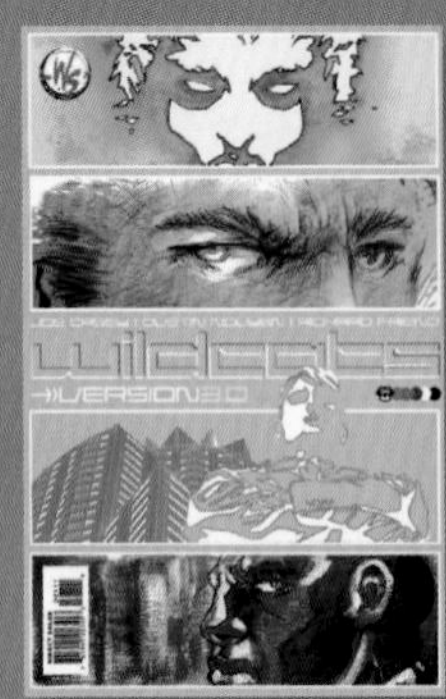
VERSION 3.0

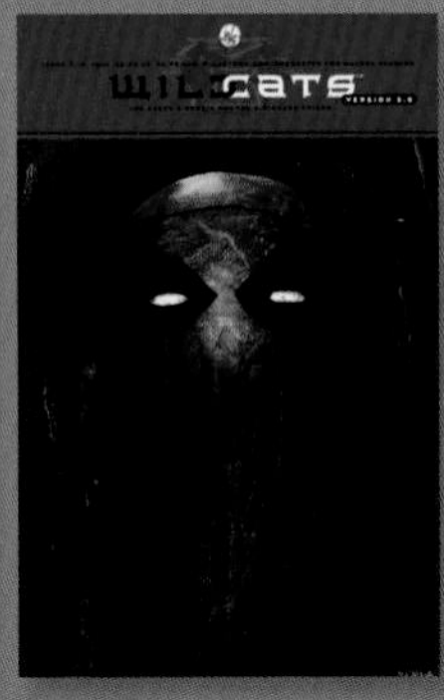

Wildcats

Wildcats

WILDCATS VERSION 3.0

WILDCATS
Version 3.0

WILDCATS
Version 3.0
CODA WAR ONE

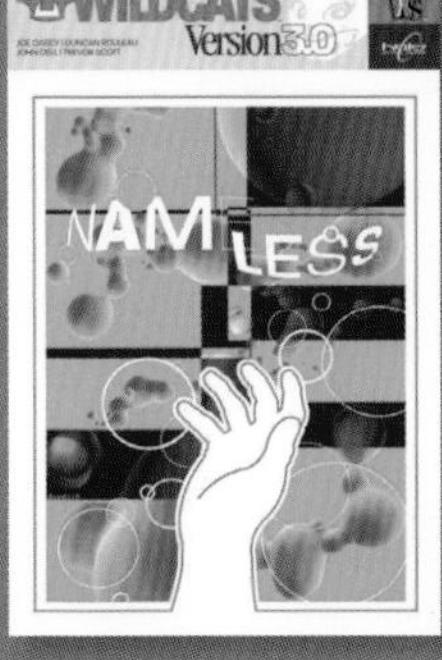
WILDCATS
Version 3.0
NAMELESS

WILDCATS
Version 3.0

WILDCATS
Version 3.0

1

Brand Building
WILDCATS
Version 3.0

Brand Building
WILDCATS
Version 3.0
Joe Casey | Dustin Nguyen | Richard Friend

2

VERSION 3.0
JOE CASEY
DUSTIN NGUYEN
RICHARD FRIEND
FULL DISCLOSURE

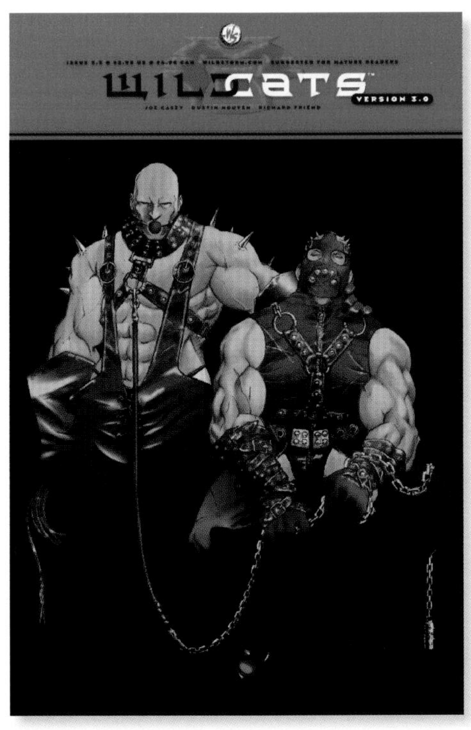
WILDCATS
VERSION 3.0
JOE CASEY · DUSTIN NGUYEN · RICHARD FRIEND

BUILD YOUR OWN GRIFTER!
ASSEMBLY REQUIRED
BATTERIES NOT INCLUDED
ISSUE 3.0 = $2.95 US = $4.65 CAN
SUGGESTED FOR MATURE READERS
WILDSTORM.COM
WILDCATS
JOE CASEY · DUSTIN NGUYEN · RICHARD FRIEND
VERSION 3.0

VERSION 3
WILDCATS
JOE CASEY
DUSTIN NGUYEN
RICHARD FRIEND

3

4

5

halo
your world... only better

6

VERSION 3.0
Wildcats

7

8

WILDCATS

Psylocke
Marvel Comics
Comic book series
2009

Captain Britain's sister and sometime **X-Man, Psylocke** has been through so many different interpretations it was difficult to know what to hang a logo on. This particular mini-series was described as "**Psylocke** does *Kill Bill* in Japan." The logo mimics the binding on the handles of Japanese swords, and ran vertically on the cover. **9** attempts to visually represent the character's telekinetic powers.

1

Psylocke

2

PSYLOCKE

3

4

PSYLOCKE

Firewords
Oxford University Press
Book cover
1999

Lettering treatment for the cover of a book of poems by authors such as Lewis Caroll and Spike Milligan who inventively play on words. I also contributed the cover design and illustrations throughout.

Armourines
Valiant Comics
Comic book series
2009

As the title suggests, the **Armourines** are a squad of armoured marines tasked by the United States government to do their dirty work in the **Valiant** universe.

The logo incorporates patriotic stars and stripes.

1 **Hewligan's Haircut**
Fleetway/2000AD
Graphic novel
1990
Writer: Peter Milligan
Artist: Jamie Hewlett
The original logo artwork, a PMT mounted on CS10 board. The cover was die-cut, the logo being printed on the title page.

2 **Opera**
Titan Books
Graphic novel
1986
Writer/artist: P. Craig Russel

3 **Chopper**
Fleetway/2000AD
1990
Writer: John Wagner
Artist: Colin MacNeil

4 5 **The Towers of Bois-Maury**
Titan Books
Graphic novel series
1985
Writer/artist: Herman Huppen

6 **True Faith**
Fleetway/2000AD
Graphic novel
1990
Writer: Garth Ennis
Artist: Warren Pleece

7 **The World of Andy Capp**
Titan Books
1990
Writer/artist: Reg Smythe and Les Lilley

8 **Troubled Souls**
9 **Few Troubles More**
Fleetway
Graphic novels
1990
Writer: Garth Ennis
Artist: John McCrea
The Northern Irish protagonists are divided by blood and religion.

10 **Sam Bronx and the Robots**
Atomic Comics/Magic Strip
Graphic novel
1989
Writer/artist: Serge Clerc

Also featured opposite:
The foil-blocked linen version of **Opera** is the limited edition hardback.
The Man from U.N.C.L.E book uses a scatter of secret files – it's a cliché, but also a loving homage. The orange version is an unused rough. The proof of Alan Moore and Oscar Zarate's *A Small Killing* exists as a very limited number of promotional copies in which the latter half of the book is blank.

1

2

3

4

5

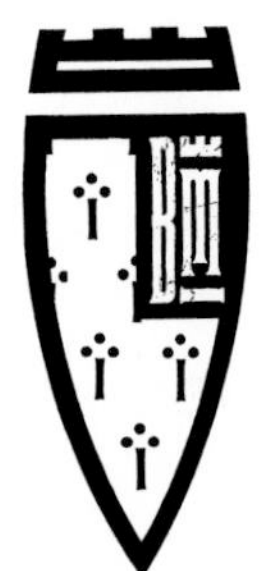

6

7

8

9

10

THE WORLD OF
ANDY CAPP

THE WORLD OF
ANDY
CAPP
Reg Smythe
WITH
LES LILLEY

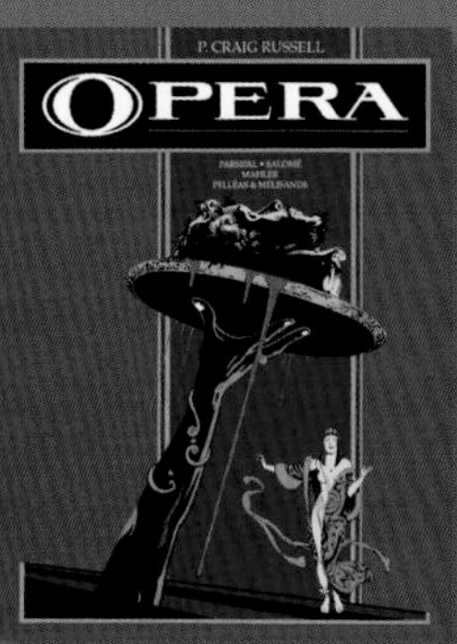
P. CRAIG RUSSELL
OPERA

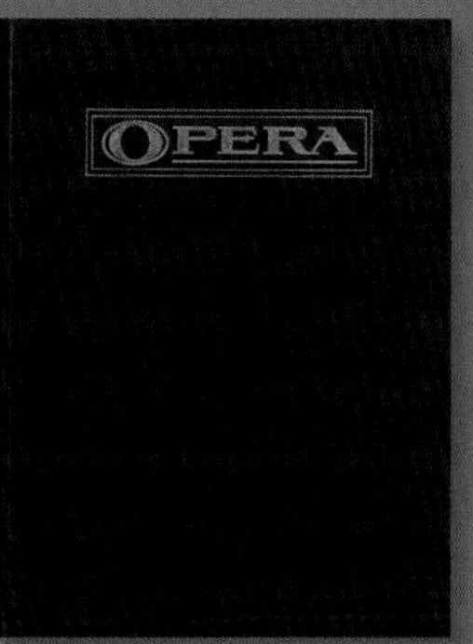
OPERA

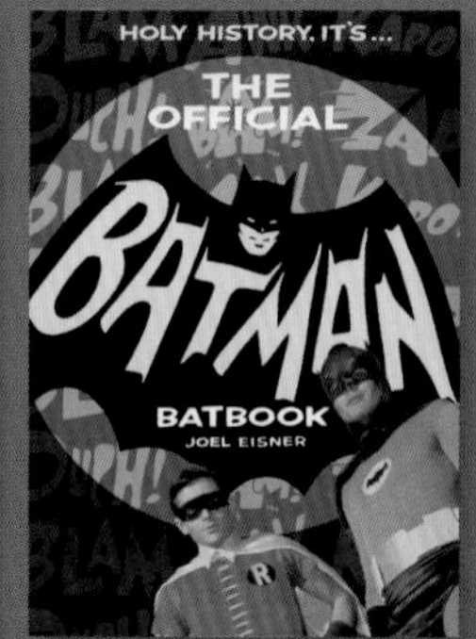
HOLY HISTORY, IT'S...
THE
OFFICIAL
BATMAN
BATBOOK
JOEL EISNER

JOHN WAGNER • COLIN MACNEIL
CHOPPER
SONG OF THE SURFER

Hermann
THE TOWERS OF
BOIS-MAURY

Hermann
THE TOWERS OF
BOIS-MAURY

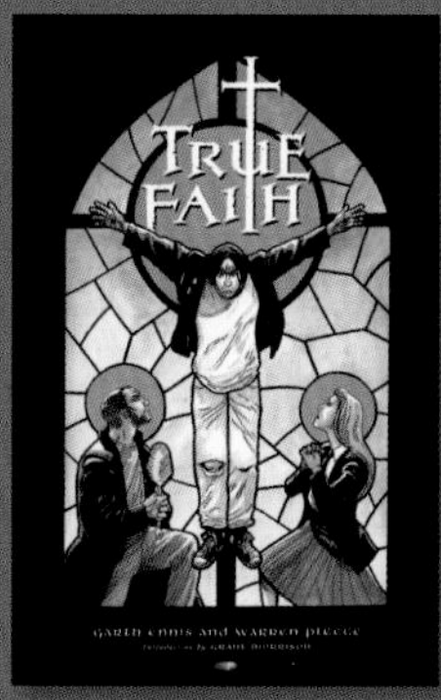
TRUE
FAITH

Hewligan's
Haircut
a story in eight partings
PETER MILLIGAN • JAMIE HEWLETT

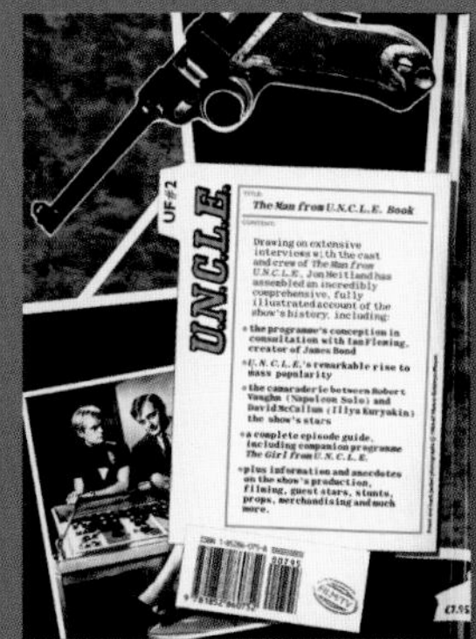
U.N.C.L.E.
The Man from U.N.C.L.E. Book

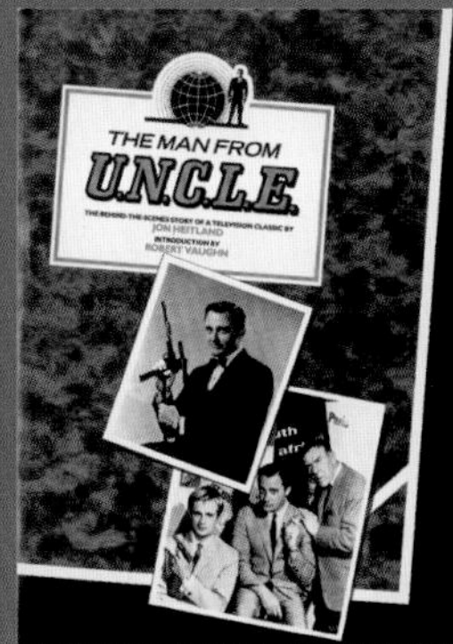
THE MAN FROM
U.N.C.L.E.
JON HEITLAND
INTRODUCTION BY
ROBERT VAUGHN

SUPERMAN
THE MAN OF TOMORROW
ALAN MOORE

ALAN MOORE OSCAR ZARATE
a small killing

THE MAN FROM
U.N.C.L.E.
JON HEITLAND
ROBERT VAUGHN

Troubled Souls

Atomic
Comics
presents
SERGE
CLERC
SAM BRONX
AND THE ROBOTS

Amato
Allan Amato
Photographer
2014

Los Angeles-based photographer Allan **Amato** specialises in powerful black and white portraiture – Nick Nolte, Terry Gilliam, Stan Lee, Al Jourgensen, Grant Morrison and ahem, Rian Hughes have all posed for him (see page 6).

I met Allan on the *Motorschiff Stubnitz,* a ship from the former East German fishing fleet. Built in 1964, it's the sole surviving vessel of its type, and now pulls into ports around Europe to be used as a floating nightclub or for corporate events. Allan was hosting a photography masterclass in its evocative industrial interior.

The logo comes in a variety of finishes which reference the ageing embossed signs attached to levers, dials and gauges throughout the ship. One was chosen for the cover; the others appear as chapter dividers throughout *Reliquary,* his sizeable monograph, which I also designed.

1

2

3

4

5

6

7

8

9

10

11

12

13

14

Xpresso
Fleetway
Comic magazine and graphic novel imprint
1991

Spun out of **Crisis** magazine, **Xpresso** was a two-issue experiment to discover whether there was a broader audience for reprinted European comic strips in the UK. I was commissioned to design the cover, logo and interior text pages.

As well as work from Lorenzo Mattotti, Milo Manara and Max Cabanes, issues also featured Americans Robert Crumb **7**, Charles Bukowski and David Lynch.

The logo features a stylised comic reader who is also the 'X' of **Xpresso**. The curved double 's' is intended to suggest steam rising from a coffee cup. The oval version **4** appeared on the covers of the graphic novels, while a text-only version was used for the magazine's masthead (**5**, with back covers also shown). The circular icons **1**, **2**, **3** were designed for different departments in the magazine, but were ultimately used more decoratively. I drew illustrations for the contents and biography pages **6**, **9**, while **8** is an unused rough.

The related graphic novel imprint **Xpresso Books** launched with **Dare**, the strip Grant Morrison and I had contributed to **Revolver**, and continued with Max Cabanes' **Heart Throbs** and Benoît Sokal's **Canardo**. The **Canardo** logo was drawn up using Aldus Freehand on publisher **Fleetway**'s first in-house Apple Mac, perhaps the first logo I'd designed with digital assistance. It was output on a low-resolution copier/printer at a large size, reduced to crisp it up on a copy camera and then spray-mounted to board, where I further adjusted it with a scalpel. This hybrid way of working, in which analogue camera-ready art was still supplied to the printer even though elements were created on a computer, was the norm for several years while repro houses and printers sluggishly caught up with the new technology.

Of the planned volumes, Federico Fellini and Milo Manara's **Trip to Tulum** progressed as far as a cover Cromalin, and Enrique Sánchez Abulí and Jordi Bernet's **Torpedo** just a logo before disappointing sales meant that the project was shelved.

1

2

3

4

5

xpresso

FORGET THE HYPE, READ THE GRAPHICS!

CRISIS PRESENTS NO. 3 • FOR MATURE COFFEETABLES • £2.25
xpresso
THE BEST OF INTERNATIONAL STRIP ART
Black Coffee in Bed

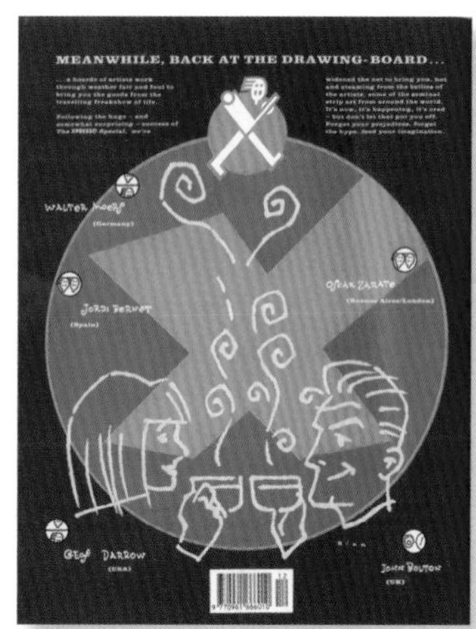
MEANWHILE, BACK AT THE DRAWING-BOARD...
Walter Moers (Germany)
Oscar Zarate (Buenos Aires/London)
Jordi Bernet (Spain)
Geof Darrow (USA)
John Bolton (UK)

6

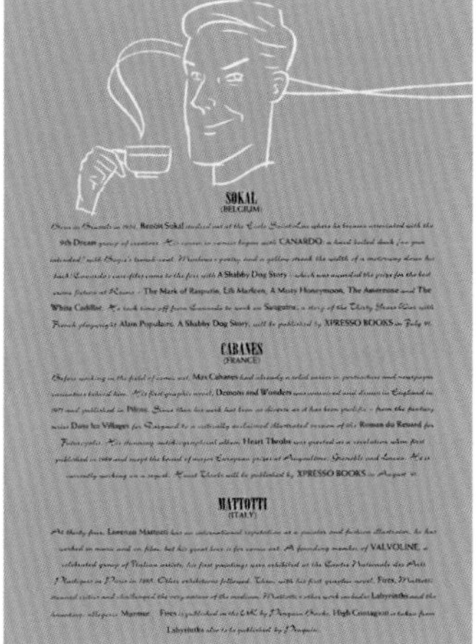
SOKAL (BELGIUM)
CABANES (FRANCE)
MATTOTTI (ITALY)

MENU
xpresso

7

BRING ME YOUR LOVE
CHARLES BUKOWSKI
ROBERT CRUMB

8

9

xpresso Bios

Canardo
Heart Throbs
Trip to Tulum
Dare
Fleetway/Xpresso
Graphic novels
1991

Canardo
Writer/artist: Benoît Sokal
Heart Throbs
Writer/artist: Max Cabanes
Trip to Tulum
Writer: Federico Fellini
Artist: Milo Manara
Dare
Writer: Grant Morrison
Artist: Rian Hughes

2 is the original artwork for the **Canardo** logo, a hybrid of digital output and paste-up. For **Heart Throbs**, the lettering was drawn out on toilet paper with a marker pen several times, the best letters assembled, and the result put under the copy camera **3**.

Trip to Tulum had previously been serialised in **Crisis**. The book did not progress beyond this cover Cromalin. **Dare** just made it under the wire before the line folded. Shown here is the cover proof and the original title spread.

Note the unobtrusive trade dress, consisting of a spine stripe with the **Xpresso** logo positioned bottom left on each volume.

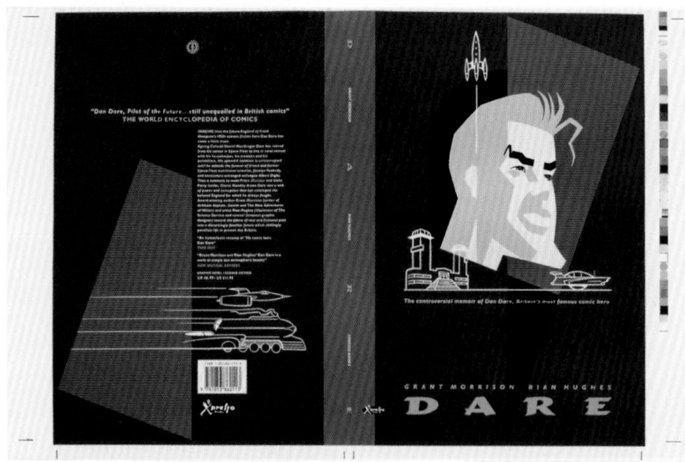

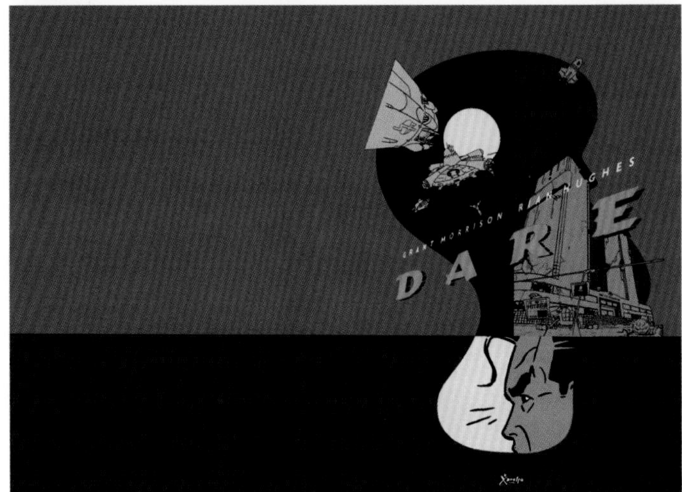

1

2

CABANES ♡ HEART THROBS

3

Dare
ProGlo Edizioni
2007
Fantagraphics
1991
Fleetway
1989

The main image is new a **Dan Dare** logo for the 2007 Italian edition, for which I also drew a new cover and interior spreads.

1 was for the original strip I drew for **Revolver** in 1989/90 (written by Grant Morrison), **2** for the graphic novel and **3** was used on Fantagraphics' US reprints, for which I also drew new covers.

1 and **2** adapt the original logo from Frank Hampson's legendary run in the **Eagle**, itself derived from Cartoon Bold, a hot-metal face released in 1936 by the Bauer foundry.

1

2

D A R E

3

DARE

4

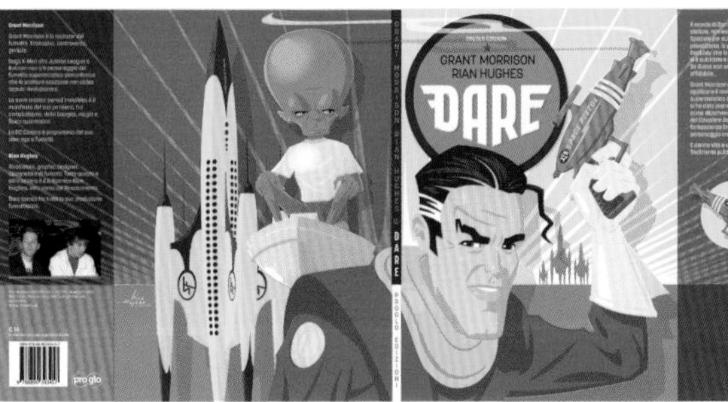

Speakeasy
Nigel Curson/John Brown
Magazine
1988/1989

1

SPEAKEASY

2

SPEAKEASY

3

GUTTERSNIPES GRAFFITI SUBSCRIPTIONS DRIVEL NEXT ISSUE TALES FROM THE SCRIPT
SPEAK-OUT OUTPUT CLASSIFIEDS CHARTS MARKETPLACE SCAN SHIPPING GUIDE

I designed **Speakeasy** twice. The "organ of the comics world" was a news monthly in newspaper format, edited by Nigel Curson. The first time was in 1988, courtesy of a puff-piece on **Fleetway**'s **Crisis** launch (a comic that I had also designed), which for the first time allowed them the budget for a full-colour cover **7**. The photocopy here **6** is from the original artwork, pasted up on CS10 board.

This was intended to set the magazine's style; however, my careful type choices and rigorous grid went out the window the very next issue. I had used one font, Neuzeit, in two weights; this was swapped for a mix of Avant Garde, Futura and a knockoff of Dynamo squished to 50% of its width.

The second time was a year later, when the magazine was picked up by John Brown, publishers of *Viz*. John asked me to redesign the logo (my previous version had been dropped by this point), lay out the covers and provide section headers **3**. For coverlines, I used a hand-drawn font – later digitised as *Crash Bang Wallop* **9** – that I laid out letter by letter. The interior of the magazine was pasted up by Titan Books' in-house studio.

5 is my original mock-up, using a *Zenith* illustration by Steve Yeowell and my own sketch of *Krazy Kat*. I also created Mylar F. Snug **8**, their fanboy mascot, who appeared in his own strip inside. **4** is a counter dispenser – this one has water stains from a studio flood. The main image is the original Rubylith and Rotring pen artwork for the logo, without the duplicated 'E', 'A' and 'S'.

I drew **Dan Dare** for issue 109's cover, in which Grant Morrison and I were interviewed at Angoulême, the French comics festival. I was proud to discover that 115 had been impounded by the Obscene Publications Squad in a raid on a comic shop.

I stepped down from design duties on issue 117, after which I watched the magazine merrily degenerate into typographic chaos for a second time.

4

5

6

7

8

9 **CRASH BANG WALLOP**
Light *Light Italic*
Medium ***Medium Italic***
Contoured
Highlight

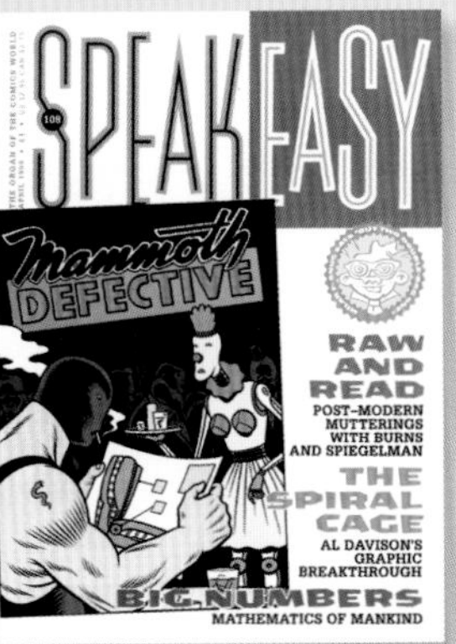

Recherché
Boutique hotel suppliers
2009

Recherché was a website supplying lighting, furniture and interior design that had originally been commissioned for boutique hotels to the general public.

There is a familiar language of hairline serif Didones **2**, **3** and light extended sans **4** which are associated with refinement and glamour through their use in the fashion and cosmetics industries, but I was looking for a more unique interpretation. The final logo is an elegant, lively script reminiscent of a signature – design shorthand for the personal touch. The upright of the 'R' is repeated at the other end in the acute accent, and these two vertical strokes are echoed in the backslanted uprights of the two 'h's.

1

2

Recherché
LONDON

3

Recherché
LONDON

4

RECHERCHÉ

5

6

7

8

9

10

Recherché

11

12

13

14

15

16

17

18

Alex Wanderer
Keith Kopnicki
Comic book
2012

Described as "Stephen King meets *The Goonies* with a little bit of *ET* and *Close Encounters* thrown in", **Alex Wanderer** was a coming-of-age story starring a 12-year-old boy.

1

2

3

4

War Mother
Valiant Comics
Comic book series
2016

The working title for this character from **Valiant**'s **4001 A.D.** crossover event was *War Marshall*. The design is heavily influenced by the style of David Mack's cover art for the issue.

The letters were drawn repeatedly with a marker pen, and the best examples assembled in Photoshop.

1

2

3

4

1%
Valiant Comics
Comic book
2013

The **1%** are a super-rich secret cabal from the **Archer & Armstrong** series who worship all things financial from their secret headquarters underneath the New York Stock Exchange.

The logo references the fine intaglio rules of lettering on banknotes and the dot-matrix displays of the trading floor.

1

2

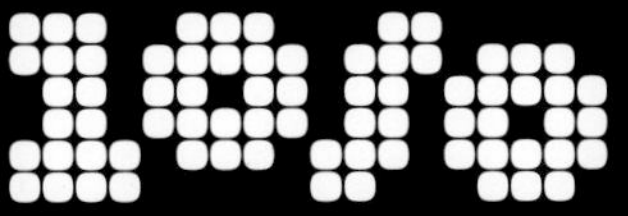

3

4

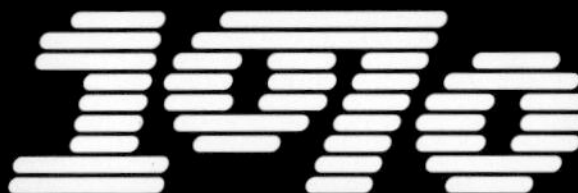

5

6

7

8

Freedom
Club night
1999

Wings are an obvious metaphor for freedom. **8** increases the letterspacing left to right to suggest an escape, or breaking into a run. The final logo (main image) also has an aspirational star.

1

2

3

4

5

6

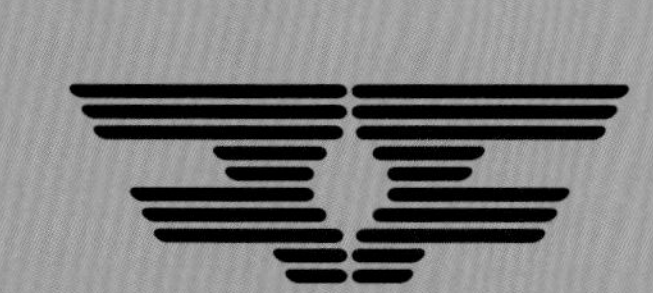

7

8

FREE D O M

1

2

3

4

5

6

7

8

9

10

1 **Rayguns and Rocketships**
Korero Press
Book cover logo
2015

2 **Space Wings**
Korero Press
Book cover proposed incidental logo
2015

3 **Birthright**
Skybound/Image
Comic book series
2014

4 **Mister Terrific**
DC Comics
Comic book series
2011

5 **Pyjamarama**
Bloomsbury
Book cover
1996

6 **Count on us**
DC Comics
Retailer incentive event
2001

7 **Enemy Ace: War in Heaven**
DC Comics
Comic book prestige series
2001

8 **Yesterday's Tomorrows**
Knockabout/Image
Graphic novel
2007
Writer: Various
Artist: Rian Hughes

9 **Toybox**
Rian Hughes/Device
Coningsby Gallery
Exhibition of limited edition prints
Proposed logo
2003

10 **Toybox**
Rian Hughes/Device
Coningsby Gallery
Exhibition of limited edition prints
2003

Manifest Destiny
Skybound
Comic book
2013

Manifest Destiny by Chris Dingess, with art by Matthew Roberts, follows the Lewis and Clark expedition westward across America in 1804 – only to find the frontier is inhabited by monsters.

The brief called for "something contemporary, with a historical bent". This 'old but new' or 'traditional but modern' request will be familiar to many designers.

The original script was titled "Lewis and Clark", but was later changed to **Manifest Destiny.** The script version **4** is based on the lettering from the Declaration of Independence, whereas **1**, **2** borrow from vintage banknotes and land deeds, and **3** and **5** evoke raw timber planks.

The chosen logo (main image) is a linked slab serif based on wood type models, with an interlock treatment and a small amount of distressing.

1

2

3

4

5

6

1 **The Winchell Riots**
Marsupial Management
2010
The logo for Oxford-based band **The Winchell Riots** appeared on a series of sleeves I also designed, released on their own Peter the Great label.

2 **Money Man**
Design In Action
House insurance brochure
2001

3 **Westrock**
Property developer
2010

4 **Vertigo #1**
DC Comics
First issue cover flash, incorporating the Vertigo logo by Richard Bruning
2004

5 **Valiant First**
Valiant Comics
Promotion
2013

6 **Slash**
Unknown
c1987

7 **Black Woods**
Proposed T-shirt motif
2001

8 **G-Spot**
G-Spot Magazine
Proposed logo
2000

9 **Droid Profile**
2000AD/Fleetway
Self-portrait
1994

10 **Superbaby Girl**
DC Comics
Merchandise motif
2004

11 **Superbaby Boy**
DC Comics
Merchandise motif
2004

12 **Mr. Positive**
Matador
Advertising mascot
Unknown brand
1992

1

2

3

4

5

6

7

8

9

10

11

12

Robots!
Caption 2013
Comic festival motif
2013

'Robots!' was the 2013 theme for the long-running Oxford comics and small press convention. My design was used on the programme cover and promotional T-shirts.

Tokyo Project
Mark Doyle
CD series/club night
2005

1

2

3

4

5

6

7

8

9

10

11

12

13

14

15

16

17

18

19

Tokyo Project
Mark Doyle
CD series/club night
2005

Mark Doyle, creator of the hugely successful **Hed Kandi** club nights and CD compilations, had received backing to set up his own label and club brand after Jazz FM sold **Hed Kandi** to Ministry of Sound.

The logo needed to be "simple enough to be reproduced as decorations inside clubs, yet cool enough to feature on clothing, jewellery, and most importantly, the front of our CDs".

The original brief foregrounded the Japanese connotations: "*Blade Runner*-style cityscapes, manga-influenced pop styles and traditional Japanese cherry blossoms and temples". I dutifully wheeled out all these somewhat clichéd motifs, adding origami, geishas and lilies, though ultimately this geographic specificity was dropped in favour of the final designs.

Of the first round (previous page), **1** and **2** look more like a bikini on a red sunburned behind than the pebbles they are supposed to resemble.

As the compilations would cover a similar range of styles of music as **Hed Kandi**, a series of related variant logos was required: **Tokyo Disco**, **Tokyo Extreme**, **Tokyo Chill**, **Tokyo Beach** and **Tokyo Deep**.

The project later metamorphosed into **Fierce Angel**.

1

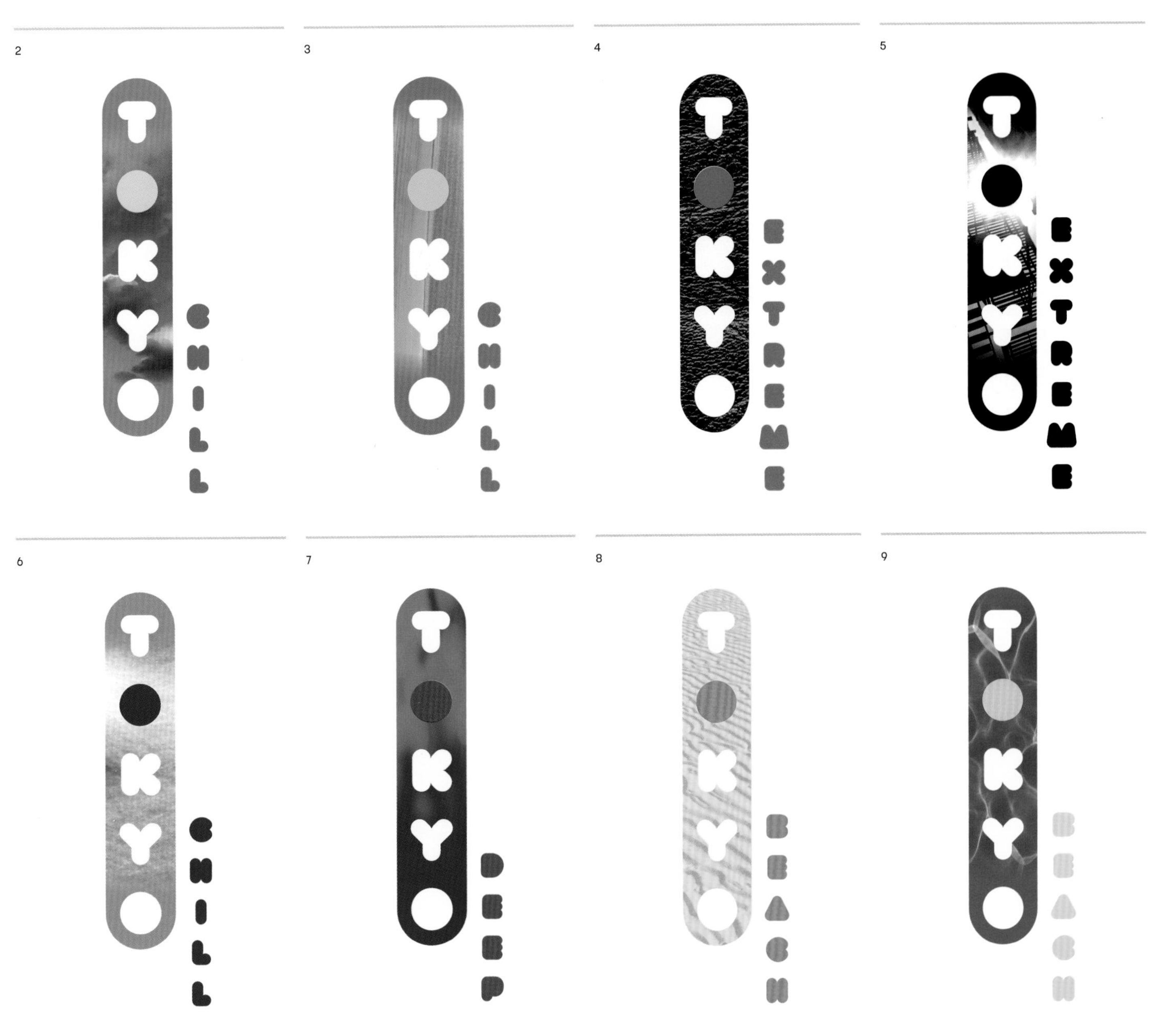
2
T
K
Y
CHILL
3
T
K
Y
CHILL
4
T
K
Y
EXTREME
5
T
K
Y
EXTREME
6
T
K
Y
CHILL
7
T
K
Y
DEEP
8
T
K
Y
BEACH
9
T
K
Y
BEACH

UNITY
VALIANT
ARMOR HUNTERS
THE UNITED
REVENGE OF THE ARMOR HUNTERS
MULTIPLE HARVEY AWARD NOMINEE

Unity
Valiant Comics
Comic book series
2013

Unity is **Valiant**'s team book – effectively their **Avengers** or **Justice League**, bringing together their most popular characters. As part of the design exploration, I was asked to revisit the original logo from **Valiant**'s first incarnation, a simple blocky affair similar to **4**.

The perspective is intended to graphically illustrate a coming together, as are the lines that sweep up and unite in the 'I' in **2**, **5** and **6**.

The final logo is an unfussy heavy sans, the interior 'spark' colour keyed to the art each issue.

The Valiant trade dress - the credits, logo position, barcode, issue number and so on – is designed to be consistent across the whole **Valiant** line. The first run of issues featured the **Valiant** branding to the fore, top left; after a year or so, when it had been firmly established, I introduced a redesign in which it ran across the top of the cover in a smaller size on a consistent black panel, along with the credits. This moved the emphasis to the title.

Many comic covers arbitrarily reposition the various design elements issue to issue, often using a bewildering variety of fonts. This tendency to chaotic inconsistency is a missed opportunity to create a stronger brand.

1

2

3

4

5

6

7

8

1 **Pogo Lean Gogo**
Band
Logo proposal
2000

2 **A to Z**
Clairefontaine
Stationery
2008

3 **XX**
Book cover
2016
Author: Rian Hughes

4 **New Agenda Arts Trust**
Arts charity
Logo proposal
2001

5 **A Retro Scientific Thriller**
Korero Press
Book cover incidental logo
2016

6 **Swanky Modes**
Idée Fixe
Greetings card range
2001

7 **Daisy Hicks**
Stylorouge/Concept Music
Recording artist
Logo proposal
2000

8 **Ciao!**
Device
Dazzle font promotional image
2005

9 **Orange World**
Proposed logo
c1994

10 **Help My Child to Talk**
Speech therapy organisation
2014

11 **Duo**
Clairefontaine
2009
Brand for a set of notebooks and storage boxes featuring my illustrations

12 **Slogan**
Clairefontaine
2009
Brand for a stationery and desk accessory range featuring my designs

1

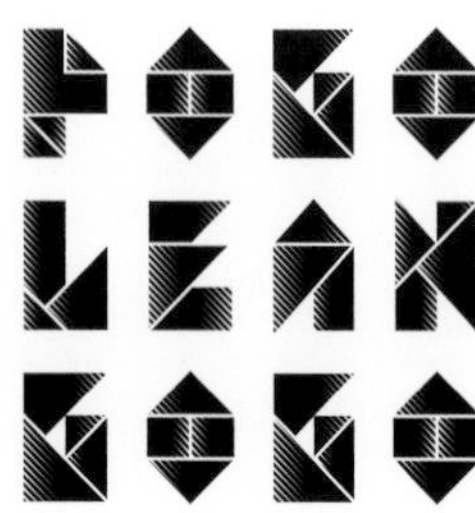

2

3

4

5

6

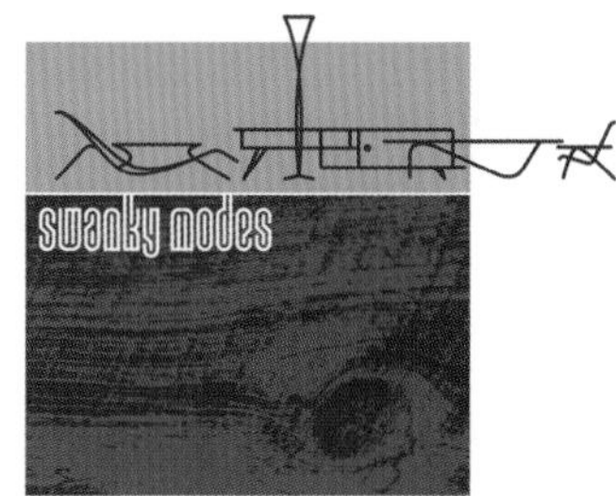

7

8

9

10

11

12

First Base
Fast-food outlet
P&O Stena Cruise Line
1999

Logo and incidental imagery for a cruise liner's on-board fast-food outlet. The type is Outlander, one of my early FontFont releases, and the faces are similar to the icons I designed for *2000AD*'s credits.

Soda
Fleetway
Proposed comic book
c1990

In the **Crisis**/**Revolver** enthusiasm for new titles, **Fleetway** planned to launch an all-ages comic called **Soda** that would reprint classic European strips, many of which had never been translated.

The title didn't progress beyond this cover Cromalin, here scanned from a colour photocopy. Both logos shown were cut from Rubylith; the **Soda** logo is scanned from a sheet of yellowing PMT film.

1 

Communications Now
Telecommunications Publishing
Magazine masthead
1986

Tony Fletcher's **Starship Enterprises** was in the same office as *What Telephone?* magazine, who asked me to rebrand them as **Communications Now**. It was almost titled "Telecommunications Now", which would have added another four letters to an already cramped masthead.

The logo was drawn up with Rotring pen and Rubylith on board, then copied down for the final paste-up. It has a certain Neville Brody-esque geometry. Options for the cover image were limited to shots supplied by the manufacturers or stock photography; nothing dates faster. Phone on beige marble? Classy. Venetian blind? Oh yes. Article on fibre-optics? How about a 1970s lamp?

The archetypal smug yuppie **1** was then in the ascendant..

1 

Fax User
Telecommunications Publishing
Magazine masthead
1986

Fax User was a quarterly magazine spun out of **Communications Now** to target the then-emerging fax machine market. The design uses a similar white border, inset image and blocks of colour. The letterspaced Trade Gothic set in a panel below was a visual tick I had picked up in the advertising agency I briefly worked for after graduation.

The logo itself **1** was passed through a fax, giving it a stepped 8-bit edge; this was lost when reproduced at smaller sizes, and was pretty subtle even on the actual cover, looking uncharitably like a printing error.

Sample headline: "Electronic mail: myth or reality?"

Fax machines do not make the most exciting subjects for cover photography.

Colin J. Smith
Gingerbread Monkey
Visual effects
2014

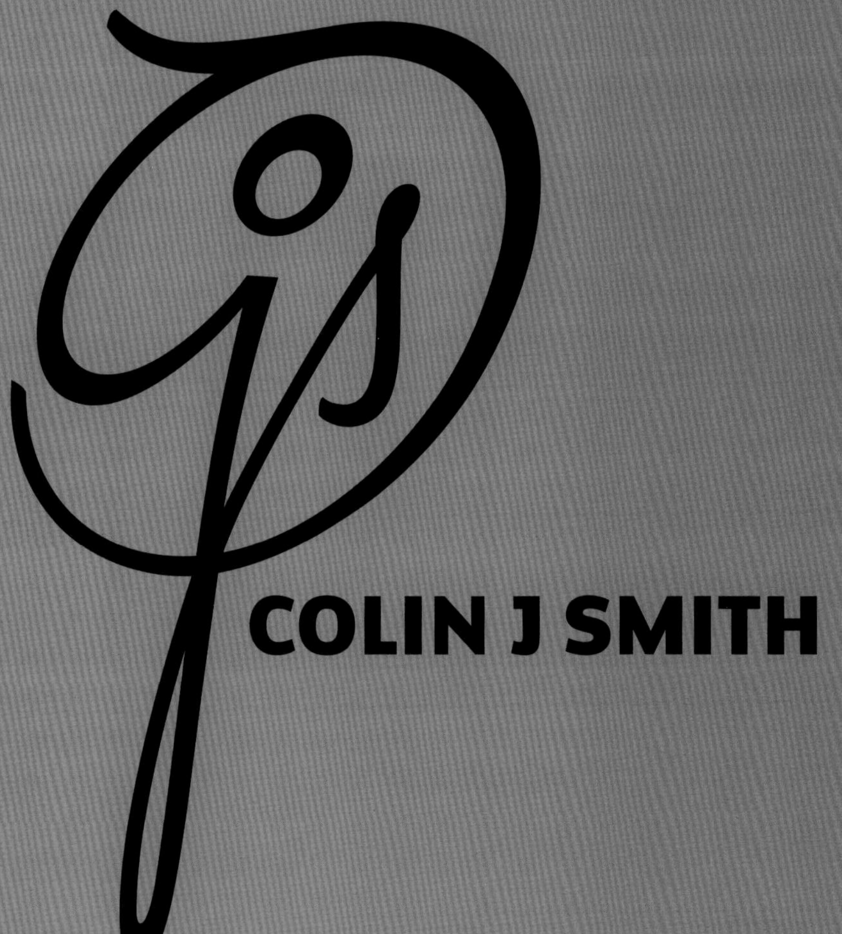

Colin J. Smith is a photographer and visual effects designer specialising in 3D and motion graphics. The chosen logo is a monogram and also a caricature.

The client did not realise that it was a portrait of him until more than a year later, during which time he'd been using it on his stationery, website and email footer.

1

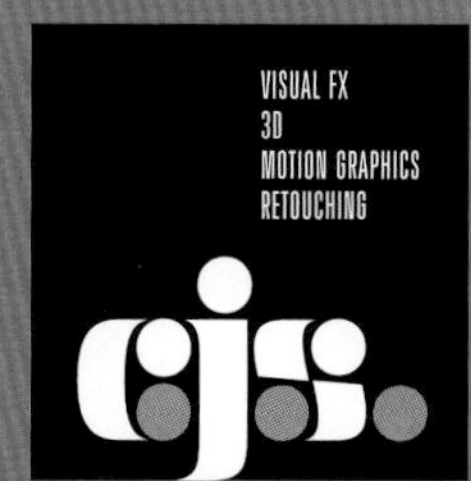

2

3

4

Mac Dings
Mac User magazine
Reviews and section icons
1994

Glasgow Science Centre
GSC/999 (agency)
Exhibition icons
2001

The Mac Man
The Mac magazine
Section icons
1995

PC icons
Microsoft
Poster advertising campaign icons
2000

Mixmag ratings
Mixmag
Music magazine review icons
1997

Toyota icons
Toyota brochure and website icons
1996

Voluptuous Panic
Turnaround Distribution
Nightclub event
2009

Turnaround are a well-established UK distributor of alternative books, magazines and small press publications. The theme for their 25th birthday extravaganza at The Scala, an old cinema in King's Cross, was taken from **Voluptuous Panic**, a book on the nightlife of Weimar Berlin, and featured burlesque and Dadaist entertainment from outfits like the Tiger Lilies.

The logo has a ruler-and-compass construction that pays homage to Fortunato Depero, while incorporating early Deco inlines.

Girlfrenzy!
DC Comics
Comic book line
1998

Girlfrenzy! was a seven-issue series that threw the spotlight on **DC Comics**' female characters. I mocked up a couple of covers,with off-centre compositions and simple, graphic blocks of colour. I particularly liked The Secret, floating in her purple blankness.

The **Girlfrenzy!** logo appeared in a panel across the top to brand the range, and instead of a disparate set of logos a clean and consistent Helvetica Extended was used. The design was overseen by DC's Curtis King.

Girlfrenzy!

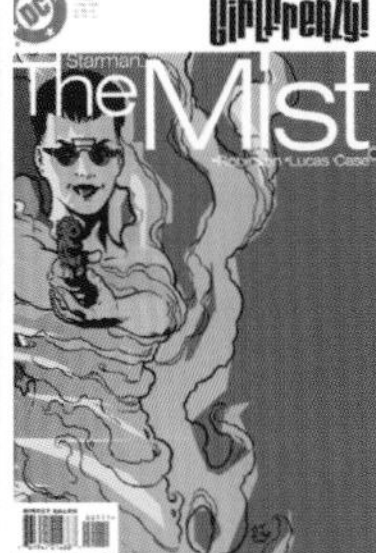

Guy Ornadel
Automatic Records
CD sleeve
1999

Icon from the *Licenced to Thrill* album.

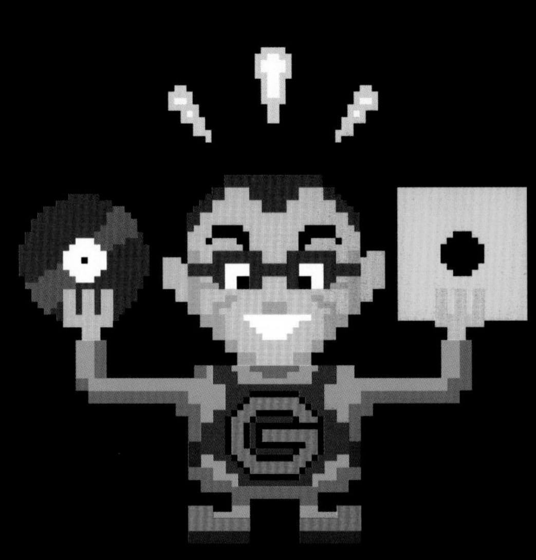

Hellblazer
Titan Books
Graphic novel series
1989

Logo and design for **Titan Books**' UK reprints of the **DC Comics** series by Jamie Delano, which spun out of Alan Moore's seminal run on *Swamp Thing*. The cover illustrations are mixed media assemblages by Dave McKean, drawn before he began to explore the possibilities of Photoshop.

1-4 were drawn on layout paper with a brush. **5** shows the adjustments to a rough achieved with a scalpel and spray mount – this would then be photocopied and faxed to the client.

The random rectangles around the final logo are artefacts produced by repeatedly photocopying the type to distress it, reversing it each time.

1

2

3

4

5

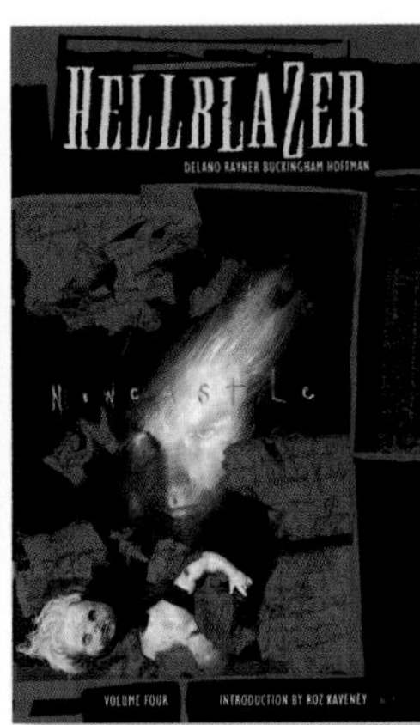

VALIANT
RAI
JAPAN IN THE 41st CENTURY!
MATT KINDT
CLAYTON CRAIN
VALIANT
RAI
JAPAN IN THE 41st CENTURY!
MATT KINDT
CLAYTON CRAIN
VALIANT
1
RAI
JAPAN IN THE 41st CENTURY!
MATT KINDT
CLAYTON CRAIN
VALIANT
2
RAI
JAPAN IN THE 41st CENTURY!
MATT KINDT
CLAYTON CRAIN
VALIANT
RAI
MATT KINDT
CLAYTON CRAIN
VALIANT
2
RAI
JAPAN IN THE 41st CENTURY!
MATT KINDT
CLAYTON CRAIN
VALIANT
RAI
JAPAN IN THE 41st CENTURY!
MATT KINDT
CLAYTON CRAIN
VALIANT
RAI
JAPAN IN THE 41st CENTURY!
MATT KINDT
CLAYTON CRAIN
VALIANT
RAI
MATT KINDT
CLAYTON CRAIN
VALIANT
4
RAI
SECOND PRINTING
MATT KINDT
CLAYTON CRAIN
VALIANT
5
RAI
PLUS EDITION
VALIANT
5
RAI
SCAN THE QR CODE WITH YOUR MOBILE DEVICE TO HEAR RAI SPEAK
VALIANT
5
RAI
MATT KINDT
CLAYTON CRAIN
VALIANT
6
RAI
BIG TROUBLE IN NEW JAPAN!
MATT KINDT
CLAYTON CRAIN
VALIANT
RAI
BIG TROUBLE IN NEW JAPAN!
MATT KINDT
CLAYTON CRAIN
VALIANT
RAI
BIG TROUBLE IN NEW JAPAN!
MATT KINDT
CLAYTON CRAIN
VALIANT
7
RAI
EVE OF DESTRUCTION
MATT KINDT
CLAYTON CRAIN
VALIANT
7
RAI
EVE OF DESTRUCTION
MATT KINDT
CLAYTON CRAIN
VALIANT
9
RAI
THE ORPHAN
PART 1
MATT KINDT
CLAYTON CRAIN
VALIANT
#10
RAI
MATT KINDT
CLAYTON CRAIN
VALIANT
11
RAI
MATT KINDT
CLAYTON CRAIN
VALIANT
12
RAI
MATT KINDT
CLAYTON CRAIN
VALIANT
WELCOME TO NEW JAPAN
RAI
VALIANT
BATTLE FOR NEW JAPAN
RAI

Rai
Valiant Comics
Comic book series
2014

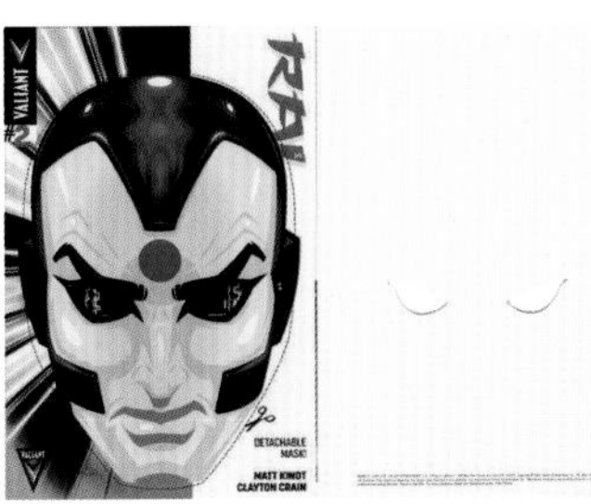

1

"In 4001 A.D., the island nation of Japan hangs in geosynchronous orbit. Here, **Rai** enforces the law. They say he's a spirit, the ghost of Japan."

For Matt Kindt and Clayton Crain's reboot of one of the most popular characters from **Valiant**'s original run, I began with a rationalisation of the existing logo **2**, **3**. The final version (main image) is a geometric reworking of gestural calligraphic brushstrokes, and also references the shape of the hero's swords.

The logo ran vertically to the right of each cover, another somewhat unsubtle reference to Japanese typography. The loose brush design top right comes from the original logo, and means 'spirit'– **Rai** was originally going to be titled 'Rising Spirit'. The final logo retains the same dimensions as the other Valiant logos so that it can be seamlessly used on the established trade paperback design; 'futureproofing' a logo by considering all the uses it might be put to avoids backing the designer into an awkward corner further down the line. (As **Valiant** began to use other designers, this consistency was unfortunately lost).

I drew the mask cover for issue 2. There is a rare misprint in which the eyes are die-cut, rather than perforated **1**. Copies were recalled, but many ended up on eBay.

2 3 4 5

Ninjak
Valiant Comics
Comic book series
2012

Ninja spy **Ninjak**, alter ego of British playboy Colin King, is another of **Valiant**'s rebooted characters from the original incarnation of the company in the 1990s. In 2013 **Ninjak** appeared in **Unity**, written by Matt Kindt, and in 2014 graduated again to his own series.

The final logo uses the four circles from the character's costume and typeforms based on his square-edged swords. The exclamation mark did not make the final cut.

1

2

3

4

5

6

7

8

9

10

11

12

Ninja-K
Valiant Comics
Comic book series
2017

For **Ninjak**'s 2017 reboot, the tone of the book shifted towards a British spy drama. MI-6 has honed its secret division of ninjas into one of the nation's most effective weapons. Ninja-A was the Queen's discreet weapon of choice during WWI, Ninja-E the globetrotting secret agent who pulled the Cold War back from the brink of armageddon; most recently, **Ninja-K**, aka Colin King, has taken up the mantle.

The logo required a slight tweak, the retention of the sword and maybe a suggestion of the Union Jack.

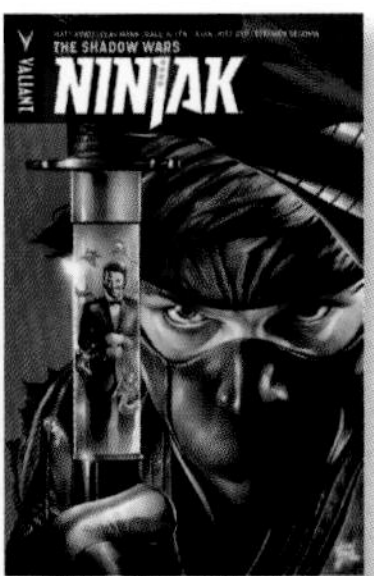

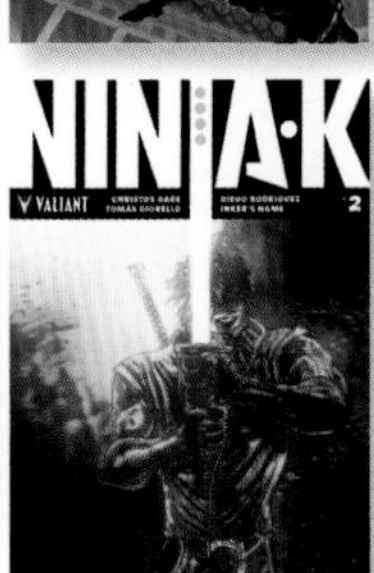

1

2

3

4

5

6

Teen Titans
Warner Animation
Cartoon title proposal
2002

1

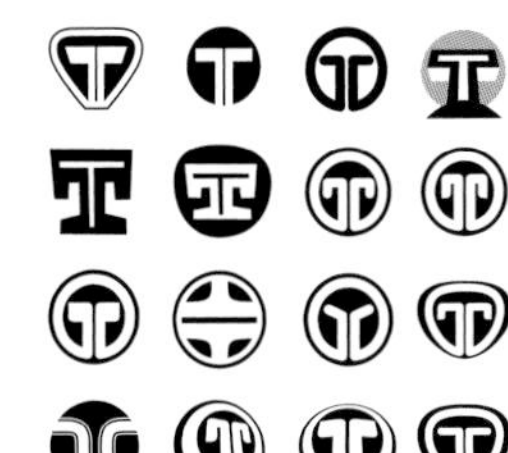

Teen Titans is an American animated television series produced by Glen Murakami, based on the **DC Comics** characters I vividly remember from Marv Wolfman and George Pérez' comics run. Having enjoyed Glen's work on the animated **Batman** and **Superman** shows with Bruce Timm, I was excited to be asked to design the show's logo.

The style of the show was influenced by Japanese anime, with its own stylistic twist. Glen wanted to steer away from the original blocky comic book masthead, and asked for something a bit "Saul Bass, but modern, not retro". From a practical standpoint, a logo that could work both on one line and 'stacked' would be more versatile in use.

Though I went through several rounds, I don't think I nailed what they were after. Although I did try a few Saul Bass-influenced designs **7**, I avoided overtly retro 1950s styles and was trying for something that had the curves of late 1960s or early 1970s modernism – not too cartoony. Some of these had a Japanese influence **11**, and others also use an interlock style in which parts of letters extend over or under their neighbours **2-5**. Ideas for a **Teen Titans** 'double T' icon that could sit alongside the type were also developed **1**.

After listening to a few rounds of feedback, an approved version (opposite) was arrived at. In the end this wasn't used – the logo that appears in the final title sequence was designed in-house. It works brilliantly in context with the energetic Puffy Ami Yumi soundtrack, but looks much more retro in style than I imagined they were after.

2

3

4

5

6

7

8

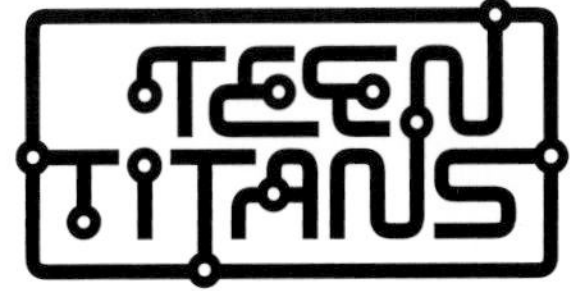

9

10

11

12

13

1

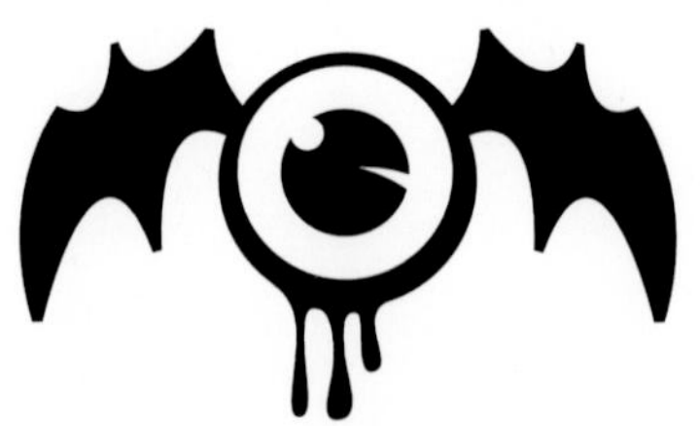

2

3

4

5

6

7

8

9

10

1 **Horror**
Maxim magazine (US)
Film article icon
2004

2 **Harada**
Valiant Comics
Comic book character
2013

3 **Great Britain**
Device
2004
Proposed national flag for Great Britain – England, Wales and Scotland, but excluding Northern Ireland

4 **Pop's Top Ten**
The Chickenhouse
Book category icons
2002

5 **Clever Kidz**
Atmosphere
CD cover
1995

6 **Wired and Tired**
Wired magazine
Column icons
1996

7 **What's Hot What's Not**
Good Food magazine
Section header
1998

8 **Hero and Zero**
MacUser magazine
Dennis Publishing
Column header icons
1994

9 **Zone**
Device
T-shirt motif
1998
Based on Via Face Don, a Mecanorma dry transfer face by Hans Donner and Sylvia Trenker from 1980

10 **Black Chip**
Vortex Comics
Doc Chaos incidental logo
1990
Writer: Dave Thorpe
Artist: Stephen Sampson

Freak Boarders
Freak Borders
Toy range
2001

The **Freakboarders** were a collection of 12cm (5-in) high toy skate/surf action figures who came boxed with tricks and accessories.

As well as the logo, I also designed the packaging.

1

2

New Mutants
Marvel Comics
Comic book series
2009

The **New Mutants**, a kind of Teen **X-Men**, featured the younger generation of students from Professor Charles Xavier's School for Gifted Youngsters. I read the original series, written by Chris Claremont with art by Bob McLeod and some beautiful experimental work from Bill Sienkiewicz.

In 2009 a third volume of the **New Mutants** was launched, written by Zeb Wells and pencilled by Diogenes Neves, for which I was asked to design the logo. I had little to go on conceptually, other than the team roster – it didn't need to tie in stylistically with the **X-Men** logo (as the later **Young X-Men** did), and I found it hard to get a handle on a logical design direction. When this happens, the temptation is to simply push shapes around until they look nice, which is when you should really take yourself away from the screen, pour a vodka and orange and think about the job more deeply. However, after working with just the internal symmetries of the letters rather than trying to articulate something about the story or the characters, I was pleased with the rhythms of **5** and **6**.

The chosen version has a subtle chisel effect, which was dropped after a few issues. **Marvel** tend to lay out covers in Photoshop rather than in Illustrator or Indesign, which offer more sophisticated vector and alignment control, so though logos are usually supplied as EPS files with the differently coloured elements grouped or on separate layers, once pulled into Photoshop such details can be lost, or buried under a profusion of shadows and effects. The final covers also suffered from a clutter of other design elements – the credits, barcode, price etc. – that had little typographic or positional consistency.

Though I often provide stand-alone logos, a cohesive trade dress in which the supporting elements are elegantly organised can make or break a design.

1

2

3

4

5

6

7

8

9

10

11

12

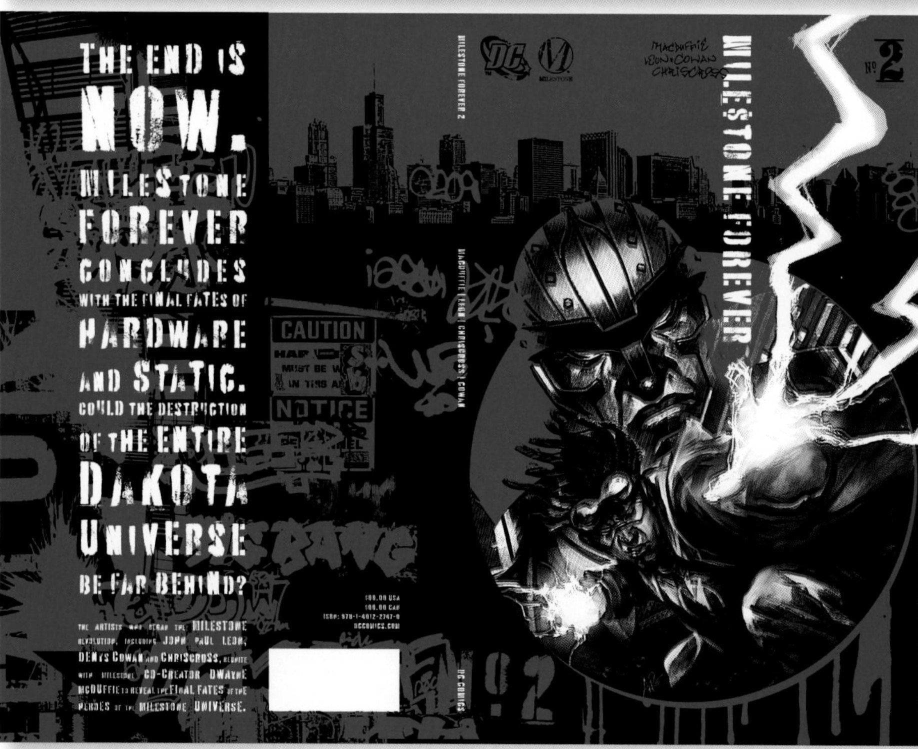

Milestone Forever
DC Comics
Comic book series
2009

Milestone was founded in 1993 by Dwayne McDuffie, Denys Cowan, Michael Davis and Derek T. Dingle, who felt that minorities were under-represented in American comics. Their most popular character is **Static Shock**, who went on to star in an award-winning cartoon series.

In 2010 DC released **Milestone Forever**, in which events that lead to its merger with the DC Universe play out. I was asked to design a stand-alone logo, though it quickly evolved into an overall trade dress. I also submitted ideas for an updated **Milestone** logo, but the original version was retained on the cover for buyer recognition, with my new version used as an endpaper motif (opposite).

The cover art had already been coloured, but it did look a bit like any other mainstream superhero book. A more punchy two-colour urban graffiti approach seemed to be an appropriate way to set them apart. For the backgrounds I used photographs I'd taken around Manhattan as a stand-in for Dakota, changing them to high-contrast black and white in Photoshop.

The lettering used for the logo and on the back cover is Battery Park, a Device font based on a photograph of a plumber's van I took through the rainy window of a New York taxi **1**.

1

MILESTONE
FOREVER

MILESTONE FOREVER
MILESTONE
MILESTONE

Honeyz
Mercury Records
Band
Proposed logo
2001

From an era when group names had to end in a 'z', **Honeyz** were touted as an R&B alternative to the Spice Girls and a rival to American girl group Destiny's Child. Later relaunched as a trio, at the 2000 **Maxim** magazine awards they picked up The Best British Girl Band gong.

The logo proposals cover the immediately obvious – a logo made from poured honey **2** – to psychedelic Art Nouveau tie-dye colour gradations.

None were used.

1

2

3

4

5

6

7

8

Anders
Kristof Spaey
Comic book series
2014

In this tale, the character's powers derive from an agent available in dilute amounts in a soda brand **4**. It escapes from the petri dish into the surrounding cover artwork, like an infection.

1

2

3

4

Huzzah!
Huzzah! Entertainment
Production company
2013

The double 'Z' used here is similar to Malcolm Garrett's classic Buzzcocks logo.

1

2

3

4

Lakesville
Mike Lake
Comic and related projects company
2000

A literal interpretation of the company name as a city skyline, in night and day variants.

Travel Choice icons
First Travel/Design House
Travel agent branding
2000

Agency Design House commissioned a set of icons to accompany their redesign of the logo and fascia of high-street travel agents First Travel, who renamed themselves **Travel Choice**.

These were extended from the original suite of holiday types – ski, sun, city break, etc. – to include other travel-related services such as currency, car hire, weather reports and so on.

1

2

3

4

5

6

7

8

9

10

11

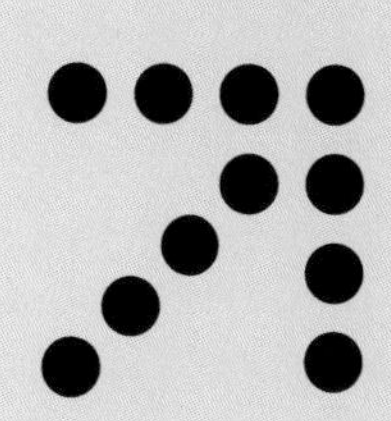

12

13

14

15

16

Planet X
Million Dollar
T-shirt range
1993

Planet X was a branded range of T-shirts for the King's Road boutique. The shirts came with a swing ticket **3** that opened into a small booklet which set out the philosophy of the label. The little alien became a kind of unofficial Device mascot **1**, his head appearing on the business cards **2** I had printed for the ill-fated studio in London's Wardour Street I shared with Steve Cook and others, the story of which is related in the introduction.

7 are the original marker-pen roughs.

1

2

3

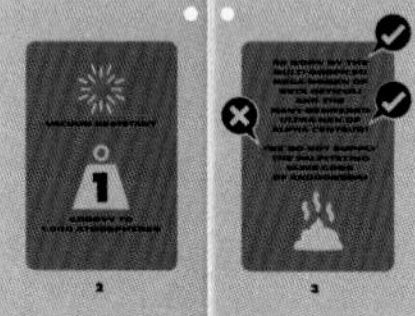

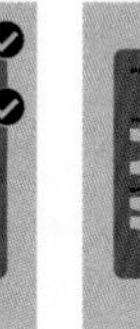

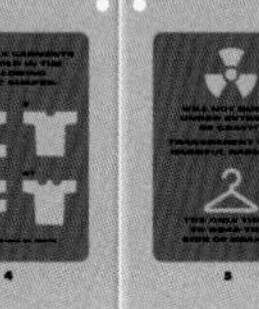

4

5

6

7

Fierce Angel
Mark Doyle
Record label and club night
Proposed logo
2005

Fierce Angel was the successor to **Hed Kandi** founder Mark Doyle's **Tokyo Disco** club nights and CD releases..

1

2

3

4

1 Anderson, Psi Division
Titan Books
Graphic novel series
1987
Writers: John Wagner, Alan Grant
Later volumes were designed in-house at Titan Books by Mark Cox

2 Skizz
Titan Books
Graphic novel
1989
Writer: Alan Moore
Artist: Jim Baikie

3 Love and Rockets
Titan Books
Graphic novel
1987
Writer/artist: Jaime Hernandez
Probably my favourite comic of all time

4 AARGH!
Mad Love
1988
'Artists Against Rampant Government Homophobia' benefit comic

5 Ape Sex
Titan Books
Graphic novel
1989
Writer/artist: Jamie Hernandez

6 Human Diastrophism
Titan Books
Graphic novel
1989
Writer/artist: Gilbert Hernandez

7 The Complete Gerry Anderson Episode Guide
Titan Books
Book cover
1989
Shown opposite is an unpublished proof. Thunderbird 1 was changed to Scott Tracy for the final printed version

8 Fantastic Television
Titan Books
Book cover
1987
Writers: Gary Gerani and Paul H. Schulz

Also featured opposite:
Batman: Year One
The UK edition of Frank Miller's finest Batman story. The first edition was turquoise, the second purple – or it might be the other way around.

1

2

3

Love & Rockets

4

5

Ape Sex

6

Human Diastrophism

7

8

ANDERSON
PSI
DIVISION
BOOK 1
WAGNER + GRANT

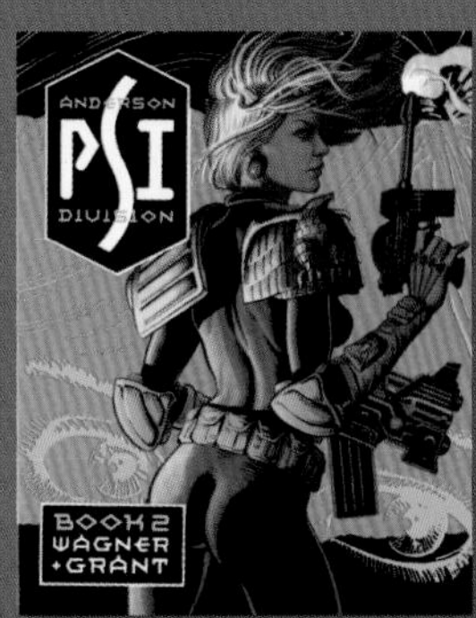
ANDERSON
PSI
DIVISION
BOOK 2
WAGNER + GRANT

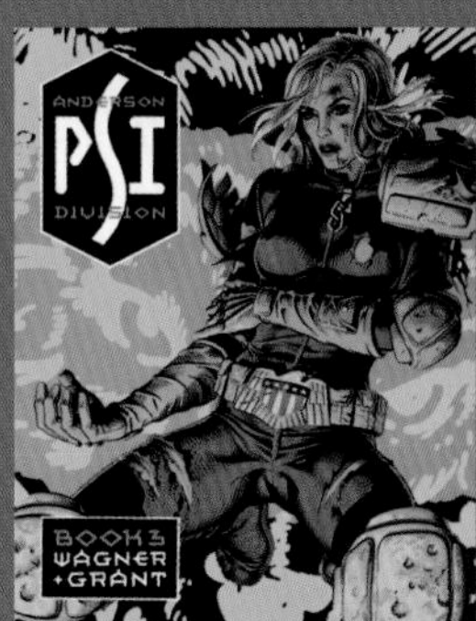
ANDERSON
PSI
DIVISION
BOOK 3
WAGNER + GRANT

ANDERSON
PSI
DIVISION
BOOK 4
BY ALAN GRANT

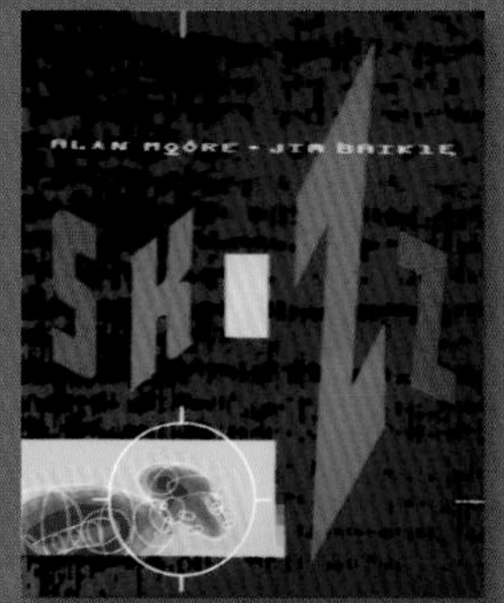
ALAN MOORE • JIM BAIKIE

JAIME HERNANDEZ
Love & Rockets

Heartbreak Soup

GILBERT HERNANDEZ
Heartbreak Soup

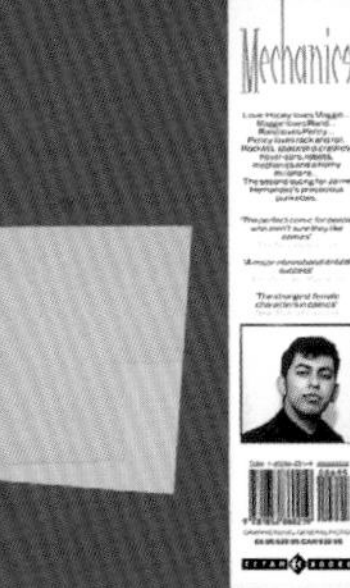
Mechanics

JAIME HERNANDEZ
Mechanics

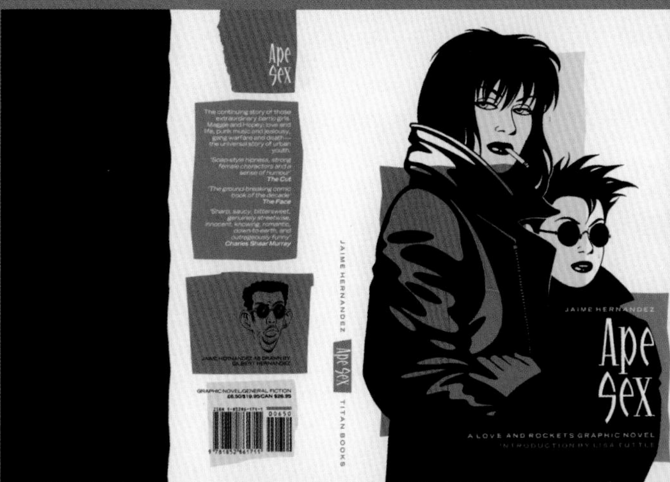
Ape Sex
JAIME HERNANDEZ
Ape Sex
A LOVE AND ROCKETS GRAPHIC NOVEL
INTRODUCTION BY LISA TUTTLE
TITAN BOOKS

Human Diastrophism
GILBERT HERNANDEZ
Human Diastrophism
A HEARTBREAK SOUP GRAPHIC NOVEL
INTRODUCTION BY MARY GENTLE
TITAN BOOKS

STAND BY FOR ACTION!

FIREBALL XL5
STINGRAY
SECRET SERVICE
UFO
THE COMPLETE
GERRY ANDERSON
EPISODE GUIDE

BATMAN
YEAR ONE

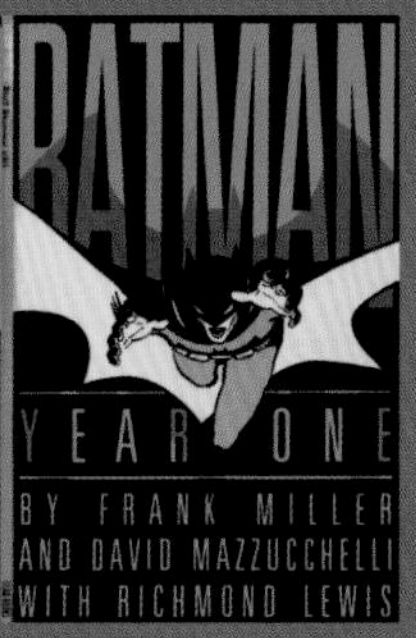
BATMAN
YEAR ONE
BY FRANK MILLER
AND DAVID MAZZUCCHELLI
WITH RICHMOND LEWIS

BATMAN
YEAR ONE
BY FRANK MILLER
AND DAVID MAZZUCCHELLI
WITH RICHMOND LEWIS

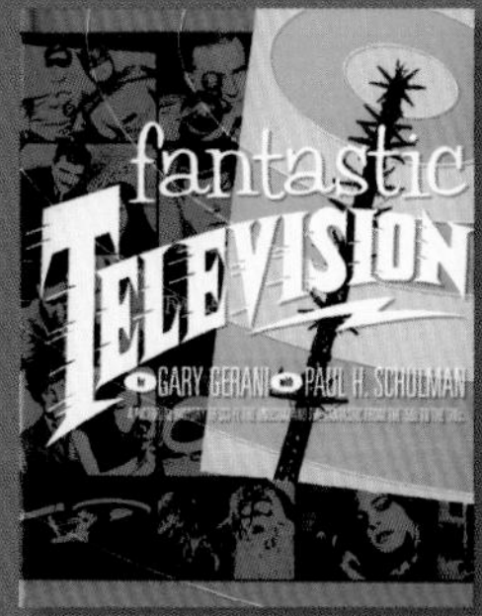
fantastic
TELEVISION
GARY GERANI
PAUL H. SCHULMAN

Animal Man
DC Comics
Comic book
1993

Commissioned during Jamie Delano and Steve Pugh's run, the logo plays with the differences between a human and an animal eye, and the neat stacking of 'mal' and 'man'. Though I preferred the cleaner and simpler main logo, ultimately the one chosen **4** kept the angled scratches from the previous design for continuity.

This logo was designed while I was still getting to grips with an early version of Aldus Freehand, and so the designs were sketched out with pen and paper and faxed to DC for approval first **1**, **2**, **3**.

1

2

3

4

Is It
Frazer Irving
Sketchbook collection series
2017

Frazer Irving, teller of tall tales and wearer of the woollen beanie, came to my attention with his finely detailed work on *Necronauts* in *2000AD*. He has one of the most unusual and evocative senses of colour and light I've seen in comics. **Is It** collects his more experimental and personal work. The logo changes issue to issue.

1

2

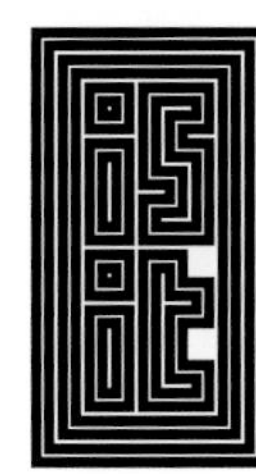

3

4

5

6

Blackfish
Blackfish Publishing
Magazine publisher
2006

1

BLACKFISH

2

3

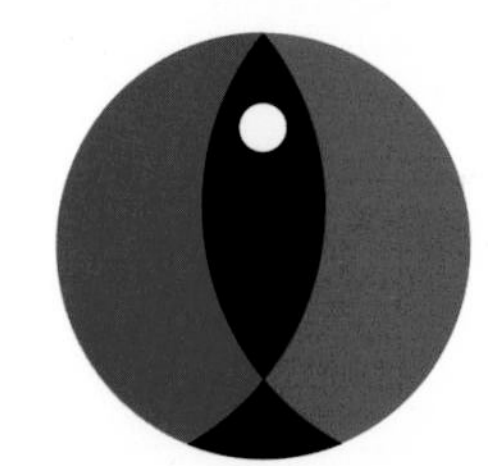

4

5

BLACKFISH

6

7

8

9

blackfish

10

11

12

13

BLACKFISH

14

15

16

17

BLACKFISH

18

19

Matt Bielby is an experienced magazine editor and publisher who was responsible for launching some of Future Publishing's most successful magazines: *Total Film, PC Gamer* and the best-selling SF title *SFX*, for the launch of which I created a space cadet mascot and drew many illustrations.

In 2006 Matt launched his own publishing company, **Blackfish**. Their inaugural magazine was to be an SF title called *Death Ray*.

A **blackfish** is an old nautical term for a killer whale, and Matt had something in black and white with a bright colour highlight in mind, preferably contained in a circular shape to make it easy to drop onto the cover, website and stationery as a 'bullet'.

Several options explore a killer whale's distinctive markings, some with the outline omitted around the white areas **11**, as well as other kinds of fish that just happened to be black **8**, **10**. The skeletal fossil, taken from a dried fish I'd photographed on the harbour pavement in Essaouira, Morocco, had the wrong connotations for a vibrant new company **4**, **5**, while **3** reminds me of a tinned tuna brand.

The simple graphic loop **2**, **6**, **15** was initially popular, having a clean, corporate clarity that lends itself to repeat patterns and other playful adaptations. **7**, **12** and **17** look too much like a surfing brand, while **9** looks too twee.

The anglerfish had the right blend of attitude, character and credibility, and fitted the company's motto "We Go Deeper". I liked the textured version **14**; the final version (main image) uses a simplified yellow and black colour scheme.

An accompanying 'heatfish' **18**, **19** was developed for the website.

Johnny DC
DC Comics
Mascot
2004

Johnny DC originally appeared as a mascot in advertisements in Silver Age **DC Comics** to promote new and upcoming titles **1**. In the 1980s he hosted a regular feature called 'DCI with Johnny DC'.

Then in 2004 **Johnny** was reinvented to brand **DC Comics**' children's titles, a line based on licensed Warner Bros. and Cartoon Network animated TV series and kid-friendly versions of other **DC Comics** superheroes. He would appear on the cover and host the letters page.

For the redesign of this strange character who is part boy, part anorexic pixie, I had to decide what to keep and what we could lose. The mortar board seemed anachronistic, so that was dropped. His only other feature of note (apart from his face and the DC bullet) was a tuft of hair; I suggested turning this into a Superman-style kiss-curl.

Using the DC bullet as his body made him less versatile **6**, **7**, and as he was to appear on the cover, he would have to be quite large for the DC brand to be visible. The solution was to give the DC logo a slight perspective and turn it into **Johnny's** speech balloon.

I created a set of key poses that could be employed across the different genres: comedy, action/adventure, superhero and spooky mystery, each supplied in a range of bright candy colours that avoided straight primaries.

As part of the new trade dress that identified the line **2**, **Johnny** sat in the top left of the cover, looking across or reacting to the action in the illustration. A banner ran along the top and held the credits, issue number, price and the **Comic Code Authority** seal. The font used is Blackcurrant, a Device design which had the requisite sense of fun.

For the interior pages, I created more poses and 'marginals' **8-10**, **14**, **18**, **22** that could be dropped in to add interest.

Later, Richard Bruning's new DC 'swoosh' logo replaced the original Milton Glaser version in Johnny's speech bubble.

3

4

5

6

7

1

2

8

9

10

11

12

13

14

15

16

17

18

19

20

21

22

23

24

25

Space Mutts
Pan Macmillan Publishing
Book cover
Proposed logo
2010

Michael Broad's children's novel pits alien cats hell-bent on world domination against the best interplanetary canine defence force in the universe – The **Space Mutts.**

The logo features a space-helmeted dog in a kennel with rocket engines attached. **1**, **2** and **4** feature Device fonts Straker and Data 90, both of which reference early computer 'optical-recognition' fonts such as OCR-A and their unusual placement of the thick and thin strokes.

1

2

3

4

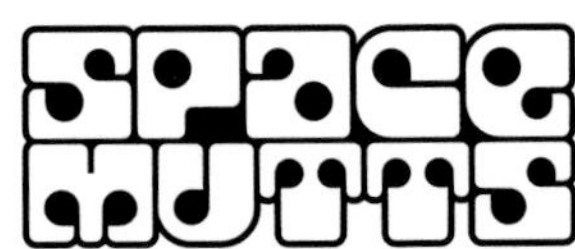

The Intimates
Wildstorm Comics
Comic book series
2005

The Intimates, a 12-issue series written by Joe Casey with art by Jim Lee and Giuseppe Camuncoli, followed the lives of super-powered teenagers in a school called the Seminary, focussing on the characters rather than the heroics.

I designed the logo and trade dress to look more like a teen magazine than a comic, while Joe wrote satirical cover lines for each issue. The fonts used are my own designs, September and Contour.

The comic was launched with a signing at Wizardworld in Fort Worth, Texas. Due to a room number mix-up, Richard Hatch of *Battlestar Galactica* fame, who was staying in the room next to ours, inadvertently paid our (not insignificant) bar bill. I didn't discover this until I was back in England. I owe you a drink in the afterlife, Captain Apollo.

The copy of the first issue shown here has been signed by the contributors. Cover artist Jim Lee humorously berates me for putting type across Destra's 'bristols.' He has a point.

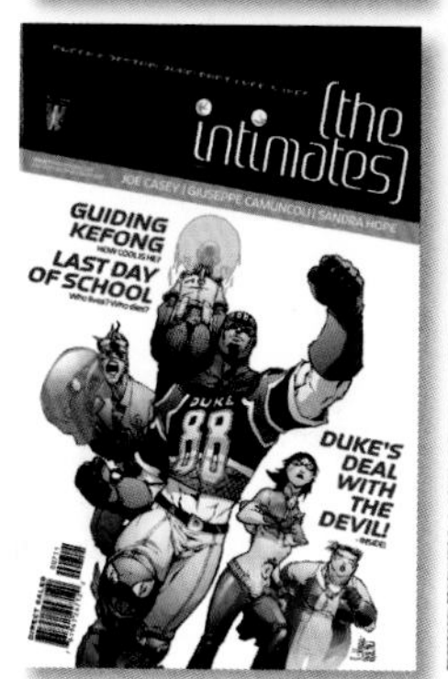

To Be Space
Hristina Milanova
Interior wall-hanging decorative displays
2010

Created for an interior designer's range of meditative wall-mounted backlit displays, the logo is based on an 'S' for space that, on its side, doubles as an infinity symbol. The loop takes you through the colours of the spectrum and back again, much like the ever-changing light show of the displays themselves.

Automatic Records
Transient Records
Record label
2000

A simplified redesign of my original logo for **Automatic**, a dance music label from **Transient Records**, that updates the original's launderette logo imagery.

1

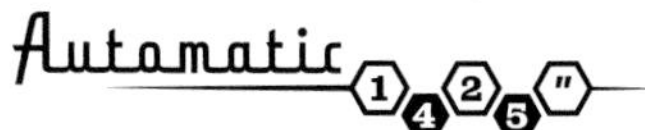

2

3

4

5

6

7

8

Vengeance of the Moon Knight
Marvel Comics
Comic book series
2009

VENGEANCE OF THE
MOON
KNIGHT

Created by Doug Moench and Don Perlin, **Moon Knight** first appeared in *Werewolf by Night* #32 in 1975 – though I vividly remember the character from the 1980s run, celebrated for the experimental art of Bill Sienkiewicz.

The editor described this 2009 reboot, written by Gregg Hurwitz and drawn by Jerome Opena, as "a pretty dark, urban horror, crime noir", and asked that I try and incorporate some aspect of the character's costume.

I avoided a straight update of any of the original logos, as nostalgia aside they weren't particularly distinguished. For the first round, the front runner was the logo opposite, which managed to neatly incorporate the "Vengeance of the" tagline and use the pointed 'O's, with a white triangle between them, to suggest the manner in which **Moon Knight's** eyes are shaded by his cowl. The unusual shapes this produces are taken through to the other letters, lending them an interesting rhythm of curves and lines. The result is sleek and masculine. I also explored the more obvious crescent moon motif, which had been used on the previous iteration.

The best designs tend to arise from an understanding and explication of the unique aspects of the character, and there are often just a few conceptually rigorous contenders for the best solution.

Here, I produced well over 80 designs over three or four rounds (one or two is usually sufficient) but could not get a handle on what **Marvel** were after. This was mainly due to a lack of detailed feedback, and requests to "see more options, please".

Eventually I managed to tease out some direction by asking very specific questions on how they felt about each one. Did they want something more traditional? More avant-garde? More dramatic? More elegant? More comic book? Less comic book? Design at its best is a collaborative process, but without that conversation the most conceptually strong work tends to get lost.

The final logo is overleaf.

1

2

3

4

5

6

7

8

9

10

11

12

Vengeance of the Moon Knight
Marvel Comics
Comic book series
2009

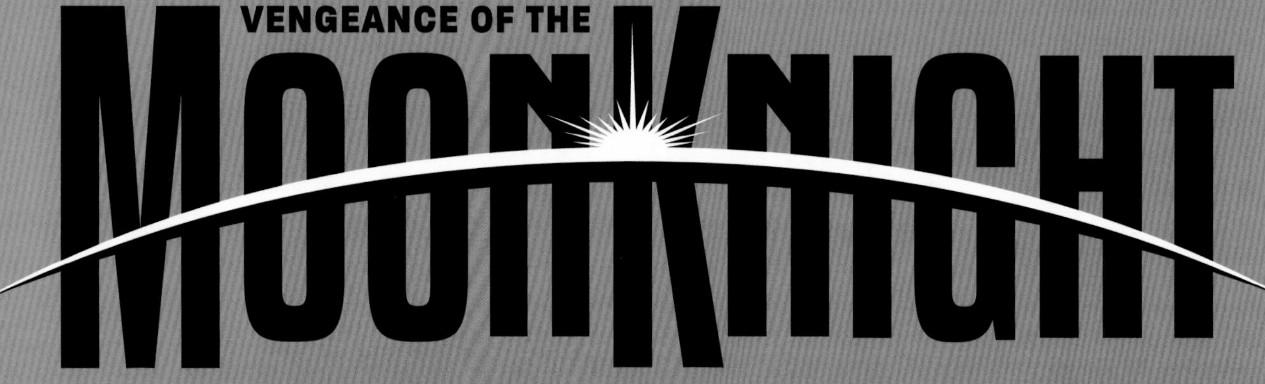

The final logo runs both words on one line, necessitating a condensed but still readable design that's perhaps reminiscent of a New York skyline. The larger 'M' and 'K' serve to break up the lettering into two distinct words, and 'Vengeance of the' is neatly tucked in the space created between them. The white overlay is the light shining over the edge of the crescent moon, with a central 'flash' positioned centrally on the upright of the 'K'. This is underscored with a black arc that also serves as the crossbar for the 'G'. Another iteration (not shown) also used the black arc as the crossbar on the 'H', but this read as two 'I's.

Stacking the two words one above the other, as seen in **1**, **2**, **3**, **4** and **11**, gives a squarer format which can be harder to incorporate on the cover, especially if the art has already been commissioned. More unusually proportioned logos are possible of course, but in these cases it helps if the cover artist sees the design before they start, so that can leave the appropriate amount of space.

Though I gave instructions on its use, it took a few issues for **Marvel** to get the hang of the logo in print. The overlaid curve and 'flash', which I'd requested be white or a light colour, was given a black outline or dropped altogether (not shown). In both instances, it just didn't read as light peeking over the crescent moon.

This is a problem inherent in logos that have a design concept that necessitates they are used in a specific fashion, and though I generally supply instructions and sample layouts showing a logo in situ with suggested colourways, these sometimes don't make it through the chain of command to the in-house designer at the coalface. One solution is to avoid anything that requires special attention – to, in effect, make it foolproof, but that does limit the design options.

Thankfully this is a rare event.

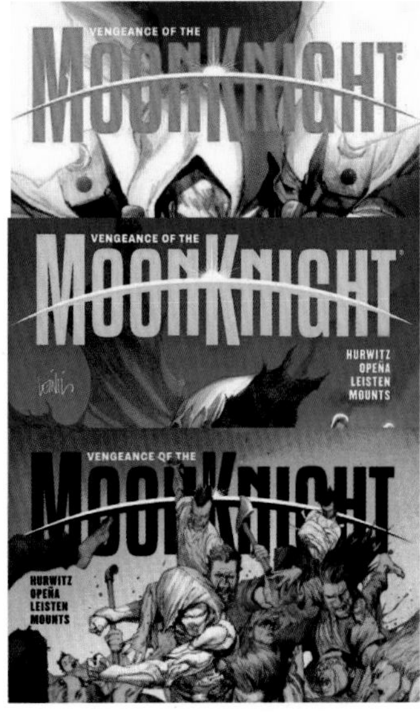

1

MOON KNIGHT

2

MOON KNIGHT

3

MOON KNIGHT

4

MOON KNIGHT

5

MOON KNIGHT

6

MOON KNIGHT

7

MOON KNIGHT

8

MOON KNIGHT

9

VENGEANCE OF THE MOON KNIGHT

10

VENGEANCE OF THE MOON KNIGHT

11

MOON KNIGHT

12

MOON KNIGHT

Organised Chaos
Clairefontaine
Stationery and accessories
2000

A motif for a range of signature designs that bore my name produced for French stationery company **Clairefontaine**. The range included wastepaper baskets **2**, pencil cases, a rucksak and a series of notepads **3**. **1** is the base of the wastepaper basket.

1

2

My Works of Unique and Timeless Genius
Behold the Legend
Please Write In Me
Fresh White Sheets
Playtime for the Soul
Fill Me Up
Who What When Where
Get It Together
Clairefontaine
Stationery and accessories
2000

A set of slogans and type treatments for a range of stationery and accessories from **Clairefontaine**. The first six covers shown below are blank or lined notebooks; the seventh is an address book and the eighth a diary.

1

PHILIP PULLMAN
NORTHERN LIGHTS

2

PHILIP PULLMAN
HIS DARK MATERIALS

3

PHILIP PULLMAN
THE SUBTLE KNIFE

4

PHILIP PULLMAN
THE AMBER SPYGLASS

5

“MIT DEM TAXI INS INTERNET”

6

“HOLT SIE AB INS INTERNET”

7

8

9

10

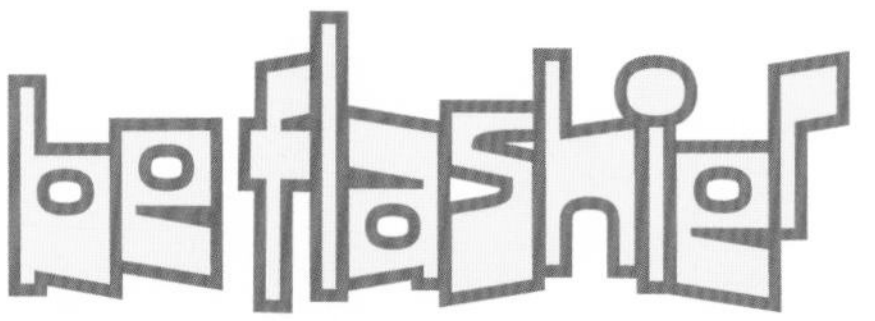

1 **Philip Pullman: Northern Lights**
2 **Philip Pullman: His Dark Materials**
3 **Philip Pullman: The Subtle Knife**
4 **Philip Pullman: The Amber Spyglass**
BBC
Radio drama CD series
2002
Custom type for a CD box set of the radio dramatisation of Pullman's *His Dark Materials* trilogy, which I also designed and illustrated

5 6 **Yellowgate**
Publicis (Switzerland)
Posters and press advertisements
2010
Custom type for a series of internet provider advertisements, for which I also provided the illustrations

7 **Be Cooler**
8 **Be Smarter**
9 **Be Karma**
10 **Be Flashier**
Ericsson/Young and Rubicam
Advertising campaign
1999
Part of a series of custom type treatments for an advertising campaign for which I also provided the illustrations

Wonder Woman
DC Comics
Comic book
Proposed logo
1992

1

2

3

4

5

6

7

One of my first commissions for **DC Comics** and designed a year before I bought my first Mac, this **Wonder Woman** logo did not progress beyond these initial sketches. Commissioned by Tom Peyer for a relaunch in which Brian Bolland took over the covers, my favourite design **6** was worked into his first sketch, but in the end a logo designed in-house was used.

I chose to reference the classic looping script of the original from 1942 in **1** and **6**, though with a contemporary twist, while others **5**, **7** borrow from the double-'W' of her chest emblem and the stars on her shorts.

These days, it is rare that I produce sketches to this degree of finish. Post-Mac, I tend to go from loose thumbnails in which I pin down the basic concept directly to Adobe Illustrator – though hypocritically I advise students not to do this. Do as I say, not as I do.

Priors
Eye Industries
Band logo proposal
2009

The logo concepts for Parisian band **Priors** encompassed cut-outs, folded paper, doodles and origami. They were keen on something that looked "hand-made, school art-class or home crafted".

The final version (main image) has a clean, stacked frame into which different textural and photographic elements relating to the band's interests were dropped.

1

2

3

4

5

PRIORS

6

7

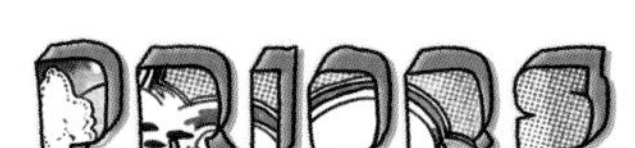

8

9

10

11

12

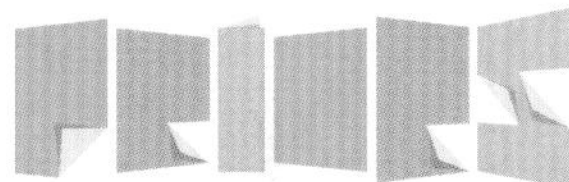

13

14

15

16

17

18

19

20

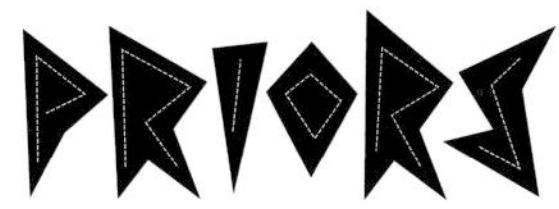

Wednesday Comics
DC Comics
Weekly newspaper-sized comic
2009

Conceived by **DC Comics**' editorial art director Mark Chiarello, **Wednesday Comics** was a 12-issue weekly anthology that was issued in an unusual 14″ x 20″ tabloid newspaper format, allowing artists to create large Sunday paper sized layouts. Each page featured a different story by a different creative team, and it folded down twice to a regular American comic size.

Mark's original sketch **2** referenced old newspaper mastheads, and was my starting point. The final logo dropped the row of heads as they tended to duplicate the round vignettes below, though they were kept for the version seen when the paper is folded out **1**, here held by DC's publisher Bob Wayne, whose nominative determinism makes him the man for the job. The logo switched colour between red and black each issue. The final covers (opposite) were assembled by DC's Kenny Lopez from my original template **16**.

I also designed the oversized hardback collection **3**.

1

2

3

4

5

6

7

8

9

10

11

12

13

14

15

COMICS
WEDNESDAY
COMICS

WEDNESDAY
COMICS

WEDNESDAY
COMICS

WEDNESDAY
COMICS

WEDNESDAY
COMICS

16

THE WORLD'S GREATEST HEROES
WEDNESDAY
THE WORLD'S GREATEST COMICS!
DC
COMICS
OCT 21, 2008
$2.99

BAD BOYS NC
©
BAD BOYS INC
©
BB

Scorch
Bad Boys Inc/A+M Records
Band mascot
1993

Formed by record producer Ian Levine, **Bad Boys Inc.** were squarely aimed at the young pop market. Jeremy Pearce and Graham Tunna, art directors at A+M Records, commissioned a mascot to be used on their sleeves, on merchandise and on stage as a backdrop.

The name **Scorch** was chosen via a competition in *Smash Hits*, a fondly remembered British pop fortnightly with offices in Carnaby Street that I briefly worked for shortly after leaving art college, designing spreads for such luminaries as The Belle Stars and Jimmy the Hoover, and decorative backgrounds for song lyrics.

Scorch appeared on picture discs, stickers **10**, Japanese releases **11**, in a Santa hat for Christmas **8**, **9**, and in a 'Bazooka Joe' style comic that was used as an inlay in the CD. He was Cupid for Valentine's day **2**, **5**, and Atlas for the single *More to This World* **4**.

Scorch sits squarely between a logo and an illustration, but then strict boundaries between type, illustration and graphics do often blur – and that can only be a good thing.

The final layouts were designed in-house by Jeremy and Graham at A+M.

1

2

3

4

5

6

7

8

9

10

11

12

Pink Floyd
Stylorouge
CD Box set
Proposed logos
1992

A proposed set of logos for a **Pink Floyd** box set reissue, taking images from each classic album and morphing them into each other. Art directed by Mark Caylor at Stylorouge.

Until a few years ago, I had never listened to *Dark Side of the Moon*. Others in the studio were incredulous, and insisted I listen to it there and then. We had it on rotation for several weeks, and yes, it is a classic.

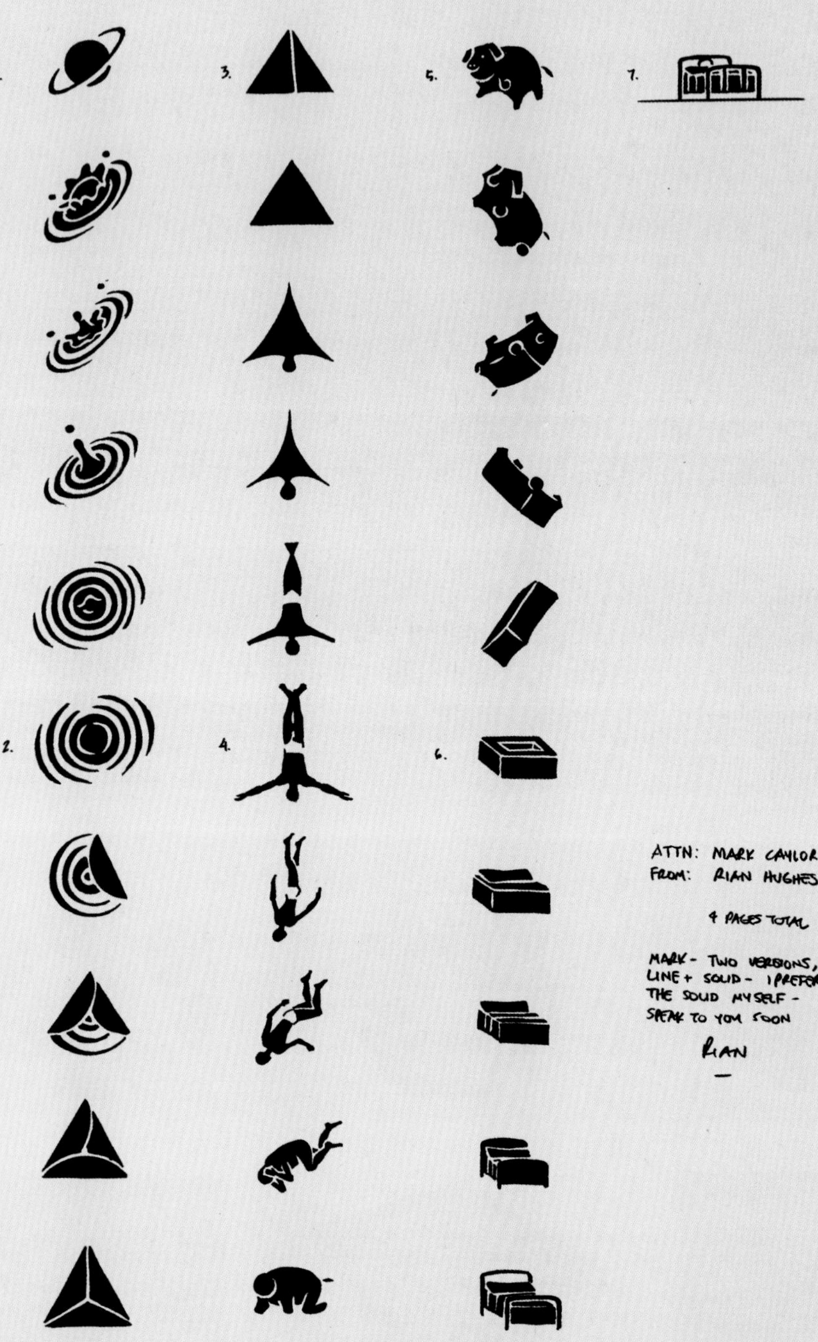

Super Freaks
Elsa Charettier/IDW
Comic book series
2017

Super Freaks is a comic book aimed at a young adult audience. The pitch is simple: "In a world where superheroes have disappeared overnight, their loser teenage sidekicks have to deal with the biggest crisis Earth has ever known all on their own". Writer Elsa Charettier asked for something "cool and bad-ass" to suit the diverse roster of misfits.

The first design **1** was deemed hard to read. The favourite from the second round has a clean but lively 'graf' edge. I supplied a set of potential colourways **3** to illustrate how it might work with Margaux Saltel's brightly coloured art.

1

2

3

4

5

6

7

Dot London
London and Partners/Mayor of London
London internet domain
2016

For the launch of the new .london internet domain, London and Partners, London's official not-for-profit promotional organisation, commissioned work from 20 London-based digital and traditional artists including Yoni Alter, Stuart Semple, Duggie Fields and myself.

The results were displayed on flyposters **2**, **3** and in exhibitions around London, including a converted shop in Covent Garden, St Christopher's Place, Box Park Shoreditch, and hanging from the ceiling of Borough Market's Market Hall **1**.

The only criterion was that each piece should be circular. My design was adapted from an earlier Device T-shirt, itself derived from an unsolicited proposal for a logo that attempted to do for London what Milton Glazer's classic 'I ❤ NY' design did for New York. That version from 2007 came with a short graphic explanation rather than a lengthy written essay **4**, and was returned by then-Mayor of London Ken Livingstone's office because "they already had a logo". I pointed out that the existing design was for the Mayor's office rather than the city itself, and so was unlikely to be adopted by souvenir T-shirt and tourist tat vendors in Trafalgar Square, the true litmus test for the success of a design such as this.

The next mayor, Boris Johnson, subsequently issued a call for proposals for a London logo, but unfortunately I found out about this two days after the deadline. I suggested in an email that as I'd originally delivered my design when Livingstone was in office I was actually *early*, but unfortunately this did not swing it and I was excluded from the judging.

Their loss was Dot London's gain. The imposition of the circular shape turned out to be an improvement. An animated version in which the heart pulses, changing to a dot and back, can be seen on their website.

1

2

3

4

Steed and Mrs Peel
Acme Press
Comic book series
1990

Written by Grant Morrison and drawn by **Robo-Hunter** and *Halo Jones* artist Ian Gibson, this series featured Steed, Emma Peel, and in the final volume, Tara King. I presume the title was chosen to avoid confusion with **Marvel**'s **Avengers.**

I sketched out the covers as I saw them: just the figures on white backgrounds, with colour kept to the centrally placed logo into which a different geometric pattern is dropped each issue, and Ian graciously worked from my roughs.

The story was called *The Great Game,* and the back cover numbers the three issues by the turn of a playing card featuring a bowler hat and goblet motif. The '52 Club' design on the back of the pack was taken directly from my year's LCP (London College of Printing, now London College of Communication) graduation catalogue. Photography by John R. Ward. **1** is the title spread, **2** a promotional poster.

STEED AND MRS PEEL

1

2

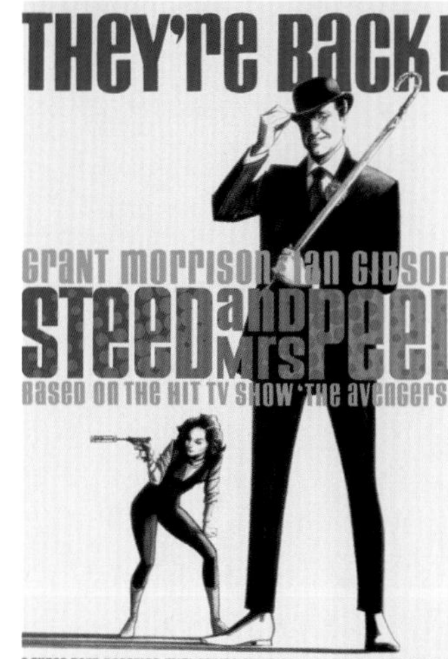

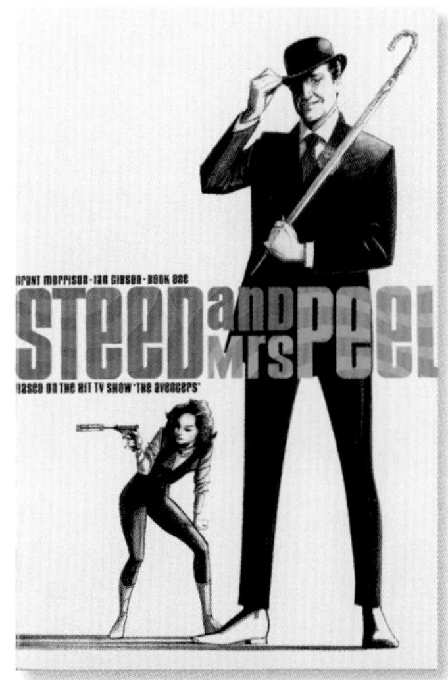

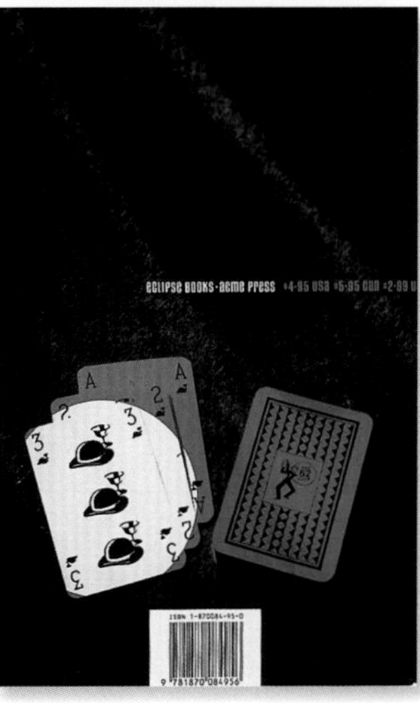

Freddie Stevenson
Juicy Musical Creations
Singer/songwriter
2006

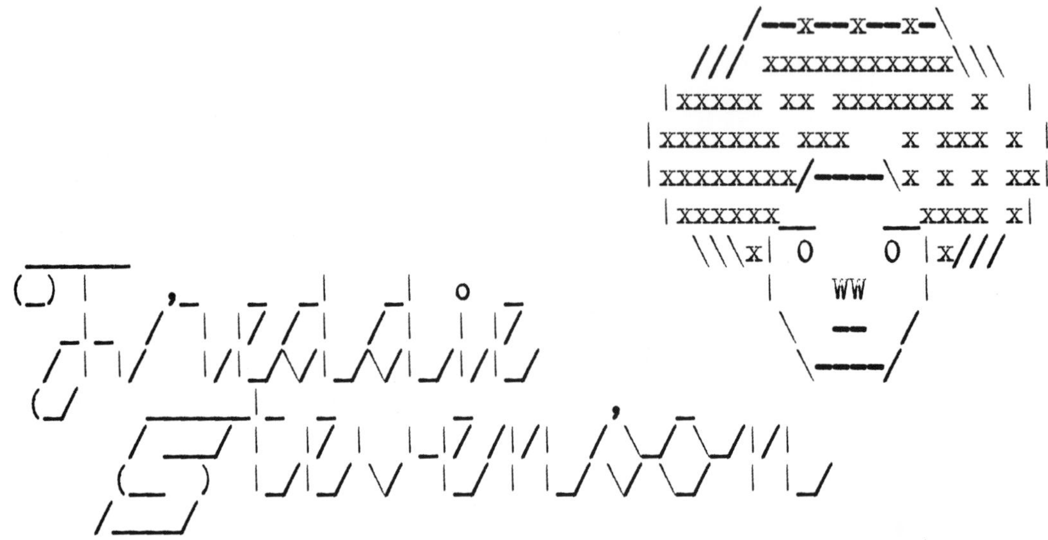

Freddie Stevenson forgoes complicated production techniques for a stripped-down acoustic guitar sound. The typewriter execution of the logo reflects this homespun singer/songwriter's DIY ethos. I took the concept through to my design of the CD packaging **3-6**, in which both the portraits of Freddie and the song titles and text are all created with a typewriter. Winner of a *Communication Arts* Award of Excellence.

1

2

3

4

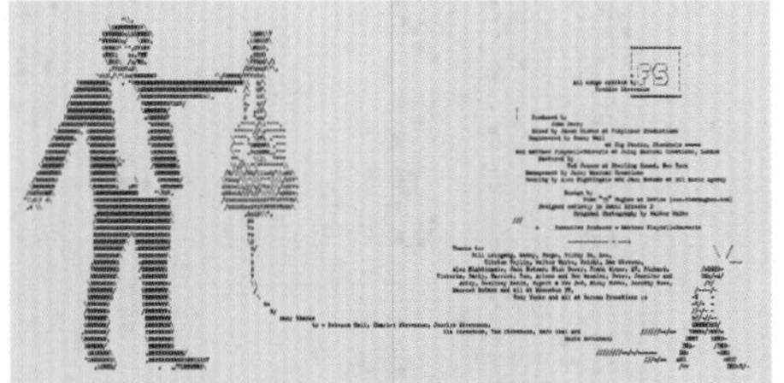

5

6

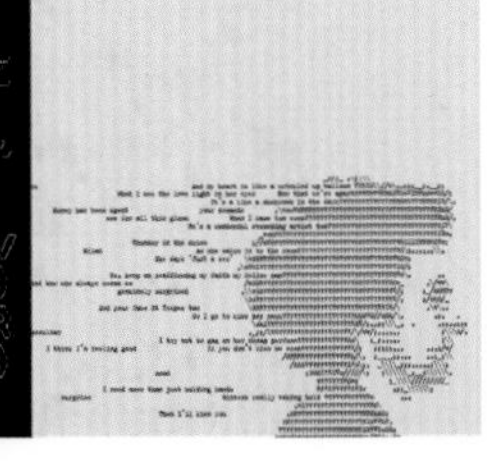

Robodojo
Wildstorm Comics
Comic book series
2002

Robodojo was a series written by veteran writer Marv Wolfman. Five of the brightest young minds in robotics create the next generation of giant robots, built for heavy labour. "Lots of rock 'em sock 'em giant robot action and girls with purple hair", as the brief explained.

For the chosen logo, I imagined what the branding applied to the actual mecha suits might look like, incorporating geometric elements from the suit designs and a Japanese science fiction aesthetic.

1

2

3

4

5

6

7

8

Hot Choice
FDG
Cable TV channel
Logo proposal
2001

1

2

3

4

Hot Choice was an adult pay-per-view network based in the USA. They requested a logo that would be bold and brash and incorporate a character who was suggestive and sexy, but not pornographic.

The logos featured winking cats, playful devils, neon (long a graphic trope suggestive of louche establishments) and hot pinks, reds and oranges.

5

Radical
Radical Surf
Surfing equipment and clothing store
Proposed logo
2001

1

2

3

4

5

6

7

8

Harbinger
Valiant Comics
Comic book series
2011

Published as part of the original line in 1992, **Harbinger** was the first logo I was asked to design for **Valiant**'s reboot in 2012.

The series is named after the corporation run by its antagonist – The **Harbinger** Foundation – suggesting that it should have a strong, clean, corporate feel. As the original **Harbinger** logo evolved it always maintained the bird element in some form, something I definitely wanted to retain.

For the final design (main image) the bird is placed at the end of a line that bisects the letters, a small serif on the 'G' being repeated on the 'A' and 'H' to add the suggestion of a crossbar.

I drew the variant cover for issue 15, in which each character is a badge.

Version **2** was revisited for the sequel, **Harbinger: Renegade**. The final logo for this series is shown at **4**.

1

2

3

4

1

2

3

4

VALIANT
HARBINGER
#0
HARBINGER
#0
HARBINGER
#1
HARBINGER
#1
HARBINGER
#1
HARBINGER
#1
HARBINGER
#2
HARBINGER
#3
HARBINGER
#5
HARBINGER
#5
HARBINGER
#6
RISE OF THE RENEGADES!
HARBINGER
#7
HARBINGER
#7
HARBINGER
#8
HARBINGER
#8
HARBINGER
#9
HARBINGER
#10
HARBINGER WARS
HARBINGER
#12
HARBINGER WARS
HARBINGER
#12
HARBINGER WARS
HARBINGER
#13
HARBINGER WARS
HARBINGER
#14
HARBINGER
#15
HARBINGER
#15
HARBINGER
#15
HARBINGER
#16
HARBINGER
#18
HARBINGER
#18
HARBINGER
#20
HARBINGER
#21
RESISTANCE
PART TWO
HARBINGER
#22
DRIVE-IN
DEATH OF A RENEGADE
SECOND PRINTING
DEATH OF A RENEGADE
HARBINGER
#22
ANNIVERSARY SPECTACULAR!
HARBINGER
#25
HARBINGER WARS
HARBINGER
DEATH OF A RENEGADE
HARBINGER
MUERTE DE UN RENEGADO
HARBINGER

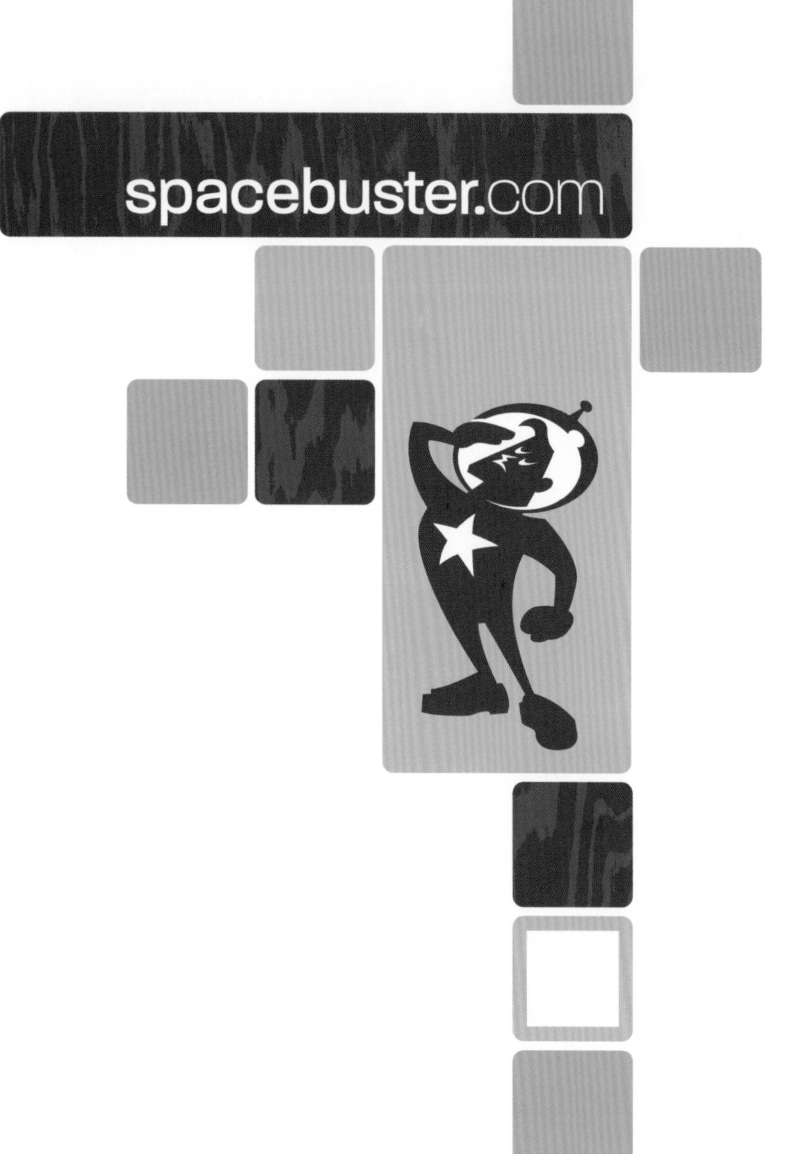

Spacebuster
View (agency)
Storage facilities
2001

A combined logo and stand-alone character for the self-storage company **Spacebuster**. The modular arrangement was flexible, and would be freely rearranged **2**, **3** for each use to mimic stacked boxes and the flexibility of the available space.

An earlier working title was Space Doctor **1**. The font is Paralucent, one of my most popular Device Fonts releases.

1

2

3

Soda Club
Stylorouge/Concept Music
Single
2002

The logos for dance anthem *Show Me You Love Me* riff on fizzy drinks labels and bubbles. The single cover also featured my illustration of the outfit, a female vocalist backed by two male dancers. The tune is based around a sample from Sub Sub feat. Melanie Williams' 1993 hit *Ain't No Love (Ain't No Use)*, which in turn samples Revelation's *Good Morning Starshine* from 1979.

1

2

3

4

5

6

7

8

American Century
DC Comics/Vertigo
Comic book series
2000

Co-written by Howard Chaykin and David Tischman, **American Century** was published under **DC Comics**' more adult-themed Vertigo imprint. Intended as a "left-wing version of Steve Canyon" set in the 1950s, the story concerned an American former pilot who fakes his own death. As the character goes on the run from Hollywood via Chicago to New York, Chaykin explores the culture of the period.

Early logo ideas referenced the lettering found on US aircraft **1**, while the chosen design (main image) evokes vintage American cigarette packaging. The unused design **1** was later adapted for an **Enemy Ace** series. The type derives from Ainsdale, a Device font.

The logo was supplied as an overall trade dress. Later covers were painted by Glen Orbik, in a noir paperback style.

1

Starship Enterprises
Tony Fletcher/Starship Enterprises
Tour programmes
1985

Tony Fletcher, editor of school fanzine turned professional music monthly *Jamming!*, was also in the business of managing bands and writing and editing tour programmes. This was the logo for this side venture, scanned from the original letterhead.

Spider-Man
BLT Associates
Film titles
Logo proposal
2002

Spider-Man: Family Business
Marvel Comics
Original graphic novel
2013

This logo was commissioned indirectly for the first of Sam Raimi's hugely enjoyable **Spider-Man** trilogy by BLT Associates. Though I was thrilled to be involved, none of my ideas were used; the final logo for the film was of the 'extended, letterspaced brushed chrome' variety that has become the default for this kind of movie.

The 'cityscape' version of the logo (opposite) was finally used in my design for 2013's **Family Business**, a **Spider-Man** original graphic novel by Mark Waid, James Robinson and Gabriele Dell'Otto. Note the spider hanging further down on its thread each time, and finally falling.

I vividly recall a set vist during the filming of the runaway train scene in *Spider-Man 2*. There was Spidey, crouching dramatically on the cab in an archetypal pose against a green screen. I got chills as my inner geek screamed "It's Spider-Man!" like a demented eight-year-old, though of course outwardly I kept my cool.

1

2

3

4

5

THE AMAZING
SPIDER-MAN

6

7

8

SPIDERMAN

9

10

SPIDERMAN

Someone has Spider-Man in their crosshairs, and the only person in the Marvel Universe who can save him is... Peter Parker's sister?!
AMAZING SPIDER-MAN
FAMILY BUSINESS

Tell me a Spider-Man story. And make it a good one.
We all know Spidey.
He's been part of our culture for more than half a century. He's in comic books, movies, and cartoons. Action figures, lunchboxes, and pajamas. And we all know his story...

Biographies

Behind the Scenes

Page 17
Page 31

Avengers: Endless Wartime
Augmented Reality
Free Digital copy

Sketchy Theatre
Life Drawing Society
Drawing events
2013

WAR
Wakeboard Association of Ranzo
Italian wakeboarding club
2011

Marvel/Harley Davidson
Marvel Comics
Merchandise
2015

The Last Drop
Maxim magazine (US)
Article header
2002

1 Skulls of the Shogun
17-Bit
Video game
2012

2 MacUser
MacUser magazine
Magazine article icon
1998

3 Silent Night of the Living Dead
New Millennium Theatre Company
Theatre production
2013

4 Caution: Hung Like a Fruit Bat
Stuff magazine
Sticker
2000
From a set of free stickers
given away with the magazine

5 Styloroughe Fish
Stylorouge
Promotional T-shirt and 'pizza box'
1998

6 Club Spirit
Distillers
Incidental animation logo
1998

7 Brave
Device
T-shirt motif
2015

8 Batman and the Signal
DC Comics
Comic book series
2017

9 UFO Pilot
Stuff magazine
Sticker
2000
From a set of free stickers
given away with the magazine

10 Molly Moon
Harper Collins
Children's book series
Proposed logo
2010

11 Brrp!
Tizer/Lowe Howard Spink
Advertisement
1991

12 Furlong PR
Public relations company
2005

1

2

3

4

5

6

7

8

9

10

11

12

Aliens
Dark Horse
Comic book magazine
1992

1

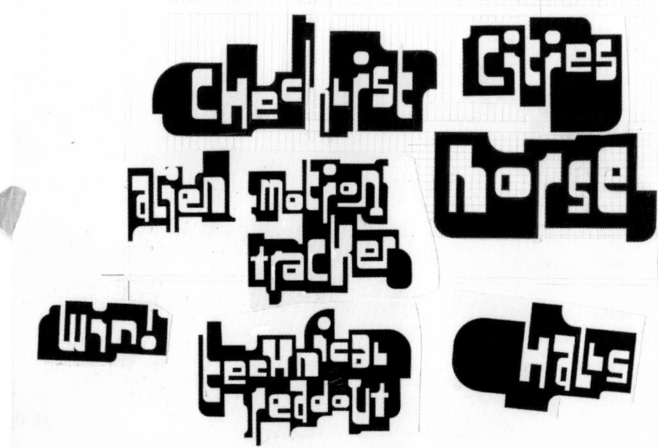

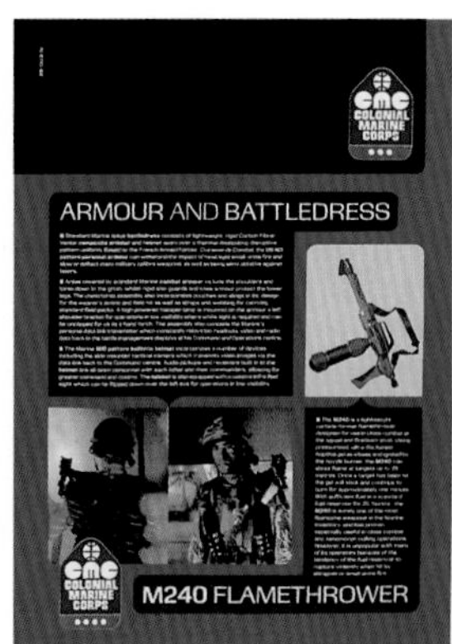

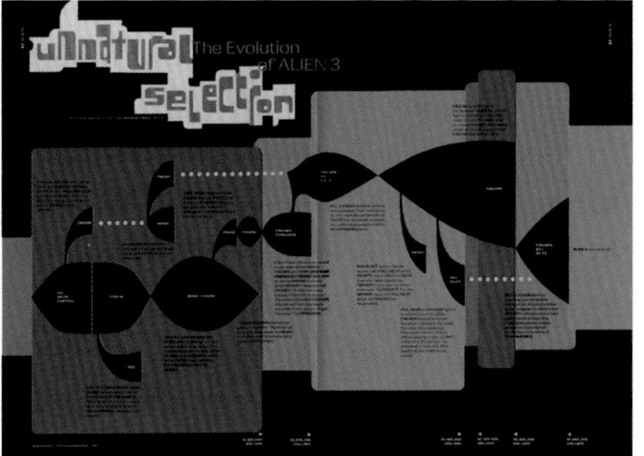

I designed the UK **Aliens** magazine for two issues after the newly formed international branch of Dark Horse Comics took over from fly-by-night publisher Trident.

There was one more issue due to be published, Volume 1 Number 17, before their relaunch, and I was asked to design it in the same amateurish style that had been used previously. I just couldn't bring myself to do it, so the redesign actually began with the last issue of Volume 1, and Volume 2, Number 1 followed on after.

I drew the article headers by hand with a Rotring pen and a parallel motion on a drawing board at the Clerkenwell studio I briefly shared with Trevor Jackson (Bite It!), Machine and Graham Tunna. After I'd accumulated quite a selection of letters, I began to cut and paste them together to save time. They became ever more ornate, and perhaps too overcomplicated. The air in East London was so filthy that if I left artwork out over the weekend it'd be covered with black soot on Monday morning, which would smudge as I worked.

The **Aliens** logo is based closely on the one from the James Cameron movie. I respaced the letters, bringing them closer together to give it more impact on the cover. This being pre-Photoshop, the printer couldn't duplicate the glow around the 'I', so it was reduced to a simple graphic lens shape.

Titan Books' in-house studio took over from Volume 2, issue 2, and after struggling to duplicate my design dropped all but the most superficial elements for the rest of the run.

Batgirl
DC Comics
Comic book series
2000

The first solo **Batgirl** title to be published didn't feature Commissioner Gordon's daughter Barbara Gordon, the more familiar version of the character, but Cassandra Cain. Deprived of human contact during her childhood and conditioned to become an assassin, she is a mute whose cowl covers her mouth. Written by Kelley Puckett and Scott Peterson, with art by Damion Scott and Robert Campanella, the title was an altogether darker affair.

My early versions of the logo **1**, **2** were rightly considered to be too light-hearted, and bore a resemblance to the logo from the Adam West **Batman** TV show, the third season of which introduced Barbara Gordon's **Batgirl**.

The more feminine shape to the cowl **6**, **8** was changed to a more dramatic and moody silhouette and lowered into the cape, again to better reflect Cain's character, and from a practical point of view to resolve the empty space to the top right of the logo that would otherwise be left when it was placed on the cover. This reduced space was put to good use as the regular position for the credits.

There was a lively discussion about whether lowercase type was essentially feminine or not; while the perceived gender of different styles of type is an essay in itself, for the final version we settled on uppercase.

For the *War Games* crossover, it was given a stencil treatment. The final covers were designed in-house at DC using the then-current standard trade dress.

1

2

3

4

5

6

7

8

This Way Up
Amphora Arts
Australia and New Zealand
Festival of Literature and Arts
2014

1

2

3

4

5

6

7

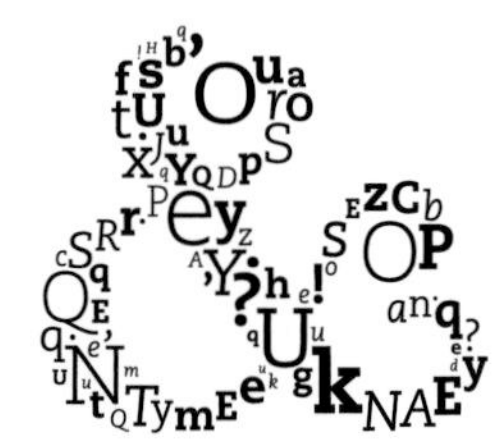

8

9

10

This Way Up is an annual festival and year-round website celebrating the arts, literature and culture of Australia and New Zealand. As well as a strong brand, the requirement was for on-site signage and a brochure, leaflets, posters, T-shirts, and elements for the festival website. The curator wanted to subvert the usual stereotypes and focus on the storytellers, creators, musicians and speakers and their current place in the world, politically, socially and culturally.

The festival was to be called the 'Australia & New Zealand Festival of Literature & Arts', and needed a recognisable symbol which could eventually be used both with and without text. As part of the design I was asked to come up with a strapline that embodied the spirit of the festival. The name was already a bit wordy, so the first logos attempt to make the title more digestible by breaking it up into units using colour and different weights of my Device font Paralucent for emphasis.

1, **2** used the variant 'Australia and New Zealand Festival of Arts and Literature', but the acronym was dangerously close to a profanity.

I proposed renaming the event the shorter and more memorable **This Way Up**, with the original lengthy but more descriptive title as the strapline.

As there was no budget for photography, a modular approach was developed into which existing photographs of the speakers and the venues could be dropped, with a duotone treatment lending them more stylistic cohesion.

The final logo (right) is based on a packing crate label and does repurpose a particular down-under cliché – that everything there is upside-down. The two arrows represent the two countries, Australia and New Zealand, while the label itself references travel, and more specifically both the journeys settlers took from the UK and elsewhere and the journey that the speakers and performers, including Aboriginal and Maori, have taken to the UK to perform.

The ampersand was a repeating motif both in 'Australia & New Zealand' and 'Literature & Arts', so it was used throughout in different styles to represent each thread of the festival in the brochure and signage **4**-**7**, **9**. Special Maori and Aboriginal ampersands were commissioned.

11 is a poster concept for the 2014 festival with an early iteration of the logo; **12** is the cover of the brochure. **13** is a poster for 2015's event. I was ably assisted on the roll-out by Ben Gilbey.

11

12

13

Hed Kandi
Jazz FM/Mark Doyle
Record label and club events
1998

New clients come by the strangest of routes. I'll let **Hed Kandi** creator Mark Doyle himself tell the story:

"When I was much younger I ran a club night on Friday at Haven Stables in Ealing Broadway. I needed a hip and trendy flyer to hand out, so I used Stock Aitken Waterman's **Roadblock** sleeve, which also became the name of the night.

"One night while DJing I was tapped on the shoulder by a young man who wanted a word. He had designed the **Roadblock** sleeve, happened to live in Ealing, and was less than impressed. There wasn't a lot I could do, other than promise him that one day I'd pay him back.

"Fast-forward to early 1999. I had been running Jazz FM Records, and after several smooth jazz albums I pushed the label's boundaries with two very successful 'Nu Cool' compilations. Whilst they sold very well, they weren't quite in keeping with the label identity, so I found myself with the job of creating an entire brand from start to finish. I thought, 'who do I know that designs logos?'

"I saw Rian's work in a design magazine and gave him a call. 'Hi Rian, bit of a weird one – are you from West London, and do you remember a club in Ealing?' He replied: 'Of course, there was one place where some cheeky bastard stole my artwork for a flyer.' I admitted it was me, but I was here, ten years later, to return the favour. He turned out to be absolutely brilliant. Obviously I had no idea just how important this logo was going to be, or what it would mean to people. Call it luck or serendipity but something brought Rian and I together to create one of the most iconic logos in dance music. I've seen it tattooed onto various body parts, made into wall art, discussed in design magazines and sold on millions of CDs. It featured heavily in our club decor, and many of the production pieces we used were stolen and turned up for vast sums on eBay.

"Rian's work nailed what Hed Kandi was about in its earliest and most successful period. It's a truly memorable piece of art and I can't imagine starting that label without it."

Mark's choice of music and Jason Brooks' glamorous cover artwork **10**, **13**, **15** were instrumental in distinguishing the brand. The final logo is an abstract head with a starburst within, suggesting a rush of joy – candy for the head. It has been used on two retail shops, **Hed Kandi** bars **15** in Brighton and Clapham (and other unlicensed venues abroad), and there was even a **Hed Kandi** branded plane **13**, **14** that flew between London and Ibiza.

My Haven Stables membership card is tucked inside early **Hed Kandi** release *Back to Love* **10**, a compilation which for me defines that era.

1

2

3

4

5

6

7

8

9

10

11

12

13

14

15

hed
kandi

Blag!
Ministry of Sound
Club night
2000

A cheeky monkey mascot for a regular event at Ministry of Sound, the famous South London nightclub.

1

2

3

4

5

6

7

8

The Animalhouse
Boilerhouse
Band
2000

Formed in 1997 in Oxford, **The Animalhouse** brought together bassist Hari T and Supergrass producer Sam Williams with Mark Gardner and Laurence 'Loz' Colbert of shoegazing band Ride for a fusion of electronics and upbeat 1960s psychedelia.

I also designed the Japanese CD release **1**, for which just the paw print **5** was used. The band were notorious for not being able to make up their minds on a design direction, and so the UK release has a different sleeve.

1

2

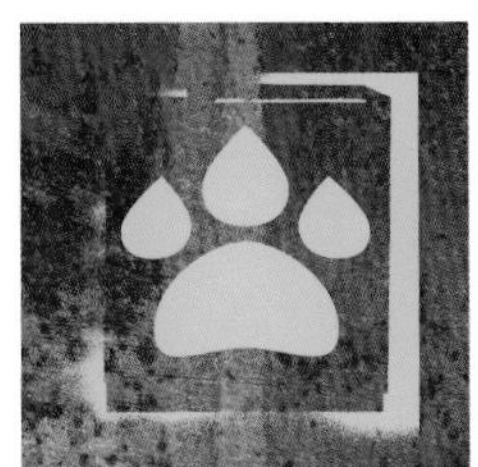

3

THE
ANIMALHOUSE

4

5

6

7

8

9

Archer & Armstrong
Valiant Comics
Comic book
2012

Relaunched as part of **Valiant**'s contemporary reboot, **Archer & Armstrong** originally debuted in 1992, written and drawn by Barry Windsor-Smith.

This incarnation by Fred Van Lente, with art by Clayton Henry, opens when Obadiah Archer is dispatched to New York by his family's religious sect to kill a hard-drinking immortal – Armstrong.

Some of the new **Valiant** logos took elements from the originals, where appropriate, while others were entirely new. To give the line a clean and contemporary appearance, every logo is white and occupies the same dimensions on the cover, diligently avoiding the usual comic book tropes of drop shadows and outlines. A transparent panel across the top ensures it is always possible to lift the logo out of any art without recourse to such effects.

The trade dress also incorporated my new **Valiant** logo, the colour of which was keyed to the art each issue, and a large issue number – **Valiant**, like many other comic companies, were keen to flag up collectable first issues of new series. On subsequent issues the size of the number was reduced.

Archer & Armstrong: Archer was a one-shot retelling Archer's origin.

ARCHER
& ARMSTRONG®

1
& ARCHER ARMSTRONG: ARCHER

2
archer & ARMSTRONG

3
ARCHER&
ARMSTRONG

4
ARCHER
ARMSTRONG

5
ARCHER
ARMSTRONG

6
Archer&
ARMSTRONG

7
Archer&
ARMSTRONG

8
ARCHER &
ARMSTRONG

9
ARCHER
ARMSTRONG

10
ARCHER
+ ARMSTRONG

11
archer and armstrong

12
·ARCHER·&·
ARMSTRONG

FORBIDDEN
PLANET

1

Named after the 1956 film, **Forbidden Planet** is a chain of shops with branches across the UK, Ireland and the US. The first small shop opened in 1978 in London's Denmark Street, where I first discovered its trove of imported US SF books, magazines and comics during the school holidays.

As the scope of the store expanded to embrace film and television, a second store was opened around the corner on St Giles High Street. Titan Books started their publishing business in the cramped basement, where I delivered early book cover designs for Mark Cox and Leigh Baulch.

In 1986 the shop relocated to a 'megastore' in New Oxford Street, at which point Jon Harrison, **Forbidden Planet**'s manager, suggested it might be time to design a new logo to replace the straight Compacta that had been used previously. Early design concepts **5**, **6** incorporated *Forbidden Planet's* iconic Robbie the Robot, who had featured in Brian Bolland's original artwork for the shop's bags. One concept involved different icons that would brand each subsection: SF, comics, horror, etc., but in the end just the rocket was used.

The extended type style of the final logo (here marked "my fave" on the original rough **7**) owes much to Aldo Novarese's Microgramma, a typeface that I remember from Gerry Anderson's TV shows and *Countdown* comic. Its 'obround' extended design projects a modernist futurism that, at the time I designed the logo, was very much at odds with the prevailing letterspaced and condensed styles.

I'm happy to find that it has weathered well, and still looks good all these years later.

8 is the letterhead; **1** a vinyl toy by Matt 'Lunartik' Jones. **9** and **10** are my designs for two anthologies by writers and artists who had signed books at the shop; **11** is the embossed slipcased limited edition.

2

5 6

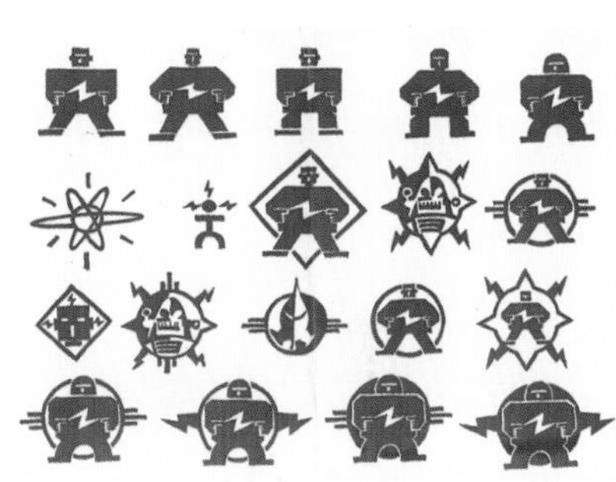

3

7 8

4

9 10 11

Crisis
Fleetway/2000AD
Comic book
1988

Crisis was a British comic magazine published from 1988 to 1991 by **Fleetway**, publishers of *2000AD*. Aimed at a more mature and politically aware audience, the comic was part of the post-*Watchmen/ Dark Knight* push to explore a wider adult market, and a contemporary of titles such as **Deadline**, **Revolver**, and *Blast!*

Edited by ex-Tharg Steve MacManus, the title launched with two serials: Pat Mills and Carlos Ezquerra's **Third World War** was a tirade against the corporate exploitation of the third world set in the near-future, while John Smith and Jim Baikie's *New Statesmen* was a superhero saga designed to be repackaged for the US market. Later issues featured work by Garth Ennis, Peter Milligan, Duncan Fegredo, Grant Morrison and others. My own **Dan Dare** strip concluded in issue 56, after the cancellation of **Revolver**.

I was tasked with the design of the logo and the layout of each issue, which included the front and back covers, the letters page, and occasionally a text piece.

The warning stripes and stencil treatment of the masthead were a direct evocation of the militaristic thrust of Mills' scripts, with the first five issues featuring Carlos' protagonists against an angular futuristic camouflage pattern. The symbols on the back covers alluded to corporate logos with a militaristic makeover.

There was a publicity blitz – advertisements in the music and style press **8** and a press kit that contained a copy of the first issue, a T-shirt and a promotional brochure **1**.

From issue six, Carlos provided full-colour covers: **6** is the rough for the redesigned layout. Later issues began to reprint European material, so the logo was letterspaced and the cover redesigned to incorporate images down the left-hand

1

2

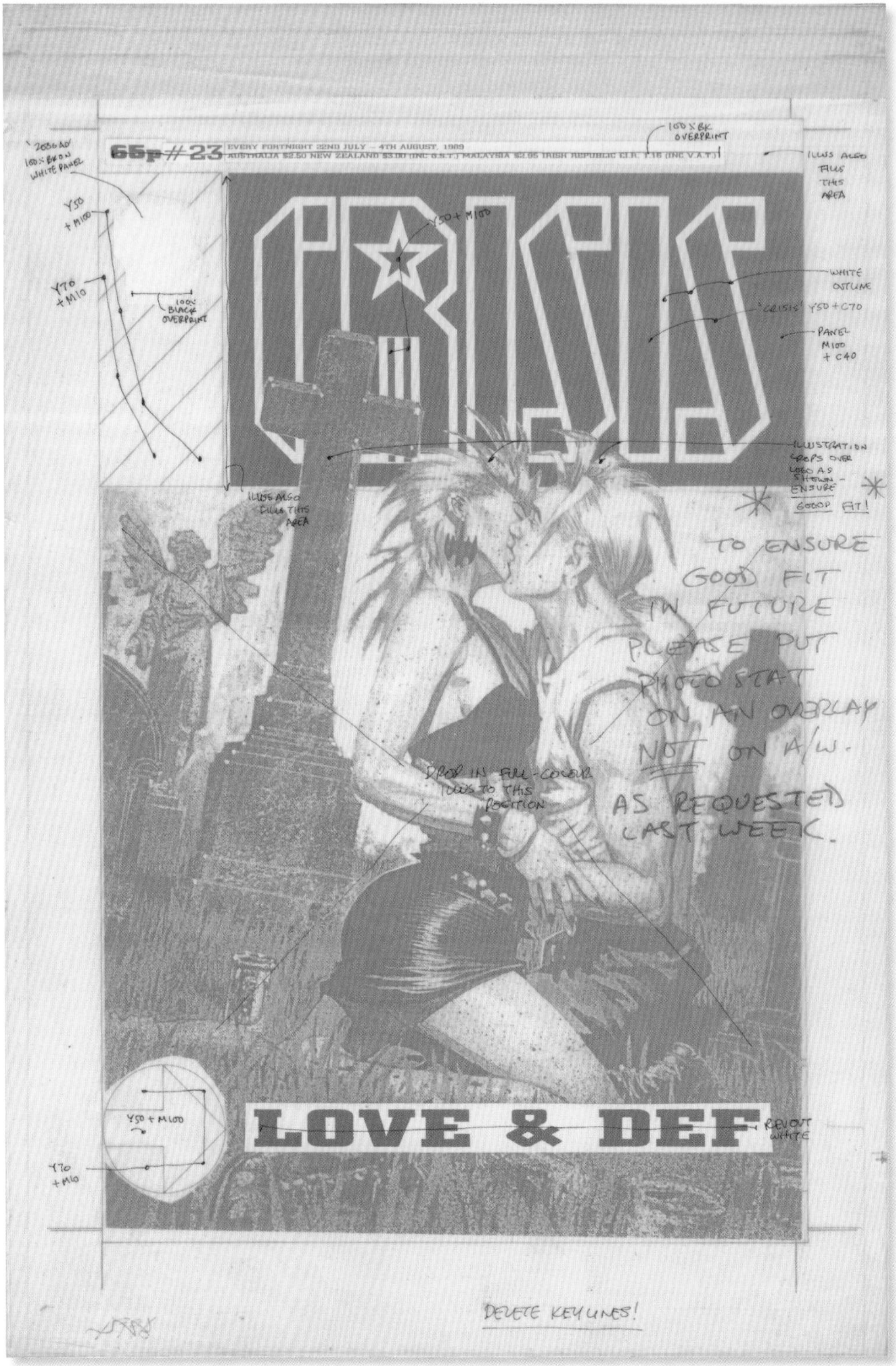

3

4

5

6

side to reflect the more varied and cosmopolitan content.

Shown opposite is the original pre-digital cover artwork for issue 23 **2** with a stat of Sean Phillips' art as a 'positional', and a note from the printer in red that I seem to have ignored first time around. The '2000AD Presents' logo top left has fallen off.

CMYK colours were indicated by percentage breakdowns in 10% increments on a tracing paper overlay; you were never sure precisely what it would look like until you saw a Cromalin, a proof made directly from the films used to expose the printing plates. Corrections at this stage would entail remaking the films, which was costly and time-consuming, and so best avoided. As a freelancer I was not in the office every day, and issues would often go straight to press without me checking these proofs beforehand.

3 is the promotional flyposter. **7** is the original logo artwork, reversed for the camera-ready paste-up. **4** and **5** are the two sets of cover-mounted stickers given away free with issues 17 and 18, using slogans from Pat's **Third World War**.

7
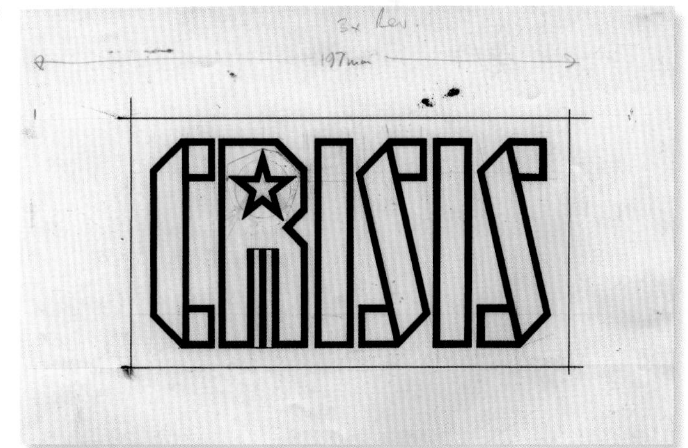

8

CRISIS
THIRD WORLD WAR
NEW STATESMEN
GOVERNMENT HOOLIGAN
APOCALYPSE COW
THIRD WORLD WARRIOR
LAGER LOUT
"I OWN U"
DANSE MACABRE
BETTER DEAD THAN RED
BASTA!
STREET FIGHTING HOMBRE
BACK IN THE U.K.
LIAT'S LAW!
SKIN MAG?
FALLS GUY
LOVE & DEF
RUDE BOYS!
KISS MY EGO!
new statesmen
TRUE FAITH
WE'RE BADS!
BABY'S IN BLACK
BAITING THE DRAGON!

CRISIS
AMNESTY INTERNATIONAL
ART & SOCIETY

CRISIS
THE BIG HEAT
AMNESTY INTERNATIONAL

CRISIS
THE DEAD SEA

CRISIS

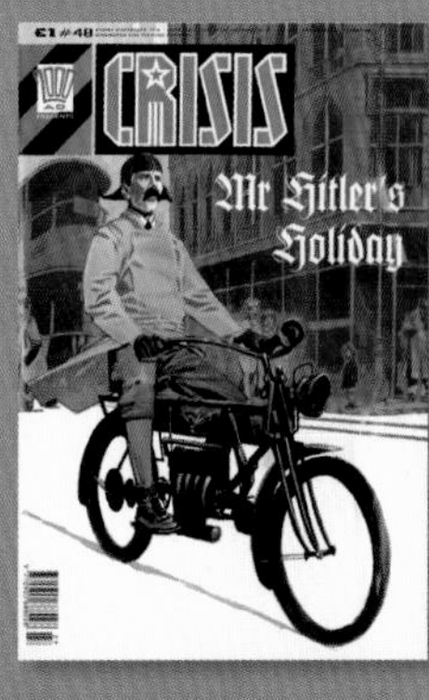
CRISIS
Mr Hitler's Holiday

CRISIS
ANOTHER TEENAGE CRISIS
SAMUEL BECKETT

CRISIS

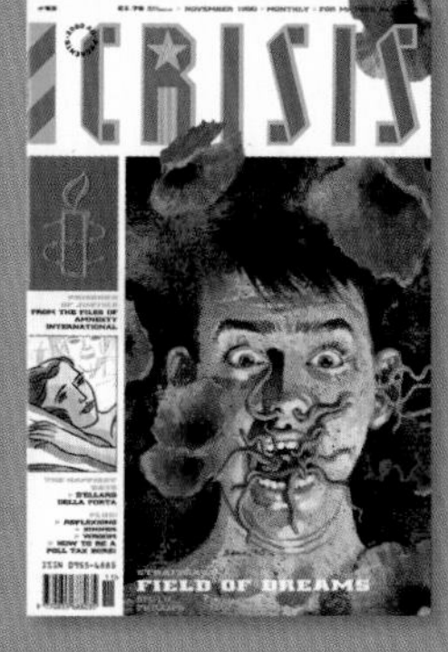
CRISIS
FIELD OF DREAMS

CRISIS
WROOM WITH A VIEW

CRISIS
CHRISTMAS ISSUE

CRISIS

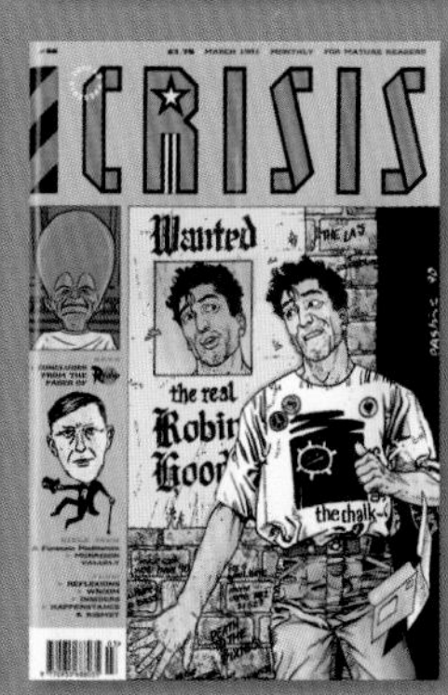
CRISIS
Wanted
the real Robin Hood

CRISIS
Morrison • Valley
BIBLE JOHN

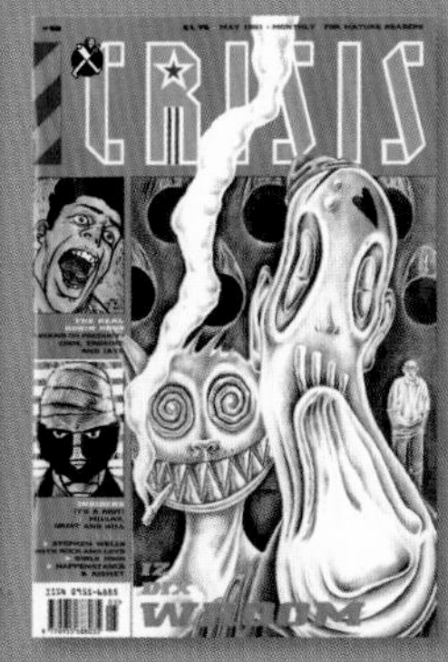
CRISIS

CRISIS
lord jim
NO-ONE HERE GETS OUT ALIVE

CRISIS
TULUM
FELLINI
MANARA

CRISIS
THE REAL ROBIN HOOD
PRINCE OF THIEVES

CRISIS
MANARA/FELLINI
TULUM

CRISIS
TALKS

CRISIS
TALKS

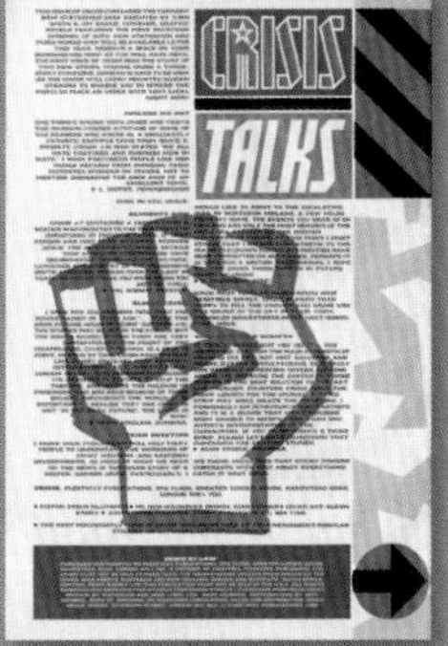
CRISIS
TALKS

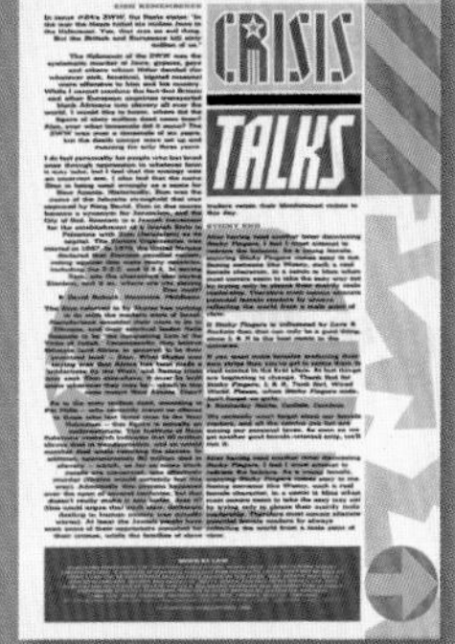
CRISIS
TALKS

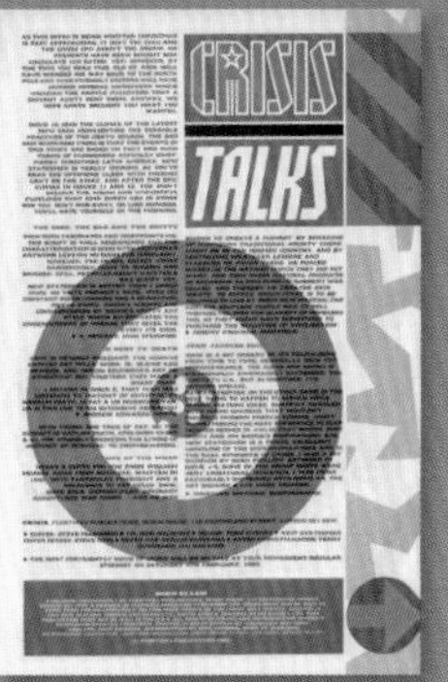
CRISIS
TALKS

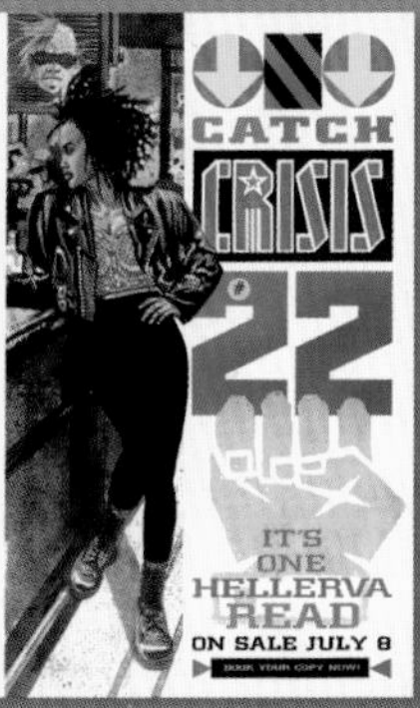
CATCH
CRISIS
22
IT'S ONE HELLERVA READ
ON SALE JULY 8

Drop-in new pic from P 5 Pic 12
DON'T USE DIALOGUE

#51 £1.75 SPAIN 450 PESETAS ★ OCTOBER 1990 ★ MONTHLY ★ FOR MATURE READERS

CRISIS
2000 AD PRESENTS

STRAITGATE ▶ SMITH PHILLIPS

THE WALL ▶ BILAL ALLEN

PLUS! ▶ VINCE JOHNSON ▶ BRECCIA ▶ ZARATE

ISSN 0955-6885

CAN YOU SEE THE REAL ME?

PAGE	ISSUE No.	TITLE	CUSTOMER	DATE
F/C	OCTOBER	CRISIS #51	FLEETWAY	0990

Shown left is the cover Cromalin for issue 51, the first of the redesigned issues that contained European reprints. Note that Sean Phillips' *Straightgate* image was changed to something much less contentious (see previous page). The main image is by Paul Johnson, 'The Wall' by Enki Bilal.

Responding to the cover art, I would often flip or distort the logo or otherwise customise it, as on issue 29 where it's treated like stained glass, issue 49 where it's flipped, or issue 27, where I waved it around as the scanning head on the photocopier moved across **2**. These effects are, of course, much easier to produce using Photoshop.

1 is a hand-drawn logo used for the initial pitch to **Fleetway**'s executives. **3** is the lettering for Sean Phillips' cover to issue 27, lifted from a vintage headline typesetting catalogue.

1

CRISIS:

2

3

Television icons
Radio Times magazine
Ratings and listings icons
2005

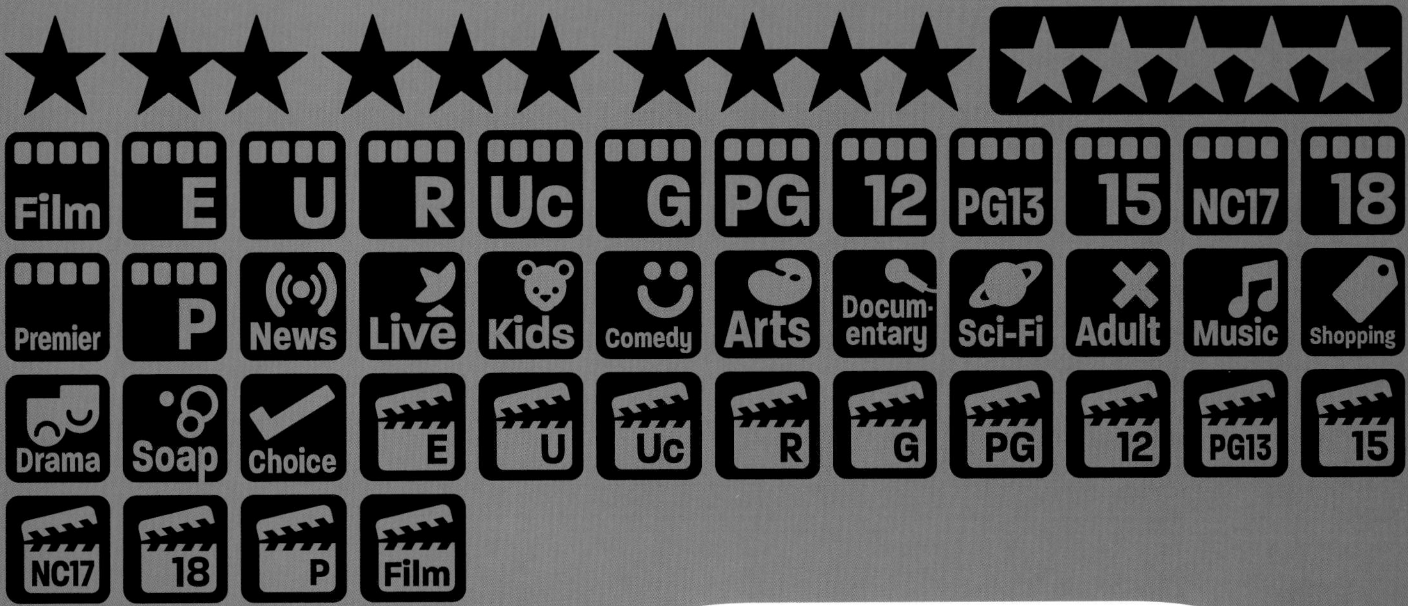

Commissioned by the long-running British TV listings magazine *Radio Times*, these icons ran at 10pt alongside the programme information and were used for many years.

The set was updated with US ratings for its release as the Device font Box Office. Note there are two 'sex/nudity' icons, with and without genitalia.

My Little Pony
Hasbro UK
Toy range
Proposed logo/character designs
1999

In my humble opinion, **My Little Pony** is a work of conceptual genius. Hair, ponies, grooming, princes and princesses, wishing wells and rainbows. It's the anti-Action Man.

Hasbro UK approached me to look at repositioning the brand to appeal to teens and adults as well as children, much in the same manner that hugely popular properties like Hello Kitty manage to cross a wide demographic range. These were some of the proposals.

I was also asked to prepare a written document in which I would set out my rationale. I set out the characters' background and the history of the world in which they lived in the manner of a comic strip outline, only later realising that what they probably wanted was a practical marketing plan.

More recently, **My Little Pony** has been relaunched, with redesigned characters, a comic book series and a successful animated TV show. I was not involved, but this reboot does bear a passing resemblance to these roughs from 1999.

The lettering evolved into a new Device font, Novak, which comes in a plain and decorative flowery version, Novak Spring.

Novak Winter
Novak Spring

1

2

3

4

5

6

7

8

9

10

11

12

MY LITTLE
PONY

Batman
Titan Books
Graphic novel series
1988/9

A six-volume series that reprints the genre-defining 1970s work of Neal Adams. The logo, as with all the type, is set at an angle; I continued this on the interior pages, which caused me some headaches. The logo **1** uses an existing bat from *Detective Comics*, with hand-drawn type laid over the top.

1

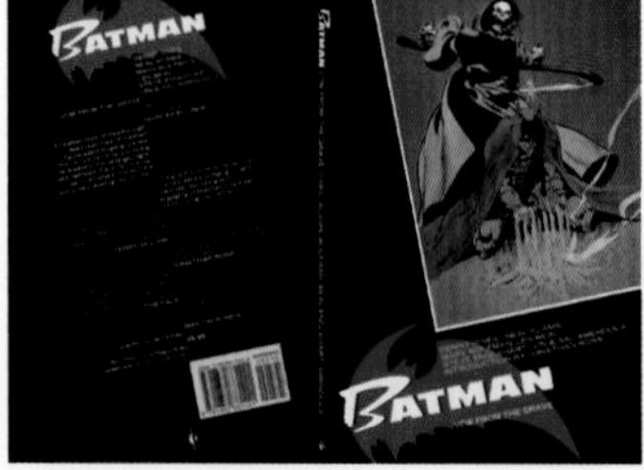

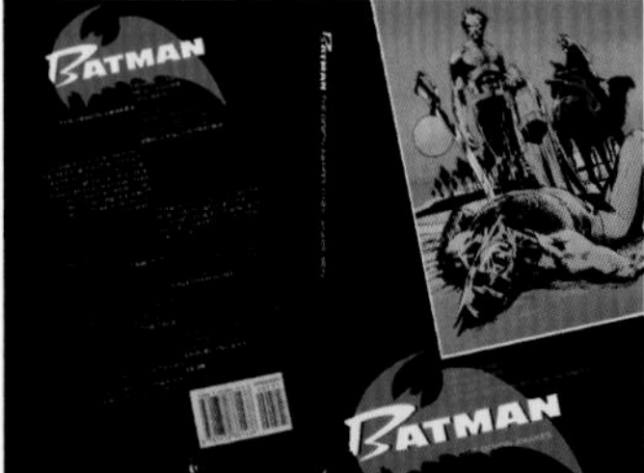

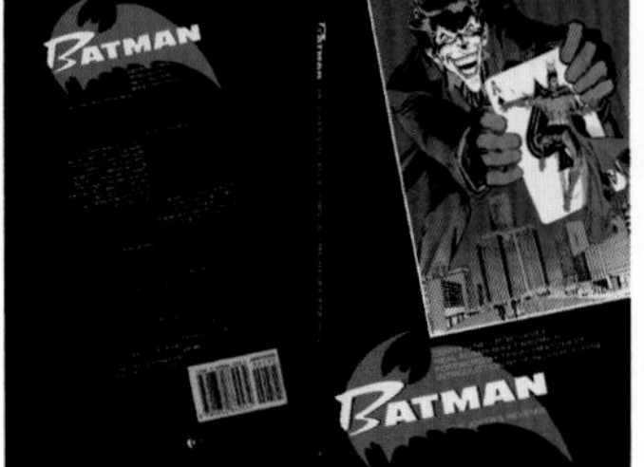

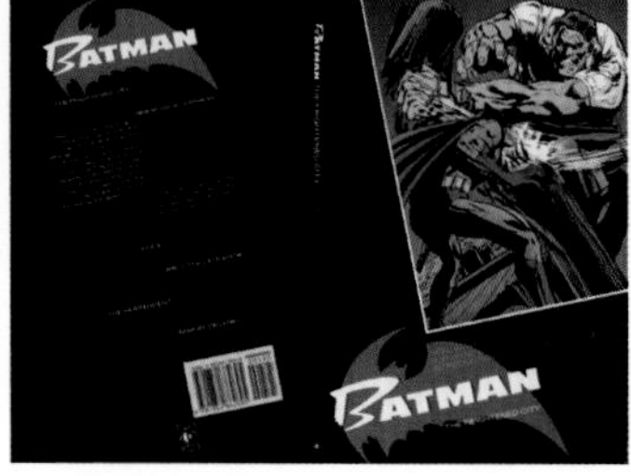

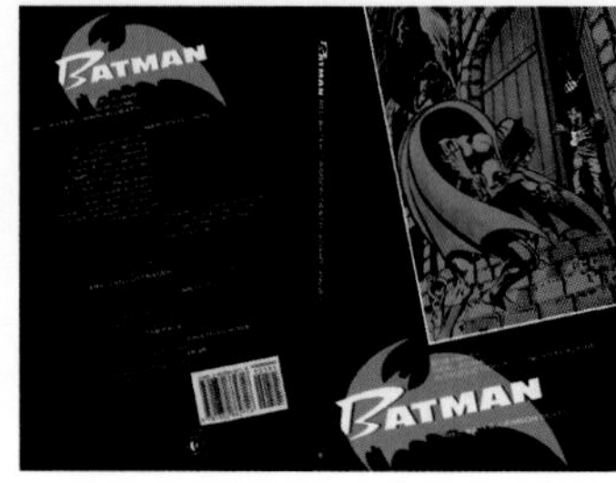

Caped Crusader Classics!
Titan Books
Graphic novel paperbacks
1988/9

These paperbacks reprinted 1950s and 1960s strips in black and white, the panels rearranged two or three to a page to fit the format. This had been done before, during the height of the Adam West TV show, presumably to get the material into bookshops. On the original UK 'Four Square' editions to which my design pays homage **1**, bizarrely the Penguin has a yellow face and hands, and the **Joker** is blue.

The logos are all vintage, supplied from the vaults of **DC Comics**, and I made sure I didn't iron out any of their kinks. In fact the **Superman** logo was purposely chosen for its wonkiness – the 'U' has the chamfered corners that were later rounded off.

For No.5 and No.7, no suitable logos existed so I drew them freehand with a pen and reduced them to size **2**.
The candy-coloured palette evokes the nostalgia of pocket-money sweet wrappers.

1

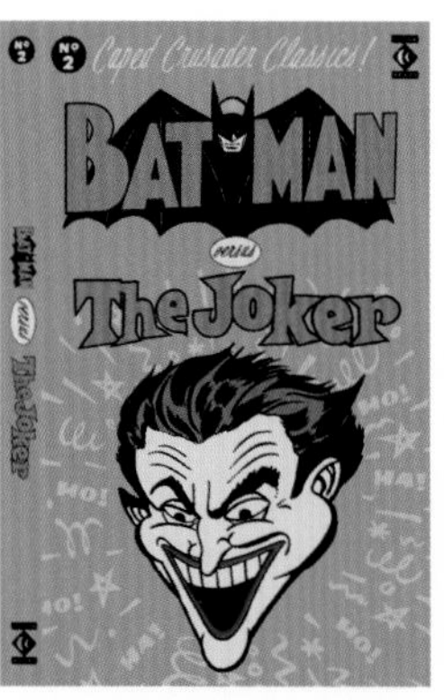

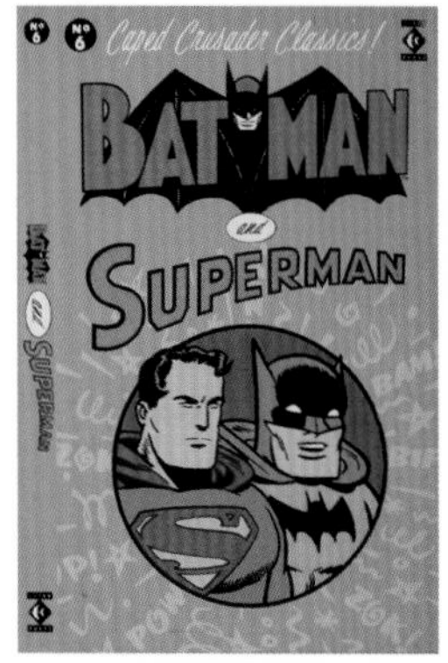

2

Woodystock
Andy Huckle
Rollercoaster Club T-shirt
2002

The L.A.W.
DC Comics
Comic book series
1999

The L.A.W. is Bob Layton and Dick Giordano's reimagining of the former Charlton heroes Blue Beetle, the Question, Sarge Steel, Nightshade, Captain Atom, Peacemaker and Judomaster, here united as an elite squad of 'living assault weapons'.

Each character was spotlighted in turn over the six issues of the series, their name being incorporated above the logo in a tab like a file card.

I also designed a bullet **4** that is a combination of the old Charlton Comics target and the then-current DC logo; I thought this was a nice touch, but it didn't make it through to the final covers.

1

2

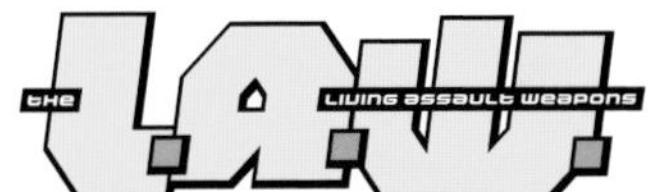

3

4

Astral Projection: Another World
Transient Records
Band logo
1999

Goa trance gurus Avi Nissim and Lior Perlmutter are **Astral Projection**, signed in the UK to **Transient Records**.

The sleeves for the late-1990s trance scene were steeped in colourful psychedelic computer imagery – fractals, shiny chrome and druggy kaleidoscopic Photoshop montages.

Without being a direct copy, the logo pays tribute to the kind of late 1960s or early 1970s typography typified by Roger Dean or the organic curves of the Art Nouveau movement. The photography is by Israeli writer, director and cinematographer Ori Gruder. The curvy icon in the circle combines an 'a' and a 'p', in imitation of a yin/yang symbol.

In 2010 I met Roger in his enormous studio in East Sussex, converted from a barn and looking very much like a high-fantasy wizard's inner sanctum. Maria Cabardo (**Smolhaus**) and I were on our way to interview him for the **Better Things** documentary when my car broke down in nearby Lewes. Gentleman that he is, Roger came out to rescue us.

1

2

3

4

Charlie Lankester and the Mojo Killers
Midmoor Music/White Tiger Management
CD cover
2012

Charlie Lankester and the Mojo Killers' brand of blues and rock are showcased on the album *Song in a Minor Key* and the singles taken from it, *Spinning of the Wheel* and *Brixton Road*. The band's influences include Black Rebel Motorcycle Club, Tom Waits, Nick Cave and mariachi music.

With his striking hat and beard, Charlie was halfway to being a logo already. The final version is abstracted from a high-contrast photograph.

The type is taken from stencilled letters I photographed on the back of an airport bus in Lima, Peru **1**. The flyposter **2** and CD sleeve **3** were printed in a metallic bronze and black.

1

2

3

Underground Toys
Forbidden Planet International
Toy manufacturers and distributors
2005

1

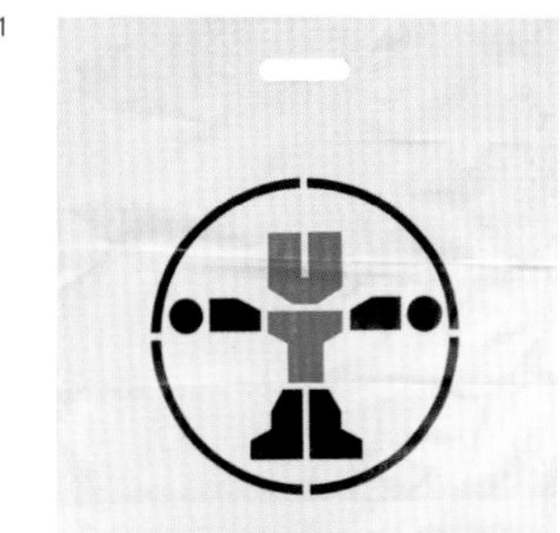

Underground Toys is a designer, manufacturer and distributor of licensed products from Disney, Star Wars, **Marvel** and others, with offices in the UK, US and Hong Kong. Kenny Penman of Forbidden Planet International, who had previously looked after Grant Morrison, Mark Millar and myself on signing tours of Dublin, Limerick and elsewhere, asked me to come up with an icon and type treatment that could work together or separately, in the manner of the **Forbidden Planet** type and rocket symbol.

I proposed a character made from the 'U' and 'T' of **Underground Toys**, arms outstretched in a classic 'Vitruvian Man' pose. Representing a simplified articulated action figure, it's iconic and immediately recognisable, but universal enough to be paired with any type of toy.

The type shares stylistic similarities with the figure, echoing the separate body parts with an angular stencil treatment.

2 was a variation in which the figure takes on different poses.

2

Bitch Planet
Milkfed Criminal Masterminds/Image Comics
Comic book series
2014

Created by writer Kelly Sue DeConnick and artist Valentine De Landro, **Bitch Planet** is a feminist drama set in an off-world prison for 'non-compliant' women that riffs on the clichés of 1960s and 1970s exploitation movies. Kelly Sue describes it as being "born of a deep and abiding love for exploitation and women-in-prison films".

The design conveys this through purposefully unsophisticated period-inspired type and a logo with a hefty drop shadow and dramatic perspective, effects that I usually tend to avoid. The fonts are genuine 'Filmotype' period designs, digitised as part of a revival project run by American type designer Stuart Sandler, mixed with fonts of my own that were inspired by my research for the *Custom Lettering of the '60s and '70s* book.

Having designed the cover, I then overprinted an off-white paper texture, added scuffed ink effects, and knocked the colours out of register.

Some covers were reused for the trade paperback collections, and others are second printings for which I've created new colourways.

1

BITCH
PLANET

2

bitch
planet

3

BITCH
PLANET

4

bitch
planet

ARE YOU WOMAN ENOUGH TO SURVIVE...
BITCH PLANET
GIRL GANGS...
CAGED AND ENRAGED!
GHOST VARIANT
DECONNICK • DE LANDRO
PETER • COWLES

ARE YOU WOMAN ENOUGH TO SURVIVE...
BITCH PLANET
GIRL GANGS...
CAGED AND ENRAGED!
DECONNICK • DE LANDRO
PETER • COWLES

ARE YOU WOMAN ENOUGH TO SURVIVE...
BITCH PLANET
GIRL GANGS...
CAGED AND ENRAGED!
DECONNICK • DE LANDRO
PETER • COWLES

ARE YOU WOMAN ENOUGH TO SURVIVE...
BITCH PLANET
GIRLS! GIRLS! GIRLS!
...FIGHTING FOR THEIR LIVES...
DECONNICK DE LANDRO PETER COWLES
AND THEIR FREEDOM!

ARE YOU WOMAN ENOUGH TO SURVIVE...
BITCH PLANET
DON'T TELL ME
TO SMILE
GIRLS! GIRLS! GIRLS!
FIGHTING FOR THEIR LIVES...
AND THEIR FREEDOM!
DECONNICK • DE LANDRO • PETER • COWLES

ARE YOU WOMAN ENOUGH TO SURVIVE...
BITCH PLANET
DECONNICK • WILSON IV • PETER • COWLES
BOLD, BEAUTIFUL AND...
BAAAAAAD!
THE SECRET ORIGIN OF
PENNY ROLLE

ARE YOU WOMAN ENOUGH TO SURVIVE...
BITCH PLANET
DECONNICK WILSON IV PETER COWLES

BITCH PLANET
SHAME THEM – MAIM THEM –
TRY TO CONTAIN THEM –
STAND BACK –
SHE'S GONNA...
BLOW!
DECONNICK • DE LANDRO • PETER • COWLES

ARE YOU WOMAN ENOUGH TO SURVIVE...
BITCH PLANET
STEEL YOUR SELVES FOR HEARTBREAK
WHICH WIP WILL RIP?!
DECONNICK • DE LANDRO • PETER • COWLES

ARE YOU WOMAN ENOUGH TO SURVIVE...
BITCH PLANET
BOUND BY LAW...
DOWN FOR JUSTICE...
DECONNICK SOMA
FITZPATRICK COWLES
MEIKO MAKI IS AN
EXTRAORDINARY MACHINE!

ARE YOU WOMAN ENOUGH TO SURVIVE...
BITCH PLANET
DECONNICK DE LANDRO
FITZPATRICK COWLES
PRESIDENT BITCH
PART ONE
ELEANOR DOANE
DREAM ON

ARE YOU WOMAN ENOUGH TO SURVIVE...
BITCH PLANET
PRESIDENT BITCH
SHE'S BEEN CLEANING UP OTHER PEOPLE'S MESSES FOR YEARS
CORRUPTION
INJUSTICE

ARE YOU WOMAN ENOUGH TO SURVIVE...
BITCH PLANET
DECONNICK DE LANDRO FITZPATRICK COWLES
VOTE
PRESIDENT BITCH

ARE YOU WOMAN ENOUGH TO SURVIVE...
BOOK TWO
BITCH PLANET
PRESIDENT BITCH
YOU CAN'T JAIL THE REVOLUTION

SEULE UNE VRAIE FEMME PEUT SURVIVRE À...
BITCH PLANET
EXTRAORDINARY MACHINE
DECONNICK • DE LANDRO
WILSON IV • PETER • COWLES

ARE YOU WOMAN ENOUGH TO SURVIVE...
BOOK ONE
BITCH PLANET
EXTRAORDINARY MACHINE
GIRL GANGS...
CAGED AND ENRAGED!
DECONNICK
DE LANDRO
WILSON IV
PETER
COWLES

ARE YOU WOMAN ENOUGH TO SURVIVE...
BOOK TWO
BITCH PLANET
DECONNICK DE LANDRO SOMA FITZPATRICK COWLES
VOTE
PRESIDENT BITCH

BITCH PLANET
TRIPLE FEATURE!
SISTERS

BITCH PLANET
TRIPLE FEATURE!
WHAT'S LOVE GOT TO DO WITH IT?
THIS IS GOOD FOR YOU
MISS TWEEN NECK COMPETITION
CLARK
HENDERSON
GRAYSON
COWLES
3 BIG STORIES...
IN 1 BOOK!

BITCH PLANET
TRIPLE FEATURE!
THOSE PEOPLE
BIG GAME
LOVE, HONOR & OBEY
3 BIG STORIES IN ONE BOOK!
COWLES

BITCH PLANET
TRIPLE FEATURE!
LIFE of a SPORTSMAN
BODYMOD
TO BE FREE
COWLES
3 BIG STORIES

BITCH PLANET
TRIPLE FEATURE
EVERYONE'S GRANDMA IS A LITTLE BIT FEMINIST
FRACTION
CHARRETIER
MIRROR, MIRROR
TSOEI
GUTEKUNST
BASIC BITCH
NYAMBI
VISIONS
COWLES
3 BIG STORIES IN ONE BOOK!

BITCH PLANET
BOOK ONE
TRIPLE FEATURE!
SCATHING SATIRE!

Damian, Son of Batman
DC Comics
Comic book
2014

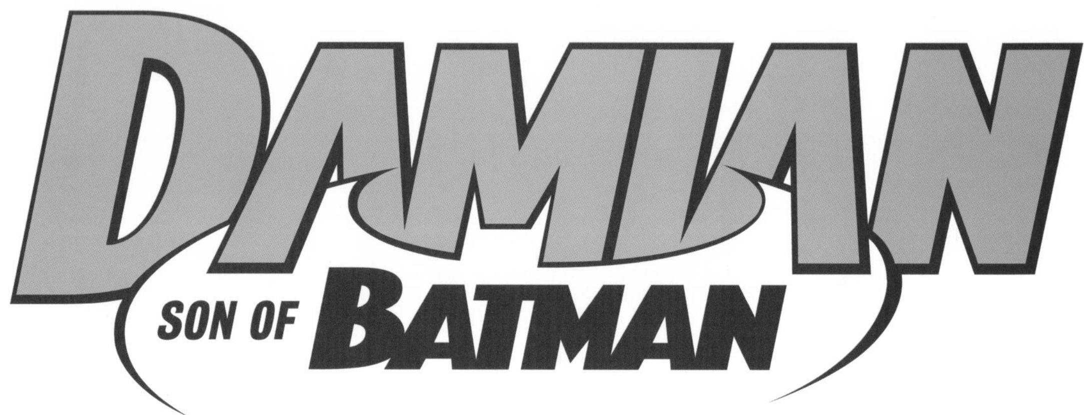

Ten-year-old Damian Wayne is the result of a tryst between **Batman** and Talia al Ghul, daughter of long-standing Bat villain Ra's al Ghul.

Damian, Son of Batman editor Mike Marts was looking for something that had a family feel to the logo I had previously designed.

The 'A's identical positions in both names, a graphic gift that was too good to pass up, was explored in the first designs **1.** For the final version, the outlined bat shape, open at the bottom, curves up to become the crossbars on the two 'A's, while the ears of **Batman**'s cowl are described by the negative space under the 'M'. Look closely – because of the 'I', the two 'A's are not equidistant from the 'M' in **Damian**, so some stretching of the left side of the cape, the larger 'D' and italicising the whole was required to balance the final design.

For purely nostalgic reasons, '**Batman**' retains the unusual reversed-stress 'A's of the original logo.

1

2

3

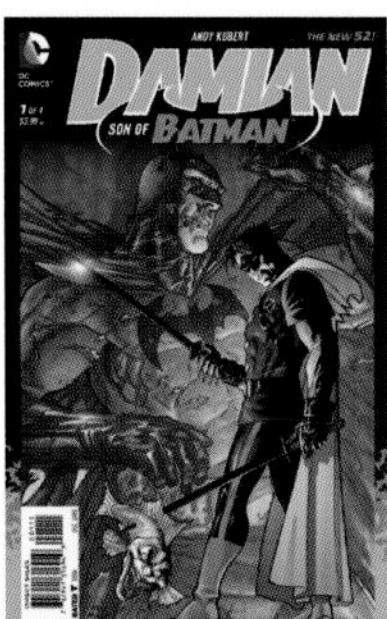

DC Comics
Publisher
Unsolicited logo proposals
2002

Though I'd not been asked by **DC Comics** to redesign their logo, I thought I'd give it a shot. In 2002 the Milton Glazer 'bullet' was still in use, and I was finding it had certain limitations. The fine outline did not reproduce well at small sizes or on the Web, and I felt the 'DC' was too small within the heavy circle.

These are some of my suggestions. Not all of these would work in situ on a cover without an enclosing outline; not all of them are beautiful. Several are far too close to the US shoe brand, while others are too complex. None were used.

Richard Bruning's 'spin' logo would appear in 2005; this would be replaced by Landor's short-lived 'peel' version, before a return to a simpler circular design in 2016.

The two at the bottom did get used, at a tiny size amongst other logos as part of the cover designs for **Flex Mentallo** and the **Tangent** series, so although they were seen in print they were not 'official' DC logos.

The Chap
The Chap magazine
Magazine masthead
2010

Since 1999, **The Chap** has been championing the rights of that increasingly marginalised species of Englishman – the gentleman. **The Chap** believes that a society without courteous behaviour and proper headwear is a society on the brink of moral and sartorial collapse, and seeks to reinstate such indispensable practices as hat doffing, giving up one's seat to a lady and the regular use of the trouser press.

The Chap also holds the annual Chap Olympiad, featuring Cad Slapping, Umbrella Jousting, Not-Playing-Tennis and Moustache Tug-of-War.

For my bespoke redressing of the magazine, betweeded editor Gustav Temple sent me a selection of post-war 'make do and mend' posters, Pifco logos and knitting patterns featuring men in cableknit jumpers for inspiration. At our first meeting in Lewes, **The Chap**'s home town, I was recovering after an extended stag weekend in Brighton. I fear I may have looked somewhat bedraggled, and not **Chap** material at all.

The type is adapted from the Device font Capitol, which I also used for the coverlines each issue. Katie Moorman designed the interiors. The pipe-smoking mascot was retained with a subtle polish, and later appeared on **Chap** cufflinks and hand-made brogues **2**, **3**.

Early concepts toyed with a script 'the', oversized logos and bold illustrations suggested by the work of Edward Hynes for the covers of the pocket-sized post-war *Men Only* magazine **1**.

We ended up using black and white photographs, but I did draw Oscar Wilde for the 'Dandy Descendants' issue. The Steve McQueen and Patrick Macnee covers were my favourites.

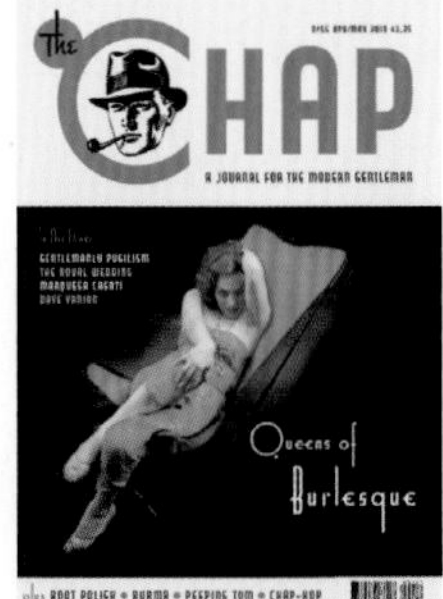

1

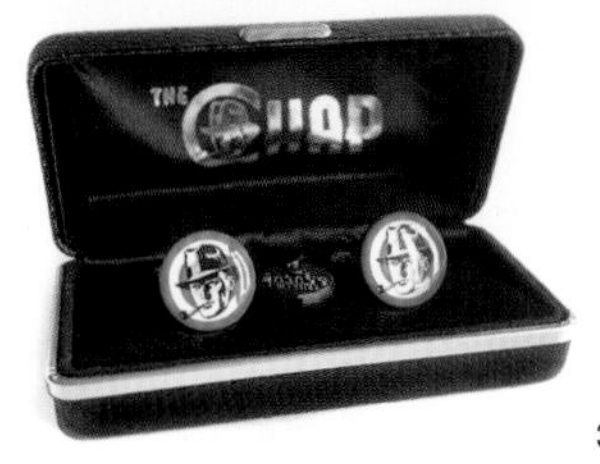

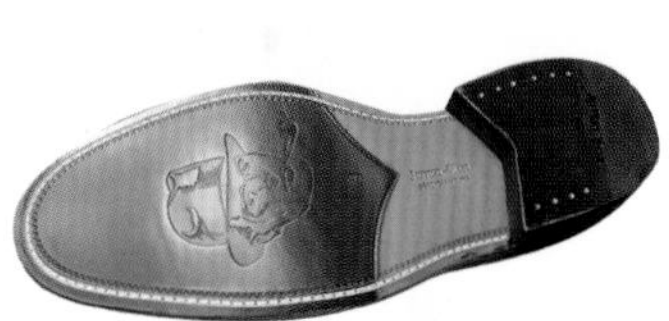

2

3

3

4

5

6

THE CHAP
A JOURNAL FOR THE MODERN GENTLEMAN
In This Issue:
the MAD QUEEN of MADAGASCAR
GORDON BENNETT
C.W. STONEKING
BELL the BUTLER
the Correspondents
plus CHIVALRY • CHAP-HOP • DAREDEVILS • ELECTRO-SWING

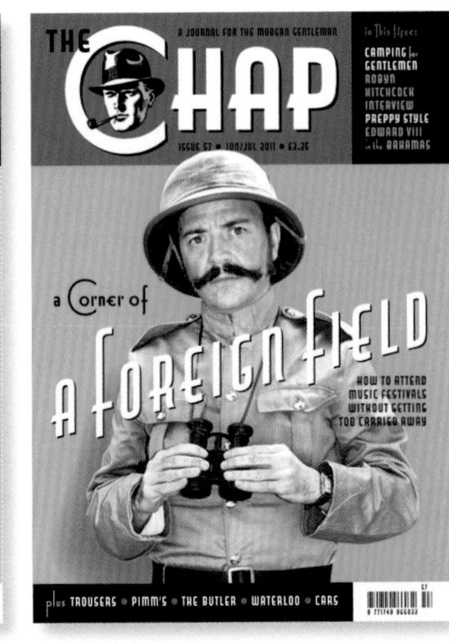
THE CHAP
A JOURNAL FOR THE MODERN GENTLEMAN
In This Issue:
CAMPING for GENTLEMEN
ROBYN HITCHCOCK INTERVIEW
PREPPY STYLE
EDWARD VIII in the BAHAMAS
a Corner of
A FOREIGN FIELD
HOW TO ATTEND MUSIC FESTIVALS WITHOUT GETTING TOO CARRIED AWAY
plus TROUSERS • PIMM'S • THE BUTLER • WATERLOO • CARS

THE CHAP
A JOURNAL FOR THE MODERN GENTLEMAN
In This Issue:
PHIL DANIELS
JOHN BLASHFORD-SNELL
JIM MOLLISON
BARBARA CARTLAND
MODS + FOKKERS
FROM BRIGHTON BEACH TO THE BATTLE OF BRITAIN
plus AIRLINE TIPPLES • SANDALS • DOFFING • BROOKLANDS

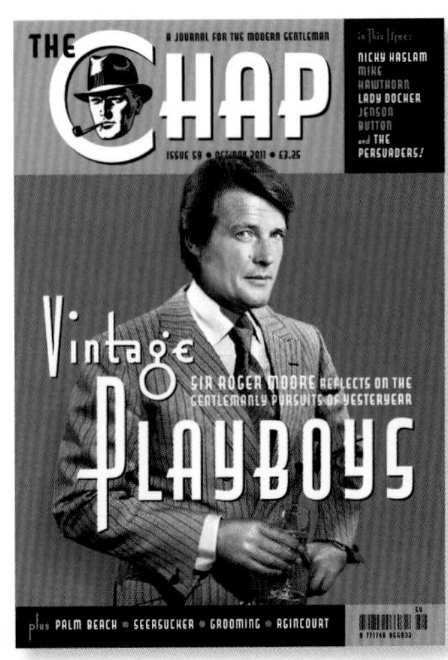
THE CHAP
A JOURNAL FOR THE MODERN GENTLEMAN
In This Issue:
NICKY HASLAM
MIKE HAWTHORN
LADY DOCKER
JENSON BUTTON
and THE PERSUADERS!
Vintage PLAYBOYS
SIR ROGER MOORE REFLECTS ON THE GENTLEMANLY PURSUITS OF YESTERYEAR
plus PALM BEACH • SEERSUCKER • GROOMING • AGINCOURT

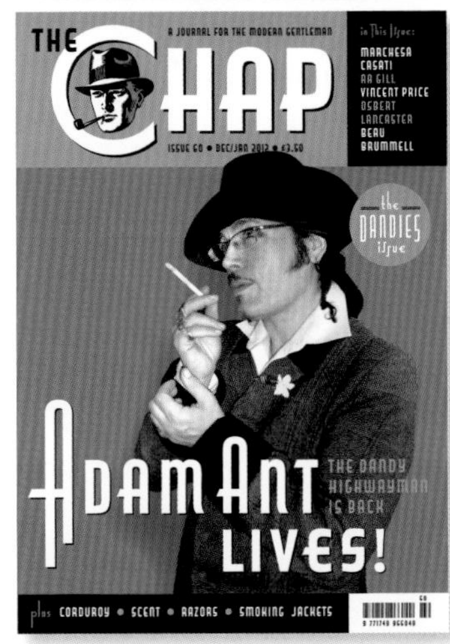
THE CHAP
A JOURNAL FOR THE MODERN GENTLEMAN
In This Issue:
MARCHESA CASATI
ERIC GILL
VINCENT PRICE
OSBERT LANCASTER
BEAU BRUMMELL
the DANDIES issue
ADAM ANT LIVES!
THE DANDY HIGHWAYMAN IS BACK
plus CORDUROY • SCENT • RAZORS • SMOKING JACKETS

THE CHAP
A JOURNAL FOR THE MODERN GENTLEMAN
In This Issue:
GEORGE MALLORY
CAROL CLEVELAND
JOLLY OLLY
CRICKET'S FASHION FAUX PAS
Diana Dors
BRING BACK THE BLONDE BOMBSHELL!
plus DUELLING • LOVE POTIONS • TANGO • GAMBLING

THE CHAP
A JOURNAL FOR THE MODERN GENTLEMAN
In This Issue:
DANIEL RADCLIFFE
ROBERT RANKIN
VINTAGE DATING
BENJAMIN DISRAELI
H. G. WELLS CONFRONTS THE MODERN WORLD:
THE DIFFIDENCE ENGINE
plus STEAMPUNK • CAPES • YOUTH TRIBES • RACING TIPS

THE CHAP
A JOURNAL FOR THE MODERN GENTLEMAN
In This Issue:
the AUSTERITY OLYMPICS
JACK JOHNSON
POCKET WATCHES
the CHAP OLYMPICS
CHRIS EUBANK ON PUGILISM, DANDYISM AND GENTLEMANLY SPORTSMEN
PLEASED TO BEAT YOU!
plus CRICKET • ROYAL ASCOT • CROQUET • SPORTING TIPPLES

THE CHAP
A JOURNAL FOR THE MODERN GENTLEMAN
In This Issue:
KEITH FLOYD
RICHARD BRIERS
BARRY HUMPHRIES
GEORGE IV
MRS. DALLOWAY
the HORN of PLENTY
a CORNUCOPIA OF FEASTS, LUNCHES
AND GARRULOUS GOURMANDS
plus CRICKET • CHAP LUNCHES • GLORIOUS GOODWOOD

THE CHAP
A JOURNAL FOR THE MODERN GENTLEMAN
In This Issue:
JACK KEROUAC
ALLEN GINSBERG
WILLIAM S BURROUGHS
THE FIFTH BEATNIK
HOW TO BE A HIPSTER WITHOUT LETTING YOUR STANDARDS OR YOUR WAISTBAND DOWN
The WELL-DRESSED Beatnik
plus MICHAEL HOROVITZ • THE BERET • RATIONAL DRESS

THE CHAP
A JOURNAL FOR THE MODERN GENTLEMAN
In This Issue:
SIR PATRICK MOORE
ZINO DAVIDOFF
TIM BROOKE-TAYLOR
THE MARQUESS OF ANGLESEY
THE LINEAGE OF THIS MOST PECULIARLY BRITISH BREED OF GENTLEMAN
ECCENTRIC CIRCLES
plus SLIPPERS • CRICKET • GAMBLING • PUNCHES

THE CHAP
A JOURNAL FOR THE MODERN GENTLEMAN
In This Issue:
TERRY-THOMAS
DARUMA
BUDDHA
FRANKIE DETTORI
JOLLY OLLY SMITH
WHY BEN MILLER COULDN'T BE BOTHERED TO HAVE A SHAVE BEFORE BEING INTERVIEWED
HOW TO BUILD A MEDIUM-SIZED HADRON COLLIDER IN YOUR SHED
Well Random, ISN'T IT?
plus TAXIDERMY • CUT-THROAT RAZORS • PARACELSUS

THE CHAP
A JOURNAL FOR THE MODERN GENTLEMAN
BLESS MY SOUL!
BRIAN BLESSED ON HIS OTHER CAREER AS MOUNTAINEER AND CHUM TO THE DALAI LAMA
plus PROSECCO • CUT-THROAT RAZORS • THE SEDUCTION ENGINE

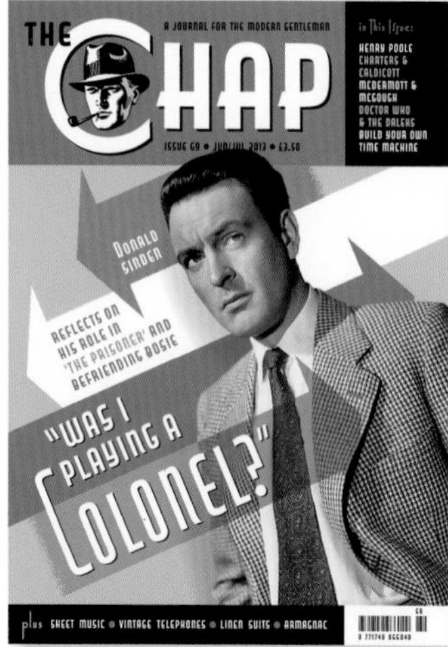
THE CHAP
A JOURNAL FOR THE MODERN GENTLEMAN
DONALD SINDEN
REFLECTS ON HIS ROLE IN 'THE PRISONER' AND BEFRIENDING BOSIE
"WAS I PLAYING A COLONEL?"
plus SHEET MUSIC • VINTAGE TELEPHONES • LINEN SUITS • ARMAGNAC

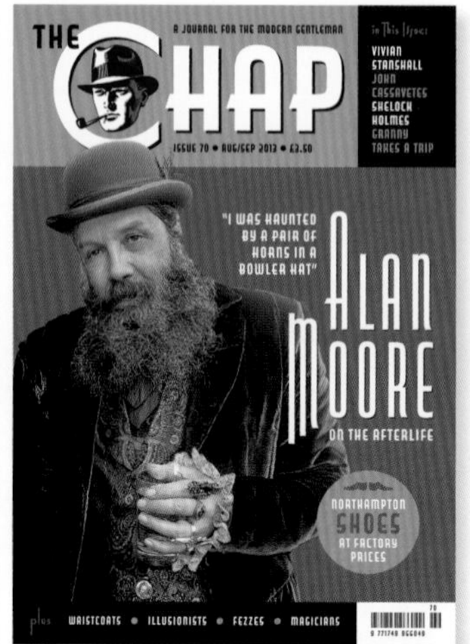
THE CHAP
A JOURNAL FOR THE MODERN GENTLEMAN
"I WAS HAUNTED BY A PAIR OF HORNS IN A BOWLER HAT"
ALAN MOORE
ON THE AFTERLIFE
NORTHAMPTON SHOES AT FACTORY PRICES
plus WAISTCOATS • ILLUSIONISTS • FEZZES • MAGICIANS

THE CHAP
A JOURNAL FOR THE MODERN GENTLEMAN
RIDING HABIT
JILLY COOPER
ON HER STABLE OF EQUINE BESTSELLERS
plus OPERA DIVAS • GROOMING • CANAPÉS • GOODWOOD REVIVAL

THE CHAP
A JOURNAL FOR THE MODERN GENTLEMAN
FELINE WOMAN
THE LEGEND OF EARTHA KITT
PURRS ON VIA A REVEALING NEW BIOGRAPHY
plus MENS' OVERCOATS • TEQUILA • WRISTWATCHES • RAFFLES

THE CHAP
A JOURNAL FOR THE MODERN GENTLEMAN
THE STEVE MC QUEEN AFFAIR
HOW THE ACTOR GOT SPRUCED UP FOR HIS FINEST ROLE
plus HERMITS • INTERIORS • RECLUSES • LIP WEASELS

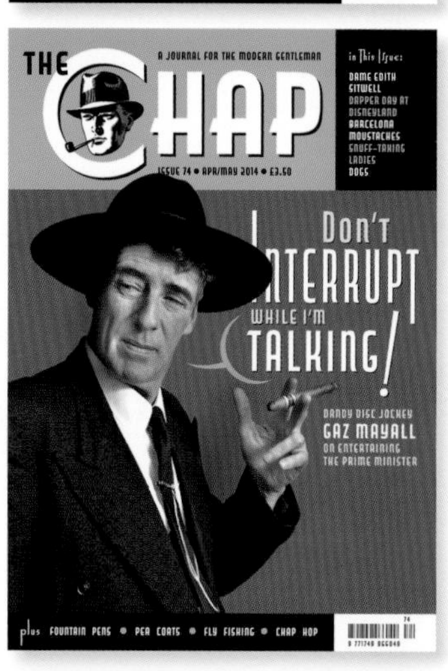
THE CHAP
A JOURNAL FOR THE MODERN GENTLEMAN
DON'T INTERRUPT WHILE I'M TALKING!
DANDY DISC JOCKEY GAZ MAYALL ON ENTERTAINING THE PRIME MINISTER
plus FOUNTAIN PENS • PEA COATS • FLY FISHING • CHAP HOP

THE CHAP
A JOURNAL FOR THE MODERN GENTLEMAN
75
RACHEL JOHNSON
SPILLS THE BEANS ON BEING THE LITTLE SISTER OF BORIS
I'm a BOY with BREASTS
plus MARTIN KEMP • CYCLING SHOES • DANDY PIPES • IT GIRLS

THE CHAP
A JOURNAL FOR THE MODERN GENTLEMAN
MONTE CARLO & BUST
Cricket made him Cry
JOAN LE MESURIER
plus SAFETY RAZORS • GENTLEMANLY SCENTS • POCKET SQUARES

THE CHAP
A JOURNAL FOR THE MODERN GENTLEMAN
FOOD & DRINK SPECIAL
EDWARD DAVENPORT
a Scandal in FITZROVIA
plus CHAMPAGNE • TRENCH COATS • FOOD SONGS • BRITISH BEER

THE CHAP
A JOURNAL FOR THE MODERN GENTLEMAN
THE CINEMATIC LEGEND REVEALS NOTHING LESS THAN THE SECRET OF LIFE
TERENCE STAMP
plus THE BUTLER • GHOST STORIES • WALKING BOOTS • SCENTS

THE CHAP
A JOURNAL FOR THE MODERN GENTLEMAN
MERLIN HOLLAND:
OSCAR WILDE'S GRANDSON ON THE TRIALS OF BEING A
Dandy DESCENDANT
plus BRACES • SABRAGE • CRICKET • SHAVING BRUSHES • BOOZE

THE CHAP
A JOURNAL FOR THE MODERN GENTLEMAN
ISSUE 80 • APR/MAY 2015 • £3.95
in This Issue:
DANZIGER
GOLDWASSER
BROUGHTON BOOTS
HARRINGTON JACKETS
WELL-DRESSED RAPPERS
SHERLOCK HOLMES 1965
PARDON ME, SIR!
VIC DARKWOOD
RETURNS FROM THE WILDS TO EXPLAIN THE ETIQUETTE OF YAWNS, ERUPTIONS, SNEEZES AND OTHER INVOLUNTARY BODILY SPASMS
plus GLOVES • DEMOB SUITS • THE BUTLER • THE LIP WEASEL

THE CHAP
A JOURNAL FOR THE MODERN GENTLEMAN
ISSUE 81 • JUN/JUL 2015 • £3.95
in This Issue:
THE ETIQUETTE OF INHERITED WEALTH
SCHOOL FOR CHIVALRY
SPENCERS
TROUSERS
UGLY HAND COMPETITION
BERLIN BORDELLOS
JOHNNY DEAN
TALKS MENSWEAR, BOUNDERS, PIPES AND THE SUPERNATURAL WITH ATTERS
I ALWAYS WANTED TO BE A RAKEHELL
AIR TRAVEL • CUBAN CIGARS • ORSON WELLES

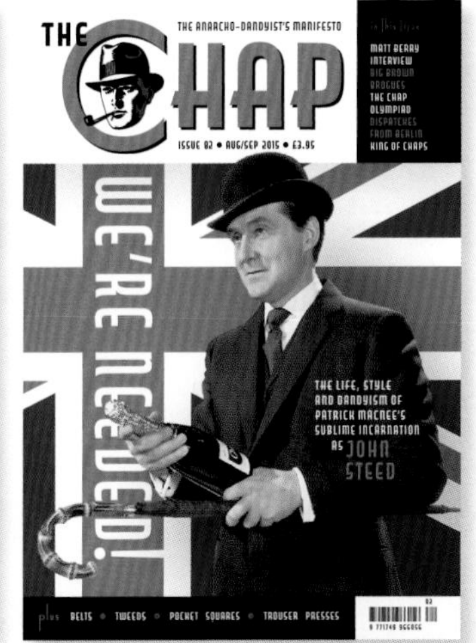
THE CHAP
THE ANARCHO-DANDYIST'S MANIFESTO
ISSUE 82 • AUG/SEP 2015 • £3.95
in This Issue:
MATT BERRY INTERVIEW
BIG BROWN BROGUES
THE CHAP OLYMPIAD
DISPATCHES FROM BERLIN
KING OF CHAPS
WE'RE NEEDED!
THE LIFE, STYLE AND DANDYISM OF PATRICK MACNEE'S SUBLIME INCARNATION AS JOHN STEED
plus BELTS • TWEEDS • POCKET SQUARES • TROUSER PRESSES

THE CHAP
THE ANARCHO-DANDYIST'S MANIFESTO
ISSUE 83 • OCT/NOV 2015 • £4.25
in This Issue:
THE HOLLYWOOD CRICKET CLUB
BARBOUR JACKETS
THE TOMB OF BEAU BRUMMELL
CARRYING ONE'S UMBRELLA
DRINKING FOR CHAPS
KENDO NAGASAKI
REVEALS EVERYTHING EXCEPT HIS FACE EXCLUSIVELY TO THE CHAP
MASKED AVENGER
plus FLAT CAPS • MUSIC HALL SWELLS • LESLIE HOWARD

THE CHAP
THE ANARCHO-DANDYIST'S MANIFESTO
ISSUE 84 • DEC/JAN 2016 • £4.25
in This Issue:
STEVE MCQUEEN AT LE MANS
DRINKING FOR CHAPS
CRICKET IN THE SOUTH PACIFIC
NAT KING COLE
THE BRITISH PUB & ITS VARIOUS USES
KATY MANNING
ON HER LIFE IN OTHER DIMENSIONS AS DOCTOR WHO SIDEKICK JO GRANT AND HER LONG-TERM RELATIONSHIP WITH A DALEK
LORD, IS THAT THE TIME?
plus NORFOLK JACKETS • SATCHELS • SMOKING JACKETS

THE CHAP
THE ANARCHO-DANDYIST'S MANIFESTO
ISSUE 85 • FEB/MAR 2016 • £4.25
in This Issue:
MILITARY WATCHES
SCENT FOR GENTLEMEN
ONLINE DATING ETIQUETTE
EXTREME CRICKET
DUFFLE COATS
MYCROFT MILVERTON
REVEALS THE MYSTICAL SECRETS OF ELECTRONIC GENTLEMEN'S PIPES
A FULL HEAD OF STEAM
plus SWIFT SHOES • THREE TENORS • DUELLING SCARS

THE CHAP
THE ANARCHO-DANDYIST'S MANIFESTO
ISSUE 86 • APR/MAY 2016 • £4.25
in This Issue:
TOM SIX INTERVIEW
GRESHAM BLAKE
FAIR ISLE SWEATERS
JEWISH MENSWEAR
THE ORIGINS OF HARLEM JAZZ
CHAPPIST BERLIN
EMMA PEEL
OUR NEW DOCTOR OF DANDYISM LOOKS AT THE DELICIOUS ANDROGYNY OF TELEVISION'S SEXIEST SIDEKICK
plus TROUSERS • WATCHES • CRICKET • SOCKS • CLERICS

THE CHAP
THE ANARCHO-DANDYIST'S MANIFESTO
ISSUE 87 • JUN/JUL 2016 • £4.25
in This Issue:
MARLENE DIETRICH
WORKWEAR
THE HUMBLE PLIMSOLL
THE NOBLE SAFETY RAZOR
SIR ALAN WHICKER
Carry on BEAMING
60s LEGEND
FENELLA FIELDING
GIVES EVERYONE PERMISSION TO SMOKE
plus SPECTACLES • PINCE NEZ • LORGNETTES • SUNGLASSES

THE CHAP
THE ANARCHO-DANDYIST'S MANIFESTO
ISSUE 88 • AUG/SEP 2016 • £4.25
in This Issue:
OLLY SMITH INTERVIEW
PEAKY BLINDERS COMPETITION RESULTS
ALAN CLARKE
KHAKI TROUSERS
THE ART OF CONVERSATION
Oh, Jackie!
HOW JACQUELINE BOUVIER KENNEDY ONASSIS MOVED FROM THE LIMELIGHT INTO THE SHADOWS OF HER OWN IMAGE
plus SCARVES • MARGATE • CRICKET • WORKWEAR

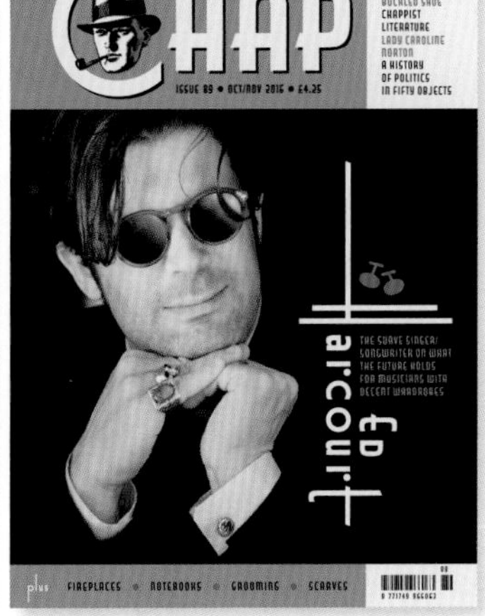
THE CHAP
THE ANARCHO-DANDYIST'S MANIFESTO
ISSUE 89 • OCT/NOV 2016 • £4.25
in This Issue:
THE MONKSTRAP BUCKLED SHOE
CHAPPIST LITERATURE
LADY CAROLINE NORTON
A HISTORY OF POLITICS IN FIFTY OBJECTS
Ed Harcourt
THE SUAVE SINGER/SONGWRITER ON WHAT THE FUTURE HOLDS FOR MUSICIANS WITH DECENT WARDROBES
plus FIREPLACES • NOTEBOOKS • GROOMING • SCARVES

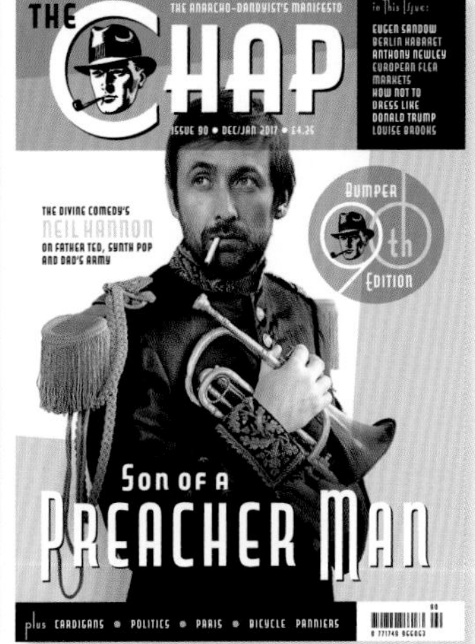
THE CHAP
THE ANARCHO-DANDYIST'S MANIFESTO
ISSUE 90 • DEC/JAN 2017 • £4.25
in This Issue:
EUGEN SANDOW
BERLIN KABARET
ANTHONY NEWLEY
EUROPEAN FLEA MARKETS
HOW NOT TO DRESS LIKE DONALD TRUMP
LOUISE BROOKS
THE DIVINE COMEDY'S
NEIL HANNON
ON FATHER TED, SYNTH POP AND DAD'S ARMY
BUMPER 90th EDITION
SON OF A PREACHER MAN
plus CARDIGANS • POLITICS • PARIS • BICYCLE PANNIERS

THE CHAP
THE ANARCHO-DANDYIST'S MANIFESTO
ISSUE 91 • SPRING 2017 • £4.25
in This Issue:
OXFORD SHOES
SHETLAND SWEATERS
SITUATIONISM FOR CHAPS
POLITICAL SEX SCANDALS
THE STRAY CAT DRUMMER'S LIFE AS A ROCKABILLY REBEL
SLIM JIM PHANTOM
plus BOOK REVIEWS • CRICKET • BERLIN • UNDERPANTS

X-Men/Uncanny X-Men
Marvel Comics
Comic book series
2006

I remember when there was just one **X-Men** comic, and it was **Uncanny**. **Marvel**'s best-selling mutant soap opera now has numerous spin-off titles, but the two longest-running are the original **Uncanny X-Men** and the adjectiveless **X-Men**.

I was asked to look at rebranding these two titles as a pair. **Marvel** wanted to reinstate the little box with the member's heads in that ran all though the fondly remembered Chris Claremont run, and I mocked up an unused trade dress to this effect.

The very first version of the logo informed **5**, and I tried alternatives to the shrinking perspective for **7** and **8**. Versions **9**, **10** and **11** keep the 3D effect, but use different type treatments.

Though I explored numerous unusual options, the logo that was chosen is very similar to the version from 1968 designed by Jim Steranko, minus the blocky 3D effect. **1** and **12** were personal favourites, but in the end a modernising polish of an old classic was chosen over a revolution.

1

2

3

4

5

6

7

8

9

10

11

12

X-Men/Uncanny X-Men
Marvel Comics
Comic book series
2006

More of my unused **X-Men** and **Uncanny X-Men** ideas and cover mock-ups, illustrating how the small character heads and credits could be incorporated into a new **Marvel** trade dress. Art by Billy Tan and John Watson.

The chosen logo was later adapted for several other X-titles (opposite).

1

2

3

4

5

6

7

8

9

10

11

12

X-Men: Kingbreaker
Marvel Comics
Comic book series
2009

Young X-Men
Marvel Comics
Comic book series
2008

X-Men: Endangered Species
Marvel Comics
Comic book series
2007

X-Men: Emperor Vulcan
Marvel Comics
Comic book series
2007

X-Men Legacy
Marvel Comics
Comic book series
2008

X-Men: Original Sin
Marvel Comics
Comic book series
2008

Outlands
Rollickin'
Animated feature film
2016

Outlands is an animated CG feature with "Arabian influences and some plasma punk tech". It features two friends who set off in search of mystical treasure, only to end up on opposite sides of a battlefield.

1

2

3

4

1

THE GIRL WHO WOULD BE
DEATH
CAITLIN R. KIERNAN DEAN ORMSTON

2

3

4

5

6

SAM WILLIAMS
EUROPATRON

7

8

9

10

1 **The Girl Who Would be Death**
DC Comics
Comic book
1998
Writer: Caitlin R Kiernan
Artist: Dean Ormston

2 **Crossroads**
Pop One/Sub Rosa Films
Film title
2014

3 **In the Powder Room**
Maxim magazine (US)
Section header
2004

4 **Device Instant Lettering**
Device Fonts
Website header
1998
Designed to mimic ageing Letraset

5 **Nihilism/Faith**
Gallery exhibition
2003

6 **Europatron**
Sam Williams
Album
Proposed logo
2015

7 **Modern Boy**
Device
T-shirt motif
2011

8 **Great Escapes**
You magazine
Article header
1997
You is the *Mail on Sunday* newspaper's colour supplement

9 **The Science Service**
Magic Strip
Graphic novel
1987
Writer: John Freeman
Artist: Rian Hughes
This is the original logo artwork, drawn up on gridded CS10 board, for my first graphic novel

10 **Ascension Plus**
Record label
2000
Dance music label from the Rising High stable

The Face of Maxim
Maxim magazine (US)
Feature
2006

Maxim is a 'lad's mag', focussing on sex, cars, style and gadgets in a light-hearted manner. The US edition ran a competition to find a model who would be the 'face' of the magazine.

Some of my designs look a little like cosmetic packaging – the inkier rough treatments were intended to give them a bit more attitude.

1

2

3

4

5

6

7

8

Grip
DC Comics/Vertigo
Comic book series
2000

Written and drawn by **Love and Rockets** co-creator Gilbert Hernandez, **Grip: The Strange World of Men** is a genre mash-up: "When Mike Chang wakes up with a lipstick smudge, someone else's suit and amnesia, he's thrown into a world of criminal gangs, crime fighters, skin swappers, and a one-eyed girl with bizarre powers."

I've followed the Hernandez brothers' **Love and Rockets** almost since its inception, where Gilbert's *Heartbreak Soup* stories left a big impression on me.

I designed the original UK collections, and was very pleased to be asked to work on this project.

Unfortunately the final logo was less than impressive: intended to look like lipstick on a mirror or a finger drawn through blood, the chosen version (main image) was simplified further in-house by the removal of the interior shape.

Sorry, Gilbert!

1

2

3

4

5

Originals
Clarks Shoes/Turner Duckworth
Shoe range packaging
2004

Playful logos suggesting the heritage of a long-established range of shoes from Clarks, the venerable English shoe-maker.

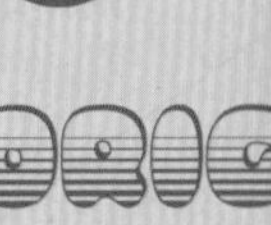

Seaguy
DC Comics
Comic book series
2004

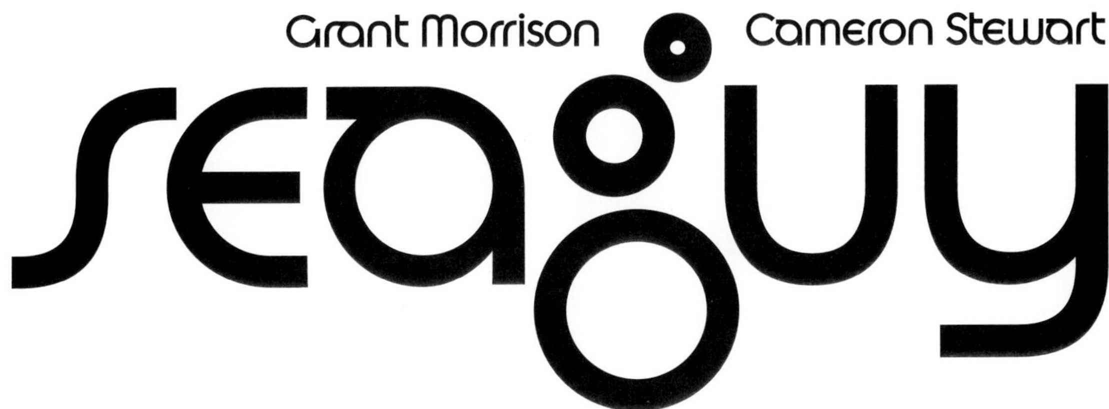

1

2

Seaguy is a Vertigo title written by Grant Morrison and drawn by Cameron Stuart. Taking a lighter, more surreal tone than many of Morrison's titles, it features a non-superpowered hero in a scuba suit and his sidekick Chubby Da Choona.

The original logo ideas tended to the playful, exploring wetsuit branding styles **5** and the seahorse shapes, waves and bubbles you might find in a seaside amusement park **2**, **6**.

The chosen logo is cleaner, in keeping with Cameron's character designs. The lowercase 'g' is formed from three rising bubbles.

3

4

5

6

Transient Records
Logo proposal
2000

Transient Records, the West London trance and club label, had been using a logo originally designed for an air-conditioning company they'd found in a book from the 1950s. I suggested that the basic design, which nicely summed up the meditative nature of much of their music, could be updated so as to make it their own.

Ultimately the original version was retained as it was widely recognised.

Dollfab
John Nee
Proposed logo
2007

Dollfab was to be a site that allowed users to design paper dolls and then print them out, share them with other users, and embed them as widgets in social networking sites.

The concept soon mutated into **Collabricator** (overleaf).

1

2

3

4

5

6

7

8

Collabricator
John Nee
Proposed logo
2007

Collabricator is an extension of the **Dollfab** concept (previous spread).

Overlapping speech balloons illustrate communication and sharing in **5** and **7-15**; cogs mesh, sometimes with one tooth elongated to resemble a speech balloon's tail as in **7-10** and **12-15**. The name-change shifted the focus from dolls to a more unisex design that emphasised collaboration. **4** uses the classic folded-paper method of multiplying figures. **6** shows the development from outline to three-dimensional object. The symmetry of the two 'o's is leveraged for **5** and **8-15**.

Some of these are probably too complex, especially for the Web where resolution can be an issue. The final logo (main image) uses a figure stepping out from a sheet of paper.

The lettering evolved into the extensive font family Urbane, my take on the geometric moderne of Futura, Spartan and Elegant Sans.

1

2

3

4

5

6

7

8

9

10

11

12

13

14

15

1 Haloes
The Hallmark Partnership
Law firm advertisement
2000

2 Grotesque 9
Type designer's social club
2017
An eight-member club of mainly London-based UK type designers, with 'floating honorary guest member'

3 Pop Kill
Comic book series
2017
Based on a design by Dave Johnson

4 Get Up and Give
BBC
Fundraising phone-in
1997

5 Intelligencia
Incidental logo
2016
From my novel *XX*

6 Vid View You
Valiant Comics
Incidental logo
2014
From the Valiant title Rai

7 Wheel World
John McInnes
In-story character badge
2012

8 Suburban Xpress
Fashion brand
Proposed logo
2014

9 Oscar Wilde
The Chap magazine
Incidental logo
2015

10 Faerie Worlds
Maxim magazine (US)
Article header
2008

11 Retro Gaming
PC Format
Future Publishing
Article header
1995

12 Alan King
Personal mark
2011

1

2

3

4

5

6

7

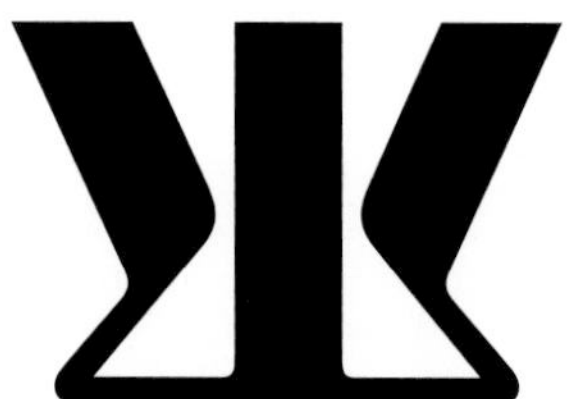

8

9

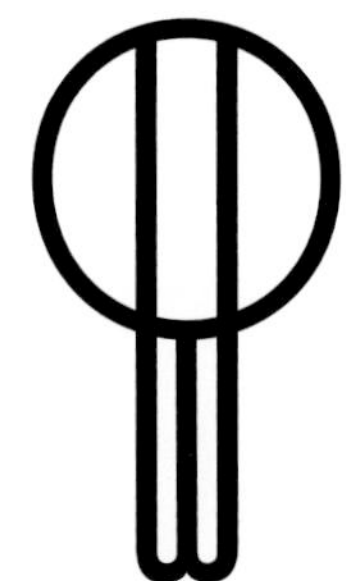

10

11

12

Skintime Aesthetics
Cosmetic clinic
2007

Skintime Aesthetics provides treatments to improve the appearance of lines, wrinkles, scarring and stretch marks, using injectables like Botox and fillers, LED phototherapy and microskin needling.

4 has a repeated 'S' in the hair; **3** uses the famous optical illusion in which the negative space between two profiles resembles a goblet, here parlayed into a fountain of youth.

1

2

3

4

Gorillas in ya Midst
Device
T-shirt motif
2005

GORILLAS IN YA MIDST

Savage
Valiant Comics
Comic book series
Proposed logo
2017

The story relates how the character's name was taken from the back of a football shirt, a reference I was asked to explore. I discovered that letters and numbers on modern sports kits are no longer in the traditional outlined 'collegiate' style, so I avoided what I saw as a cliché.

The final logo, which I didn't design, is in this style; this was one of those cases where the obvious choice was probably the best choice.

1

2

3

4

H.A.R.D Corps
Valiant Comics
Comic book series
2011

In the original series, **H.A.R.D.Corps** (Harbinger Active Resistance Division) operatives were human **Harbinger** hunters with chips implanted in their heads which enabled them to temporarily access **Harbinger** powers.

Valiant's 2011 reboot (which was eventually folded into **Bloodshot and H.A.R.D Corps,** for which a hybrid logo was designed) kept to this basic premise.

The brief was to update the original logo, so I opted to keep the 'heartbeat' motif and extend it throughout the rest of the letters.

1

2

3

4

1 2 **The Valiant Chronicles**
Valiant Comics
Web series
Proposed logos
2016

3 **Potato Printing**
Kinkajou
2015
Author: Rian Hughes
Incidental type from the *Get Lettering* book, actually printed with potatoes – though I forgot to cut the letters in reverse. This was easily rectified by flipping the scan in Photoshop.

4 **Miss Moustache**
Image Comics
Incidental logo
2012
From *Soho Dives Soho Divas,* my collection of burlesque-themed designs and illustrations

5 **Curves and Angles**
The Modernist Gentleman's Cultural Art Pamphlet
Incidental logo
2014
From *Soho Burlesque,* my unpublished sequel to *Soho Dives, Soho Divas*

6 **Spiffy Designs**
Self-promotional set of cards
1989

7 **Beware: MP3s Are Killing Illegal Taping**
Limited edition print
2000
Update of the 'Home Taping is Killing Music' campaign

8 **Dishy Lilli**
Incidental logo
2014
From *Soho Burlesque,* my unpublished sequel to *Soho Dives, Soho Divas*

9 **Is It Art?**
Computer Arts magazine
Article icon
1995

10 **Karmachanics**
Million Dollar
T-shirt motif
1994

11 **World Car**
Car magazine
1996

12 **Head/Heart**
Incidental logo
2014
From *Soho Burlesqueque.*

1

THE VALIANT CHRONICLES

2

3

POTATO PRINTING

4

5

6

7

8

9

10

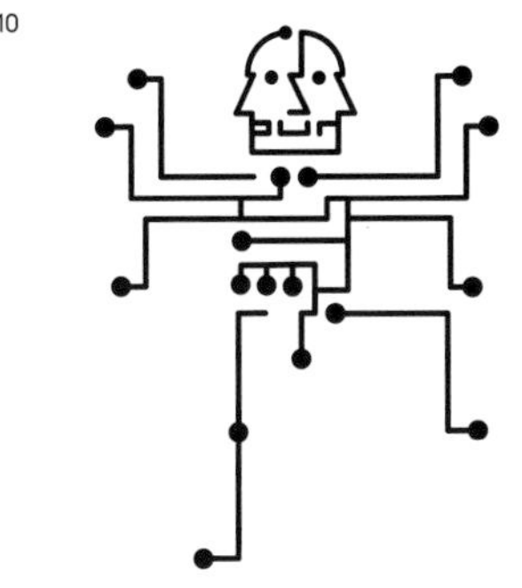

11

12

Maxim Mascot
Maxim magazine
Brand extension proposal
2002

The American edition of *Maxim* magazine was interested in developing a mascot or mark that they could license as part of a brand extension, along the lines of *Esquire* magazine's Esky or the *Playboy* rabbit.

The 'M' is taken from the magazine's masthead. The project did not develop beyond these concepts.

1

2

3

4

5

6

7

8

9

10

Ocean
Wildstorm Comics
Comic book series
2004

Ocean is a six-issue mini-series written by Warren Ellis, with pencils by Chris Sprouse and inks by Karl Story. Originally commissioned as a film script, it was adapted into a comic series and subsequently collected as a graphic novel.

In the ocean below the ice that covers Jupiter's moon Europa, scientists have discovered strange artifacts which may be coffins containing a non-human race. Special weapons inspector Nathan Kane is sent to Cold Harbor, a research station in orbit around Europa, to investigate.

The final logo (main image) plays with the backlit planet, its small ring and the moon. Other ideas adapted Chris Sprouse's designs for the cryogenic coffins **1**. The type is based on the Device font Rogue, originally developed as a custom font for the UK lad's mag *Loaded*. For consistency, this was also used for the credits.

The final covers of the series and the collection were designed in-house. Most of these reverse the logo and/or add a heavy outline, effects which unfortunately undermined the basic concept of Jupiter and Europa lit from behind.

1

2

3

Lord Havok and the Extremists
DC Comics
Comic book series
2000

Written by Frank Tieri with art by Liam Sharp, the **Lord Havok and the Extremists** mini-series was spun out of *Countdown,* another title, and so featured a 'Countdown presents' banner across the top.

Titles which are part of large company-wide crossover events often sport a plethora of stylistically unrelated logos. Though this can be avoided by judicious forward planning in the design, unfortunately it's not always possible.

1

2

3

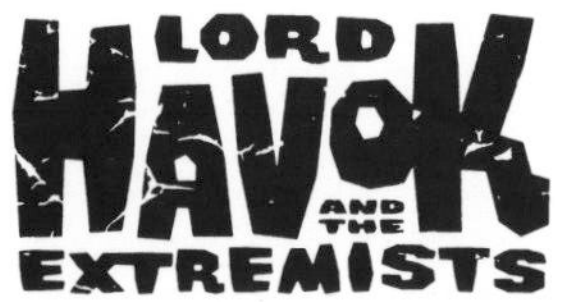

4

Mega City Comics
Comic shop
1991

Mega City Comics, the long-established store in London's Camden Town, is named after Joe Dredd's home town. The logo is shown here on a carrier bag.

1 is the original artwork, cut from Rubylith in negative. This was then put under the PMT camera and reversed. Note the addition of curves on 'Mega' on the printed version. **2** is the marker-pen sketch, **3** is a black and white version that was used in trade advertising.

The logo was applied to everything except the shop fascia itself. This still bears the original hand-painted logo, which has now almost completely weathered away.

1

2

3

Dynamo Development Labs
Design consultancy
2007

Dynamo Development Labs is a design consultancy and development studio working primarily for the toy and entertainment industries.

The identity was required to have a retro/modern feel (the 'traditional but contemporary' request many designers will be familiar with) and incorporate a satellite which could stand alone as an icon. There was also to be a sister brand called **Go Go Dynamo 2**.

I borrowed some Futurist imagery for **7**, and extended the idea of the satellite into a hybrid spark plug for **2**, **9**, **10** and **12** – a time-honoured metaphor for ideas and creativity, and in this context appropriately machine-age.

The final logo opted for a more straightforward depiction of a dynamo.

1

2

3

4

5

6

7

8

9

10

11

12

13

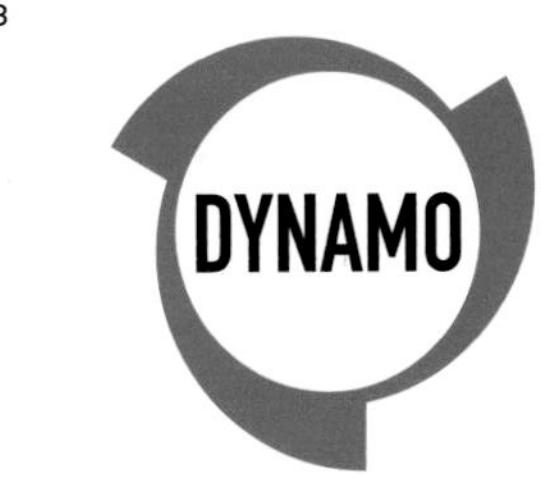

14

15

16

17

18

Credit Card icons
Fleetway
2000AD comic credits
1993

1

Steve Cook, art director for the legendary UK comic *2000AD,* commissioned several custom fonts for the title and its spin-off specials. Since the earliest issues, a '*2000AD* Credit Card' **1** on the first page of each strip has listed the writer and artist droids. For the 1993 redesign, these icons were supplied as part of a symbol font called Scrotnig Hexes, 'Scrotnig' meaning 'good or exciting' in alien editor Tharg's native Betelgeusian.

English comics' creative teams rarely extended beyond a writer, artist and letterer, but in the interests of completeness a colourist, inker, penciller, designer and photographer were also part of the set.

Inker

Photographer

Penciller

Letterer

Writer

Artist

Colourist

Designer

Atomic Chimp
Greg Thompson
Comic book
2007

Influenced by 1930s movie serials and Looney Tunes cartoons, **Atomic Chimp** is an SF adventure strip written by Greg Thompson with art by Matthew Humphreys.

Greg had sent me a sketch based on the original Action Comics logo, which I worked up as an option **2**, but it was felt that the final logo (main image) better encapsulated the tone of the comic.

1

2

Maxim's NFL Smackdown
Maxim magazine
Magazine section logo
2003

A logo for *Maxim* magazine's coverage of the US National Football League. The font is the Device design Westway.

1

2

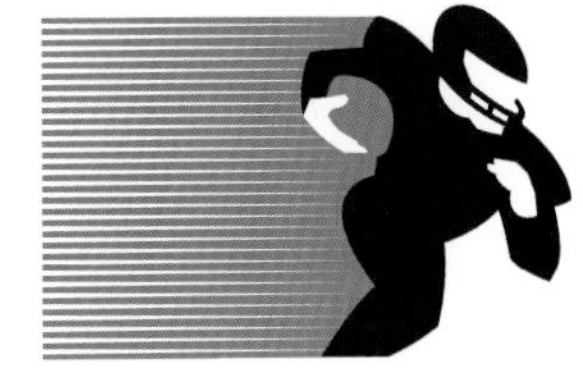

3

John '00' Fleming
Transient Records
DJ compilation album and personal mark
1998

Designed for Ministry of Sound and Godskitchen DJ John '00' Fleming's compilation album *Licensed to Thrill,* these logos play with his 'Joof' nickname, mixing decks and 8-bit graphics.

1

2

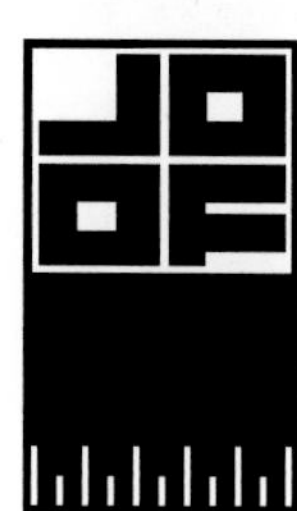

3

4

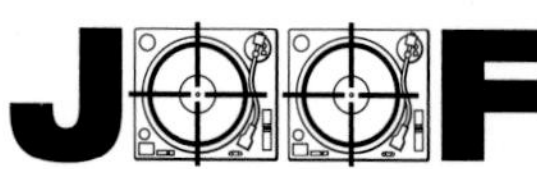

5

6

Kick Angel
Mercury Records/Stylorouge
Band
Proposed logo
2000

Logo proposals for a female three-piece signed to Mercury Records.

1

2

3

4

5

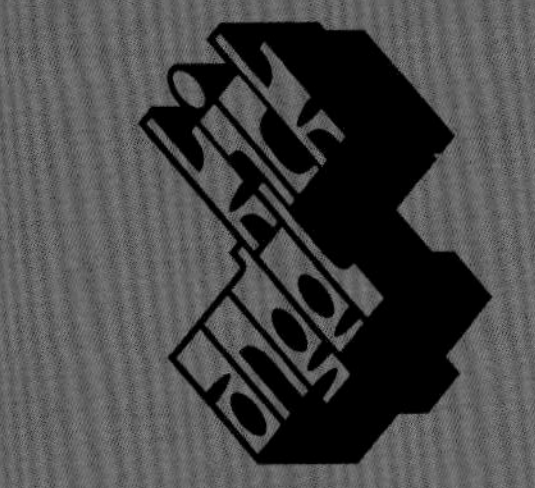

6

7

8

Pout and About
New Woman magazine
Lip gloss packaging
2000

Logos and illustration for a pair of cover-mounted lip gloss tins, given away free with an issue of *New Woman*.

Dale Walker, the art editor, commissioned many illustrations for the magazine from me in the early 2000s.

Orange
Mobile telecommunications
Advertising icons
1995

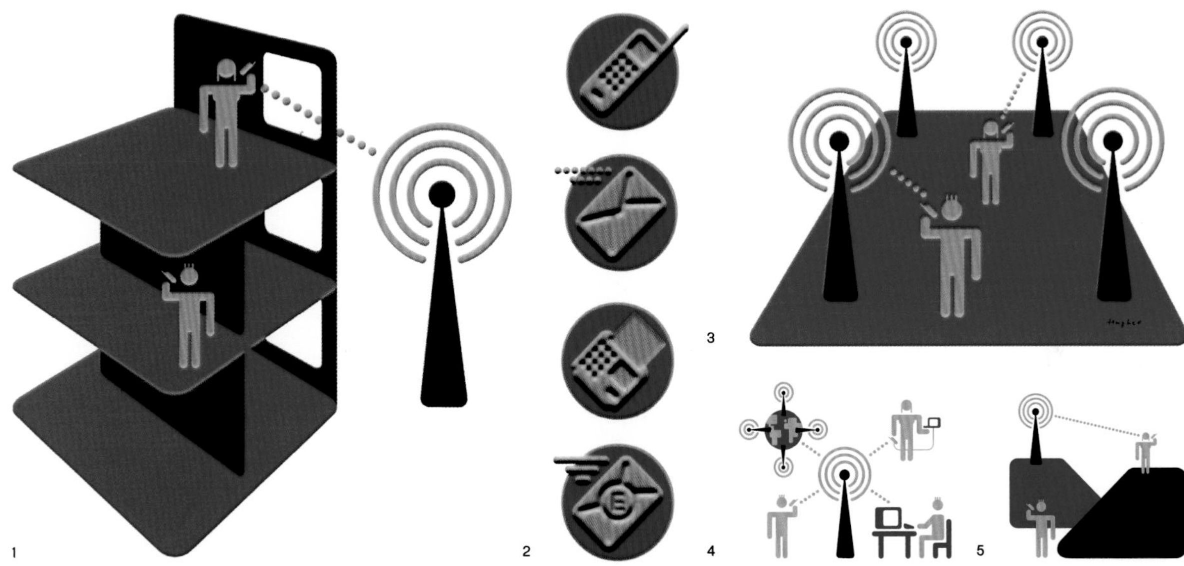

Film Review Icons
Maxim magazine (US)
2000

A set of humorous icons for American men's magazine *Maxim*'s film roundup.

1 Gratifying Violence
2 Hot Babe Alert
3 Zoinks, Ghosts!
4 Full-Frontal Nudity
5 Adorable Kid Warning
6 Chock-full O' Stunts
7 For Girlfriends Only
8 Historical Intrigue
9 Big Star On Board
10 Adorable Gay Character
11 Set in NYC
12 Backstabbing for Profit
13 More Hot Babes
14 More Gratifying Violence
15 Horrific Acts

The All-New Atom
DC Comics
Comic book series
2006

The **All-New Atom** spotlighted the fourth Atom, Ryan Choi. The logo references the original Silver Age version by Ira Schnapp, which had an unusual square 'O'. I added a shrinking perspective and a chisel shadow. In use, the top of the 'A' is designed to bleed off the top of the cover.

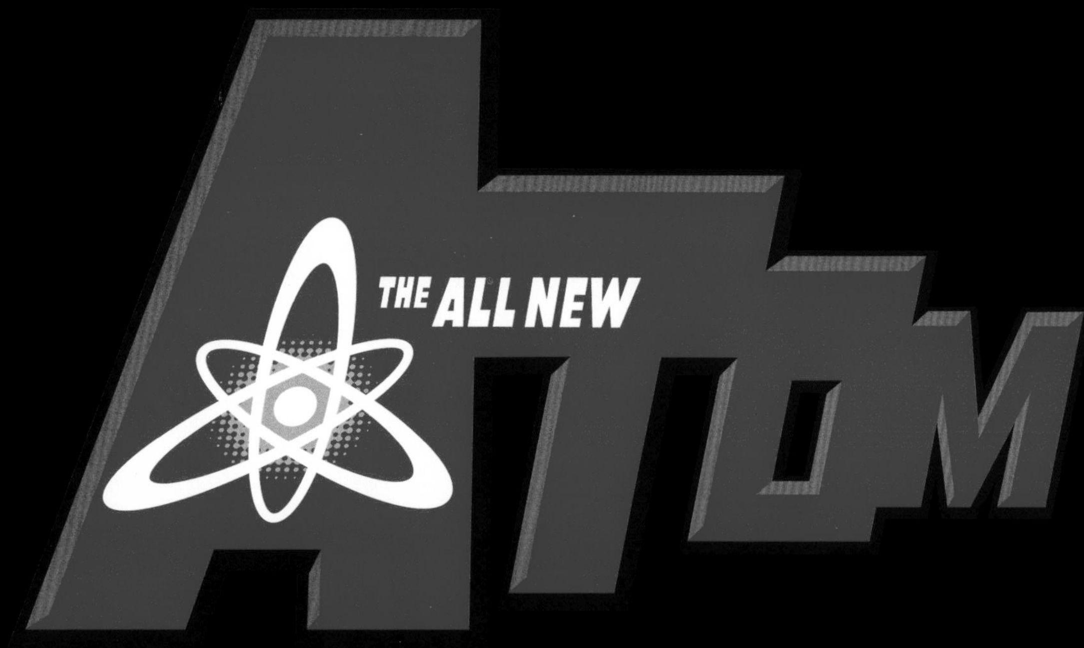

Wolverine: Weapon X
Marvel Comics
Comic book series
2008

Wolverine, one of **Marvel**'s most popular characters, has several titles to his name: **Wolverine, Wolverine: Weapon X**, and **Dark Wolverine**. **Dark Wolverine** focuses on Daken, Wolverine's son. **Wolverine: Weapon X** was released to coincide with the **Wolverine** movie.

As the two new titles were directly related to each other, it was suggested that the **Dark Wolverine** logo might be a degraded version of the **Weapon X** version.

Some of my first round of ideas **7**, **12**, **15** were rightly considered too 'cartoony', and as I usually try and push comic book logos away from genre clichés unless specifically producing a pastiche, I felt like I was indeed heading in the wrong direction.

Nevertheless, for the next batch of ideas I embraced sharp pointed serifs and slashes, which I'd carefully avoided first time around. As editor Jon Barber pointed out, when it comes to Wolverine, "There's, um, no overdoing the slashes!"

The **Weapon X** tagline was designed in the same type style, though less condensed for ease of use on the cover.

1

2

3

4

5

6

7

8

9

10

11

12

13

14

15

16

Wolverine/Dark Wolverine
Marvel Comics
Comic book series
2008

Further concepts for **Wolverine**, and the eroded 'dark' version of the logo. **10** is far too Germanic; **1** too ecclesiastical. **5** uses the slashes to offset elements of the letters; **2** has a scratched dog tag.

I thought **3**, **8** and **11** were unusual solutions. The more mainstream versions that were chosen are shown opposite.

1

WOLVERINE

2

WOLVERINE

3

4

5

WOLVERINE

6

7

WOLVERINE

8

9

Wolverine

10

Wolverine

11

WOLVERINE

12

WOLVERINE

DARK
WOLVERINE

X-Ray Kid
Jeff Matsuda
Games design company
Proposed logo
2008

X-Ray Kid Studios is an entertainment company specializing in video game development, comic books and television production. Based in Seattle and Newport Beach, California, the company produced art for Google's 'Lively' project.

The logo needed to suggest fun, but with a certain attitude. Despite the name, they did not want to be seen as a studio that was skewed towards projects aimed at children.

I explored letters made of bones, a development of their existing space-suited character, and several based on skulls, some using the 'X' below in the manner of a skull and crossbones.

Though I presented several rounds of designs, none were chosen.

1

2

3

4

5

6

7

8

9

10

11

12

Batman: The Return of Bruce Wayne
DC Comics
Comic book series
2010

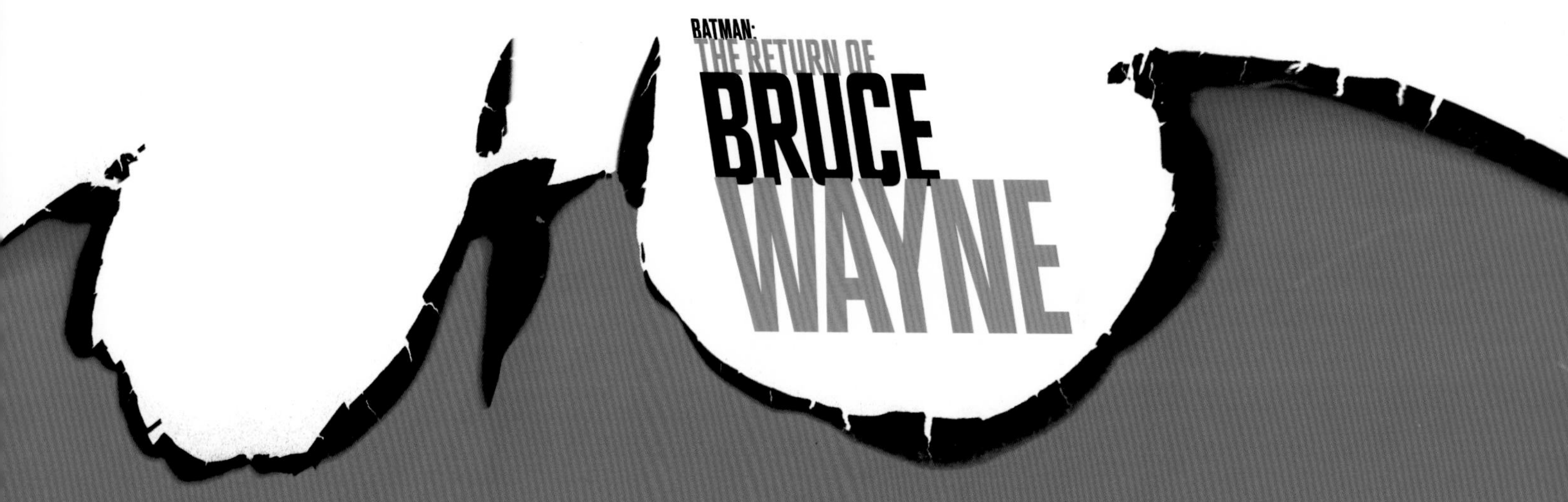

Batman: The Return of Bruce Wayne was a six-issue limited series written by my old collaborator Grant Morrison and featuring a team of rotating artists. The series picks up from #12 and details the journey Bruce Wayne takes through the timestream of the DC Universe back to the present day after being deposited in the distant past by Darkseid in *Final Crisis*.

The logo was created by burning the edge of several sheets of paper, scanning in the results and carefully patching together a bat from the best parts of each. As the series covered pre-history to the current day, I originally wanted to avoid any type style that could be associated with a specific time period and suggested a hand-drawn treatment **1**.

No-one seemed to respond to this idea, so I fell back on aged woodtype **2** and a stonemason's serif **4** to suggest the ravages of the ages.

The final version (opposite) uses a clean backslanted geometric sans, which on reflection does sit back in the mix in a reasonably understated fashion and let the burned bat symbol come to the fore. Each line is set at a larger point size, a somewhat obvious metaphor for a return from the past. The final version moves '**Batman**' to the left of the burned bat's ears to lend it more prominence.

Andy Kubert's covers also subtly repeat the bat motif across the backgrounds of the six issues, while variant covers featured each time period's version of Bruce Wayne, from left to right by Chris Sprouse, Frazer Irving, Yanick Paquette, Georges Jeanty and Ryan Sook. The final covers were laid out on my template by Kenny Lopez at **DC Comics**.

1

2

BATMAN:
RETURN OF
BRUCE
WAYNE

3

BATMAN
RETURN OF
BRUCE
WAYNE

4

BATMAN:
RETURN OF
BRUCE
WAYNE

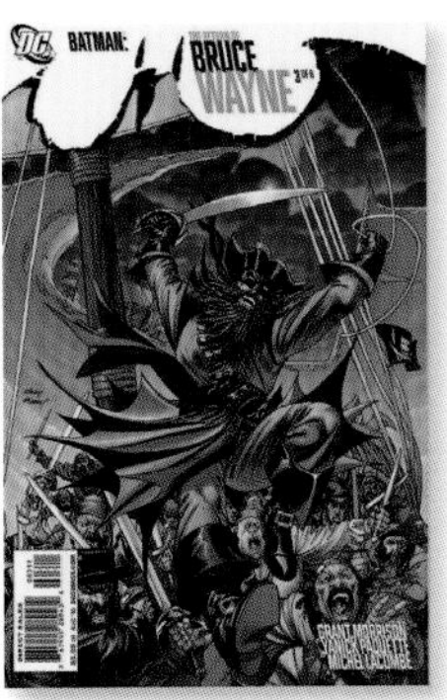

Fem-I-Nine
Matt Haley
Comic book series
2016

In Matt Haley's SF comic, a group of children have been sent to colonize another planet. They are the only option – the adults keep mysteriously dying en route. An android, accidentally awakened early, helps one of the young astronauts survive and make it to her final destination.

I based the design on a mission patch. Centering the letters around the '9' on one line was not easy **1**, **2**: 'Fem' is three letters, and 'Nine' four. The 'I' is not precisely central, but it *looks* central – which is what matters.

The white shape in the background of the final version is a starburst. The swirly type **4** was considered too psychedelic.

1

2

3

4

Knockabout Comics
Publisher
1985

Venerable UK publisher **Knockabout** grew out of the underground comics boom of the 1960s and 1970s, first importing works by the likes of Robert Crumb and Gilbert Sheldon, then as Hassle Free Press publishing their own line of collections and original material. The anthology title **Knockabout** featured short stories by a broad selection of UK talent such as Hunt Emerson, Bryan Talbot, Mike Matthews and Graham Higgins.

They are still going strong, publishing work by Krent Able and Brian Bolland, *The League of Extraordinary Gentlemen* by Alan Moore and Kevin O'Neill, my own collection of early strips *Yesterday's Tomorrows*, and translations of European albums.

My designs for the publisher were produced using the traditional tools of the trade: paste-up on CS10 board. The logos were cut from Rubylith, a red transparent photo-opaque film, or drawn by hand with a brush or Rapidograph, then copied down to size using a PMT (photo-mechanical transfer) camera to crisp them up for reproduction. As a branding feature, each cover had a zigzag down the left-hand side into which a repeat pattern was dropped.

Knockabout's editorial office was in their warehouse in Acklam Road, London, just off Portobello Road Market. As related in the introduction, I discovered a stash of vintage Artype lettering sheets on a market stall one lunchtime, and these were pressed into use. Budgets were tiny, headline typesetting was expensive, and we had to improvise.

The font used across the top of the **Knockabout** anthologies is Filmotype Modern, which I digitised in 2011 from the original Typositor film strips as part of Stuart Sandler's revival project.

Underground comics' obsession with sex and drugs meant that police busts were a regular occurrence – moral guardian Mary Whitehouse took a special interest in **Outrageous Tales from the Old Testament.** To meet legal defence costs, publishers Tony and Carol Bennett published a *Trial Special,* ran fundraisers and jumped out of planes for sponsorship.

Shown here is the original artwork for the **Knockabout** logo, drawn by hand at A3 size. I also drew a sans **1** and an outline version **2**, which I copied onto film and then layered **3**.

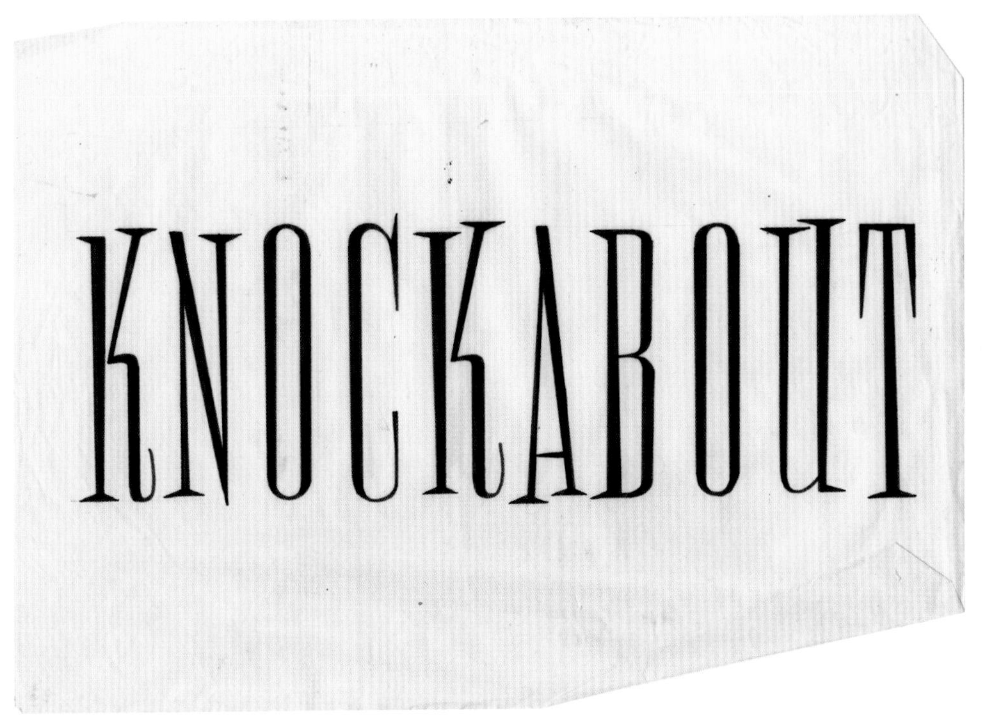

1

KNOCKABOUT

2

KNOCKABOUT

3

KNOCKABOUT

Jazz Funnies
Knockabout Comics
Graphic novel
1986
Writer/artist: Hunt Emerson

Philbert Desanex' 100,000th Dream
Knockabout Comics
Comic book
1989
Writer/artist: Gilbert Sheldon

Puss Puss
Knockabout Comics
Comic book
1994
Writer/artist: Hunt Emerson

The Fabulous Furry Freak Brothers
Knockabout Comics
Freak Brothers #0 comic
1986
Writer/artist: Gilbert Sheldon

Peter Pank
Knockabout Comics
Graphic novel
1992
Writer/artist: Max

Puss Puss
Knockabout Comics
Comic book
Proposed logo
1994

Shown opposite is a selection of **Knockabout** covers.

The Robert Crumb titles were also available as limited edition, foil-stamped signed hardbacks. **Calculus Cat** collected strips from the **Knockabout** anthology and Paul Gravett and Peter Stanbury's *Escape* magazine, where my own early strips also saw print. The logo here is very much based on Hunt's lettering style. **Jazz Funnies** collects the Max Zillion strips from the **Knockabout** anthology. The second **Jazz Funnies** cover was for a reprint that didn't materialise – shown is a scan taken from a photocopy of a Cromalin. In **Hard To Swallow**, Hunt illustrated John Dowie's stand-up routines. **Startling Planet** collected Hunt's paranormal strips from *Fortean Times* magazine. The **Knockabout** anthology ran for many years, and alongside established underground artists like Gilbert Sheldon and Kim Deitch featured many UK 'alternative' and small-press creators.

Firkin originally ran in the top shelf magazine *Fiesta*. **Oink!** collects material from the magazine of the same name in two small paperback books, and uses a redrawn version of the existing logo that brings it into line with the other **Knockabout** titles. **The Collected Fat Freddy's Cat** also repackaged existing strips in paperback format.

The covers for the two-volume **Complete Freak Brothers** reuse images from a silkscreen print and an old cover, with a logo based on a customised version of the Device font Laydeez Nite. It's quite hard to read, as Gilbert helpfully notes in a sketch he drew for me on the title page **1**.

For the **Freak Brothers Omnibus** and the **Fat Freddy's Cat Omnibus**, I laboriously hand drew the logo and accompanying type to make it look as if the entire cover was one illustration.

1

my troubles with
WOMEN
Robert Crumb

R. Crumb's
AMERICA
Robert Crumb

R. Crumb draws the
Blues
Robert Crumb

my troubles with
WOMEN
Robert Crumb

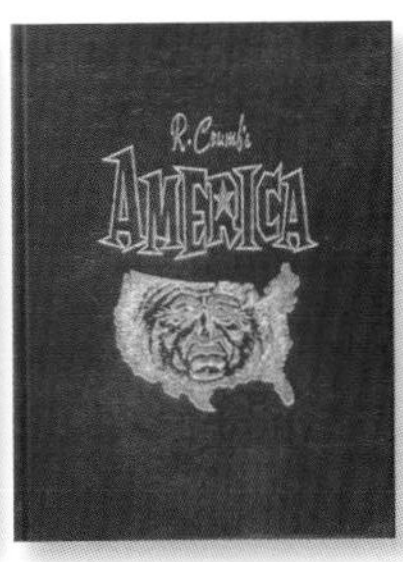
R. Crumb's
AMERICA

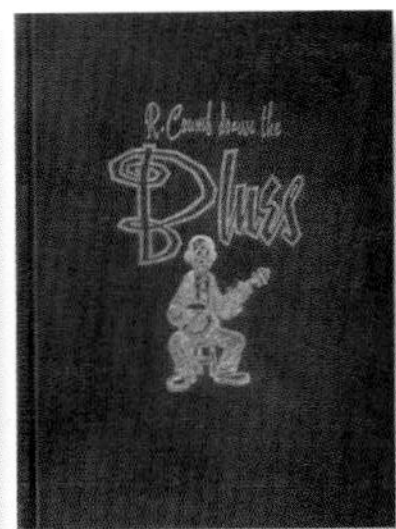
R. Crumb draws the
Blues

THE FABULOUS FURRY
FREAK
BROTHERS
IN THE IDIOTS ABROAD

HUNT EMERSON'S
CALCULUS CAT
DEATH TO TELEVISION!!

HUNT EMERSON
JAZZ funnies
BUS STOP
MAX ZILLION
ALTO EGO

JAZZ
FUNNIES
MAX ZILLION

OUTRAGEOUS TALES FROM THE
Old Testament
HUMAN SACRIFICE
MURDER
Wrath of GOD
Deadly Tent Pegs
ENORMOUS BOILS
JUDGES KINGS AND PROPHETS

Philbert Desanex'
100,000th
DREAM
Gilbert Shelton

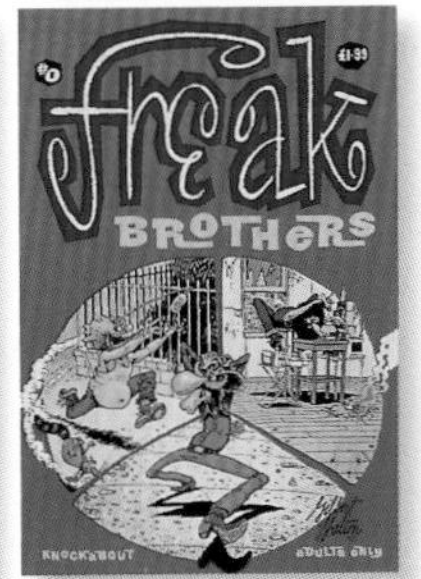
Freak
BROTHERS
KNOCKABOUT
ADULTS ONLY

Famous Tales of
FAT FREDDY'S
CAT
Gilbert Shelton
"The Funniest Cat in Comics"

HARD TO
SWALLOW
JOHN DOWIE
HUNT EMERSON

STARTLING
planet
RAIN OF KISSES!
emerson-higgins

GLACIAL GLAMOUR AND REFRIGERATED RABBITS
KNOCKABOUT

DAYDREAMS AND NIGHT FEARS
KNOCKABOUT
GILBERT SHELTON
HUNT EMERSON
JACK ALARUM
GRAHAM HIGGINS

THERE'S A FUNNY SPELL IN HERE
KNOCKABOUT

The Collected
FAT FREDDY'S
CAT
BOOK TWO
GILBERT SHELTON

The Collected
FAT FREDDY'S
CAT
BOOK ONE
GILBERT SHELTON

HUNT EMERSON · TYM MANLEY
FIRKIN
GUIDE TO HUMAN SEXUAL BEHAVIOUR
ADULTS ONLY

HUNT EMERSON · TYM MANLEY
FIRKIN
GUIDE TO HUMAN SEXUAL BEHAVIOUR
I'M ONLY DOIN' ME JOB....
DNA
ADULTS ONLY

HUNT EMERSON · TYM MANLEY
FIRKIN
GUIDE TO HUMAN SEXUAL BEHAVIOUR

HUNT EMERSON · TYM MANLEY
FIRKIN
GUIDE TO HUMAN SEXUAL BEHAVIOUR

From the pages of
OINK!
Uncle Pigg's
CRACKLING
Tales
1

From the pages of
OINK!
2
Uncle Pigg's
CRACKLING
Tales

PUSSPUSS

MAX
PETER
PANK

FREAK
BROTHERS

FREAK
BROTHERS

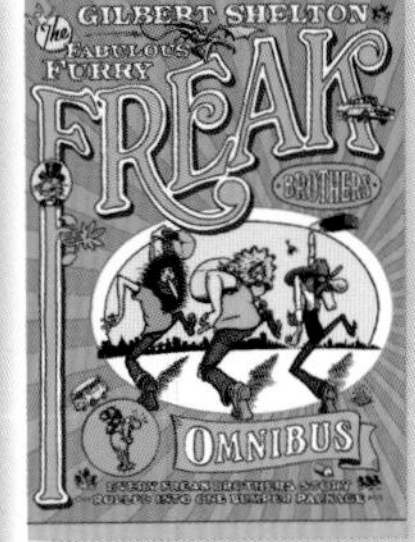
GILBERT SHELTON
The FABULOUS FURRY
FREAK
BROTHERS
OMNIBUS

GILBERT SHELTON
FAT FREDDY'S
CAT
OMNIBUS
THE FUNNIEST CAT IN COMICS

THE BEST OF
WONDER
WART-HOG
GILBERT SHELTON

FIFTY FREAKIN YEARS
FABULOUS FURRY
FREAK
BROTHERS
GILBERT SHELTON

R. Crumb's America
Knockabout Comics
Graphic novel
1994
Writer/artist: Robert Crumb

My Troubles with Women
Knockabout Comics
Graphic novel
1990
Writer/artist: Robert Crumb

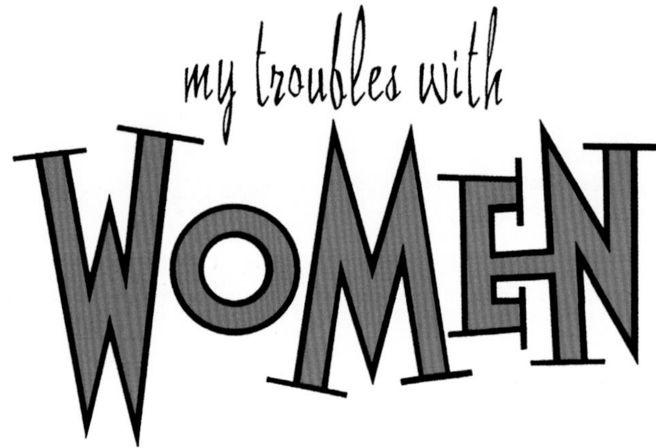

Startling Planet
Knockabout Comics
Comic book
1989
Writers/artists: Hunt Emerson and Graham Higgins

R. Crumb draws the Blues
Knockabout Comics
Graphic novel
1992
Writer/artist: Robert Crumb

1 Jester
Knockabout Comics
Paperback book imprint
1988

2 Hard to Swallow
Knockabout Comics
Book cover
1988
Writer: John Dowie
Artist: Hunt Emerson

3 Ceasefire
Knockabout Comics
Comic book anthology
1991

4 Famous Tales of Fat Freddy's Cat
Knockabout Comics
Book cover
1994
Writer/artist: Gilbert Sheldon

5 Firkin
Knockabout Comics
Comic book series
1989
Writer: Tym Manley
Artist: Hunt Emerson

6 Firkin
Knockabout Comics
Comic book series
Proposed logo
1989
Writer: Tym Manley
Artist: Hunt Emerson

7 Trombone
Knockabout Comics
Comic book anthology
1990

8 The Fabulous Furry Freak Brothers
Knockabout Comics
Graphic novel
1986
Writer/artist: Gilbert Sheldon

9 Outrageous Tales from the Old Testament
Knockabout Comics
Graphic novel anthology
1987

10 Crack Editions
Knockabout Comics
Graphic novel imprint
1986

1

Jester

2

HARD TO SWALLOW

3

CEASEFIRE

4

5

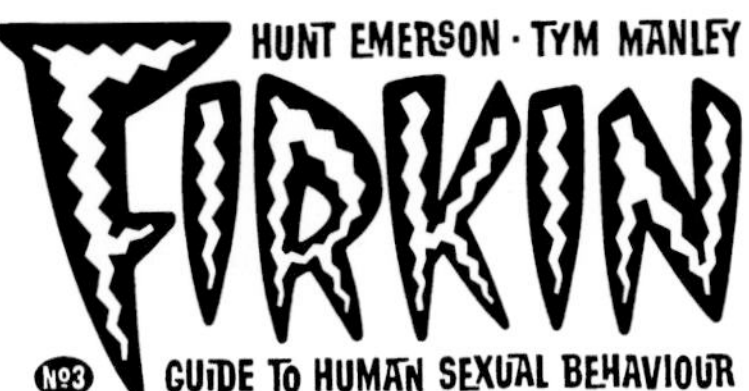

6

FIRKIN

7

International Comic Humour
TROMBONE

8

9

10

OUTBREAKS
OF VIOLETS
RANDOM ACTS OF KINDNESS
MTV EUROPE MUSIC AWARDS
LIMITED 1995 EDITION

Outbreaks of Violets
MTV Europe
Music Awards brochure
1995

Written by Alan Moore and illustrated by an international cross-section of comics talent, the brochure for the 1995 MTV Europe Music Awards, or EMAs for short, came in two versions. The simpler (but still fancy) standard version was bound with two brass screws and given away at the event; the hardback, linen-hinged version was designed to resemble a folio, and was limited to 50 copies that were presented to top advertisers and other luminaries.

The theme we were given was "random acts of kindness" – Alan wrote the text for a set of 24 cards that chart an escalating "outbreak of reasonableness", culminating in a build-up of World's Greatest Dad mugs and the dropping of the Platonic Bomb. These are presented as actual cards in the limited edition, while they are printed as part of the book itself in the standard edition. MTV executives read parts of Alan's script aloud to each other at the presentation, laughing as they did so. Each artist also produced a print with their own interpretation.

At the awards ceremony, the screws proved too much of a temptation: the dancefloor at the afterparty was quickly carpeted with loose pages. This could be why it is probably the rarest Alan Moore title in existence: a copy of the standard edition fetched £800 on eBay. To my knowledge, no copies of the limited edition have come up for sale.

The artists involved were Mique Beltran, Max Cabanes, Mick McMahon, Baru, Francesca Ghermandi, Javier Mariscal, Jean-Philippe Stassen, Kellie Strøm, François Avril, Isabel Kreitz, Rachael Ball, Max Andersson, Stefano Ricci, Francois Boucq, Jamie Hewlett, Max, Edmond Baudoin, Ed Pinsent, Loustal, John M. Burns, Joakim Pirinen, Lorenzo Mattotti, Christian Gorny and Ever Meulen.

The covers are made from a recycled stock in which flecks of newsprint can be seen, and which yellows very quickly. The illustration of the friendly devil on the sticker on the front was drawn with a brush, and then auotraced. I also created a custom font, Metropol Noir, which was later released as part of the Device range.

Frank Wynne served as editor, cajoling artists, charming printers and pulling the whole complex project together. It ended up winning a couple of industry awards.

Cover art credits

Credits given in main text, except:
18 **Shadowman**
#0 Khari Evans; #0 Dave Johnson [variant cover]; #1 Dave Johnson [variant cover]; #2 Patrick Zircher; #2 Dave Johnson [variant cover]; #4 Patrick Zircher; #4 Dave Johnson [variant cover]; #5 Rafael Grampá; #5, 6 Dave Johnson [variant covers]; #6-8 Patrick Zircher; #9 Dave Johnson [variant cover]; #9 Andrew Robinson; #10 Riley Rossmo [variant cover]; #10 Roberto De La Torre, David Baron, Matt Milla ; #11 Rian Hughes [variant cover]; #12 Dave Johnson [variant cover]; #12 Kekai Kotaki; #13X Stephane Perger; #14, 15 Roberto De La Torre; #15 Mike Allred; #16 Russell Dauterman, Jordie Bellaire; **Shadowman: End Times** #1, 2 Jeff Dekal; #2 Trevor McCarthy [variant cover]; #3 Lewis LaRosa; #3 Russell Dauterman; **Shadowman TPB** #1, 2 Patrick Zircher; #3 Dave Johnson; #4 Roberto De La Torre; **Shadowman: End Times TPB** Giuseppe Camuncoli;
22 **The Spirit**
#1 Darwyn Cooke, J. Bone, Dave Stewart [3 variant covers]; #2, 3, 6-8, 10, 11 Darwyn Cooke, J. Bone, Dave Stewart; #14 Jordi Bernet, Dave Stewart; #16 Bruce Timm, Dave Stewart; #17, #18 Paul Smith, Lee Loughridge
27 **Batman, Incorporated**
#0, 2 Chris Burnham, Nathan Fairbairn; #2 Cameron Stewart [variant cover]; #5, 8, 9, 12 Chris Burnham, Nathan Fairbairn
34 **Harbinger: Bleeding Monk**
#0 Clayton Henry
37 **Armor Hunters**
#1-4 Trevor Hairsine; **Armor Hunters: Bloodshot** #1 Trevor Hairsine; **Armor Hunters: Harbinger** #1 Trevor Hairsine; #1 Blank [variant cover]; #1 Clayton Crain; #2 Rian Hughes; #3 Doug Braithwaite; #4 Clayton Henry; **Armor Hunters: Aftermath** #1 Mico Suayan; #1 Diego Bernard [variant cover]; #1 Brent Peeples [variant cover]; **Armor Hunters: Bloodshot:** #1 Clayton Crain; #2-3 Philip Tan; **Armor Hunters: Harbinger** #1 Clayton Crain; #1-2 Lewis LaRosa; #2 CAFU [variant cover]
38 **Nameless**
#1-6 Chris Burnham, Nathan Fairbairn
55 **Batman and Robin** #1 Frank Quitely; #1 Frank Quitely [second printing variant]; #2-3, 6, 8 Frank Quitely; #8 Cameron Stewart
58 **Jonny Double**
#1-3 Mark Chiarello
62 **X-O Manowar**
#1 Esad Ribic; #1 Cary Nord [pullbox exclusive variant]; #1 Cary Nord [third printing black and white variant]; #6 Patrick Zircher [second printing black and white variant]; #9 Trevor Hairsine; #9 Clayton Crain [variant cover]; #11 Clayton Crain; #12 Marko Djurdjevic; #13 Trevor Hairsine; #14 Arturo Lozzi ; #15 José Ladrönn [variant cover]; #22 Lewis LaRosa; #27 Diego Bernard [variant cover]; #27 Miguel Sepulveda; #28 Diego Bernard; #29 CAFU; #29 Juan Doe [variant cover]; #30 Raul Allen [variant cover]; #30 Clayton Henry [variant cover]; #30 Rafa Sandoval [variant cover]; #31 Emanuela Lupacchino [variant cover]; #33 ChrisCross [variant cover]; #34 Lewis LaRosa; #35 Lewis LaRosa; #36 Rafa Sandoval; #37 Stephen Segovia, Brian Reber; #39 Brent Peeples [variant cover]; #41 Jefte Palo, Jordie Bellaire [variant cover]; #47 Khoi Pham [variant cover]; #50 Kaare Andrews [variant cover]; #50 Chip Zdarsky [variant cover]; #50 Marcos Martin [variant cover]; **X-O Manowar TPB** #6 Jelena Kevic Djurdjevic; #8 Raul Allen; #11 Phil Jimenez
66 **Britannia**
#1, 2 Cary Nord; #2 Dave Johnson [variant cover]; #3 Cary Nord; #3 Dave Johnson [variant cover]; #4 Cary Nord; #4 Dave Johnson [variant cover]
69 **Mythic**
#1 John McCrea; #1 John McCrea [variant cover]; #1 Matteo Scalera, Moreno DiNisio [variant cover]; #2 John McCrea; #2 Declan Shalvey, Kelly Fitzpatrick [variant cover]; #3 Sean Murphy [San Diego Comic-Con variant]; #3 John McCrea; #3 Duncan Fegredo [variant cover]; #4 John McCrea; #4 Goran Parlov [variant cover]; #5 John McCrea, Rian Hughes; #5 Brian Churilla [variant cover]; #6 John McCrea, Rian Hughes; #6 Gene Ha [variant cover]; #7 John McCrea; #7 Steve Pugh [variant cover]; #8 John McCrea, Rian Hughes; #8 Mike Huddleston [variant cover]; **Mythic TPB** John McCrea [cover]; Rian Hughes [opening spread]
82 **Tangent Comics: Year 1**
Green Lantern #1 J. H. Williams III; **The Joker** #1 Matt Haley; **Sea Devils** #1 Vince Giarrano; **Doom Patrol** #1 Sean Chen; **Metal Men** #1 Ron Marz; **The Atom** #1 Paul Ryan; **Flash** #1 Gary Frank; **Nightwing** #1 Jan Duursema; **Secret Six** #1 Tom Grummett
83 **Tangent Comics: Year 2**
JLA #1 Darryl Banks; **Tales of the Green Lantern** #1 J. H. Williams III; **Wonder Woman** #1 Angel Unzueta; **The Joker's Wild** #1 Tom Simmons; **Nightwing: Night Force** #1 Jan Duursema; **The Batman** #1 Klaus Janson; **Flash** #1 Paul Pelletier; **Powergirl** #1 Dusty Abell; **The Superman** #1 Jackson Guice
97 **Bizarro**
Bizarro World Jaime Hernandez, Coco Shinomiya; **Bizarro Comics** Matt Groening
102 **Harbinger Wars**
#3 Patrick Zircher; #4 Stephane Perger [variant cover]; #4 Juan Doe [variant cover]
102 **Harbinger: Omegas**
#1 Lewis LaRosa; #2 Glenn Fabry, Adam Brown [variant cover]; #3 Lewis LaRosa, Brian Reber; #3 Glenn Fabry, Adam Brown [variant cover]
108 **The Invisibles**
#1 Rian Hughes; #2-25 Sean Phillips
111 **Strange Tales**
#1 Jaime Hernandez; #2 Ivan Brunetti
112 **Eternal Warrior**
#1 Clayton Crain; #1 Dave Bullock [variant cover]; #2 Clayton Crain; #3 J.G. Jones; #7 Lewis LaRosa [variant cover]; #8 Lewis LaRosa
129 **James Bond 007**
James Bond 007: Vargr #1 Dom Reardon; #1 Jason Masters [variant cover]; #1 Glenn Fabry [variant cover]; #1 Rian Hughes [variant cover]; #1 Dan Panosian [variant cover]; #1 Gabriel Hardman [variant cover]; #1 Dennis Calero [variant cover]; #1 Dennis Calero [variant cover]; #1 Ben Oliver [variant cover]; #1 Dennis Calero [variant cover]; #2, 3, 5, 6 Dom Reardon; **James Bond 007: Eidolon** #7, 9, 10 Dom Reardon; **James Bond 007: Hammerhead** #1 Ron Salas [variant cover] #2 Francesco Francavilla; **James Bond 007: Black Box** #1 Dom Reardon; #2 Dom Reardon [variant cover]; #4 Dom Reardon; **James Bond 007: Kill Chain** #1 Juan Doe [variant cover]; #1 Greg Smallwood
131 **Days Missing**
#1-4 Frazer Irving [variant covers]
134 **Eternity**
#1 Jelena Kevic-Djurdjevic; #1 Trevor Hairsine [variant cover]; #1 Felipe Massafera [variant cover]
136 **Eagle/Dan Dare**
Volume 6 #42 Frank Hampson studio
137 **The Death-Defying Doctor Mirage**
#1-3 Travel Foreman; #4, 5 Kevin Wada
137 **The Death-Defying Doctor Mirage: Second Lives**
#1 Jelena Kevic Djurdjevic [variant cover]; #1 Travel Foreman
144 **I Hate Fairyland**
#1-5 Skottie Young
159 **Outcast**
#1, 3, 8, 10, 14, 15, 18 Paul Azaceta, Elizabeth Breitweiser
173 **Captain America Reborn**
#1-6 Bryan Hitch, Jackson "Butch" Guice
183 **Shade, the Changing Man**
#51-53 Sean Phillips
203 **Flex Mentallo**
#1-4 Frank Quitely
206 **Ivar, Timewalker**
#1-9 Raul Allen; #9 Al Barrionuevo, Sandra Molina [variant cover]; #9-12 Raul Allen [Cover A]; #12 Kano [variant cover]
217 **Valiant** [various]
Valiant Masters: Bloodshot Barry Windsor-Smith; **Valiant Masters: X-O Manowar** Joe Quesada; **Valiant Masters: Rai** Joe St. Pierre; **Must Read Valiant** #1, 2 Various; **Deluxe Edition: Bloodshot Reborn** Juan Doe; **Deluxe Edition: X-O Manowar** Cary Nord; **Deluxe Edition: Bloodshot** Esad Ribic; **Deluxe Edition: Shadowman** Russell Dauterman; **Deluxe Edition: Harbinger** Mico Suayan; **Deluxe Edition: Rai** Clayton Crain
222 **Jacked**
#1-6 Glenn Fabry, Ryan Brown
229 **Turok**
#1 Bart Sears; #1 Craig Rousseau [variant cover]; #1 Rob Liefeld [variant cover]; #1 Jae Lee [variant cover]; #2, 3 Jae Lee; #4 Ardian Syaf [variant cover]; #5 Jae Lee [variant cover]; #5 Bart Sears; #6 Jae Lee [variant cover]; #6 Bart Sears; #7, 9 Jae Lee [variant cover]; #10 Bart Sears; #10, 11 Jae Lee [variant cover]; #11 Bart Sears; #12 Jae Lee [variant cover]
231 **Magnus, Robot Fighter**
#1 Joe Bennett [variant cover]; #1 Gabriel Hardman; #1 José Malaga [second printing cover]; #2 Emanuela Lupacchino [variant cover]; #3 Stephen Segovia [variant cover]; #4 Emanuela Lupacchino [variant cover]; #5 Cory Smith [variant cover]; #6 Gabriel Hardman; #7, 8 Cory Smith [variant covers]; #9 Jonathan Ang Lau; #9 Cory Smith [variant cover]; #10, 11 Jonathan Lau; #11 Cory Smith [variant cover]; #12 Jonathan Lau; #12 Cory Smith [variant cover]; #0 Gabriel Hardman
232 **Solar, Man of the Atom**
#1 Juan Doe
232 **The Occult Files of Doctor Spektor**
#1 Christian Ward
237 **The Multiversity**
#1 Ivan Reis, Joe Prado; #1 Chris Burnham, Nathan Fairbairn [variant cover]; #1 Brian Hitch [History of the Multiverse variant cover]; **Society of Super-Heroes** #1 Chris Sprouse, Dave McCaig; #1 Frazer Irving [variant cover]; #1 Guillem March, Tomeu Morey [History of the Multiverse variant cover]; #1 Chris Sprouse [variant cover]; **The Just** #1 Ben Oliver; #1 Ben Oliver [variant cover]; #1 Eduardo Risso [varinat cover]; **Pax Americana** #1 Frank Quitely, Nathan Fairbairn; #1 Frank Quitely [sketch variant cover]; #1 Michael Cho [variant cover]; #1 Jae Lee [variant cover]; #1 Patrick Gleason [History of the Multiverse variant cover]; **Thunderworld Adventures** #1 Cameron Stewart, Nathan Fairbairn; #1 Cameron Stewart [variant cover]; #1 Cliff Chiang [variant cover]; #1 Cully Hamner [History of the Multiverse variant cover]; **Multiversity Guidebook** #1 Tom Fowler [variant cover]; #1 Phil Jimenez, Dave McCaig [variant cover]; #1 Rian Hughes; #1 Rian Hughes [second printing cover]; Rian Hughes [sketch variant cover]; Mastermen #1 Jim Lee, #1 Jim Lee [sketch variant cover]; #1 Aaron Kuder, Nathan Fairbairn; #1 Howard Porter, Tomeu Morey [History of the Multiverse variant cover]; **Ultra Comics** #1 Doug Mahnke; #1 Doug Mahnke [sketch variant cover]; #1 Yanick Paquette, Nathan Fairbairn [History of the Multiverse variant cover]; #1 Duncan Rouleau; **Multiversity** #2 Ivan Reis, Joe Prado; #2 Michael Allred, Laura Allred [variant cover]; Francis Manapul [History of the Multiverse variant cover]
242 **Judge Dredd: Definitive Editions Future Crime** Bil Maher; **Bad Science** Brendan McCarthy; **Hall of Justice** Rich Larson; **Metal Fatigue** Dave Dorman
243 **Third World War**
#1 Duncan Fegredo; #2 Glenn Fabry; #3 Sean Phillips; #4 Paul Johnson; #6 Glen Fabry
245 **Kid Eternity**
#1-3 Duncan Fegredo
246 **4001 AD**
Clayton Crain [cover roughs]
248 **Eternal Warrior: Days of Steel**
#1 Bryan Hitch; #1 Cary Nord [variant cover]; #1 Rafa Sandoval Cover [variant cover]; #2 Rafael Albuquerque [variant cover]; #3 Trevor Hairsine, Brian Reber; #3 Al Barrionuevo, David Baron [variant cover]
250 **Bloodshot**
#0 Dave Bullock; #1 Arturo Lozzi; #1 Esad Ribic [variant cover]; #1 David Aja [variant cover]; #1 Mico Suayan [variant cover]; #2, 6 Arturo Lozzi; #7 Kalman Andrasofszky; #9 Clayton Henry; #10 Mico Suayan; #11 Kalman Andrasofskzy; #11 Matthew Clark [variant cover]; #12 Kalman Andrasofszky; #13 Dave Bullock; #14 J. G. Jones; #15 Emanuela Lupacchino; #16 Patrick Zircher; #16 ChrisCross [variant cover]; #17 Riley Rossmo; #18 Cully Hamner [variant cover]; #20, 21 Jorge Molina [variant covers]; #22 Lewis LaRosa; #22 Riley Rossmo [variant cover]; #22 Roberto De La Torre [variant cover]; #24 Rafa Sandoval; #25 Lewis LaRosa; #25 Bryan Hitch [variant cover]; #25 Rafael Albuquerque [variant cover]; **Bloodshot: Reborn** #1 Juan Doe; #1 Lewis LaRosa [variant cover]; #2, 4, 8, 9 Dave Johnson [variant covers]
261 **Fantastic Four**
Mark Bagley, Steve McNiven; animated TV show image, Leonard Kirk [cover roughs]
267 **Revolver**
#1 Rian Hughes; #2 Brendan McCarthy; #3 Floyd Hughes; #4 Warren Pleece; #5 Steve Parkhouse; #6 Rian Hughes; #7 Shaky Kane; **Revolver Horror Special** John Bolton [cover], Rian Hughes [contents spread]; 277 **Revolver Romance Special** Brian Bolland [cover], Rian Hughes [contents spread]
283 **Vertigo Voices**
Face #1 Duncan Fegredo; **The Eaters** #1 Dean Ormston; **Kill Your Boyfriend** #1 Philip Bond
286 **Tank Girl**
#1 Jamie Hewlett [dummy cover]
290 **Kid Eternity**
#1-8, 11, 12, 14, 16 Sean Phillips
297 **Deadline**
#69 Jamie Hewlett; #70 Steve Whittaker; #71 #Ilya [Ed Hillier]
304 **Utopia/Exodus**
Jae Lee, Terry Dodson [cover roughs]; **Dark Avengers/Uncanny X-Men: Utopia** #1 Marc Silvestri; #1 Terry Dodson [variant cover]; **The Uncanny X-Men** #513 Simone Bianchi, Simone Peruzzi [variant cover], #513 Terry Dodson; #514 Simone Bianchi; **Dark Avengers/ Uncanny X-Men: Exodus** #1 Steve McNiven; **Dark Avengers/Uncanny X-Men: Utopia** #1 Simone Bianchi [variant cover]; Jae Lee [variant cover]; **Dark Avengers** #7 Mike Deodato; #7 Simone Bianchi, Simone Peruzzi [variant cover]; #8 Simone Bianchi, Simone Peruzzi; **Dark Avengers/Uncanny X-Men: Exodus** #1 Simone Bianchi
359 **The Mighty**
#1, 2, 4, 7, 9 Dave Johnson
366 **DC Focus**
Touch #3 Tomer Hanuka; **Fraction** #1 Tomer Hanuka; **Hard Time** #1 Tomer Hanuka; **Kinetic** #4 Tomer Hanuka
367 **Hard Time**
#2, 4 Tomer Hanuka; #5, 6 Brian Hurtt
369 **Touch**
#1, 2 Tomer Hanuka; #4 Brian Hurtt
371 **Kinetic**
#2, 3 Tomer Hanuka; #7 Warren Pleece
372 **Fraction**
#2 Tomer Hanuka; #5, 6 Timothy Green II
376 **Batgirl**
#1-3, 5 Phil Noto; #11 Stanley Lau; #18, 19, 23 Dustin Nguyen
382 **Quantum and Woody**
#1 Ryan Sook; #2 Rian Hughes [variant cover]; #2 Ryan Sook; #2 Tom Fowler [variant cover]; #10 Kano; #0 Tom Fowler
385 **Wildcats**
#1-6, 8, 12, 15, 16, 18-20, 22-24 Dustin Nguyen
386 **Wildcats**
#7, 9, 11 Dustin Nguyen
391 **Various**
Andy Capp Reg Smythe; **Opera** P. Craig Russell; **Chopper** Colin MacNeil; **Bois-Maury** Hermann; **True Faith** Warren Pleece; **Hewligan's Haircut** Jamie Hewlett, photo John Ward; **Superman: The Man of Tomorrow** John Higgins; **A Small Killing** Oscar Zarate; **Troubled Souls** John McCrea; **Sam Bronx and the Robots** Serge Clerc
395 **Xpresso**
#1 Milo Manara; #2 John Bolton; back cover and interior line illustrations Rian Hughes; **Bring Me Your Love** Robert Crumb
396 **Various**
Trip to Tulum Milo Manara; **Heart Throbs** Max Cabanes; **Dare** Rian Hughes
399 **Speakeasy**
#91 Carlos Ezquerra; #107 Steve Yeowell; #108 Charles Burns; #109 Rian Hughes; #110 Dave Gibbons; #112 Brain Talbot; #113 Jamie Hewlett; #115 Brendan McCarthy; #116 Kevin O'Neill; #117 John Bolton
412 **Unity**
#1 Travel Foreman [variant cover]; #1 J.G. Jones [variant cover] #3 Dougie Braithwaite; #3 Shane Davis, Michelle Delecki [variant cover]; #3 J.G. Jones [variant cover]; #4 Clayton Crain; #4 Riley Rossmo [variant cover]; #5 Philip Tan [variant cover]; #5 Mico Suayan [variant cover]; #6 Raul Allen [variant cover]; #7 Dave Bullock [variant cover]; #8 Mico Suayan; #9 Mico Suayan; #9 Stephen Segovia [variant cover]; #10 Mico Suayan; #10 Russell Dauterman [variant cover]; #10 Donovan Santiago [variant cover]; #11 Raul Allen; #11 CAFU [variant cover]; #15 Raul Allen; #16 Antonio Fuso [variant cover]; #17 Lewis LaRosa, Brian Reber; #17 Juan Jose Ryp, Hi-Fi [variant cover]; #18 Joe Eisma, Allen Passalaqua [variant cover]; #18 Pere Pérez, David Baron; #19 Kano [variant cover]; #20, 21 Kano; #22 Diego Bernard, Sandro Ribeiro, Allen Passalaqua; #22 Jeff Dekal [variant cover]; #24 Diego Bernard, Allen Passalaqua; #23 Bilquis Evely, Mat Lopes; **Unity TPB** #3 Mico Suayan; #4 Lewis LaRosa; #7 Bilquis Evely
415 **Soda**
nn Franquin
419 **Girl Frenzy**
Superman: Lois Lane #1 Leonard Kirk; **Batman: Batgirl** #1 Leonard Kirk; **JLA: Tomorrow Woman** #1 Leonard Kirk; **Wonder Woman: Donna Troy** #1 Leonard Kirk; **Birds of Prey: The Ravens** #1 Leonard Kirk; **Young Justice: The Secret #1** Leonard Kirk
422 **Rai**
#1 Clayton Crain; #1 Bryan Hitch [variant cover]; #1 Raul Allen [variant cover]; #2 Mico Suayan [variant cover]; #2 Rian Hughes [variant cover]; #2 Raul Allen; #3 Raul Allen; #3 Clayton Crain [variant cover]; #4 Clayton Crain; #4 Clayton Crain [second printing variant cover];

#5 Clayton Crain; #5 Mico Suayan [variant cover]; #5 David Mack [variant cover]; #6 Clayton Crain; #6 Miguel Sepulveda, David Baron [variant cover]; #6 Cary Nord, Matthew Wilson [variant cover]; #7 Clayton Crain; #7 Rafael Albuquerque [variant cover]; #9-12 Ryan Sook [variant covers]; **Rai TPB** #1, 2 Clayton Crain
425 **Ninjak**
Ninjak TPB #1 Lewis LaRosa, Brian Reber #2 Mico Suayan, Ulises Arreola; #4 Lewis LaRosa, Brian Reber; **Ninja-K** #1 Tonci Zonjić; #1 Lucas Troya [varinat cover]; #1 David Mack; #2 Lucas Troya [variant cover]; #2 Ben Templesmith [variant cover]; #2 Trevor Hairsine
441 **Various**
Anderson, Psi Division #1-3 Garry Leach; #5 John Bolton
Skizz #1 Jim Baikie; **Love & Rockets** Jaime Hernandez; **Heartbreak Soup** Gilbert Hernandez; **Mechanics** Jaime Hernandez; **Ape Sex** Jaime Hernandez; **Human Diastrophism** Gilbert Hernandez; **Batman: Year One** David Mazzucchelli
449 **The Intimates**
#1-6 Jim Lee; #7-12 Giuseppe Camuncoli
455 **Moon Knight**
#1, 4, 6 Leinil Francis Yu
475 **Harbinger**
#0 Mico Suayan [second printing variant cover]; #0 Lewis Larosa [variant cover]; #1 Patrick Zircher [second printing variant cover]; #1 Dougie Braithwaite [variant cover]; #1 Jelena Kevic-Djurdjevic [variant cover]; #1 Mico Suayan [variant cover]; #2 Arturo Lozzi; #3 Patrick Zircher [variant cover]; #5 David Aja [variant cover]; #5 Mico Suayan; #6 Mico Suayan; #7 Mico Suayan; #7 Emanuela Lupacchino [variant cover]; #8 Mico Suayan;#8 Jeff Lemire [variant cover]; #9, 10 Mico Suayan; #12 Amy Reeder; #12 Khari Evans [varinat cover]; #13, 14 Patrick Zircher [variant cover]; #15 Barry Kitson; #15 Rian Hughes [variant cover]; #15 Trevor Hairsine [variant cover]; #16 Zach Montoya [variant cover]; #18 Matthew Walsh; #18 Andrew Robinson [variant cover]; #20 Zach Montoya [variant cover]; #21 Zachary Montoya; #22 Michael Walsh [Wondercon Convention cover]; #22 Joe Eisma [second printing variant cover]; #25 Barry Kitson [variant cover]; **Harbinger TPB** #3 Khari Evans; #5 Khari Evans, Mico Suayan; #5 Michael Walsh
478 **American Century**
#1 -3 Howard Chaykin; #11, 12 Glen Orbik
485 **Aliens**
Volume 1 #17 Chris Cunningham; Volume 2 #1 John Bolton; 'Next Issue' linework Kelley Jones
487 **Batgirl**
#15, 17, 18 Damion Scott; #35 James Jean; #37 Damion Scott; #45, 57 James Jean
494 **Archer & Armstrong**
#1 Clayton Henry [variant cover]; #1 Mico Suayan; #1 Clayton Henry [second printing variant cover]; #2 Arturo Lozzi; #2 Patrick Zircher [variant cover]; #3 Arturo Lozzi; #3 David Aja [variant cover]; #5 Patrick Zircher; #5 Emanuela Lupacchino [variant cover]; #5 Emanuela Lupacchino [variant cover]; #6 Emanuela Lupacchino; #7 Clayton Henry [variant cover]; #8, 9 Emanuela Lupacchino; #9 Tom Fowler [variant cover]; #10 Andrew Robinson [variant cover]; #0 Clayton Henry; **Archer & Armstrong: Archer** #0 Clayton Henry
500 **Crisis**
#1-5, 7, 9, 10, 12 Carlos Ezquerra; #13, 14 Glenn Fabry; #15, 19 Simon Bisley; #20 Brendan McCarthy; #22 Glenn Fabry; #23 Sean Phillips; #26 Glen Fabry; #27, 28 Sean Phillips; #29 Warren Pleece; #30, 34 Sean Phillips; #36, 38 Glenn Fabry; #39 Sean Phillps; #40, 43 Glenn Fabry; #45 Dave Hine; #48 Steve Yeowell; #49 Warren Pleece; #51 Paul Johnson; #52 Sean Phillips; #53 Dix; #54 Paul Johnson; #55 José Munoz; #56 Gary Erskine; #57 Daniel Vallely; #58 Dix; #59 Steve Sampson; #60 Milo Manara; #61 Gary Erskine; #63 Milo Manara
506 **Batman**
Caped Crusader Classics! #1-6 Bob Kane (ghosted?), **Batman** #1-6 Neal Adams
513 **Bitch Planet**
#1 Valentine De Landro [Ghost variant cover] Image Firsts: Bitch Planet #1 Valentine De Landro [second printing variant cover]; #1, 2 Valentine De Landro; #2 Kate Leth [second printing variant cover]; #3 Valentine De Landro; #3 Avon [second printing variant cover]; #4-9 Valentine De Landro; **Bitch Planet TPB** #1, 2 Valentine De Landro; **Bitch Planet** [French edition] #1 Valentine De Landro; **Bitch Planet Triple Feature** #1-5 Valentine De Landro; **Bitch Planet Triple Feature TPB** #1 Valentine De Landro
514 **Damian: Son of Batman**
#1, 2 Andy Kubert; #3 Dustin Nguyen [variant cover]; #4 Mick Gray [variant cover]; #4 Andy Kubert
559 **Batman: The Return of Bruce Wayne**
#1-6 Andy Kubert; #1 Chris Sprouse, Karl Story [variant cover]; #2 Frazer Irving [variant cover]; #3 Yanick Paquette, Michel Lacombe [variant cover]; #4 Cameron Stewart [variant cover]; #5 Ryan Sook [variant cover]; #6 Bill Sienkiewicz, Lee Garbett [variant cover]
563 **Knockabout Comics**
My Troubles with Women, R. Crumb's America, R. Crumb Draws the Blues Robert Crumb; **The Fabulous Furry Freak Brothers in Idiots Abroad** Gilbert Shelton; **Calculus Cat, Jazz Funnies** Hunt Emerson; **Outrageous Tales from the Old Testament** various; **Philbert Desanex' 100,000 Dream, Freak Brothers #0, Fat Freddy's Cat** Gilbert Shelton; **Hard To Swallow, Startling Planet** Hunt Emerson; **Knockabout** #11 Max; #12 Graham Higgins; #13 Mike Matthews; **The Collected Fat Freddy's Cat** Gilbert Shelton **Firkin** Hunt Emerson; **Oink!** Tony Husband; **Pusspuss** Hunt Emerson; **Peter Pank** Max; **Freak Brothers Omnibus, Fat Freddy's Cat Omnibus, The Best of Wonder Warthog, Fifty Freakin' Years with the Fabulous Furry Freak Brothers** Gilbert Shelton

Further reading

Books by Rian Hughes
[edited selection]

XX
In preparation
I Am A Number
Top Shelf [US] 2017
Custom Lettering of the '20s and '30s
Korero Press [UK] 2017
Get Lettering
Kinkajou [UK] 2016
Get Mapmaking
Kinkajou [UK] 2016
112 Hours
Device [UK] 2014
Lifestyle Illustration of the '50s
Goodman Fiell [UK] 2013
Tales from Beyond Science
Image [US] 2012
Soho Dives, Soho Divas
Image [US] 2012
Hardware: The Definitive SF Works of Chris Foss
with Imogene Foss, Titan Books [UK] 2012
Cult-ure: Ideas Can Be Dangerous
Fiell [UK] 2010
Custom Lettering of the '40s and '50s
Fiell [UK] 2010
On The Line
with Rick Wright
Image Comics [US] 2010
Yesterday's Tomorrows
with Raymond Chandler, Grant Morrison, John Freeman, Tom DeHaven, Chris Reynolds
Image Comics [US] 2010
Lifestyle Illustration of the '60s
Fiell [UK] 2010
Custom Lettering of the '60s and '70s
Fiell [UK] 2010
Ugenia Lavender
Children's books by Geri Halliwell, six volumes
Pan Macmillian [UK] 2009
Yesterday's Tomorrows (hardback limited edition)
Knockabout Gosh [UK] 2007
Ten Year Itch
(collects font designs)
Device [UK] 2005
Art, Commercial
Die Gestalten Verlag [Germany] 2001
Firewords: A Book of Wordplay Poems
ed. John Foster, Oxford University Press [UK] 2000
Dare
with Grant Morrison, Xpresso/Fleetway [UK] 1992
Edizioni Proglioni [Italy] 2010
The Science Service
with John Freeman, Acme/Various, [UK/US, France, Holland, Belgium] 1989

Collections and anthologies
[edited selection]

The Thing Artbook
Printed in Blood [US] 2017
Best of Heavy Metal: Volume 1
Grant Morrison/various, Heavy Metal Magazine [US] 2017
Crepax: Valentina (limited edition)
Fantagraphics [US] 2017
The Story of Emoji
Gavin Lucas, Prestel [UK] 2016
Script Fonts
Geum-Hee Hong and Karin Schmidt-Friederichs, Laurence King [UK] 2016
Batman: Facts and Stats from the Classic TV Show
Y. Y. Flurch, Titan Books [UK] 2016
Mad Max Fury Road: Inspired Artists
DC Comics [US] 2015
Is She Available?
Igor Goldkind, Subversion Factory [US] 2015
The Multiversity
Grant Morrison/various, DC Comics [US] 2015
Vertigo: CMYK
DC Comics [US] 2015
Batman Black and White: Volume 4
DC Comics [US] 2015
Graphic Design x 100
ed. Dorian Lucas, Braun [Germany] 2014
Design: Logo
Paul Howalt and Von Glitschka, Rockport [US] 2014
Skulls
Ilya, Robinson [UK] 2014
50 Years of Illustration
Lawrence Zeegen, Laurence King [UK] 2014
Hoax: Psychosis Blues
Ravi Thornton, Ziggy's Wish [UK] 2014
A1 Annual: Volume 1
ed. Dave Elliott, Titan [UK] 2014
Happy!
Grant Morrison, Darick Robertson, Image 2013
Incredible Tretchikoff
Boris Gorelik
Art/Books [UK] 2013
Comics Sketchbooks
Steven Heller, Thames and Hudson [UK] 2012
Numbers in Graphic Design
Roger Fawcett-Tang, Laurence King [UK] 2012
Pop Psychedelic
BigBros Workshop, Last Gasp [US] 2012
Logolounge Master Library 1, 2, 4
Catherine Fishel and Bill Gardner, Rockport [US] 2011, 2012
The Dictionary of Graphic Design and Designers
Alan Livingston and Isabelle Livingston, Thames and Hudson [UK] 2012
Damn Good: Top Designers Discuss Their All-Time Favorite Projects
Tim Lapetino and Jason Adam, North Light Books [US] 2012
Characters: An Eclectic Alphabet
Will Foley [UK] 2012
Nelson
ed. Rob Davis, Woodrow Phoenix, Blank Slate [UK] 2011
Winner of the 'Best Book Award' at the British Comic Awards 2011
Typography Sketchbooks
Steven Heller and Lita Talarico, Thames and Hudson [UK], Princeton Architectural Press [US] 2011
Typo Shirt One
Index Books, ed Magma Design [Spain] 2011
Creative Characters: MyFonts Interviews
ed. Jan Mittendorp, BIS [Holland] 2010
Sci-Fi Art Now
ed. John Freeman, Ilex Press [UK] 2010
Design for the Greater Good
Peleg Top and Jonathan Cleveland, Collins Design [US] 2010
Illustration Now
ed. Julius Wiedemann, Taschen [Germany] 2009
Sketchbook: Conceptual Drawings from the World's Most Influential Designers
Timothy O'Donnell, Rockport 2009
Drip, Dot, Swirl
Von Glitschka, HOW books [US] 2009
Really Good Logos, Explained
with Margo Chase, Ron Miriello, Alex White, Rotovision [US] 2009
Market Smart
Jim Gilmarten, Collins Design [US] 2009
Marketing Illustration: New Venues, New Styles, New Methods
Marshall Arisman and Steven Heller Allworth Press [US] 2009
Comic Art Now
Dez Skinn, Ilex Press [UK] 2008
Grids: Creative Solutions for Graphic Design
Lucienne Roberts, John Wiley & Sons [US] 2008
Vector Graphics and Illustration: A Masterclass
Steven Withrow and Jack Harris, Rotovision [US] 2008
Logo a Lot
Bnn, Ram Distribution [Japan] 2008
Crumble. Crackle. Burn
Von Glitschka, HOW books [US] 2007
Made with FontFont
Bis [Germany] 2007
Swallow 3
ed. Asley Wood, IDW [US] 2007
Contemporary Graphic Design
Charlotte and Peter Fiell, Taschen [Germany] 2007
Big Book of Fashion Illustration: A World Sourcebook of Contemporary Illustration
Martin Dawber, Batsford [UK] 2007
Illustration: A Theoretical and Contextual Perspective
Alan Male, AVA [UK] 2007
Project: Romantic
AdHouse Books [US] 2006
Indie Fonts 3
Rotovision [US] 2006
The Secret Life of Logos
Leslie Carbarga, HOW Books [US] 2006
Mascotte 2
Delicatessen, Happy Books [Italy] 2006
Visual Thinking
Mark Wigan, AVA [UK] 2006
Text and Image
Mark Wigan, AVA [UK] 2006
Business Cards 2: Ways of Saying Hello
Liz Farrelly and Michael Dorrian, Laurence King, [UK] 2006
Color Harmony: Logos
Christopher Simmons, Rockport [US] 2006
Commercial Illustration: Mixing Traditional Approaches and New Techniques
Ian Noble, Rockport [UK] 2006
A-Z of Type Designers
Neil Macmillan, Laurence King [UK] 2005
401 Design Meditations: Wisdom, Insights, and Intriguing Thoughts from 150 Leading Designers
Catharine Fishel, Rockport [US] 2005
200 Best Illustrators Worldwide
Lurzer's Archive [Germany] 2005
Type 1
Laurence King [UK] 2005
Logo, Font and Lettering Bible
Leslie Cabarga, Writer's Digest Books [US] 2004
The Typographic Experiment: Radical Innovation in Contemporary Type Design
Teal Triggs, Thames and Hudson [UK] 2004
Images 28
The Association of Illustrators [UK] 2004
Picture Perfect: Fusions of Illustration and Design
Ian Noble, Rotovision [UK] 2003
Logolounge
Volumes 1, 2, 3, 5, 7 Rockport [US] 2003/12
The Complete Guide to Digital Illustration
Steve Caplin, Adam Banks and Nigel Holmes
Watson-Guptill [US] 2003
Designing Typefaces
David Earls, Rotovision [US] 2002
The Encyclopedia of Cartooning Techniques
Steve Whitaker, Sterling Publishing [UK] 2002
Pictoplasma
Hendrik Hellige and Michael Mischler, DGV [Germany] 2001
Logo World
PIE books [Japan] 2001
Packaging: Graphics + Design
Renee Phillips, Rockport [UK] 2001
Visible Music
PIE Books [Japan] 2000
Extreme Fonts
Spencer Drate, HarperCollins Design [US] 2000
New Logo and Trademark Design
PIE books [Japan] 2000
Emotional/Digital
Thames and Hudson [UK] 1999
The European Design Annual 4
Rotovision [UK] 1999
Illustration
Yolanda Zappaterra, Rotovision [UK] 1998
100% Illustrator
Smart Books [Switzerland] 1997
New Typographics 2
PIE Books [Japan] 1997
1, 2 and 3 Color Graphics
PIE books [Japan] 1996
Timing Zero
PIE books [Japan] 1996

Print articles
[edited selection]
Key • In-depth article

• **Circular 18** [UK] The Typographic Circle magazine, 2014
Rian Hughes inverview
Computer Arts [UK] November 2014
My design space is . . .
Computer Arts [UK] October 2014
The Future of Design Education
Creative Review [UK] July 2012
Mmmmm . . . Dingbats
Your Days Are Numbered [UK] #2, May 2012
Rian Hughes inverview
Creative Review [UK] October 2012
Monograph (booklet sent to subscribers only)
• **Re:Vox** [UK] April 2012
Rian Hughes: The New European
Ultrabold: The Journal of St Bride Library [UK] #12, Autumn 2012
Inspirational Pages
Design Week [UK] 23 June 2011
Designers make sense of London's changing transport

Creative Review [UK] July 2010
Retro Renderings (Custom Lettering of the '60s and '70s)
Digital Arts [UK] February 2010
Brand New Retro
Spaceship Away [UK] #22, 2010
Rian Hughes – Daring to be Different
Stella [UK] October 2010
Reader, I Swooned
(Lifestyle Illustration of the '60s)
Wired [UK] January 2010
Design: Comics Get Serious
Digital Arts [UK] November 2009
Keep Your Desk Tidy
• **Eye** [UK] Type Special #71, Spring 2009
Drawn to be Wild
• **Baseline** [UK] Summer 2009
Rian Hughes' 500 Faces
by Steven Heller
• **Ultrabold: The Journal of St Bride Library** [UK] #6, Summer 2009
Vintage Custom Lettering
The Comics Journal [US] #295, January 2009
Yesterday's Tomorrows
Reddition: Verlag für Graphische Literatur #47 [Germany] May 2008
Yves Chaland und die Nouvelle Ligne Claire
Computer Arts [UK] #147, April 2008
Industrial Romantic
Digital Arts [UK] September 2008
Character Building
• **Novum** [German/English text] July 2007
The Simple Joy of Creation
• **Design Week** [UK] 12 July 2007
Back to the Future: The Visions of Rian Hughes (cover story)
• **Ultrabold: The Journal of St Bride Library** [UK] #3, Autumn 2007
Paralucent: Beyond Clear
Page [Germany] May 2006
Zehn Jahre Rian Hughes
Typo: typografie a grafický design [Czech Republic] #20, April 2006
Device Fonts: Ten Year Itch
Digit magazine [UK] April-May 2006
Device Fonts
Grafik [UK] June 2006
Anatomy of a Typeface: Ministry
• **Ultrabold: The Journal of St Bride Library** [UK] #1, Autumn 2006
Ministry: A New 14-Weight Sans Family
Computer Arts Projects [UK] #86, Typography Special, July 2006
Type of Our Times
Territory magazine #5, 2006 [Malaysia]
Japan Fever (cover story)
Eye #55, Spring 2005
Manual: A Book about Hands by George Hardie (review)
Computer Arts Projects [UK] August 2005
Essential Advice from the World's Best Designers
Page [Germany] February 2005
Motorcity – ornament für groß jungs
ENE 0: Ensayo Del Diseño [Mexico] #2, March 2004
Rian Hughes
Alt Pick magazine [US] Spring/Summer 2004
Conspiracy + Collaboration
Intro [Germany] #112, December 2003/January 2004
Eagle Flies Again [UK] #10, Spring 2004
Dark Dare
• **X Funs** [Taiwan] #7, 2003
Interview with Device (cover story)
Design Week [UK] 25 December 2003
Character Reference

Mac Format [UK] March 2002
Showcase: Rian Hughes
Eye [UK] #39, Spring 2001
Meanwhile, in the weird world of art
Computer Arts [UK] Winter 2000
A Taste of Paradise
Creative Review [UK] September 2000
What's new in Type Design: Range
Emag: The *Sydney Morning Herald* magazine [Australia] March 2000
Font Fashion
Design Week [UK] 31 March 2000
Illustration: Eurostar
Computer Arts Special [UK] #15 2000
Essential Typography
Desktop [Australia] April 2000
Young Turks
• **Semper Mac** [US] December 1999
Interview: Rian Hughes
Creative Review [UK] June 1999
What's new: Gran Turismo
Publish [US] April 1999
New Faces
• **Graphics International** [UK] #51, January 1998
Designer profile: Rian Hughes
• **Design Week** [UK] 9 February 1998
Man and Superman
Publish [UK] April 1998
New Faces
Campaign [UK] 1 May 1988
Private View: Carland
Page [Germany], 1998
Creative Technology [UK] March 1997
Virgin Safety Video
Creative Review [UK] February 1997
The world's first fully-animated in-flight safety video
Creative Technology February 1996
Folio: MTV Europe Awards Brochure
FontShop 96:2 Het Buzz [Netherlands] February 1996
Spektakel Device Fonts, en onderzoek van Rian Hughes
Design Week 15 December 1995
MTV Europe Awards Brochure
Computer Arts #1 December 1995
Profiles: Rian Hughes
Creative Technology [UK] June 1995
Comic Hero (cover story)
The Mac [UK] October 1995
A Mac of my Own
Campaign [UK] Press Advertising Awards issue, 1995
Newquay Steam
The Mac [UK] February 1995
Character Building
• **Circular 5** [UK] #5, 1995
Modified Outrageous
Creative Technology [UK] January 1995
Folio: On The Line
Creative Technology [UK] September 1994
Folio: R. Crumb's America
Design Week [UK] Type Special, September 1994
Face to Face
• **Comic World** #18, August 1993
Spotlight: Martin Conaghan talks to Rian Hughes
Design Week [UK] 21 May 1993
Design Week Diary: Spiffy Designs
Frankly [UK] #4, 1993
Rian Hughes interview
Design Week [UK] 26 November 1993
The Bare Necessities
Evening Standard [UK], Friday 6 September 1991
The Big Draw
Academy [UK] #19, 1991
Dare
Comics International [UK] December 1990
Fleetway axes experimental title Revolver

New Musical Express [UK] 7 July 1990
Loaded!
Skeleton Crew [UK] August 1990
Revolver
• **Speakeasy** [UK] #109 May 1990
The Future is Now
The Independent on Sunday [UK] 1 July 1990
The adult comic comes of age
Flypost [UK] August 1990
Cut 'n' Mix Comix
City Limits [UK] May 9, 1989
Freeze-frames and after
The Indy [UK] September 1989
The Science Service
New Musical Express [UK] 16 December 1989
Def Com One: Hughes' Baby
Arkensword [UK] #22 1987
Secret Service
Creative Review [UK] September 1984
What's New in Design
(College project)

Online articles [edited selection]
• **AIGA, New York**
Tea and Biscuits lecture [video]
https://vimeo.com/49475623
• **Wikipedia**
https://en.wikipedia.org/wiki/Rian_Hughes
• **MyFonts**
Creative Characters interview
http://www.myfonts.com/newsletters/cc/200904.html
Huffington Post
Soho Dives, Soho Divas
https://tinyurl.com/yc8qucf8
Print
Beyond the Graphic Novel: Is She Available?
https://tinyurl.com/j3mac4v
The Seedy Beauty of the Soho Diva
https://tinyurl.com/ybugusm6
Typostrate
Custom Lettering of the '20s and '30s
https://tinyurl.com/ycpl5fr6
• **Resonance FM**
British Mavericks podcast interview
http://podcasts.resonancefm.com/archives/2846
• **Forbidden Planet Blog**
Yesterday's Tomorrows
https://tinyurl.com/yaaoq2jk
Typographica
Interview: Rian Hughes
https://tinyurl.com/y7d42l9n
Bleeding Cool
Soho Dives, Soho Divas
https://tinyurl.com/yantfw2w
Rian Hughes' Shadowman logos
https://tinyurl.com/y7lnbjty
Dave Gibbons, Rian Hughes, Garry Leach and more at Image Duplicator
http://tinyurl.com/ycuqoxb8
Rian Hughes' new Valiant logo
https://tinyurl.com/ycvfq5rr
CBR
Conversing on Comics with Rian Hughes
http://tinyurl.com/yaok4sh8
Committed: Rian Hughes – Designs for the Future
https://tinyurl.com/y8uv7lvf
Committed: Covers with Depth
https://tinyurl.com/y8faa6l9
YouTube
Fiell: *Rian Hughes on being a Graphic Designer*
https://www.youtube.com/watch?v=B-0-xD0-qzw
Fiell: *Rian Hughes on 'Cult-Ure: Ideas Can Be Dangerous'*
https://www.youtube.com/watch?v=qN-ILX-7Zew

DC: *How The Multiversity Sets Up the Future of DC*
https://www.youtube.com/watch?v=6BYcxALtnsM
Fiell: *1960s Illustration Techniques*
http://tinyurl.com/yb6s4jnk
• **Logolounge**
Rian Hughes
https://www.logolounge.com/articles/rian-hughes
Creative Bloq
Exclusive access to Batman and Spider-Man logo creator's workspace
http://tinyurl.com/y9q8kg5r
Great Krypton!
Designing a Tangent (interview)
Part 1 http://tinyurl.com/yaabvf4u
Part 2 http://tinyurl.com/yaatlxoh
BBC News
Grant Morrison and Rian Hughes' 'The Key'
http://www.bbc.co.uk/news/magazine-26730067
http://www.bbc.co.uk/news/magazine-26784218
BoingBoing
Soho Dives, Soho Divas: Sketching London's Burlesque Artistes
https://tinyurl.com/yctgy3xz
• **AIGA**
Belief in Yesterdays: An Interview with Rian Hughes
http://tinyurl.com/ycpayqlg
3AM
Rian Hughes Device
https://tinyurl.com/ybp4a6qt
Newsarama
Rian Hughes on his Comics Future Past
https://tinyurl.com/yb9grav7
New York Times
Yesterday's Tomorrows
https://tinyurl.com/yb73lw4y

Exhibitions [edited selection]
Tributes to Valentina
Group exhibition
Sarjakuvakeskus Comics Center Helsinki [Finland] 2017
Dot to Dot
Group exhibition held at various sites across London: The Trunk at The Artworks, Elephant and Castle; One New Change, City of London; The Market Hall Exhibition, Borough Market; The Covent Garden Digital Dot Room; Boxpark Shoreditch. London [UK] 2016
Typo Circle 40
40th anniversary show, featuring posters and ephemera
Protein Gallery, Shoreditch, London [UK] 2016
David Bowie Tribute
The Museum of Soho, in collaboration with The British Record Shop Archive and Spindle Magazine
Zero One, London [UK] 2016
The Cartoon Museum, London [UK] 2016
ICE Brighton [UK] 2017
Phono+Graphic
Group exhibition curated by Sean Phillips
60 vinyl record covers by 60 comic book artists
Nuvango Gallery, Toronto [Canada] 2016
Kendal Museum, Lakes International Comic Art Festival [UK] 2015
50 Years of Illustration
Group exhibition curated by Lawrence Zeegen
Upper Street Gallery, London College of Communication, London [UK] 2014
Les Rencontres Chaland
Group exhibition curated by Yves Chaland's widow, Isabelle Chaland
Nerac [France] 2014
Comics Unmasked
Group exhibition curated by John Harris Dunning and Paul Gravett,
The British Library [UK] 2014
Sequential City
Group exhibition
Baxter and Bailey, London [UK] 2013
Show Us Your Type: London
Group exhibition
Central St Martins, London [UK] 2013
Image Duplicator
Group exhibition curated by Rian Hughes and Jason Atomic as a riposte to the Tate's Lichtenstein retrospective, with proceeds going to the Hero Initiative
Orbital Gallery, London [UK] 2013
BT ArtBox
One of 40 customised phone boxes displayed across London, auctioned for ChildLine's 25th anniversary. Artists included Zaha Hadid, Malcolm Garrett, Peter Blake and Zandra Rhodes. Rian's was in Soho Square London [UK] 2012
Sense and the City
Group exhibition including work by Syd Mead, Le Corbusier and Archigram
London Transport Museum [UK] 2012
Types for the New Century
Group exhibition
Stationers' Hall, London [UK] 2012
University of the West of England, Bristol [UK] 2012
University of Northumbria, Newcastle [UK] 2012
Bauhaus in Weimar [Germany] 2012
Museum für Druck-kunst, Leipzig [Germany] 2013
Chipping Camden Literary Festival [UK] 2013
KLDW Typo-Graphics
Group exhibition
National Art Gallery, Kuala Lumpur [Malaysia] 2010
In Search of the Atom Style
Group exhibition curated by Paul Gravett, also featuring Serge Clerc, Yves Chaland, Ever Meulen, Woodrow Phoenix, François Avril and others
The Atomium, Brussels [Belgium] 2009
Making History: LCC and the School of Graphic Design
Group exhibition of alumni work
Well Gallery, London College of Communication (LCP), London [UK] 2005
Toybox
Solo show of limited edition prints
Coningsby Gallery, London [UK] 2003
Powerhouse::uk
Group exhibition
Horse Guard's Parade, London [UK] 1999
Cafe Casbar
Solo show
Smith's Gallery, Covent Garden, London [UK] 1990
Film and Strip
Group exhibition
Air Gallery, London [UK] 1987

Awards [edited selection]
The entry costs for industry awards can be higher than the fee for the job itself, which means I rarely enter them. Most of the following were submitted by the clients themselves, whom I thank:
Communication Arts Award of Excellence
Typography Annual 2013
for Freddie Stevenson *On The Line* CD
Broadcasting Design Awards: Gold Award 1996
for MTV Europe Music Awards brochure, 1995
AP&PB Best Use of Print Award
for MTV Europe Music Awards brochure, 1995
New York Art Director's Club: Merit Award
for *Mystery in Space* book jacket, 2000
Campaign Press Advertising Awards: Best Use of Typography
for Newquay Steam advertisements, 1995

Talks [edited selection]
Design Museum London [UK] 2017
Cultural Salon: What is Freedom?
Design Museum London [UK] 2017
Cultural Salon: Fear and Love
St Bride Foundation London [UK] 2017
Eye Magazine's Type Tuesday: Fists, Fleurons and Emojis
2000AD: 40 Years of Thrill-Power Festival London [UK] 2017
The Look of 2000AD
The House of Illustration
London [UK] 2015
Lifestyle Illustration's Stylish Heyday
Vision Bristol Bristol [UK] 2014
Adventures in Pop Culture Design
Lakes International Comic Art Festival
Kendall [UK] 2014
Design Demon: Rian Hughes
Barbican London [UK] 2013
Hyper-Pop
Royal College of Art London [UK] 2012
Red Tape: Local Global
Literary Dundee Festival
University of Dundee [Scotland] 2012
Typo London: Social
Institute of Education, London [UK] 2012
Typo London: Places
Institute of Education, London [UK] 2011
The Bookseller Conference
The British Library, London [UK] 2012
The Typographic Circle
JWT, London [UK] 2011
Institute of Contemporary Arts London [UK] 2010
Grant Morrison: Walking with Gods
The Artworkers' Guild London [UK] 2010
The Letter Exchange Lecture Series: Type Exotica
Dundee Literary Festival
University of Dundee [Scotland] 2010
Kuala Lumpur Design Week
Kuala Lumpur [Malaysia] 2010
CPH:TYPO 09
Copenhagen [Denmark] 2009
Typo Berlin Berlin [Germany] 2008
13th International Design Conference
St Bride Foundation London [UK] 2008
The 7th Annual Friends of St Bride Conference
The Artworker's Guild London [UK] 2007
Font Fight!
The Art Directors Club New York [US] 2007
Design, Tea and Biscuits
[https://vimeo.com/49475623]
Institute of Contemporary Arts London [UK] 2007
The Image-Soaked Future

Juries [edited selection]
D&AD 50
Typography Jury foreman, 2012

Industry associations
Wynkyn de Worde Society
Double Crown Club
Grotesque 9
Miniox dek Thargo ("Slave of Tharg")

Index

Figures in *italic* refer to illustrations